A HISTORY OF
Box Elder County

A HISTORY OF *Box Elder County*

Frederick M. Huchel

1999
Utah State Historical Society
Box Elder County Commission

ISBN 0-913738-09-3
Library of Congress Catalog Card Number 98-61321
Map by Automated Geographic Reference Center—State of Utah
Printed in the United States of America

Utah State Historical Society
300 Rio Grande
Salt Lake City, Utah 84101-1182

To my ancestors, who suffered and sacrificed, and made it possible for me to be born in Box Elder County: Niels Andersen and his son Martin Andersen, who came from Denmark; William Evans and his wife, Mary Jordan Evans (and her parents David Jordan and Margaret Watkins Jordan), who came from Wales to make a home in Brigham City.

Contents

Acknowledgments ix

General Introduction xiii

Chapter 1 The Natural Setting 1

Chapter 2 Man Before History 28

Chapter 3 Trappers, Explorers, Goldseekers 43

Chapter 4 The Saints Come Marching In 63

Chapter 5 The Cooperative and the United Order Movement 88

Chapter 6 The Transcontinental Railroad 105

Chapter 7 Corinne: The City of the Ungodly 123

Chapter 8 The Box Elder Tabernacle 146

Chapter 9 The Non-LDS Churches in Box Elder County 166

Chapter 10 Into the Twentieth Century 188

CHAPTER 11 Box Elder County in the Last Half of the Twentieth Century 266

CHAPTER 12 Reflections on Box Elder County at the end of the 20th Century 293

CHAPTER 13 The Towns of Box Elder 305

SELECTED BIBLIOGRAPHY 429

INDEX 437

Acknowledgments

My greatest fear in writing this book has been neglecting to acknowledge someone whose help made it possible.

First, there are my parents, who instilled in me a love for learning and for history. My first grade teacher, Ella Angebauer Long, taught me to love to read. My junior high school English teacher, Ferrin Allen, taught me the basics of grammar. If I can write, I owe it to Jordan Larsen, the best high school English teacher Utah has ever had. For an interest in and understanding of history, I owe a debt to D. A. Olsen, whose history classes at Box Elder High School were actually interesting.

In college I had three mentors. Dr. Larry C. Porter taught me the intricacies of the history of the Church of Jesus Christ of Latter-day Saints. Dr. Le Grande Davies taught me how to think. He showed me how to view history as a continuum and to understand parallels and connections. Le Grande and I remained friends. It was with him that I first saw and explored Box Elder's Sun Tunnels. In the early planning stages of this volume he rendered invaluable assistance. My greatest debt, though, is to Professor Hugh Nibley who taught me the importance of language and what history *is.* He taught me *why* history is important. Dr. Nibley taught me that history is not lists and chronicles and chronologies. Its message comes in comparisons, parallels, relationships, and its *lessons.*

In the preparation of this history, county commissioner Frank Nishiguchi must receive top billing for starting and nurturing the project. He has been a good friend and facilitator. Then there is Lorna. Lorna Ravenberg has kept the wheels turning and facilitated the project in uncounted ways.

High on the list are the members of the Box Elder History Committee put together by Frank Nishiguchi. They were responsible for gathering information on their own communities, and making the compilation job possible. Each one performed a great work. Without their hours of research and labor, the job would have been too large, and I would have been overwhelmed. Some of them deserve special mention. Keith Andersen of Bothwell took two days out of his busy life to give me the tour of his life of western Box Elder County. I was absolutely amazed at the things and places and people he knows. Then there was the invaluable day I spent with Gale Welling, learning about Fielding and Collinston and Cutler Dam. Merlin Larsen took me on a tour of the pictographs and anciently inhabited caves of the Promontory.

I must also thank my friend and neighbor Fred Cannon for a first-hand look—and nearly all my information—on the Great Lucin Cutoff Trestle.

Many almost-forgotten stories and anecdotes are stored in the encyclopedic mind of Lewis Howell Jones, Jr. His insights have been invaluable.

LuAnn Adams and her staff in the county clerk-recorder's office provided valuable assistance in entering into the computer the community histories. County surveyor Denton Beecher provided maps and measurements.

Then there are Kent Powell and Craig Fuller at the Utah State Historical Society, without whose untold hours of labor this project would not have come to pass. Their help and patience deserve an award.

A special note of thanks is due to my friends since high school days. William G. "Bill" Jones provided me a second home in Corinne, and access to the marvelous history of that town. James R. "Sam" Bass got me seriously into the history of the transcontinental railroad. It has become a lifelong love. It was with Sam that I explored much of the county first-hand in our teens.

I am indebted to Kane County historian Alan C. DeMille for considerable on-site instruction concerning the Orderville United Order of Zion.

I must thank the staff at Golden Spike National Historic Site, who have given me free access to their files and collections, and an opportunity to see the inner workings of the park: Superintendent Bruce Powell, administrative assistant Kathleen Gonder, chief ranger Rick Wilson, ranger John Moeykens, and engineer Bob Dowty, as well as many who have served there before them. Then, there is the late Bernice Gibbs Anderson. I learned from her things about Corinne and the transcontinental railroad that no one else knew.

I am indebted to Ann Buttars and the staff of Utah State University Merrill Library's Special Collections, and her predecessor, the late, encyclopedic Jeff Simmonds

A special thanks is due to Sarah Yates, editor of the *Box Elder News and Journal,* who opened her files to this project, and to Eva Bingham of Honeyville, who provided an editing pen and many helpful suggestions.

My deepest thanks go to my wife and sweetheart, Cherie, for her help, her love, her support, her encouragement, and her sacrifice and dedication in bringing order to my files, and to our children, Kamalla and Daxton, for being patient while I took so much time typing, typing, typing.

General Introduction

When Utah was granted statehood on 4 January 1896, twenty-seven counties comprised the nation's new forty-fifth state. Subsequently two counties, Duchesne in 1914 and Daggett in 1917, were created. These twenty-nine counties have been the stage on which much of the history of Utah has been played.

Recognizing the importance of Utah's counties, the Utah State Legislature established in 1991 a Centennial History Project to write and publish county histories as part of Utah's statehood centennial commemoration. The Division of State History was given the assignment to administer the project. The county commissioners, or their designees, were responsible for selecting the author or authors for their individual histories, and funds were provided by the state legislature to cover most research and writing costs as well as to provide each public school and library with a copy of each history. Writers worked under general guidelines provided by the Division of State History and in cooperation with county history committees. The counties also established a Utah Centennial County History Council to help develop policies for distribution of state-appropriated funds and plans for publication.

Each volume in the series reflects the scholarship and interpretation of the individual author. The general guidelines provided by the Utah State Legislature included coverage of five broad themes encompassing the economic, religious, educational, social, and political history of the county. Authors were encouraged to cover a vast period of time stretching from geologic and prehistoric times to the present. Since Utah's statehood centennial celebration falls just four years before the arrival of the twenty-first century, authors were encouraged to give particular attention to the history of their respective counties during the twentieth century.

Still, each history is at best a brief synopsis of what has transpired within the political boundaries of each county. No history can do justice to every theme or event or individual that is part of an area's past. Readers are asked to consider these volumes as an introduction to the history of the county, for it is expected that other researchers and writers will extend beyond the limits of time, space, and detail imposed on this volume to add to the wealth of knowledge about the county and its people. In understanding the history of our counties, we come to understand better the history of our state, our nation, our world, and ourselves.

In addition to the authors, local history committee members, and county commissioners, who deserve praise for their outstanding efforts and important contributions, special recognition is given to Joseph Francis, chairman of the Morgan County Historical Society, for his role in conceiving the idea of the centennial county history project and for his energetic efforts in working with the Utah State Legislature and State of Utah officials to make the project a reality. Mr. Francis is proof that one person does make a difference.

ALLAN KENT POWELL
CRAIG FULLER
GENERAL EDITORS

BOX ELDER COUNTY

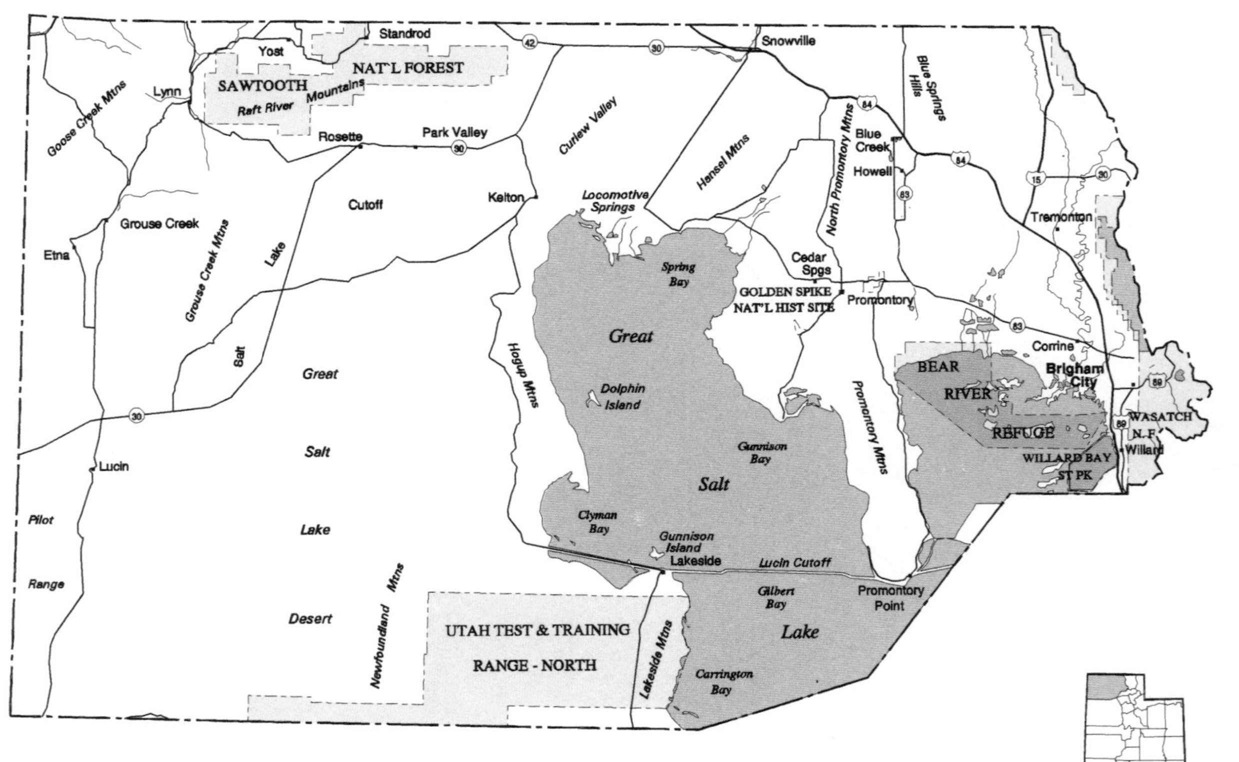

CHAPTER 1

THE NATURAL SETTING

The northwestern corner of Utah, the area which comprises Box Elder County, is a vast land of stark contrasts. Its terrain ranges from alkali flat to desert to scrub oak-covered foothills to aspen-sloped and pine-crowned mountains to barren subalpine crags. The county is named for the large number of Box Elder trees growing in Box Elder Canyon at the time of settlement.

Box Elder County is the fourth largest county in Utah at 5,594 square miles—only San Juan, Tooele, and Millard counties are larger. The county covers about 5,600 square miles, depending on the level of the Great Salt Lake. Approximately 48 percent of the county is privately owned which is double that of private land ownership statewide. The largest federal land agency in the county is the Bureau of Land Management which controls 2,041 square miles, followed by the United States Forest Service, the Department of Defense, the Fish and Wildlife Service, Bureau of Reclamation, National Park Service, and Indian tribes.

Box Elder County is rich in history, geology, flora, fauna, technology, and has a heritage of human habitation, dating from prehistoric times. The diverse climate, topography, and geology have helped shape the lives of generations of people—from prehistoric peoples to present generations.

Within Box Elder County's boundaries lies the bulk of Utah's (and North America's) saltiest permanent body of water, the Great Salt Lake, one of the chief geographic features of the Great Basin and the Intermountain West. The Great Basin is a series of closed basins, each bounded by north—south trending mountains.

Box Elder County is located in the northeast corner of the very large Great Basin physiographic province. The eastern boundary of the county follows exactly the eastern boundary of the Great Basin. The northern boundary of the county is nearly the northern boundary of the hydrologic Great Basin. The northern county line follows the 42nd parallel of latitude, covering nearly two degrees of longitude—nearly 100 miles—from just west of the 112th degree to just beyond the 114th degree west longitude. The western county boundary, which also forms the Utah-Nevada stateline, extends exactly one full degree, or about 84 miles, from 41 degrees north to 42 degrees north. The county's southern boundary—from the west—follows the 41st parallel to the west shoreline of Great Salt Lake and Carrington Bay. From there it angles north to the middle of the lake, then northerly to a point just west of Utah Hot Springs. from there east to the crest of the Wellsville and Clarkston Mountain Ranges then north to the 42nd parallel.

The Great Basin hydrologic province of the North American continent is a quarter-million square mile area of the western North American continent which has no outlet to the sea. Among the lakes located within this hydrologic basin are Utah and the Great Salt Lakes. There is also a physiographic Great Basin, with boundaries slightly more constricted than those of the hydrologic Great Basin.[1] The western border of the physiographic Great Basin is formed by the snow-capped ridge of the Sierra Nevada, the highest range in the continental United States. The great wall of the Sierra Nevada Mountains stretches diagonally from the Klamath region of southern Oregon and northern California to the Mojave Desert in southeastern California, walling in the Great Basin on the west.

On the north, a less-well-defined boundary meanders east from the Sierra Nevada Mountains across the low mountain ridges which mark the lava-covered country defining the Snake River Plains of southeastern Oregon and southern Idaho. Streams which arise on the northern slope of these mountains flow into the Columbia River including the small annual steams of Goose Creek, Birch Creek, the Raft River, and Johnson and George creeks located in the extreme northwest corner of Box Elder County.

The southern rim of the physiographic Great Basin Province is ragged and indistinct, caused by erosional encroachment of the great Colorado River drainage. Utah tributaries with names such as Paria, Rio Virgin, Kanab Creek and Muddy empty into the Colorado River through deep canyons called Parunuweap, Mukuntuweap, and Meadow Valley Wash. The basin rim is also defined by plateaus with Paiute names such as Markugunt and Paunsagunt, and the formidable Black Ridge in Washington County which was such an obstacle to the Mormon pioneers who settled in Utah's Dixie. The Pine Valley and Bull Valley mountains form the watershed in southwestern Utah.[2]

The eastern perimeter of the physiographic Great Basin is formed by another well-defined wall of mountains, the great diagonal upthrust of the high gentling rolling High Plateaus which encompass the Wellsville and Clarkston Mountains in Box Elder County. The hydrologic Great Basin province is similar nearly to the just described physiographic province. The hydrologic Great Basin stretches farther eastward taking in the drainage of the Bear River which has its headwaters in the Uinta Mountains—the only major east-west trending mountain range in the United States.

One of the major features of the Great Basin is the Great Salt Lake, a remnant of Lake Bonneville, a prehistoric Ice Age lake which filled much of the area west of the Wasatch Mountains to what is now the Utah-Nevada state line.

The elevation of Box Elder County ranges from 4,200 feet (the "standard" level of Great Salt Lake) to nearly 10,000 feet. Dunn Peak in the Raft River Mountains reaches 9,925 feet, Willard Peak attains an elevation of 9,764 feet, and Box Elder Peak rises to 9,372 feet above sea level.

Geology and Topography

The most noticeable geologic features of Box Elder County are its mountains and the valley of the Great Salt Lake.The mountainous boundary which forms the eastern border of Box Elder County is a result of one of the unseen features of the area: the Wasatch Fault Zone which extends from Malad City, Idaho on the north to Nephi on the south and paralleling Interstate 15 for about two hundred miles. The uplift begun in the Miocene epoch continues today. The Wellsville Mountains mark the northern end of the Wasatch Range proper. The greater Wasatch Fault line extends much farther in both directions.[3]

The eastern boundary of Box Elder County is delineated by the craggy Wellsville and Clarkston Mountains, separated by a six -mile sag where the Bear River flows through the Bear River Narrows from Cache County to Box Elder County. These mountains tower over the communities of Brigham City, Harper Ward, Honeyville, Deweyville, Collinston, Fielding, Plymouth, Washakie, and Portage It is claimed that using the measurement of base-width to height, the Wellsville Mountains are the steepest in the world. Anyone who has walked the knife-edged ridge of the Wellsvilles and looked down the western slope would surely tend to agree. Though the western face of the Wellsville Mountains looks out over the vast Bear River Valley, its eastern foothills are punctuated south of Cache Valley by two small valleys: Dry Lake, and Mantua.

The Wellsville and Clarkston Mountains—the latter part of the Malad Range—are composed mostly of marine sedimentary rock laid down during the Cambrian-Silurian-Dovonian-Pennsylvanian Periods when much of the western United States continent was submerged under an ancient sea. On the east side of both mountain ranges are outcroppings of non-marine sedimentary rock layed down during the more recent Tertiary Period. The Wellsville Mountains are known for deposits of trilobites and other Devonian fossils. Minerals, including copper, silver, lead, zinc, antimony, and gold, have been found in the Wellsville Mountains, principally in Cataract, Baker, and Antimony Canyons northeast of Brigham City.

The mountains are tilted to the east, exposing layers upon layers of rock strata. The mountains have been forced upward and tilted by numerous ancient seismic events. The fault scarp shows in the rugged west face of Wellsville Mountain, while the eastern face is covered with topsoil and is heavily vegetated. One of the interesting features of the east side of the Wellsville Mountains is Dry Lake in Cache County where runoff from the east side of the Wellsville Mountains collects in the spring. When Grove K. Gilbert made his survey in October 1879, he noted that Dry Lake (which he called Boxelder Lake) was—as it is at that time every year—dry. As he followed Box Elder Creek down the canyon, he postulated that the creek had begun to build a delta on the edge of the mountain at or just before the Provo Epoch of Lake Bonneville. He noted that "the Provo delta was rather small and its upper surface was nearly obliterated by the next. The same proximate obliteration was the fate of several other deltas whose remnants remain only at the extreme right or left."[4]

Dry Lake in Cache County is a basin which gathers spring runoff. In the summer of the great wet year 1983, the level of Dry Lake rose until US Highway 89—which has traversed Dry Lake Valley since 1947, when the highway was re-aligned from Sardine canyon to Wellsville Canyon—was under water, and the roadbed had to be raised. It is said by local old-timers that there is a "drain" of sorts at the east edge of dry lake through which the waters of the lake percolate, providing the source for springs which issue from the western foothills of the Wellsville Mountains, from Brigham City to Collinston.[5]

Five miles east of Brigham City and on the east side of the Wellsville Mountains lies Mantua Valley, once known as "the Little Valley." Many of the springs in Mantua Valley provide culinary water not only for the town of Mantua but for Brigham City as well. Mantua Reservoir, built in the 1960s, impounds runoff for Brigham City's irrigation system. Though a boon for Brigham City, the reservoir has raised the water table in Mantua Valley to the point that home construction and agriculture have been adversely affected.

West of the Wellsville Mountains is the lower Bear River Valley, one of several valleys that compose a group of Wasatch Front valleys—Utah Valley, Salt Lake Valley, and the Malad River Valley. Each of the valleys is separated by east-west tending spurs and salients of the Wasatch Mountains. The Pleasant View salient separates the less well-defined valley of Weber County and the lower Bear River Valley located in Box Elder County.

At the far northwestern corner of the county are the Raft River, Goose Creek, and Grouse Creek Mountains. Between them and the Wellsville and Clarkston Mountains in the northern section of the county are a series of north-south mountains and valleys. Moving west is the broad Bear River Valley. The Bear River valley blends into the Malad River Valley north of Fielding and Riverside. It is here in these two valleys that most of the agriculture takes place. Farther west, are other mountain ranges (including Little and Curtain, West Hills and Blue Springs Hills), playas, valleys, and streams.

On the west side of Blue Creek Valley rise the North Promontory Hills, which stretch southward becomingthe Promontory Mountains. The Promontory separates the two "arms" of the the Great Salt Lake and, along with Fremont and Antelope Islands, divides the lake north to south. West of the North Promontory range is Hansel Valley, delimited on the west by the Hansel Mountains.[6]

Between I-15 and Utah Highway 30 is the expansive Curlew Valley, punctuated by Cedar Hill and the Wildcat hills to the west. The next major ridge begins with the eastern slope of the Raft River Mountains on the north, continuing in the Baker Hills and the Hogup Mountains, which run down the western edge of the Great Salt Lake. West of the Baker Hills rise such landmarks as Red Dome, the Matlin Hills, Terrace Mountain, and Pigeon Mountain, far to the west, which were to give their names to sidings on the old transcontinental railroad route.

West of Curlew Valley, south of the Raft River Range, and north of Red Dome and the Matlin Mountains is Park Valley, where the settlements of Park Valley and Rosette are nestled.

The next major range in Box Elder County, proceeding west, are the Grouse Creek Mountains, which intersect the Raft River Mountains on the north. The Raft Rivers comprise the major mountain range in northwestern Box Elder County, and extend north from Rosette and Park Valley to the state line. The highest peak in the the Raft River Range is 9,890 feet above sea level.

The Raft River Mountains coalesce into the Goose Creek

Mountains, their peaks and crags broken up by the Upper Raft River Valley (just north of the Raft River Mountains), Junction Valley (separating the northern Raft Rivers from the Goose Creek Range,) the spectacular Cotton Thomas Basin, and the Grouse Creek Valley, to the west of the Grouse Creek range.

In the far northwest corner of Box Elder County lies the expansive Yost Valley, which extends north into Idaho. From the isolated community of Yost, one can see across the valley the tiny community of Almo, Idaho, as well as glimpse to the northwest one of the chief landmarks of the California Trail: The Twin Sisters (known during the Gold Rush as the Castle Rocks or the Steeple Rocks).

The Raft River Range is metamorphic in nature and consists of the oldest rocks in Utah, more than two billion years old, according to geologists.[7] There is also evidence of glacial activity in the Raft River and Grouse Creek Mountains.[8]

The northern slopes of the Goose Creek, Grouse Creek, and Raft River ranges constitute the only portion of Box Elder County not in the Great Basin. They are part of the Snake River Plain and drainage which is a tributary to the mighty Columbia River.[9]

At the southern edge of Box Elder County, rising from the playa of the Great Salt Lake Desert, are (west from the western edge of the lake) the Lakeside Mountains, the Newfoundland Mountains, and the Silver Island Mountains, which are continued to the north in the Little Pigeon Mountains, just south of Pigeon Mountain proper.

In southwestern Box Elder County is evidence of considerable ancient volcanic activity, which can be seen from I-15 between Tremonton and Blue Creek, and on U-30 between Snowville and Lucin, including some volcanic buttes or cones rising from the valley floor. There is said to be a volcanic dike in the Promontory Range near the southern tip of Promontory Point.

Igneous intrusions are also found in the Pilot Range, on Crater Island, in the Grouse Greek Mountains, at the north end of the Newfoundland Mountains, in the Raft River Range, and in the Wasatch Range. Significant exposures of extrusives are found at the north end of the Pilot Range, in the Goose Creek Mountains, Hogup Mountains, Wildcat Hills, Summer Ranch Mountains (Hansel Mountains) and in the North Promontory Mountains.[10]

Copper, zinc, and silver were discovered near the south end of the Promontory Range at the turn of the twentieth century. By World War I, the Lakeview Mining Company was the largest producer of zinc ore in the county.[11]

Minerals were discovered in the Grouse Creek Mountains as early as 1860. In July 1874 the Ashbrook Mining District was organized. It is the second most important mining district in the county.[12]

To the east in the Raft River Mountains are the Park Valley, Yost, and Clear Creek Mining districts. The districts produced a variety of minerals including copper, gold, lead, silver, and tungsten.

In the southern half of the Grouse Creek Mountains is the Rosebud Mining District. One of the newest mining districts in the county, there was little mining activity here before 1900. Tungsten has been the major ore mined, although the district has produced smaller amounts of lead, silver, and copper.

The Curlew Valley is a wide tract of level land north of the Great Salt Lake and between the Raft River and Hansel Mountains. It is part of a much larger area that extends into southern Idaho. The valley lacks the soil and vegetation typical of the Great Salt Lake Desert to the south.[13] Dividing the Curlew and Malad valleys is a series of low, north-trending ranges and narrow valleys that are significantly different from surrounding sections of the county. The topography is best described "as rolling or rounded [with] few outcrops of bare rock [and] is typical of the weathering and erosion of the Oquirrh Formation that produces mainly small, blocky fragments."[14] Large accumulations of gravel and sand are found in this section of the county and along Lake Bonneville shorelines.[15]

West of Great Salt Lake, dividing the lake bed from the Great Salt Lake Desert to the west, lie the Hogup and Terrace mountains on the north and the Lakeside mountains on the south. Between these mountain ranges is a convenient open area for the tracks of the old Southern Pacific's Lucin Cutoff, now part of the larger Union Pacific Railroad system. West of the Great Salt Lake is the Great Salt Lake Desert. It is composed of sand, mud, and salt, punctuated by the Newfoundland Mountains and other smaller mountains.

The Newfoundland Mountains were formed, like other mountain ranges in the Great Basin, from ancient sea deposits. The

Newfoundland Mountains and the Silver Island Mountains have igneous intrusions; as a result there have occurred mining activities in both mountain ranges, primarily tungsten as well as limited amounts of copper, gold, silver, lead, and molybdenum. The Newfoundland Mining District was established in the early 1870s. Mining activities occurred mostly during the first two decades of the twentieth century.

Mining activities commenced in the Silver Island Mountains in the early 1870s as well. However, no real production took place until shortly after the turn of the century. The Silver Island Mining District encompasses the entire mountain range which extends into northwest Tooele County. Much of the mining activity in the Box Elder County section of the Silver Island Mountains has taken place in the smaller Crater Island District. Between 1908 and 1913, the Crater Island District produced about $90,000 in various metals. Little production occurred following World War I until 1934 when the Great Depression encouraged reworking the claims in the district. Between 1934 and 1948, less than 100 ounces of gold, more than 1,100 ounces of silver, 23,600 pounds of copper, and 91 pounds of lead at an accumulated value of more than $7,800 were produced. In the 1970s limited mining activity resumed in the district, primarily prospecting and mining tungsten and molybdenum.

Bordering the Utah (Box Elder County)Nevada State line are the Pilot Peak Mountains composed chiefly of marine sedimentary rock laid down eons ago. The mountains also have instrusive igneous rock from which deposits of copper, silver, gold, lead, and zinc have been mined. As the name of the mountain range suggests, the Pilot Peak Mountains have been an important topographical landmark for adventurers, overland travelers, explorers, and fur trappers. Zenas Leonard was one such fur trapper who, in 1833, traveled through the western part of the county from a rendezvous on Green River to California. At the Pilot Peak Mountains Leonard wrote: "After traveling a few days longer through these barren plains; we came to the mountains described by the Indian as having its peak covered with snow. It presents a most singular experience—being entirely unconnected with any other chain. It is surrounded on either side by level plains and rises abruptly to a great height, rugged and hard to ascend.

To take a view of the surrounding country from the mountain, the eye meets with nothing but a smooth, sandy, level plain. On the whole, this mountain may be set down as one of the most remarkable phenomena of nature. Its top is covered with the piñon tree, bearing a kind of seed, which the natives are very fond of, and which they collect for winter provision."[16]

Thirteen years later another group of adventurers welcomed sighting the Pilot Peak Mountains. The Edwin Bryant and William H. Russell Party was one of several emigrant groups to travel around the south end of the Great Salt Lake using Hastings Cutoff to make better time on their way to California. By August the Bryant-Russell Party had reached the southern shore of the Great Salt Lake and had crossed much of the Great Salt Lake Desert before entering present-day Box Elder County. After many hard and dry hours of travel, Bryant reached the Pilot Peak Mountains. The mountains provided welcome relief of water which at one of the springs was "very cold and pure, and tasted to us more delicious than any of the invented beverages of the epicure to him."[17]

The Pilot Peak Mountains were, in places, richly endowed with thick vegitation. Bryant wrote that a traveling companion discovered a "blade of grass" which was measured at thirty-five feet in length and the diameter about a half inch.[18]

James Clyman, one of the earliest Euro-Americans to cross the Great Salt Lake Desert, wrote of the desert east of the Pilot Peak Mountains:

> To the South and East you have a boundless salt plain without vegetation except here and there a cliff of bare rocks standing like monumental pillars to commemorate the distinction of this portion of the earth . . . [We] soon entered on the great salt plain, the first plain 6 or 7 miles wide covered in many places three inches deep in pure white salt pass . . . [t]his is the [most] desolate country perhaps on the whole globe there not being one spear of vegetation and of course no kind of animal can subsist, and it is not ascertained to what extend this immince salt and sand plain can be south of where we [are] . . . [19]

Mines were first discovered in the Pilot Peak Mountains in the

Summer of 1868, a year before the completion of the transcontinental railroad. Three years later a small smelting furnace was built at Buel City, located in the eastern foothills of the Pilot Peak Mountains. Between 1870 and 1917, over $3.2 million of metals—gold, silver, copper, lead, zinc—was mined from the igneous formations of the Pilot Peak Mountains.[20]

The Wasatch Mountains south of Brigham City are composed of Precambrian sedimentary and crystalline rock which have been metamorphosed. The Wasatch Mountains were uplifed by ancient orogeny episodes.

This section of the Wasatch Mountains has yielded a modest amount of mineral ore. The first discovery was made on the King Solomon vein in 1897. Five years later the Sierra Madre Mining District was formed. Between 1901 and 1905, the several mining claims produced 205 tons of ore containing $100 worth of gold, 152 ounces of silver, and over 3,000 pounds of copper for a total value of about $1,000.

A second mining district, the Willard Mining District, was organized near the turn of the century. Some lead-silver ore and copper were discovered. The yields from the several mining claims were insufficient to cover expenses and the claims were closed.

Over the years, there has been significant prospecting and mining activity in Box Elder County, as well as considerable commerce in rock and gravel. Between 1951 and 1974, the total mineral production was valued at $59,982,616. Of that amount, over $8.6 million worth of base metals was produced in the county. Most of the value from mining has come from construction materials, primarily stone, sand, and gravel. Nearly half the cumulative value of mineral production in Box Elder County between 1951 and 1974, came from construction of the Southern Pacific causeway from Promontory Point to Lakeside between 1956 and 1959. Over 43.7 million cubic yards of rock fill came from the quarries on the Promontory peninsula. In addition salts have also been harvested in the county. Through 1874 salts harvested from the Great Salt Lake provided 17.9 percent of the cumulative mineral value in the county.[21]

Great Salt Lake

The Great Salt Lake and the Great Salt Lake Desert dominate the county's landscape. It is the largest lake in the nation apart from the Great Lakes and is a remnant of prehistoric Lake Bonneville.

Named for a nineteenth century U.S. Army captain B.L.E. Bonneville, who never set foot in Utah, Lake Bonneville is the most recent of several ancient lakes that covered Box Elder County and western Utah. It was formed more than 50,000 years ago during the last Ice Age. Climatic changes resulted in the fluctuation of Lake Bonneville. At its largest, Lake Bonneville covered the greater part of western Utah with arms stretching into Nevada and southern Idaho. The ancient lake level rose during wet cycles and leveled off during dry spells, finally reaching it highest point, about 5,200 feet above sea level, with a depth of about 1,050 feet and carving out a shoreline at what is now known as the Bonneville Level or Bonneville Bench. At that time Lake Bonneville covered at least 75 percent of Box Elder County. After an extended period at the Bonneville Level, the lake breached Red Rock Pass (located on US Highway 91 about nineteen miles northwest of Preston, Idaho). Red Rock Pass is the lowest point in the northern rim of the Great Basin, and through it poured a tremendous flood of water and debris.

The Great Bonneville Flood, which drained and uncovered much of the land in Box Elder County, was one of the greatest geological "catastrophes" in the history of the continent. Some scientific evidence indicates that the maximum discharge was about fifteen million cubic feet per second of water passing through the Red Rock pass outlet or about three times the average flow of the Amazon River.[22] An associate of the famous John Wesley Powell and co-worker for the U.S. Geological Survey, Grove Karl Gilbert, was, in 1878, the first to report on the Great Bonneville Flood and to extensively study Lake Bonneville. Later studies of flood gauging of the Snake River Canyon in Idaho substantiates much of Gilbert's study of the Great Bonneville Flood.

After the great flood, the ancient lake level rested a while at what is called the Provo Level, before continuing to drop. The Provo Bench or Terrace is the second major level of the lake and is approximately

400 feet below the Bonneville Terrace and more than 500 feet above the current level of the Great Salt Lake. At 300 feet above the current lake level, the Stansbury Terrace—the youngest of the several major terraces—was formed.

In Box Elder County, the evidence of Lake Bonneville is visible in terraces on the Wasatch Range and most clearly on the Promontory Range, which bifurcates Great Salt Lake, dividing it into two arms—the Bear River Bay and the smaller North, South, and Willard bays on the east side; and the Gilbert, Gunnison, and Spring bays on the west.

Beginning about 25,000 years ago, Lake Bonneville receded to its current shoreline. Hydrologists and others have set the mean or standard level of the Great Salt Lake at 4,200 feet above sea level. Over the years the lake level has fluctuated with wet and dry cycles.. The historic high was equaled during the wet cycle of 1983 to 1986. Even now, the Great Salt Lake covers about 12 percent of Box Elder County's nearly 6,400 square-mile area.[23] The lake has an average depth of thirteen feet, and a maximum mean depth of thirty-five feet, though many locals claim a depth of a hundred feet just off Promontory Point.

The lapping waters of the receding Lake Bonneville coupled with periodic flooding created alluvial deposits in the county. Located at the mouths of the various canyons on the west face of the Wellsville Mountains, these alluvial deposits are composed of soil, gravel, and sand. On these alluvial fans some of the state's best fruit is grown and construction materials are mined. Brigham City is situated on one of the most prominent of ancient alluvial deposits in the county. It is the narrow band of watered land where the first settlements in nineteenth-century pioneer Utah were founded.

Elsewhere in the county are other bodies of lake-deposited silt and fanglomerate which escape the casual eye. In the valley between Corinne and the Promontory, thousands of feet of lake deposit overlie the valley bedrock. In some places the fill is 10,000 feet deep. Poking through these lake deposits are the north-south trending Little Mountain, the Newfoundland Range, Pilot Range, and the Promontory Mountains.

Water Resources

Between the Wellsville Mountains and the Malad Range to the north flows the Bear River, the Great Salt Lake's major tributary and the major source of water to irrigate eastern Box Elder County.[24] Bear River has its origin on the north flank of the Uinta Mountains. It takes a tortuous and meandering course through Utah, Wyoming, Idaho, and again into Utah. The waters of the Bear River are controlled by diversion into Bear Lake, and by Cutler Dam, one of the nation's largest hydroelectric structures when it was built in the 1920s. It is from Cutler dam that the east and west Bear River canals flow, irrigating the vast arable land in Bear River Valley which otherwise could not be irrigated from the sunken riverbed.

West of the Bear River and on the other side of the West Hills flows the Malad River, down the Malad Valley from Idaho. In the early years after the completion of the transcontinental railroad, the Malad Valley was a major freight corridor between the mines of western Montana and the railheads at Kelton and Corinne. Donald Mackenzie, a French-Canadian trapper from the Hudson's Bay Company, is credited with naming the river. While trapping for beaver on the Malad River, MacKenzie and some of his men became ill after eating beaver meat. The root word from which Malad or Malade (French for "sick') is derived is the same word from which comes our English term "malady."[25] American explorer Captain John C. Fremont called the river the Roseaux.

One of the most lovely and pastoral spots in Box Elder County is the confluence of the Bear and Malad rivers, as their serpentine paths merge in the midst of some of Utah's most picturesque and fertile agricultural land, about two miles north of Corinne. The Bear River continues past Corinne flowing leisurely through the marshes and sloughs which provide sanctuary and nesting grounds to great flocks of waterfowl—an area encompassed within Bear River Migratory Bird Refuge—before entering into the Bear River Bay, which forms the north arm of Great Salt Lake.

Though the Bear and the Malad are the largest rivers in Box Elder County, and flow through the most populous areas of the county, numerous other streams that are also vital to life and agriculture in the county. Box Elder Creek carries water from the mountains above Brigham City; Blue Creek flows through Blue Creek Valley, west of the Blue Springs Hills; Deep Creek provides needed water in Curlew Valley, as does Tenmile Creek between Black Butte and the Wildcat Hills. One of the major watercourses in western Box Elder County is Dove Creek, flowing from the junction of the Raft River Mountains and the Grouse Creek Mountains to the sinks of Dove Creek, between the Baker Hills and the Matlin Mountains and next to the long-abandoned transcontinental railroad grade built by the Central Pacific Railroad in 1869.

The Raft River range is drained by Indian Creek, Pine Creek, Black Hills Creek, Johnson Creek, George Creek, Onemile Creek, Clear Creek, Rice Creek, and Tenmile Creek. From the Grouse Creek Mountains flow Grouse Creek and its tributaries: Kimbell, Pine, and Red Butte, as well as Muddy and Rosebud creeks on the east side. The Goose Creek Mountains give rise to Basin, Joe Dahar, Cotton, and Straight creeks (all tributaries of Grouse Creek), and Hardesy, Pole, Birch, and Long creeks, which flow west or north out of Box Elder County (and out of Utah), except Long Creek, which joins Junction Creek, draining Junction Valley, and then in its turn joining the Raft River, which flows north into Idaho, a tributary of the Snake River. The north slope of the Raft River range and the west slope of the Goose Creek mountains are outside the Great Basin. The Snake River flows eventually into the great Columbia River, and finally into the Pacific Ocean.

Besides its creeks and rivers, Box Elder County is dotted with springs. Box Elder County's most significant historic route, the Salt Lake Cutoff, followed a line of springs from the base of the Wasatch and Wellsville mountains west across the Bear River Valley. The springs rise here and there across the otherwise arid valleys of Box Elder County. Springs, large and small, bear a veritable potpourri of names: Burnhope Spring, Blue Springs, Garland Springs, Cedar Springs. There are springs along the pioneer trails with names like Immigrant and Pilot. There are springs named for people: Madsen, Udy, Chambers, Callahan, Porter, and Connor. There are springs with colorful names like Crystal, Mound, Locomotive, Dipping Vat, Pole, Mahagany, Boundary, Owl, and Rabbit.

In a desert land, water is the key to settlement. Box Elder County, over the years, has gained its complement of water impoundments. The largest is Willard Bay, holding 193,300 acre-feet of water. Other Box Elder County reservoirs include Cutler, Blue Creek Reservoir, Rose Ranch Reservoir, Mantua Reervoir, Etna Reservoir, and Death Creek Reservoir. Other water impoundments include the ponds dammed up at Locomotive Springs and the Newfoundland Evaporation Basin, the short-lived lake created by the ill-fated project to pump Great Salt Lake overflow into the desert during the wet cycle of the 1980s.

Box Elder County has a significant number of hot and warm springs. Utah Hot Springs—known to local residents simply as "Hot Springs"—is located on the boundary between Box Elder and Weber counties in the Union Pacific Railroad right-of-way. At one time a resort stood on the spot, but within the last twenty years it was razed in favor of an explosives plant. The water at Utah Hot Springs is highly mineralized and its water temperature is scalding at 135° Fahrenheit.

Just north of Honeyville is Crystal Springs, Box Elder County's major hot springs resort. Earlier known as Madsen Hot Springs, Crystal Springs has been a bathing resort since the Shoshoni and their predecessors inhabited the land. In the 1970s the pools were rebuilt and a waterslide installed. A natural cold springs next to the hot springs has led to the assertion that at Crystal Springs are to be found the largest-volume hot and cold springs arising side-by-side in the United States.

Ten miles west of Corinne are the forlorn and neglected "Stinky Springs." This high-sulfur spring, officially known as Stinking Hot Springs, is a sad tale in history. It was owned in the nineteenth century by Corinne pioneer Hiram House. At his death he bequeathed the springs to Box Elder County with the stipulation that no one would ever be charged to use the healing sulfurous waters. Box Elder County officials agreed, in turn, to maintain the spring and its buildings, and keep the place clean. A subsequent owner of land around the spring moved the bathing building across the highway. Over the years Box Elder County forgot its part of the agreement and the building was allowed to disintegrate. At this writing, only the concrete pools remain, which bathers have covered with a black-plastic "tent." The site is filthy, and many people dare not go there any more. More's the pity, for waters of Stinky Springs are said to contain healing power, especially for those suffering from arthritic conditions. Many local old-timers testify of the curative powers of the waters.

Etna Hot Springs, the other major hot spring, lie on the far western border of the county. Within the past few years, its waters have been harnessed and piped to provide geothermal heat for a house built nearby.

Climate

In addition to the geography, hydrology, and topography which affected Box Elder County is its climate. Box Elder County covers exactly one degree of latitude from 41degree to 42 degree north latitude, placing the county well within what is called the Temperate Zone or mild climate. The climate is affected by the wide difference in altitude of nearly 4,500 feet, from a standard lake level of 4,200 feet above sea level at the Great Salt Lake to nearly 10,000 feet in the far northwestern corner of the county in the Raft River range.

The salinity of the lake, which never freezes, has a moderating effect upon local weather. Moisture-laden storm fronts leave the Pacific Northwest and have most of the moisture wrung out as they pass over the Sierras and the Cascades. The Wellsville Mountains force most of what moisture is left out of the clouds and on to the communities along their base giving a much higher annual amount of precipitation to Brigham City, with an average of eighteen inches a year, than locations like Corinne and the Bear Lake Migratory Bird Refuge, which average five inches or less a year.

The annual average mean temperature is nearly 51 degrees Fahrenheit, the same as Ogden and Salt Lake and three degrees warmer than Logan's 48 degrees.Brigham City's record high temperature was 108 degrees Fahrenheit in July 1931; the record low was minus 27 degrees in February 1963. The annual snowfall averages fifty-two inches a year, with the heaviest snowfall on record during 18–20 December 1929 leaving twenty-eight inches.

The county's highest official recorded temperature of 109 degrees occurred at Corinne in June and August 1940, eight degrees below the highest recorded temperature of 117 in St. George in 1985. At the other end of the scale, minus 30 degrees was recorded at the Thiokol Plant in February 1984.[26]

The frost-free season in Box Elder County (except in the mountain elevations) averages from 120 to 160 days, roughly from May to October.[27] The average date of the last frost is 14 May; and the average date of the first frost is 28 September. That gives an average of 138 consecutive days without frost in a normal growing season. The average normal annual precipitation varies from location to location, from the lake to the mountains, between thirty and thirty-nine inches at the highest elevations to less than six inches on the Great Salt Lake Desert.[28]

The moderate climate is very good for agriculture and helps explain why Box Elder County is the largest producer of winter wheat in the state and why a third of the peaches grown in Utah come from the Brigham City area. In 1992 the combined market value of all agricultural and livestock produces sold amounted to more than $138 million, placing the county fourth behind Cache, Utah, and Sanpete counties.[29]

Box Elder County has experienced its share of severe weather. A report in the *Brigham City Bugler* chronicled a storm on 29 July 1897:

> We learn from Ben Williams, the Collinston stage line proprietor, that one of the heaviest rain and hail storms occurred on the east side of Bear River flat last Thursday afternoon that ever happened in that section to the knowledge of the earliest settlers, says the Malad Enterprise. The storm came up during the afternoon and inside of two hours Bear River had risen to a point much higher than the high water mark of the regular spring floods. The whole sides of the mountain around Square Town [Plymouth] were washed clean and many acres of lucern and wheat were washed away. The water poured down from off the mountains in regular torrents and roads, bridges and fences were swept away like chaff. In some places along Bear River, where the water had overrun the banks, hail was piled over the land to a depth of 18 to 20 inches and thousands of pounds of fish were left on the shores by the receding waters. Wagon loads were gathered up by settlers on the river and thousands were left to rot in the sun. The storm only

> lasted about two hours and was mostly in the mountains, but the damage done the settlers in the valley was very large. No such storm has ever occurred in that section before.[30]

In the late 1920s through the mid-1930s the lack of precipitation in the west end of the county forced ranchers to haul thousands of gallons of water by rail to thirsty livestock. A terrific windstorm in the early 1950s toppled scores of trees, tore off roofs, and took a couple of pinnacles off the Brigham City LDS Tabernacle. Five tornados have been recorded in the county since 1847.[31] Late spring frosts and occasional hailstorms have brought economic difficulties to parts of the county. The afternoon of 31 May 1918 a hailstorm stripped young pea plants of their blossoms and an estimated 75 percent of peach, apricot, and cherry fruit was stripped from trees causing thousands of dollars in damage.[32] On 30 July 1958 a two-inch downpour in forty minutes killed 1,300 turkeys in Fielding. In Bothwell a flash flood drowned eight cattle and flooded fourteen homes.[33]

Flora and Fauna

The canyons and hillsides of Box Elder County are covered with maple trees. The scrub-oak which covers the foothills above Salt Lake City, Ogden, and Provo reaches its northern limit in Box Elder County. In the canyons and mountains are found Mountain Mahogany, Chokecherry, and Serviceberry or Shad Brush. Aspen are found higher up on the mountains between 6,500 to 8,000 feet aspen. Atop the Wellsville and Raft River Mountains are stands of Douglas Fir and Spruce. In the valleys streams are outlined by the rough-barked and gnarled-limbed Cottonwood. The desert flats are covered with native grasses, rabbitbrush , and the ubiquitous sagebrush . Box Elder County has its share of pests as well, plants such as *Salsola,* an annual forb, greasewood, and *Halogeton*—introduced to the Intermountain West from central Asia in the 1930s. Perhaps the most discussed in recent years is the cursed Dyer's Woad, also known as mustard weed. Box Elder's flora has some features of its own. One species of wild onion is found nowhere but in the area between Promontory and Thiokol.[34]

The careful observer will find a plethora of plant life in the county. From the marshes between Corinne and Blue Creek cattails and rushes have been used for many purposes. The tuberous roots of the cattail were used by Natives and pioneers alike for a potato-like food, the pollen was used as flour, and the fluff of the cattail heads made soft mattress stuffing. In addition to food or fiber, many plants have a wide variety of medicinal purposes. The leaves of sagebrush were pulverized by Indians and pioneers into a powder and was used to soothe skin chafing. Indians used sagebrush as a disinfectant. Sagebrush leaves were used to cover seeds and berries to protect them from bug and rodent attack.[35] Cocklebur leaves were boiled to a tea for use as a diuretic. Cocklebur seeds, when crushed, were used as an antiseptic for skin abrasions. Boiled leaves and spring rods of dandelion helped to dissolve kidney stones, and Mormon tea, also known as Cowboy Tea or Brigham Tea among other names, was brewed and drunk as a decongestant.[36]

In May the fields and foothills around Promontory are dotted with Utah's state flower—the Sego Lily. In far-western Box Elder County are piñon pine trees which produce pine nuts, an important food source for Native peoples.

Wildlife habitat is directly tied to the plant life of the county. This is especially true with the lower herbivores. There is, for example, a small "sagebrush vole" or meadow mice which eats primarily the leaves and bark of sagebrush. The deer mouse ranges only in the areas covered by saltbush or shadscale. While some of the smaller mammals are limited in their range, larger rodents and mammals have a much wider range in the Great Basin. The porcupine is an exception. It is found only among trees.

Some of the wider-ranging mammals found in the county are mule deer, badger, an occasional elk or moose, bobcat, an occasional puma, and perhaps (although it is rare these days) a bear. Mule deer, some scientists and other argue, are more plentiful than in the nineteenth century and earlier. Archaeological studies suggest the mule deer was rather sparse in the diet of the prehistoric Indians of the area.[37] The carnivores are not as limited in habitat as are the small herbivores, although a change in small mammal population affects, to a greater or smaller degree, the predator population.

Farther west, in the desert areas of the county, are found populations of mice in the grasslands and wheat fields, rats, and ground squirrels, as well as badgers, and coyotes. In the same area are large populations of cottontail and the black-tailed jackrabbits.

Reptiles range from horned toads and geckos to blowsnakes and rattlesnakes. Although rattlesnakes are usually limited to the rocky foothills and arid benchlands, occasionaly they are found in inhabited areas including Brigham City. More common are the watersnakes found near springs and marshy areas of the county.

Human activity has in some cases altered dramatically animal population in the county. For instance, the increased need for food and fiber by the Indians of northern Utah eliminated a very small herd of mountain bison. Large amounts of bison bones were retrieved from several archaeological sites near the mouth of the Bear River.[38]

As settlement has developed, human population grown, and hunting increased, many of the mammals which historically ranged near and around the present site of towns and cities have been hunted to lower populations or withdrawn to less populated areas. Among these are the bear, cougar, and wolf.

In the marsh areas of the county are muskrat, and higher in the mountain canyons are found beaver and their dams. Skunks are common. Less common are the weasel and the wild mink. The fresh waters of the county have limited endemic fisheries but include carp, catfish, trout, Utah chub, Utah sucker, and Bluehead

There are many birds in the county including many migratory birds that find refuge in the marshes and bird refuges along the Bear River and the Great Salt Lake. A few of the birds include: blue grouse, pheasants, mourning doves, red-winged blackbirds, meadowlarks, yellow-headed blackbirds, western screetch owl, common night hawk, northern flicker, willow flycatcher, black-capped chickadee, song sparrow, pigeon, magpie, raven, crow, hummingbird, California Gull, blue heron, loons, agrebes, cormorants, ibis, egrets, goose, snipe, curlew, and many kinds of ducks.

Geographic Place Names

It is the nature of people to give names; however, geographical names often change as one culture displaces another. So it has been in Box Elder. We have no knowledge of the names given the rivers, streams, and mountains of Box Elder by the ancient cultures. The earliest names we have for the features in Box Elder's valleys and mountains are those of the native Shoshoni, who were in possession of the land before the French-Canadian trappers, government explorers, and the Mormon settlers came.

The Bear River was known to the Shoshoni by two different names. Above Bear Lake, it was known as *tsy-guy-o-guy* (*sag-wy-og-way*), and lower Bear River was called *pe-og-wa.* Beaver Dam was *ha-na-te-ya-tih-up,* and Box Elder Creek was *wo-go-bas.* The Shoshoni called the Malad River *tope-pah* (or *tope-og-way*).[39]

The community of Portage takes its name from Portage County, Ohio, the county in which Lorenzo Snow, Box Elder County's foremost religious leader, was born. Mantua, five miles east of Brigham City, was named for Snow's birthplace. Mantua was earlier known as Flaxville (from an early agricultural venture) and Little Copenhagen (from the colony of Danes sent there to found the settlement). Snowville, in far northern Box Elder County, was named for Lorenzo Snow.

Many places in the county were named for persons. Wellsville Mountain and the town on its eastern slope were named for Daniel H. Wells, early Mormon pioneer and counselor to Brigham Young. The town of Willard was named for Willard Richards, also a counselor to Brigham Young. Porter Spring, one of the springs along the Salt Lake Cutoff, was named for early Utah lawman Orrin Porter Rockwell. Deweyville, formerly known as Empey Springs, was named for John C. Dewey, "who settled the area after William Empey left in 1864." Honeyville was so named after founder Abraham Hunsaker declined the name "Hunsakerville," but agreed to name it for his occupation as a beekeeper. [40]

One of the most intriguing area names is Hansel Valley. The evolving name of Hansel Valley indicates the orthographic transformation which can take place in the absence of written records. The Salt Lake Cutoff was pioneered in 1848 when discharged members of the Mormon Battalion returning from California after the discovery of gold at Sutter's sawmill met Captain Samuel J. Hensley, a U.S. Army captain, who, along with ten other men, were on their way west. Hensley's name, applied to the route, a spring, a mountain, and a valley in the immediate area of his meeting with the returning battalion members, was heard, orally transmitted, and became, in turn, "Hensell," "Hansel," and even "Hazel" on one map. [41]

A number of Box Elder County names are what might be called "railroad names." Some were conferred with the coming of the transcontinental railroad in 1869, others were added later. They include Kelton, Terrace, Lucin, Surban, Umbria, Metatarus, Cosmo, and Watercress. Collinston was named for Collins Fullmer, a conductor on the Utah Northern Railroad.

Perhaps the most famous of the railroad towns in Box Elder is Corinne, known derisively in surrounding Mormon communities as "The Burg on the Bear" (from its location at the spot where the transcontinental railroad crossed the Bear River). Corinne has also been labeled "The Gentile Capital of Utah" and "The City of the Ungodly."[42] There are several accounts of the derivation of the town's name. Some say it was named for a famous French actress of the time, Corinne LaVaunt. Others say the name was derived from the name of a character in a popular novel. The most plausible is that it was given the name of Corinne Williamson, the young daughter of Col. J. A. Williamson, who surveyed the town for the railroad. From the beginning, to the present day, people have had difficulties spelling the name "Corinne." Some give it two "r"s instead of two "n"s. Early on, some Corinnethian wag came up with a bit of doggerel verse to make the job easier: "Two *n*'s, an *i*, and an *e;* an *r*, an *o*, and a *c*."

A number of Box Elder County towns were settled and named during what might be called the "second tier" of Utah colonization. Around the turn of the twentieth century, dams were built, canals dug, irrigation systems constructed, and communities established on the plains of the county, where land could not be brought under irrigation in pioneer days. A whole cluster of communities bear the names of LDS church leaders during this era of commercial irrigation development including: Fielding (Joseph Fielding Smith), Penrose (Charles W. Penrose), and Thatcher (Moses Thatcher). Howell was named for politician and canal-magnate Joseph Howell. In 1903 Tremonton was settled by a group from the area of Tremont, Illinois.[43] Another community which didn't last, and didn't live up to the grand prognostications of its promotors, was Appledale, an expansive development of homes and orchards which failed when the irrigation water leached alkali and salt to the surface, killing the apple trees and crops. It was not until the later organization of the Corinne Drainage District and the laying of an extensive system of drainage tiles to drain the area that it became productive farm land.

On Promontory, besides the locations of five small communities—Promontory, North Promontory, East Promontory, Booth Valley, and Saline—each with a schoolhouse, was the mining town of Lakeview, in the Lakeview mining district, with a magnificent view of the lake, and the much later community of Little Valley, which bloomed and faded with the construction of the Southern Pacific Causeway in the late 1950s.

Other places, such as the Civilian Conservation Corps camp built in Willard Basin in the 1930s, "Chatfield's Dam" at the head of a failed irrigation project in Devil's Gate Basin, and "The Russian Settlement" near Park Valley, have been named because of a group or undertaking with which the location is associated.

Box Elder County has it share of ghost towns. Not only has the highly-touted Appledale disappeared, but so have others. Kelton, Terrace, and all their sister towns of the transcontinental railroad between Corinne and Lucin are gone. So is La Plata, the booming silver-mining town on the border between Box Elder and Cache counties in the high Bear River Mountains.

ENDNOTES

1. See Stephen Trimble, *The Sagebrush Ocean: A Natural History of the Great Basin* (Reno: University of Nevada Press, 1989), 5–8.

2. Don R. Murphy, "Physiographic Provinces," in Wayne L. Wahlquist, ed., *Atlas of Utah* (Ogden: Weber State College, 1981), 17.

3. The Wasatch Range proper extends from Mount Nebo (where Juab, Sanpete and Utah counties meet) on the south to Wellsville Mountains (dividing Box Elder and Cache counties) on the north. The greater Wasatch line, however, extends through the 400-mile length of Utah, and further, into Idaho and Arizona. Ward Roylance, *Utah: A Guide to the State* (Salt Lake City: Utah Arts Council, 1982), 20.

4. Charled B. Hunt, ed., "Pleistocene Lake Bonneville, Ancestral Great Salt Lake, as Described in the Notebooks of G. K. Gilbert, 1875–1880,"

Brigham Young University Geology Studies Vol. 29, Pt. 1 (Provo: Brigham Young University Department of Geology, 1982), 116.

5. Geologists dispute that belief, since the upthrust of the Wellsville Range would seem to direct water east instead of west.

6. The name "Hansel" is a corruption by oral transmission of "Hensley." See L. A. Fleming and A. R. Standing, "The Road to 'Fortune': The Salt Lake Cutoff," *Utah Historical Quarterly 33* (Summer 1965), 255, n 12, who give as their source Joseph Cain and Ariah C. Brower's 1851, *Mormon Way Bill to the Gold Mines.*

7. William L. Stokes, *Geology of Utah* (Salt Lake City: Utah Geological and Mineral Survey, 1986), 39.

8. Helmut H. Doelling, with Jock A. Campbell, J. Wallace Gwynn, and Lee I. Perry, "Geology and Mineral Resources of Box Elder County, Utah" *Utah Geological and Mineral Survey Bulletin* 115 (Salt Lake City: Utah Geological and Mineral Survey, 1980), 66. The Raft River Mountains and river were named after rafts used to cross the river. The Pilot Range was named by John C. Fremont. The mountains were used as a guide by overland travelers. Grouse Creek was named for the numerous sage grouse found in the valley. For a study of these and other geographic place names, see John W. Van Cott, *Utah Place Names* (Salt Lake City: University of Utah Press, 1990).

9. Stokes, *Geology of Utah,* p. 256.

10. Doelling, et al., "Geology and Mineral Resources of Box Elder County," 66.

11. Ibid., 108.

12. Ibid., 145.

13. Stokes, *Geology of Utah,* 256.

14. Ibid.

15. Ibid.

16. John C. Ewers, ed., *Adventures of Zenas Leonard Fur Trader* (Norman: University of Oklahoma Press, 1959), 67.

17. Edwin Bryant, *What I Saw in California Being the Journal of a Tour in the Years 1846, 1847* (Minneapolis: Ross & Haines, inc., 1967), 183. Pilot Peak itself, located just inside the state of Nevada, is 10,716 feet above sea level.

18. Bryant, *What I Saw In California,* 184.

19. J. Roderic Korns, "West From Fort Bridger—The Pioneering of the Immigrant Trails Across Utah, 1846–1850," *Utah Historical Quarterly,* 19 (1951): 33.

20. B.S. Butler et. al. *The Ore Deposits of Utah,* U.S. Geological Survey

Professional Papers #111 (Washington, D.C.: Government Printing Office, 1920), 489.

21. Doelling, et. al., "Geology and Mineral Resources of Box Elder County," 85–86.

22. Cort Conley, *Idaho for the Curious: A Guide* (Cambridge, ID: Backeddy Books, 1982), 507. (For more detailed information, see USGS Paper No. 596, 1968.)

23. Helmut H. Doelling, *Geology and Mineral Resources of Box Elder County,* 1.

24. The average annual flow of the Bear River measured between 1941 and 1990 at Corinne was 1.231 million acre feet. *Utah State Water Plan: Bear River Basin* (Salt Lake City: Utah Division of Water Resources, 1992), 5–6.

25. Van Cott, Utah Place Names, 242.

26. R. Clayton Brough et al., *Utah's Comprehensive Weather Almanac* (Salt Lake City, 1987). The coldest spot in the state is Peter Sinks in Logan Canyon where the temperature dropped to minus 67 degrees in February 1985.

27. E. Arlo Richardson, Gaylen L. Ashcroft, John K. Westbrook, "Freeze-Free Season" in Wahlquist, *Atlas of Utah,* 63.

28. E. Arlo Richardson, Gaylen L. Ashcroft, John K. Westbrook, "Precipitation" in Wahlquist, , *Atlas of Utah,* 66–67.

29. Agricultural census for Utah and various counties.

30. *Brigham City Bugler,* 31 July 31 1897, 1.

31. Brough, . *Utah's Comprehensive Weather Almanac,* 73.

32. *Box Elder News,* 31 May 1918.

33. Brough, *Utah's Comprehensive Weather Almanac,* 168, 182.

34. The author expresses thanks to Brigham Young University botanist Stanley L. Welsh for pointing this out.

35. Michael Moore, *Medicinal Plants of the Desert and Canyon West* (Santa Fe: Museum of New Mexico Press, 1989), 103–4.

36. Ibid., 59, 69, 109.

37. Jesse D. Jennings, *Prehistory of Utah and the Eastern Great Basin,* University of Utah Anthropological Papers, Number 98 (Salt Lake City: University of Utah Press, 1978) , 223; and Dale L. Stevens, ed., *The Great Salt Lake Desert, a Geographical Survey* (Provo: Department of Geography, 1995), 412.

38. Jennings, *Prehistory of Utah and the Eastern Great Basin,* 162, 233.

39. From "Shoshoni Place Names in Utah and Vicinity," typescript in possession of the author.

40. Van Cott, *Utah Place Names,* 110.

41. L. A. Fleming and A. R. Standing, "'The Road to 'Fortune': The Salt Lake Cutoff," Utah Historical Quarterly, 33 (Summer 1965): 255.

42. Noted Corinne historian Bernice Gibbs Anderson wrote a small history of Corinne, published with the title, "Corinne: City of the Un-Godly."

43. Ibid. See also Van Cott, *Utah Place Names,* 374.

CHAPTER 2

MAN BEFORE HISTORY

Human beings have walked the mountains and deserts, the shores and fens of earth for thousands if not millions of years. We have no exact figures concerning the length of human habitation in what is Box Elder County, but we have evidence of human occupation going back several thousand years. Men, women, and children of whom we have scant record lived and died in the mountains, valleys, caves, and on the riverbanks of the area for generations.

Our ignorance of the prehistoric inhabitants of Box Elder, except for the detritus they left, along with their mortal remains and vestiges of their habitations, is almost all-encompassing. We know nothing of their thought, religion, hopes and dreams, and plans. We can understand these cultures, totally removed from our own in time, space, and cosmos, only on *their* own terms. We can only describe the bits and pieces we find left behind.

Archaeologist David Madsen explains that prehistoric societies are usually seen " . . . in terms of extremes; either as ignorant savages blundering their way through life or as primitive spiritualists living in harmony with nature and the world around them. But the[y] . . .

were just like every human group; some were cruel and some were benevolent; some were smart and some were a little slow; some worked hard and some were lazy. They were human beings, simply that, trying to raise children in a variable and sometimes harsh landscape."[1]

Part of the gap which separates us from these ancient peoples is their intimate connection with the land, and the variation and diversity of land forms, climate, elevation, vegetation, and all the environmental variables encountered in the cyclical yearly migrations of the ancients.

That said, in the present discussion we must content ourselves with those of our culture here in these valleys and mountains of whom we have some evidence, and with the evidence we have found.

That evidence takes us back some 10,000 years, to the time of the retreat of large glaciers, the last years of Lake Bonneville, and the change from a cool-wet climate to today's warm-dry climate.[2] Any remains or evidence of human habitation of the pre-Bonneville period would have been obliterated during the 40,000 years the thousand-foot-deep lake covered the land.

The evidence we have of human habitation in our area dates from the time Lake Bonneville broke through Red Rock Pass and began its retreat, after caves and springs appeared, and after the climate warmed, becoming hospitable for human beings who occupied the area in small food-gathering groups.[3]

The lifestyle of these earliest known human residents of Box Elder prevailed through the millennia up to and including the Shoshoni, who inhabited the area upon the arrival of the early European and American explorers, and the later nineteenth-century settlers.

Anthropologists have divided the 10,000 or so years of known habitation in Box Elder and the greater Eastern Great Basin into three cultural phases: Desert Archaic, Fremont, and Late Prehistoric (also known as proto-historic).

According to the doyen of Utah archeologists, Jesse D. Jennings, "From 10,000 or more years ago, until A.D. 400, the only culture represented in Utah, as well as the rest of the Great Basin, was the Desert Archaic. That culture is characterized as a hunting-gathering one, a flexible, highly adaptive lifeway that has characterized most of man's worldwide history."[4] Their culture was not glamorous, nor complex socially, but they did develop highly specialized tools, utensils, and practices. Basket making was a highly developed craft. Jug-shaped baskets were lined with piñon gum or pitch to make them water tight. Stone tools were used to grind grains and seeds. Obsidian and other glasses were chipped to make sharp-edged projectiles. Clothing was made from animal skins and woven reeds and well-suited to the climate. Living accommodations were not permanent but varied, as groups traveled in their annual cycle for harvesting plants and hunting animals. The social order was simple but effective and was centered in the primary and extended family.[5]

Traces of their migratory patterns remain upon the landscape. Some of the ancients wintered in caves on Promontory and spent their summers in the lush Cache Valley. The traces of an ancient path can still be seen coming out of flat-bottom canyon on Wellsville Mountain, and descending to a spring near the valley floor east of Brigham City.

According to Jesse Jennings, "The Fremont culture is uniquely Utahn, having developed in the state from an Archaic base *after* the transmission of certain technological complexes across the Southwest from Mexico."[6] The innovations were primarily in the area of agriculture and included the cultivation of corn, squash, and beans.[7] Another difference between the Archaic and Fremont cultures was the making of pottery, which the Fremont did and the Archaics did not. Another Fremont innovation, made possible by agriculture, was a more sedentary lifestyle with the development of permanent housing which consisted of subterranean areas under wood-and-mud structures.

The Fremont amused themselves with gaming pieces made of bone or pottery and stone balls—between the size of a golf ball and tennis ball. Anthropologist James H. Gunnerson concludes: "The balls from the Fremont area have presumably been found associated with patterns of small pits pecked into the surface of nearly level bedrock. This association suggests some sort of game like marbles in which the balls would be rolled into the pits."[8]

The Fremont people were undoubtedly diverse in many ways. As David Madsen writes:

> Like the land, the prehistoric societies of the western Colorado Plateau and the eastern Great Basin can also be characterized by variation and diversity and are neither readily defined nor easily encapsulated within a single description. Some people were primarily settled farmers, growing corn, beans, and squash in small plots along streams at the base of mountain ranges: some were nomads, collecting wild plants and animals to support themselves; still others would shift between these lifestyles. In some areas the population was relatively dense, in others only small groups were found widely scattered across the landscape. People living in this region may even have spoken different languages or had widely divergent dialects. Yet, despite the diversity of these lifestyles and the varied geography which structured their actions, these people seem to have shared patterns of behavior and ways of living which tie them together.

Today we call these scattered groups of hunters and farmers the Fremont, but that name may be more reflective of our own need to categorize things than it is a reflection of how closely related these people were. "Fremont" is really a generic label for a people who, like the land in which they lived, are not easily described or classified.[9]

The Fremont were replaced, by A.D. 1300 by the third cultural group, again with ties to northern Mexico. The Shoshonian tribes (Shoshoni, Paiute, Gosiute, Ute) speak a Numic language, which has Uto-Aztecan roots. Their lifestyle and cultural practices were little different, even near the time of their first contact with history, in the early to mid-1800s, from those of the Desert Archaic peoples of ten thousand years before. Jesse Jennings notes that "it seems that the Shoshoni-speakers who were in possession of Utah upon first white contact were migrants from southern California and Nevada. They may have been a factor in the disappearance of the Fremont. The linguistic evidence is firm as to the time and direction of expansion of the Shoshoni-speakers; what is lacking is knowledge of the nature of the contact with the Fremont, although there is repeated evidence of dual use of camp locations by both cultures."[10]

Having defined, at least briefly, the three stages of prehistoric habitation in Box Elder, and having noted that the lifestyle of all three was substantially the same, we move to a discussion of how they lived, at least as can be reconstructed from what they left behind.

Of their food supply and eating habits, Jennings notes that

> The major foods of a gathering population were always vegetal; meat made only modest and sporadic contribution to the diet. In recent years this has been observed and verified in several archeological as well as ethnographic studies over the world. The reasons, once known, are painfully obvious. The over-riding facts are: (1) Plants are fixed in position, (2) they normally fruit every year (piñon is an exception) although abundance may vary, (3) they fruit at the same time each year, (4) collecting fruits does *not* endanger the species and their permanent availability is thus assured, and (5) much vegetal food can he saved or stored. Animals on the other hand, although highly prized, are subject to wide fluctuation in abundance due to disease cycles, over-kill, or temporary climatic change. An example of periodic scarcity is the well-known (and probably ancient) reduction and increase of the jackrabbit population over a seven or eight year cycle. Another kind of scarcity would result from a successful antelope drive; a drive decimates a local herd, so that several fawn crops are required to restore the herd to original strength before another harvest is warranted.[11]

Harvesting of vegetable foods, and thus the travel or migration schedule of the people was dependent upon and dictated by the seasonal cycle.

Most of the information about the Desert Archaic peoples has come from cave locations or sheltered overhangs, almost always located near a water source such as a seep, spring, shallow lake, or stream. Two of the most important sites are Danger Cave in Tooele County and Hogup Cave in Box Elder County. Both caves are similar. They were formed by the waters of Lake Bonneville which washed out cavities in the limestone cliffs. Both caves overlook the desert salt flats but are located close to small springs which provide water, nuture marsh plants and attract animals.[12] Hogup Cave was occupied from about 6500 B.C. to A.D. 1470.

Of more recent excavation, Hogup cave is richer in artifacts than

Danger Cave; however the Hogup Cave artifacts complement and refine the discoveries made in Danger Cave. From Hogup we learn that obsidian was superseded by jasper and chert for projectile tips after about 2000 B.C., and that basketry became less important after about A.D. 1. Hogup Cave yielded many more engraved pebbles and bone tools than Danger Cave. Hogup bone artifacts include awls, needles, and beads. Of note among the clothing items were moccasins, of which the most interesting were what are called "hock" moccasins, which we are told "were of unusual manufacture. They are one-piece, having been made from the tube or cylinder of skin removed from the hind legs of bison. The tube was made by cutting the hide all around the leg, above the hock, with a similar encircling cut well below the hock. After peeling the skin thus freed of the leg, the lower end was sewn shut. When the foot was inserted, the hock formed a naturally shaped heel, with the skin above the hock fitting loosely around the ankle. An encircling thong tie or string fastened the upper part snugly. This style of footgear is without counterpart except for one specimen from Danger Cave . . . "[13]

In Hogup Cave excavators discovered "Ten unique little bundles . . . of wrapped plant fibers . . . Each has a set of 'horns' projecting from the 'head,' the horns being bone splinters, twigs, or cactus spines. The delicate 'bodies' often have feathers attached to the lower end."[14] Jennings explains that these figures resemble and are comparable in function to the Kachina dolls of the Hopi.

We learn from the layers of cultural deposits in such places as Hogup Cave that the Desert Archaic people were "a hunter-gatherer people who lived within their environmental means. The countryside was their supermarket and source of raw materials for tools, utensils, clothing, fuel, medicine and ritual gear. . . . That supermarket included 40 species of animal. Most frequent were rabbits, but antelope, deer, bison, mountain sheep and wild birds were also harvested in addition to roots and seeds which were parched, ground, and eaten."[15]

Much of the anthropologists' understanding of the diet and health of prehistoric peoples comes from the study of human coprolites—the fecal residue left by human occupants of such locations as Danger and Hogup caves. Jennings writes:

Interesting corroboration as to diet has come from the analysis of human coprolites, the fecal residue of ancient meals. In a pilot study of Danger Cave materials, Fry (1968) has identified charred pickleweed seed, flecks and pieces of charcoal, very fine grit (eroded from the millstones during the grinding of the charred seed) and much cactus pad epidermis and tiny charred cactus spines, saltbush seeds and leaves, bulrush seeds, rabbit brush seeds and two or three kinds of animal hair (including antelope). *All* samples contained cactus scrap and pickleweed fragments, charcoal, and grit. Thus the historic Indian practice of parching small seeds by constantly swirling and moving them mixed with live coals around in a flat basketry tray is probably established as typical of the ancients. After parching, the seeds were ground, eaten as gruel or in cakes or even as dry meal. A most interesting conclusion from the dietary study was that at Danger Cave the diet became more varied (i.e., more plant species), from early to late. Even more interesting is the discovery that the coprolites contained eggs and specimens of lice (both human and nonhuman); ticks; and the egg sacs of internal parasites, such as pinworms, roundworms and the thorny-headed worm, the latter sometimes being a fatal infection. Insect parts, such as legs and wings, have also been recovered from coprolites. And, it is known ethnographically that insects, particularly the Mormon cricket that occurs in plague quantities some years, were collected by the bushel in historic times. They too were parched, ground on the mills, and the paste stored. Many fruits as well—such as choke-cherry and serviceberry—were dried, milled, and stored for later use.

The coprolites from Hogup Cave were subjected to similar dietary and parasite analysis, with very similar findings. The pickleweed and cactus appeared again to provide most of the vegetable foods in the lower levels; but after about the time of Christ, pickleweed was less popular (grass seed may have taken the place of the pickleweed seeds). Grit and charcoal continued to appear in all the specimens. As at Danger, one can note at Hogup an increase in dietary complexity through time (including the appearance of chopped grass that was removed from the paunch of such ruminants as bison and eaten). The same parasites—pin-worms and thorny-headed worms—were found in the Hogup specimens, but they were not as numerous as at Danger; there the infection was so

> bad that Fry (1970) speculates deaths in the Danger population must have occurred from this cause. In quantity these worms perforate the intestine, with resulting diarrhea, anemia, weight loss, and death.[16]

Surprisingly the Hogup studies yielded no evidence that items such as sego or camas bulbs, piñon nuts, grass seeds, or chokecherries were used by the ancient cultures even though they were important in the diet of historical tribes.

Grasshoppers were an important part of the prehistoric diet in the Box Elder County area. During excavations at Lakeside Cave under the direction of Dr. David Madsen, archaeologists found thousands of grasshopper fragments in all the layers of strata they uncovered and in the matrix of dried human feces inside the cave. An important piece in the puzzle was provided in 1985 when amateur archaeologists who had worked at the Lakeside Cave excavation found millions of dead grasshoppers piled in rows along the eastern side of the Great Salt Lake. The insects had flown or been blown into the salt water and then washed ashore "leaving neat rows of salted and sun-dried grasshoppers stretched for miles along the beach." Madsen and his associates conducted studies indicating that one person could collect an average of two hundred pounds of the grasshoppers an hour. They also analyzed the caloric content of the grasshoppers and found them to equal or exceed that of other prehistoric food sources as well as modern fast-food items. As an easily acquired, easily stored source of food for prehistoric inhabitants of the eastern side of the Great Salt Lake, the grasshoppers were apparently a staple for the counties first residents.[17]

Other insects were also used for food by the prehistoric and historic inhabitants of the area. In 1826 Peter Skene Ogden wrote of the Indians he encountered in the area: "One of their dishes, not of small size, was filled with ants. They collected them in the morning early before the thaw commences. The locusts they collect in Summer and store up for their Winter; in eating they give the preference to the former, being oily; the latter not, on this food these poor wretches drag out an existence for nearly four months of the year; they live contented and happy; this is all they require."[18]

Agriculture was the great difference between the Archaic peoples and the Fremont peoples who lived throughout much of Utah, southern Idaho, and eastern Nevada between A.D. 500 and 1300. Like the Anasazi, their contemporaries to the south, the Fremont ceased to be exclusively foragers and hunters, as had been the Archaic peoples, and began to plant, husband, and harvest corn, beans, and squash.

Other characteristics of the Fremont include their baskets, moccasins, clay figurines, and a thin-walled gray pottery. As they became more sedentary because of their cultivation of crops, the Fremont used large basin-shaped stone grinding bases (known as metates). The Fremont succeeded the Archaics in inhabiting the caves around the lake, as well as building pit houses (a shallow hole topped by poles and woven reeds or sticks above ground), where water was available, crops could be raised, and game was abundant, such as along the Bear River and other tributaries of Great Salt Lake.

Fremont artifacts have been found in the area's caves, and hundreds of sites have been identified along the Bear River and in the wetlands bordering the Great Salt Lake. Early settlers of Willard noted pit houses and other above-ground structures. At Willard Bay State Park, archaeologists have conducted excavations since 1892.[19]

One well-known Fremont site in Box Elder County is the "Orbit Inn site," located between the Brigham City airport and Utah Highway 83, just east of Interstate 15.[20] These habitation sites seem to have been occupied in two phases, 1200–500 years ago, and 500–300 years ago. David Madsen explains the basis of these marshland sites: "Along the eastern margin of the Great Basin, the snow-fed rivers of the Wasatch and Uinta mountains find their final home in the closed-basin valleys of what was once Lake Bonneville. As this water spreads out across the relatively flat Ice Age lake bottoms, it creates a number of vast oases in the midst of comparatively harsh desert environments. These large saline marsh areas constitute some of the richest ecosystems within the Fremont region and the large array of fish, waterfowl, shellfish, and marsh plants found closely spaced within these marshes provided some Fremont groups with wild resources that were as productive and reliable as any domestic crop."[21]

In addition to the pickleweed and grasses of the dry areas, the marshes provided sedges, bulrushes, cattails, mustard, chenopods, plantago, waterfowl, muskrats, fish, fresh-water mollusks, and larger animals which watered at the streams, such as bison. The marshland Fremont sites show no use of agriculture as do other Fremont sites, suggesting that the marshlands were a bounteous food source unavailable to other Fremont peoples.[22]

Sarah Yates describes the end of the local Fremont as somewhat of a mystery.

> By 1300–1350 A.D. the Fremont archaeological culture was no longer recognizable. There was an apparent abandonment of agriculture, less time spent in building permanent shelters and ceramics, and a change in the way people moved about from place to place.
>
> This has posed a mystery for archaeologists ever since the Fremont culture was first identified. Reasons for its "disappearance" are not known. A hotter climate and drought, which made farming difficult, is often given as one explanation. Another factor may have been the expanding Numic-language groups who were living in the area by historic times.
>
> Whether the Fremont left the area or were assimilated into these other cultures is not known, but the Shoshoni did not take on many of the Fremont cultural attributes such as the styles of architecture, basketry, moccasins, pottery, etc. Their shelters, for example, were circular wiki-ups rather than pit houses, and their pottery was made by slab instead of coiling.

What is known, is that archaeological evidence indicates the Shoshoni occupation began about A.D. 1250–1300. Archaeology shows considerable use of the same camps, but this could be due to the favorable locations rather than any relationship between the peoples. After all, many are the same sites where pioneers later settled, farmers plowed fields and built their homes, and cities grew.[23]

John Marwitt articulates the current position of experts that sometime between A.D. 1200 to 1300 the Fremont withdrew "from their Utah heartland eastward into the Great Plains under pressure from a (linguistically and archeologically demonstrated) Shoshonean expansion out of the southeastern Great Basin . . . it appears not unlikely that some Fremont or Fremont-influenced groups (especially those of the northern region) drifted on to the northwestern plains of Wyoming and perhaps southern Montana."[24]

The Fremont ultimately gave way to the Numic peoples which were the immediate ancestors of the historic Shoshoni, who occupied this land when the first white settlers came. Though they came later, and in some form or another "supplanted" the Fremont, the continuity of lifestyle, use of the land, exploitation of the natural resources, and habitation sites are not a series of sharp divisions, but a continuation of similarities, layered with notable differences. This is most noticeable in Hogup cave, where evidence of occupation ranges from more than ten thousand to less than fifty years ago.[25]

James Gunnerson seems to hold that the entire complex of Desert Archaic, Fremont, and Proto-Shoshonean cultures are related. Using dendrochronological and trade pottery data, he postulates that the Uto-Aztecans moved north from southern Arizona to the Kayenta area of northern Arizona. One group remained in the area to become the ancestors of the Hopi, while another continued northward over a period of a thousand years, ending up in the eastern Great Basin around 600 B.C.

After Fremont technology and its population reached a point where it was generally in balance with the environment, the climate became drier and crop failures more common. Conflicts over water developed, and the Fremont disbursed in small groups to live off the land. "It was no longer worthwhile to build substantial houses. Their heavy metates had to be abandoned. It was impractical to carry fragile pottery or if they did so, they took little pains with its manufacture because of the greater chance of breakage."[26] Gunnerson implies that the Fremont gradually metamorphosed into the Shoshonean peoples discovered by the first whites to come into the area in the early 1800s.

A final important, but little understood element of prehistoric cultures is the rock art they left behind. The Fremont rock art found in Box Elder County is on a smaller scale than that found in other parts of the state, but it is evidence of their habitation of the area. "Perhaps the greatest concentration of Box Elder County rock art is above Connor Spring southwest of Penrose-Thatcher, where Fremont-style 'graffiti' appears with and is sometimes carved over by work more characteristic of Shoshoni, pioneer and modern. Rock art is found in other locations in that area, near the Promontory Indian Caves and on the hillsides above Willard and north of Brigham City."[27]

In conclusion, we may say that during the 10,000 or more years of human habitation in Box Elder, people lived either a hunting-gathering lifestyle, occupying caves (part of the year) and following the yearly cycle of the growth and ripening of plants and the migratory patterns of wildfowl and other animals, or a more sedentary lifestyle, adding corn, beans, and squash to the diet where agriculture was viable. Evidence indicates that "these were people who sometimes went hungry, who got hurt and had colds, who cared for their children, and who loved and cared for one another."[28]

By the time the first European/American settlers came to these valleys, they found the Shoshoni, who were subject to visits or raids by Ute, Blackfoot and Flathead Indians.

Thus prehistory gave way to history, and the long period of stable societies and small changes in peoples who lived basically the same for thousands of years gave way to a society mainly of Caucasians of European extraction. The change was—in the perspective of the entire timeline—sudden, violent, and total. The newcomers, with their advanced technology and new diseases, decimated the Native peoples, and what had been thousands of years of cultural stability, based on the appropriate and sensible use of the natural resources, gave way to a society which seemed to dominate rather than co-exist with the natural habitat. The Machine Age, with its mining, paving, burning, huge garbage dumps, and all concomitant exploitation of all possible resources, was not far behind.

ENDNOTES

1. David B. Madsen, *Exploring the Fremont* (Salt Lake City: Utah Museum of Natural History, 1989), xiii.

2. Jesse D. Jennings, *Prehistory of Utah and the Eastern Great Basin,* Anthropological Papers, Number 98, University of Utah, 1978, p. 15. I acknowledge a great debt of gratitude to Sarah S. Yates in preparation of this chapter.

3. Sarah S. Yates, "Prehistoric Peoples of Box Elder County," typescript, copy in my possession.

4. Jennings, *Prehistory of Utah and the Eastern Great Basin,* 245.

5. Ibid.

6. Ibid., 246. As to the origin of the Fremont, James H. Gunnerson explains that "There are two logical possibilities with regard to the origin of the Fremont culture. It could have developed *in situ* from a Desert culture base with the addition of Anasazi traits, a theory championed by Rudy [Jack R. Rudy, *An Archaeological Survey of Western Utah,* University of Utah Anthropological Papers, No. 12, (Salt Lake City: University of Utah, 1953); Jennings and Norbeck [Jesse D. Jennings and E. Norbeck, "Great Basin Prehistory: A Review," *American Antiquity,* 21: 1–11, (Salt Lake City, 1955);, and H. M. Wormington, *A Reappraisal of the Fremont Culture,* Denver Museum of Natural History, Proceedings, no. 1 (Denver: Denver Museum of Natural History, 1955)." James H. Gunnerson, *The Fremont Culture,* Papers of the Peabody Museum of Archaeology and Ethnology, Harvard University, vol. 59, no. 2 (Cambridge, Massachusetts: The Peabody Museum, 1969), 170. Gunnerson mentions a "second possibility, that the Fremont culture represents a movement of people with a Puebloan culture into the area . . . "

7. Jennings, *Prehistory of Utah and the Eastern Great Basin,* 246. It must be noted that other plant materials were used, not only for food, but also for basketry, clothing, etc., such plants as cattails, rushes, reeds, juniper bark, willows, and so on. See Margaret A. Towle, "Use of Plant Materials Other Than Maize," in James H. Gunnerson, *The Fremont Culture,* Papers of the Peabody Museum of Archaeology and Ethnology, Harvard University, vol. 59, no. 2 (Cambridge, MA: The Peabody Museum, 1969), 207–8.

8. Gunnerson, *The Fremont Culture,* 141. Again, it is interesting that, when searching for cultural meaning for artifacts, researchers take recourse, again and again, to the Hopi and related cultures. Gunnerson notes (141) that "The bone rectangles and the pottery or stone disks could have been used together in a game like one still played by the Hopis, in which rectangular dice are thrown, and counters are moved on a course for a number of spaced determined by the way the dice fall." Some archaeologists believe that the balls were "manos" used with metates for grinding. See Madsen, *Exploring the Fremont,* 33.

9. Madsen, *Exploring the Fremont,* 2.

10. Jennings, *Prehistory of Utah and the Eastern Great Basin,* 246.

11. Ibid., 247. For a discussion of Fremont hunting, gathering, and agriculture, including the particular flora and fauna involved and the seasonal cycle itself, see David B. Madsen, "Fremont/Sevier Subsistence," in David B. Madsen, ed., *Fremont Perspectives,* Utah State Historical Society Antiquities

Section Selected Papers, No. 16 (Salt Lake City: Utah State Historical Society, 1980),. 25–33.

12. Madsen, *Exploring the Fremont,* 53.

13. Jennings, *Prehistory of Utah and the Eastern Great Basin,* 61.

14. Ibid.

15. Yates, "Prehistoric Peoples of Box Elder County," 2.

16. Jennings, *Prehistory of Utah and the Eastern Great Basin,* 85.

17. David B. Madsen, "A Grasshopper in Every Pot," Natural History (July 1989): 22.

18. Ibid., 25.

19. Yates, "Prehistoric Peoples of Box Elder County," 2.

20. As a footnote on a much more recent period in the history of Box Elder County, we cannot resist a comment about the name of the Orbit Inn site. In the early 1960s, just after Thiokol Chemical Corporation located its rocket motor plant west of Corinne, a plethora of space-related names began to adorn places in Box Elder County. Tremonton got its "Rocket Road" and some enterprising businessman built and opened a saloon on the road that all newly-arrived workers at Thiokol would have to travel to and from the plant. After a hard day building rockets, surely at least some would need a drink. The years passed, and the Orbit Inn closed, was torn down, and ceased to exist. No noticeable trace is left upon the landscape. When the nearby Fremont site was located and catalogued, the Orbit Inn was the nearest cultural feature, and gave its name to the site. Now the Orbit Inn is history, and its name, one of the most recent in Box Elder's catalogue of names, survives only as a name-tag for one of the most ancient sites of human habitation in Box Elder County.

21. Madsen, *Exploring the Fremont,* 44.

22. Ibid., 47, 49, 50. For a treatise on the relationship between the Fremont in general and the specific people who lived in the caves on the western side of Box Elder's Promontory peninsula, the reader is referred to C. Melvin Aikens, *Fremont-Promontory-Plains Relationships,* University of Utah Department of Anthropology, Anthropological Paper No. 82 (September 1966). Michael S. Berry, "Fremont Origins: A Critique" in David B. Madsen, ed., *Fremont Perspectives,* Utah State Historical Society Antiquities Section Selected Paper (Salt Lake City: Utah State Historical Society, 1980), 19 notes that Jack R. Rudy "designated the makers of Promontory ware (Steward's Promontory culture) as proto-Shoshonean and, further, he postulated that the entire western Utah sequence from pre-Puebloid hunter-gatherers through the Puebloid period to the historic Shoshoni constituted a Shoshonean cultural continuum."

23. Yates, "Prehistoric Peoples of Box Elder County," 3–4.

24. Marwitt, "A Fremont Retrospective," 11; refers to Melvin C. Aikens, *Fremont-Promontory-Plains Relationships,* University of Utah Anthropological Papers, No. 82 (Salt Lake City: University of Utah, 1966).

25. Madsen, *Exploring the Fremont,* 51.

26. Gunnerson, *The Fremont Culture,* 197.

27. Yates, "Prehistoric Peoples of Box Elder County," 4.

28. Ibid.

CHAPTER 3

TRAPPERS, EXPLORERS, GOLDSEEKERS

With the coming of European fur trappers, exploration parties sent by the federal government, and the hordes of avaricious forty-niners, the history of Box Elder moves from prehistory onto the stage of history—written history, for that is the defining factor which separates prehistory from history. There are no first-hand accounts. History, then, requires language, not only spoken, but written. The presence of a written record, and the recording of events, makes history. The ancient ones who lived off the land and migrated with the seasons, from the marshes and desert's fringe to the lush high-mountain valleys, the people whose clothing was of rabbit skins, whose feet were shod with reeds and buffalo hocks, whose weapons were made of obsidian and flint and jasper, who ate grasshoppers and crickets, ricegrass and pickleweed, and who lived in caves and wickiups kept no written records, as far as we know. They kept—nor left—no history we can decipher. They were *pre*-historic.

The first non-Indians to record their impressions of parts of Utah were the Spanish friars, Dominguez and Escalante, who traveled through as far north as Utah Lake in the summer of 1776. While the Spanish did not enter present-day Box Elder County, the area was recognized as Spanish territory in the 1819 Adams-Onis Treaty between the United States and Spain. That treaty defined the boundaries of the 1803 Louisiana Purchase and set the northern boundary of Spanish territory as the 42nd parallel—the present northern boundary of Utah's Box Elder County. The boundary remained unsurveyed and undefined, creating a contested land in northern Utah as American, British, and New Mexican fur trappers entered northern Utah in the 1820s.

The British, primarily under Peter Skene Ogden—who led several expeditions for Hudson's Bay Company and left his name on a river, mountain, valley, and city south of Box Elder County—followed the streams down from Oregon as far south as the Weber River. Another Hudson's Bay Company trapper, Donald Mackenzie named the Malad River when he and his companions became ill from eating tainted beaver meat while encamped on the river.[1]

New Mexican trappers came north primarily from Taos via the San Juan, Colorado, Green, Duchesne, and their tributary streams. Americans came west from St. Louis by way of the Missouri River.

In the winter of 1824–25, James Bridger was selected to settle bets about the course of the Bear River. The trappers knew the upper Bear (the Shoshoni *sag-wy-og-way*) through Wyoming, Idaho, and the Cache Valley, from trapping the beaver-rich streams which fed into it. They did not know the Bear River below Cache Valley, the *pe-og-wa,* the part of Bear River which did not have lush beaver-bearing streams. Bridger followed the river from Cache Valley into present day Box Elder County and southward to the mouth of the Bear River where it entered the Great Salt Lake. Bridger concluded that he had reached an arm of the Pacific Ocean because of the salty water he found.[2] He is credited with being the first American to see the Great Salt Lake; however, Etienne Provost, a fur trapper of French extraction from Taos, New Mexico reached the south end of the Great Salt Lake in the fall of 1824 after he lost eight men in a fight with Snake Indians on the Jordan River. During the winter of 1825–26, fur trappers were forced out of Cache Valley because of heavy snows. They divided into two camps, one under John Weber which wintered on the Weber River, the other, probably under Jedediah Smith, wintered on the Bear River near its mouth.

After breaking camp in late February 1826, Jedediah Smith took his men around the head of Bear River Bay and across the Bear River Mountains to explore the unknown county north and west of the Great Salt Lake. The party reached the north end of the lake where four men, James Clyman, Louis Vasquez, Moses (Black) Harris, and Henry G. Fraeb, spent twenty-four days in bull boats sailing to the south end of the lake in search of beaver-laden streams. Meanwhile, Jedediah Smith crossed into eastern Nevada, then made his way to the 1826 rendezvous in Cache Valley by an unknown route.[3]

Having explored northwest of the Great Salt Lake in the spring and early summer of 1826, Jedediah Smith decided to explore the region south and west of the lake at the conclusion of the 1826 rendezvous. Known as the Southwest Expedition, the year-long sojourn took Smith south through the center of Utah to the Virgin River, then on to California, and back across the Salt Desert in time for the 1827 rendezvous at the south end of Bear Lake. Both legs of the trip took Jedediah Smith through part of Box Elder County. George Brooks, editor of the Jedediah Smith diaries, concludes that Smith went through Box Elder Canyon and Sardine Canyon at the beginning and end of the year-long journey. Smith records in his diary at the end of the journey:

> July 1st 25 Miles North along the shore of the Lake [Great Salt Lake] Nothing material occurred.
>
> 2nd 20 Miles North East made our way to the Cache. But just before arriving there I saw some Indians on the opposite side of the creek. It was hardly worth while as I thought, to be any wise careful, so I went directly to them and found as near as I could judge by what I knew of the language to be a band of the Snakes. I learned from them that the Whites, as they term our parties, were all assembled at the little Lake, a distance of about 25 miles. There was in this camp about 200 Lodges of Indians and as the[y] were on their way to the rendevous I encamped with them.
>
> 3rd I hired a horse and a guide and at three O Clock arrived at the rendezvous. My arrival caused a considerable bustle in camp,

> for myself and party had been given up as lost. A small cannon brought up from St. Louis was loaded and fired for a salute.[4]

The fur trade continued until the streams were depleted of beaver, and the stylishness of beaver hats declined. Many former fur trappers became guides for government exploring expeditions and some of the first overland emigrants from the east.

The Bidwell-Bartleson Party

The first overland emigrant party to California was the Bartleson-Bidwell Party in 1841. The party spent nearly two weeks crossing through Box Elder County during their history-making journey. The party of sixty-one persons left Missouri in May 1841 and followed the Oregon Trail along the North Platte River to the Sweetwater River, through South Pass, and on to Fort Bridger. West of Fort Bridger, they struck the Bear River and followed it north to Soda Springs where about half the company decided to follow the known route on to Oregon while the others stuck with their original goal of California. With nine wagons, they headed south along the Bear River traveling without any guide or compass and crossing into Utah near present-day Clarkston on 16 August 1841. Historian David Bigler describes their activities and route into and across Box Elder County.

> Intending to rest in Cache County while several men sought directions at Fort Hall, the party mistakenly crossed the low range just north of the Gates of the Bear to arrive in the Great Salt Lake Valley near present Fielding. After fording the Malad River opposite Plymouth, they continued south through the future towns of Garland and Tremonton until, desperate for water, they headed east to strike the Bear River, just south of Corinne.
>
> The party then headed northwest, intersecting its own trail, to skirt the north end of the Great Salt Lake, find the Mary's River now the Humboldt), which, it was then believed, flowed from the lake to the Sacramento River, and follow it to California. They crossed the Promontory Mountains on the route of the later transcontinental railroad and passed just north of Kelton to rest at Ten Mile Spring near the base of the Raft River Mountains.
>
> Crossing Park Valley to the south of the present town, they

came on 11 September to Owl Spring, just north of Lucin, where Kentuckian Benjamin Kelsey abandoned his wagons and put his wife and baby on horseback. Two days later, the emigrants were the first of many to arrive at Pilot Peak on the Utah-Nevada border and find relief at the fresh-water springs at its base.[5]

John Bidwell, who kept a diary of the journey, offered one of the earliest written descriptions of Box Elder County. The diary entries for 13 through 27 August 1841 follow.

> F. 13th. Traveled about 10 miles in a southerly direction. It was the intention of the company to stop and hunt in cash [sic] valley, which is on bear river 3 or 4 days travel from its mouth.
>
> S. 14th. Left the river on account of the hills which obstructed our way on it, found an abundance of choke cherries, many of which were ripe, road uncommonly broken, did not reach the river, distance about 14 miles.
>
> S. 15th. Continued our journey over hills and ravines, going to almost every point of the compass, in order to pass them: The day was very warm—the grass had been very good, but it was now very parched up; having come about 15 miles, we encamped on a small stream proceeding out of the Mountains at no great distance from us. But we were surprised to see it become perfectly dry in the course of an hour, some of the guard said there was plenty of water in it about mid night.
>
> M. 16h. This morning there was abundance of water in the little stream and it was running briskly when we left it. If the water was not supplied by the melting of the snow in the mountains, it was really an interesting spring, found an abundance of choke cherries, very large and exquisitely delicious, better than any I ever eat before, distance traveled, 12 miles.
>
> T. 17th. Traveled about 16 miles; saw a large smoke rising out of the mountains before us. It had probably been raised by the Indians, as a telegraph, to waran the tribe, that their land was visited by strangers. We were unable to procure any fuel this evening, we therefore slept without fire. The Indians, found in this region, are Shoshonees, they are friendly.
>
> W. 18th. Traveled but a short distance, when we discovered that a deep-salt creek prevented our continuing near the river. In ascending this stream in search of a place to cross it, we found on

its margin a hot spring, very deep and clear. The day was very warm and we were unable to reach the river, encamped on this salt creek and suffered much for water, the water being to salt we could not drink it, distance 15 miles.

T. 19. Started early, hoping soon to find fresh water, when we could refresh ourselves and animals, but alas! The sun beamed heavy on our heads as the day advanced, and we could see nothing before us but extensive arid plains, glimmering with heat and salt, at length the plains became so impregnated with salt, that vegetation entirely ceased; the ground was in many places white as snow with salt & perfectly smooth—the mid-day sun, beaming with uncommon splendor upon these shining plains, made us fancy we could see timber upon the plains, and wherever timber is found there is water always. We marched forward with unremitted pace till we discovered it was an illusion, and lest our teams should give out we returned from S. to E, and hastened to the river which we rached in about 5 miles.

A high mountain overlooked us on the East and the river was thickly bordered with willows—grass plenty but so salt, our animals could scarcely eat it; salt glitters upon its blades like frost. Distance 20 miles.

F. 20th. Company remained here while two men went to explore the country, they returned bringing the intelligence that we were within ten miles of where the river disembogued [sic] itself into the great salt lake, this was the fruit of having no pilot—we had passed through cash valley, where we intended to have stopped and did not know it.

S. 21st. Marched off in a N.W. direction, and intersected our trail of Thursday last, having made a complete triangle in the plain. At this intersection of the trails, we left a paper elevated by a pole, that the men, returning from Fort Hall, might shun the tedious rounds we had taken. Found grass and water which answered our purpose very well, though both were salt. Distance ten miles.

S. 22nd. This morning a man (Mr. Bralaski) returned from the Fort, and said the reason, why he came alone, was, the other men had left him, because he was unable to keep up with them; he having a pack horse laden with provision. He had seen the paper at the intersection of the trails, and was guided by it to the camp, the others were undoubtedly going the rounds of the triangle, sure enough, they came up in the afternoon, having gone to the river and back, no pilot could be got at the Fort. The families, that went into Oregon, had disposed of their oxen at the fort and were going to descend the Columbia River with pack horses—they in exchange, received one horse for every ox, their wagons they could not sell. They procured flour at 50 cents a pint, sugar same price and other things in proportion, near where we were encamped here, were a few Hackberry trees.

M. 23rd. Started, bearing our course west, in order to pass the Salt Lake—passed many salt plains and springs in the forenoon, the day was hot—the hills, and land bordering on the plains, were covered with wild sage. In passing the declivity of a hill, we observed this sage had been plucked up, and arranged in long minows, extending near a mile in length. It had been done by the Indians, but for what purpose we could not imagine, unless it was to decoy game. At evening we arrived in full view of the Salt Lake, water was very scarce. Cedar grows here both on the hills and in the valleys, distance 20 miles.

T. 24th. Cattle strayed this morning to seek water—late start—day was warm—traveled about 10 miles in a W. direction, encamped where we found numerous springs, deep, clear and somewhat inpregnated with salt. The plains were snowy white with salt. Here we procured salt of the best quality. The grass, that grew in small spots on the plains, was laden with salt which had formed itself on the stalks and blades in lumps, from the size of a pea to that of a hen's egg, this was the kind we procured, it being very white, strong and pure.

W. 25th. Remained here all day.

T. 26th. Traveled all day over dry, barren plains, producing nothing but sage, or rather it ought to be called, wormwood, and which I believe will grow without water or soil. Two men were sent a head in search of water, but returned a little while before dark unsuccessful.

Our course intersected an Indian trail, which we followed directly north towards the mountains, knowing that in these dry countries, the Indian trails always lead to the nearest water. Having traveled till about 10 o'clock P.M. made a halt, and waited till morning—distance about 30 miles.

F. 27th, Daylight discovered to us a spot of green grass on the

> declivity of the mountains towards which we were advancing. 5 miles took us to this place, where we found to our great joy, an excellent spring of water and an abundance of Grass—here we determined to continue, 'till the route was explored to the head of Mary's River and run no more risks of perishing for want of water in this desolate region.[6]

The expedition reached California in early November, nearly six months after leaving western Missouri.

John C. Frémont

The first major exploration of Box Elder County under the auspices of the central government, was led by the colorful, controversial John Charles Frémont. Frémont made five expeditions to the West between 1842 And 1849. It was on his second expedition in 1843 that he past through Box Elder County, explored part of the Great Salt Lake, and named the geographical area the Great Basin. Frémont's maps were used were used by the Mormon pioneers of 1847 and his favorable report about the region was well-received by Brigham Young.[7]

Frémont's second expedition left St. Louis in May 1843. By September 1 the party had reached a stream which Frémont called the Roseaux, or Reed River.[8] The Roseaux is what we now know as the Malad River. On that date Frémont notes that

> The morning was squally and cold; the sky scattered over with clouds; and the night had been so uncomfortable, that we were not on the road until 8 o'clock. Travelling between Roseaux and Bear rivers, we continued to descend the valley, which gradually expanded, as we advanced, into a level plain of good soil, about 25 miles in breadth, between mountains 3,000 and 4,000 feet high, rising suddenly to the clouds, which all day rested upon the peaks. These gleamed out in the occasional sunlight, mantled with the snow which had fallen upon them, while it rained on us in the valley below, of which the elevation here was about 4,500 feet above the sea.[9]

Frémont's account continues, noting that "The country before us plainly indicated that we were approaching the lake, though, as the ground where we were travelling afforded no elevated point, nothing of it as yet could be seen; and at a great distance ahead were several isolated mountains, resembling islands, which they were afterwards found to be."[10] After describing the grass, brush, and shrubs, Frémont notes that they camped about 300 yards above the confluence of the Roseaux and Bear rivers.[11] After studying the river, Frémont decided to explore it from its surface. He notes, "Among the useful things which formed a portion of our equipage, was an India-rubber boat, 18 feet long, made somewhat in the form of a bark canoe of the northern lakes. The sides were formed by two air-tight cylinders, eighteen inches in diameter, connected with others forming the bow and stern. To lessen the danger from accidents to the boat, these were divided into four different compartments, and the interior space was sufficiently large to contain five or six persons, and a considerable weight of baggage."[12]

Frémont embarked in his technological marvel, along with Basil Lajeunesse, "Thinking that perhaps in the course of the day we might reach the outlet at the lake."[13] He notes that, at that time, Bear river "was from sixty to one hundred yards broad, and the water so deep, that even on the comparatively shallow points we could not reach the bottom with 15 feet."[14] After floating down the river for "five or six hours," they "came unexpectedly upon several families of *Root Diggers,* who were encamped among the rushes on the shore, and appeared very busy about several weirs or nets which had been rudely made of canes and rushes for the purpose of catching fish."[15] These were the Shoshoni. Frémont wrote: "They had the usual very large heads, remarkable among the Digger tribe, with matted hair, and were almost entirely naked; looking very poor and miserable, as if their lives had been spent in the rushes where they were, beyond which they seemed to have very little knowledge of anything."[16] After making acquaintance with the startled Indians, Frémont promised to send men to trade with them, and paddled off down the Bear. The heavily-loaded boat moved slowly, and the day ebbed without having found the river's mouth. Frémont and Lajeunesse beached their craft, cached the supplies "in the willows."[17] They climbed the bank and discovered, by their trail, that their companions had passed by earlier in the day. After following the trail for about fifteen miles they " . . . caught sight of the camp-fires among clumps of willows just as the sun had sunk behind the mountains on the west side of the valley, filling the clear sky with a golden yellow."[18] At three o'clock in the morning, Frémont sent several men and horses for the boat. They returned in the afternoon, bringing with them "a small quantity of roots, and some meat, which the Indians had told them was bear meat."[19] That afternoon they went about three miles farther down the river, but found further travel impossible, on account of the spreading out of the water in the miry delta. There, they camped for the night.

The next day the exploring party retraced their steps for about five miles, crossed the river, and camped. On the fifth, they headed for one of the island mountains about twelve miles to the south but were prevented from reaching their goal by the mud. They turned eastward following a well-beaten path along the shore of the lake to the hot springs at the foot of the Wasatch Mountains near what is now the boundary between Box Elder and Weber counties. "In about seven miles from Clear creek [probably Willard] the trail brought us to a place at the foot of the mountain where there issued with considerable force ten or twelve hot springs, highly impregnated with salt. In one of these, the thermometer stood at 136°, and in another at 132°.5; and the water, which spread in pools over the low ground, was colored red."[20] From there, Frémont and party went south, launched their India-rubber boat on Great Salt Lake, and explored Frémont Island, where Kit Carson carved his famous cross on the island's highest point and Frémont lost the cap for his telescope.

On 12 September, however, Frémont and company were back in Box Elder. The previous morning, they had breakfast on Yampah and suppered on kamas, no better fare than the poor Indians, "but a cup of good coffee still distinguished us from our *digger* acquaintances." On the twelfth, they came north past "the hot salt-springs" and camped on the creek at the mouth of Willard Canyon. There they had "a supper of sea-gulls, which Carson killed near the lake."[21]

On the thirteenth they continued north, through Bear River Valley, probably following a beaten trail. They crossed Box Elder Creek, and mention is made of North Lake. In the afternoon they came upon "five or six hot springs gushing out together, beneath a conglomerate, consisting principly of fragments of a grayish-blue limestone, efflorescing a salt upon the surface. The temperature of these springs was 134°, and the rocks in the bed were colored with a red deposite, and their was common salt crystallized on the margin." This was the spot now known as Crystal (or Madsen) Hot Springs. That night they camped on the Bear River. The company was low on food, and consequently low in spirits. An expected rendezvous with a supply group had not materialized. On the fourteenth the men "looked so forlorn, that I gave them permission to kill a fat young horse which I had purchased with goods from the Snake Indians, and they were very soon restored to gayety and good humor." Frémont and his German cartographer, Charles Preuss, were made of different stuff than the men of their cohort. Frémont records that "Mr. Preuss and myself could not yet overcome some remains of civilized prejudices, and preferred to starve a little longer; feeling as much saddened as if a crime had been committed."[22]

The next day they purchased a small quantity of food from some Snake Indians, and later acquired an antelope from another Indian for a small quantity of gun powder and some balls. That night word came of their supply train, which they met the following day with its good supply of flour, rice, dried meat, and small amount of butter.[23] Resupplied, the explorers turned northward, into the Snake and Columbia river drainage leaving both the Great Basin and Box Elder behind in their ambitious sweep of the great American West.

Howard Stansbury

The next of the government explorers to enter Box Elder history was Howard Stansbury, who gave his name—as did Frémont before him—to one of the Great Salt Lake islands. Stansbury's exploration does not follow immediately in a strict chronology of the county's history, but is grouped with Frémont and the gold-seekers here.

Stansbury was seven years older than Frémont, and was commissioned in 1849 to survey Great Salt Lake and explore the surrounding region in the wake of the discovery of gold on the American river in northern California. One of his assistants, First Lieutenant John W. Gunnison, became prominent in the history of Utah but died at the hands of Indians in Millard County in 1853.

In addition to exploring the Great Salt Lake, Stansbury was

instructed to help improve transportation in the region, first by trying to establish a better wagon road between Fort Bridger and Salt Lake City, and second by accessing potential transcontinental railroad routes in the West.[24]

In September 1849 Stansbury's party came from Cache Valley down Box Elder Canyon. Here is his description of the canyon, before it was improved for travel:

> The pass or gorge through which this little stream [Box-elder Creek] rushes down the mountain to the plains below is steep, rugged, and very narrow, being in places scarcely passable for mules. I had hoped it would afford a passage over the range for wagons, but this I soon found to be impracticable. Descending this wild pass for about two miles, we reached the lake valley, and repaired to our camp on Bear River.
>
> In crossing the Wahsatch range at this point, the lower hills on the eastern side were composed of broken conglomerate. Large boulders of serpentine were met with on the surface, and also altered sandstones and limestones. Ascending from Cache Valley, the dark limestones were found cropping out, but the surface was so completely covered with vegetable soil that no section could be obtained. The limestones seemed to form the summits of the highest elevation of the range, but as we passed through the deep gorge of Box-elder Creek, this could not be positively ascertained. No trap was observed, but large boulders of granite were seen in the sides of the pass. The rocks had been so much worn, and the surface was so covered by fallen masses, that no section of the stratification was visible.[25]

On 20 October Stansbury and company turned "more to the southward, with the intention of doubling a lofty promontory that puts into the lake from the north, and forms the western boundary of the Malade valley. In about a mile [from the emigrant road] we came upon three or four beautiful springs of clear, bright water: they were gushing out from a rocky point, (of dark limestone and coarse argillaceous sandstone, with a dip of about 20° to the east,) and unite to form a branch which runs southward some miles, and then sinks in the sand, before reaching the lake. The water was, however, warm, brackish, and entirely unfit for drinking."[26] He had apparently reached the springs at the head of Salt Creek, on the eastern end of Bothwell.

Stansbury and party then turned south, down the length of the Promontory peninsula, around the point, and north up the western side. They encamped at Promontory Point, and Stansbury rhapsodized.

> The evening was mild and bland, and the scene around us one of exciting interest. At our feet and on each side lay the waters of the Great Salt Lake, which we had so long and ardently desired to see. They were clear and calm, and stretched far to the south and west. Directly before us, and distant only a few miles, an island rose from eight hundred to one thousand feet in height, while in the distance other and larger ones shot up from the bosom of the waters, their summits appearing to reach the clouds. On the west appeared several dark spots, resembling other islands, but the dreamy haze hovering over this still and solitary sea threw its dim, uncertain veil over the more distant features of the landscape, preventing the eye from discerning any one object with distinctness, while it half revealed the whole, leaving ample scope for the imagination of the beholder. The stillness of the grave seemed to pervade both air and water; and, excepting here and there a solitary wild-duck floating motionless on the bosom of the lake, not a living thing was to be seen. The night proved perfectly serene, and a young moon shed its tremulous light upon a sea of profound, unbroken silence. I was surprised to find, although so near a body of the saltest water, none of that feeling of invigorating freshness which is always experienced when in the vicinity of the ocean. The bleak and naked shores, without a single tree to relieve the eye, presented a scene so different from what I had pictured in my imagination of the beauties of this far-famed spot. that my disappointment was extreme.[27]

We note from Stansbury's description that the Shoshoni living on the Promontory were living much as their prehistoric ancestors. The explorers came upon "a brackish spring, where there had been a camp of Indians the night before."[28] There "a quantity of some species of seeds they had been beating out lay in small heaps around, and I found an old water-bottle they had left in their haste. It was ingeniously woven of a sort of sedge-grass, coated inside with the gum of the mountain pine, by which it was rendered perfectly water-tight."[29]

The expedition turned west across Rozel Flat, then continued north, and turned northwest across Salt Wells Flat. They then traveled north to Cedar Hill, and north of it turned west, and went across the Curlew Valley, picking up the route of U.S. Highway 30 as it goes through Park Valley and Rosette. Stansbury's company then turned south (as does Highway 30), and followed generally the route of the highway east of the Goose Creek range to Lucin, and then west into what is now Nevada.

Parts of the Great Salt Lake Desert, the Great Salt Lake, and the territory around both were extensively studied scientifically for the first time from September 1849 to August 1850 by Captain Howard Stansbury from the U.S. Corps of Topographical Engineers. He, like other travelers before who ventured across the Great Salt Lake Desert, found the western sections of Box Elder County dry and difficult to traverse. Commenting on the dryness of the desert, Stansbury, at his camp located northwest of the Great Salt Lake, wrote, "The poor animals [his caravan of mules] presented this morning a forelorn appearance, having been now without a drop of water for more than twenty-four hours, during eighteen of which they had been under the saddle, with scarcely anything to eat."[30]

Along with his report, Stansbury, like Frémont before him, left a detailed map of the topography along his route, and drew in the route itself. Stansbury's survey and map were too late for Brigham Young, were immensely valuable as a survey and a report on the water, geology, flora, fauna, and indigenous inhabitants of a large segment of Box Elder.

The Salt Lake Cutoff

As news of the discovery of gold in California spread eastward, eager Argonauts came from all parts of the country, across the Great Plains, across the Rocky Mountains, following the trails used by Oregon, California, and Mormon pioneers. The California Trail divided at Fort Bridger. A northern route led from Fort Bridger to Fort Hall, then down the Snake River and up Goose Creek to the headwaters of what is now called Mary's River until it joined the

Humboldt, then along the latter stream to its sinks. The northern trail then took its course along the Truckee River from Lake Tahoe across the Sierra Nevada Mountains and into California.

The southern trail left Fort Bridger and followed the route of the Mormon pioneers to the Great Salt Lake. From there the trail bore south along the foot of the mountains until it met the Spanish Trail near Cove Fort and followed it to its terminus at Los Angeles.

There were several "cutoffs," or variant trails, some usable during certain seasons of the year, and some little more than death-traps, like the Hastings Cutoff, the route of the ill-fated Donner-Reed party across the Great Salt Lake Desert. There was, among the trails, a route north from Salt lake City through Box Elder County to Fort Hall, and then west (or east) along the Oregon and CaliforniaTrail. This road to Fort Hall was the route pioneered by Hazen Kimball, an early defector from the Mormon settlement at Salt Lake City.[31]

Another trail, known as the Salt Lake Cutoff, was opened by Captain Samuel J. Hensley and ten soldiers under his command in August 1848. Hensley and his men left Salt Lake City in early August and traveled north through Box Elder County and across the Bear River on a course parallel to present-day Interstate 84 to Snowville, then west to join the California Trail from Fort Hall in what is called Emigration Canyon, at a place called the Twin Sisters, just south of City of Rocks, Idaho. On Sunday, 27 August 1848, about ten days after leaving Salt Lake City, Hensley met a group of the returning Mormon Battalion members who had come up the Humboldt and Mary's rivers on their way to Great Salt Lake City. The battalion boys had intended to go first to Fort Hall and then south to Salt Lake City, but Hensley described the route he and his men had just followed, wrote out a waybill for the eastbound travelers, and indicated that by following the shortcut it would save the men at least eight or ten days.[32] Although Hensley's name was not applied to the cutoff, it was remembered as Hansel and applied to the Box Elder County landmarks of Hansel Valley, Hansel Spring, and the Hansel Mountains.

After leaving Hensley, the battalion members traveled two more days and met a large company, forty-eight wagons, under the command J. B. Chiles. Chiles had traveled the West before, in 1841, pioneering the route to Fort Hall via Fort Bridger, then northwestward along the Snake River to Ft. Boise, then crossing the present-day California border at Goose Lake, and following the Sacramento River south to Sutter's Fort. Upon being informed of Hensley's discovery, Chiles told the Mormon Battalion boys that there was a cutoff that was shorter yet, and gave them directions to the projected cutoff. [33] The Mormon travelers sent scouts ahead to find Chiles's route. Nine days later the main group encountered their scouts near the head of Mary's River. Chiles's fabled cutoff had been a figment of the old explorer's imagination. The boys then decided to follow the route described by Hensley.[34]

On 15 September they reached the place where Hensley's cutoff separated from the trail north to Fort Hall. That spot was the small valley dotted with spires of wind-eroded granite, a surreal landscape of fantastic shapes called Cathedral Rocks. At the point where the new cutoff left the old road was a notable landmark, mentioned by Hensley, a pair of tall rocks which one of the men, Addison Pratt, gave the name "the Twin Sisters."[35] From Cathedral Rocks, now more commonly called the City of Rocks, the Salt Lake-bound Mormon Battalion boys descended east to the site of present-day Almo, Idaho, then followed the Raft River (called by them Cajnes or Cazier Creek), through the narrows east of Almo, then southeasterly to the site of Naf. Battalion members made Hensley's trail into a road, crossing the present-day Idaho-Utah border just south of Naf, then following just south of the route of Utah highway 42, past Cedar Springs, Emigrant Springs, and Pilot Springs across what is known as the Rose Ranch. The cutoff passed south of Snowville to Hansel Spring, where the highway passes the Hansel Mountains.[36] Following a route necessary for wagons, oxen, and horses, the road continued to the next source of water, Blue Spring, then past Blind Springs to the site of Garland. From there the trail went north to the only good wagon crossing of the Malad River at Rocky Fort, west of Plymouth, then southeast through Fielding to the best ford of the Bear River, later known as Hampton's Ford. From there the road followed Hazen Kimball's track along the route of present State Highway 69, from spring to spring to the north end of what became Box Elder settlement. Where the Kotter farm is now located, the road turned east to meet Rees Spring and avoid the marshy country below the foothills. From there the road turned west and traveled along what is now Brigham City's Main Street, becoming U.S. Highway 89 south of town. The road followed the springs to secure water for men and animals.[37] At Cold Spring, near the Box Elder-Weber county line, the route of the Salt Lake Cutoff turns west, along a line which follows the springs and avoids the sand and the marshes, through Plain City, Hooper, and Syracuse, then curving east to meet U.S. Highway 89 at the Utah State University Experimental Farm near Farmington. The road then went along the foothills past Bountiful into the Salt Lake Valley.

The Hensley Cutoff became one of the major routes to the gold fields, in fact, *the* major route for summer travel. It also became the route many Mormon missionaries traveled to San Francisco to take sail for their fields of labor, particularly in the Pacific islands.

In 1849 an estimated 45,000 emigrants made their way over the California Trail. Of those, historian Brigham D. Madsen concludes that almost all of the 15,000 who went via Salt Lake City also used the Salt Lake Road.[38] Migration to California continued at a rapid pace with more than 165,000 people and nearly a million animals crossing the California Trail between 1849 and 1857. Of those California-bound immigrants, a substantial number passed through Box Elder County en route to their Eldorado.[39]

ENDNOTES

1. John W. Van Cott, *Utah Place Names* (Salt Lake City: University of Utah Press, 1990), 242.

2. Hubert Howe Bancroft, *History of Utah* (Salt Lake City: Bookcraft, Inc., 1964) [originally published in 1889 in San Francisco], 19–20.

3. Dale Morgan, *Jedediah Smith and the Opening of the West* (Indianapolis: The Bobbs-Merrill Company, Inc., 1953), 179–87.

4. George R. Brooks, ed., *The Southwest Expedition of Jedediah S. Smith* (Lincoln: University of Nebraska Press, 1977), p. 197; Fred R. Gowans, *Rocky Mountain Rendezvous* (Layton, Utah: Gibbs M. Smith, Inc., 1985), p. 13.

5. David L. Bigler, "Bartleson-Bidwell Party," in Allan Kent Powell, *Utah History Encyclopedia* (Salt Lake City: University of Utah Press, 1994), 33.

6. John Bidwell, *A Journey to California, 1841: The first emigrant party to California by wagon train, the Journal of John Bidwell* (Berkeley, CA: The Friends of the Bancroft Library, 1964), 11–12.

7. Herman J. Viola and Ralph E. Ehrenberg, "Introduction" to *John C.*

Frémont, The Exploring Expedition to the Rocky Mountains (Washington, D.C.: Smithsonian Institution Press, 1988), xii. It was not Frémont's maps or descriptions which brought the Mormons west, nor did they *cause* Brigham Young to choose the area. They helped him map his route, and showed him mountains, lakes, and rivers, but the decision to come to "the Rocky Mountains" was made by Joseph Smith, before his martyrdom in 1844. It was a part of the development of Joseph Smith's theological kingdom, not only Brigham Young's, to settle among the Native Americans in the southwest. See Andrew Karl Larson and Katharine Miles Larson, eds., *Diary of Charles L. Walker* (Logan: Utah State University Press, 1980), 522, 524; Ronald W. Walker, "Seeking the 'Remnant': The Native American During the Joseph Smith Period," *Journal of Mormon History,* 19 (Spring 1993): 1–33.

8. Frémont, *The Exploring Expedition to the Rocky Mountains,* 146.

9. Ibid., 147.

10. Ibid. These would have included Little Mountain, west of Corinne, Frémont Island, and perhaps Little Mountain west of Ogden, and Antelope Island.

11. Ibid.

12. Ibid.

13. Ibid.

14. Ibid.

15. Ibid., 148.

16. Ibid.

17. Ibid.

18. Ibid.

19. Ibid., 149.

20. Ibid., 150.

21. Ibid., 158.

22. Ibid., 159.

23. Ibid., 160.

24. Don D. Fowler, "Introduction," in Howard Stansbury, *Exploration of the Valley of the Great Salt Lake* (Washington, D.C.: Smithsonian Institution Press, 1988),. xi.

25. Stansbury, *Exploration of the Valley of the Great Salt Lake,* 97. It is for that reason that pre-historic (and historic) natives tended to make the journey from Cache Valley to Box Elder Creek via Flat Bottom Canyon, the first defile north of Box Elder Canyon. There is a well-marked trail emerging from Flat Bottom canyon on the Bonneville bench, and descending on a northerly slope, down the face of Wellsville mountain, toward a spring

nearly at the base of the hill. This trail was used, not only in prehistoric times, but in early settlement days, and particularly by Brigham City men who had been "called" to work on Logan temple in the 1880s. The route for them to Logan by foot was via Flat Bottom canyon on Monday morning and back on Saturday, according to local legend.

26. Ibid., 98–99.

27. Ibid., 101–2.

28. Ibid., 103.

29. Ibid., 103–4.

30. Ibid., 106.

31. L. A. Fleming and A. R. Standing, "The Road to 'Fortune': The Salt Lake Cutoff," *Utah Historical Quarterly*, 33 (Summer 1965): 257.

32. Ibid., 250, quoting "West from Fort Bridger" in *Utah Historical Quarterly*, 19 (1951): 250.

33. J.B. Chiles gave the east-bound Mormon Battalion members a "waybill" listing the route, the landmarks by which it could be followed, mileages, and noting springs, rivers, and sources of feed for animals.

34. George R. Stewart, *The California* Trail (Lincoln: University of Nebraska Press, 1962), 202–4; Fleming and Standing, "The Salt Lake Cutoff," 250–51.

35. Fleming and Standing, "The Salt Lake Cutoff," 204.

36. As often happens as trails become roads and place names are conferred by chance, Samuel Hensley has not been accorded the recognition he deserves. His route, which became the main route to California during the Gold Rush, traveled by tens of thousands of emigrants, became known as the Salt Lake Cutoff. Although his name was conferred on a spring, a range of mountains, and a valley, by the time it was written down, it had become Hansel Valley, Hansel Mountains, and Hansel Spring (also called Dillie Spring), short shrift given to the route's pioneer, Samuel J. Hensley.

37. One of the prominent springs in southern Box Elder is Porter Spring, just west of the tiny town of Perry. Not only was it one of the important springs along the Salt Lake Road, it bridges the gap between the nineteenth and twentieth centuries in an interesting, entrepreneurial way. In the 1850s LDS apostles Charles C. Rich and Amasa Lyman were sent to California to reclaim tithing funds collected by renegade Mormon adventurer Samuel Brannan. They took along as their guide, no doubt-bodyguard, and probable enforcer, Orrin Porter Rockwell. Rockwell had been to the California gold fields and knew the territory. After their return, Rockwell realized that money was to be better made off the gold seekers than in the gold fields. Accordingly, he homesteaded on the spring which bears his name, making it a "recruiting" place for men and animals. It was the north-

ernmost of the springs along the Salt Lake Road which had both plenty of water and plenty of grass. Travelers to the gold fields could stop a while, fatten their horses, oxen, and milk cattle (for a price, collected by the enterprising Rockwell) and then head out across the desert in much better condition. It is interesting that, in the 1970s, Porter Spring was purchased by Jay Call, descendent of Mormon pioneer Anson Call, and owner of Flying J. Mr. Call built his dream house on the edge of the pond at Porter Spring, and it serves today as his private "recruiting" place, a home in an edenic spot with a considerable heritage. [See J. Kenneth Davies, Mormon Gold (Salt Lake City: Olympus Publishing, 1984); Howard M. Carlisle, *Colonist Fathers, Corporate Sons: A Selective History of the Call Family* (Calls Trust, 1996), 190.

38. Brigham D. Madsen, ed., Exploring the Great Salt Lake: The Stansbury Expedition of 1849–50 (Salt Lake City: *University of Utah Press,* 1989), 173, note 42.

39. L. A. Fleming and A. R. Standing, "The Road to 'Fortune': The Salt Lake Cutoff," *Utah Historical Quarterly,* volume 33, number 3 [Summer 1965], p. 258 and George R. Stewart, *The California* Trail (Lincoln: University of Nebraska Press, 1962), 231–232, 319.

Chapter 4

The Saints Come Marching In

Mormon settlement of Utah began in earnest in mid 1847, as a wagon-train moved laboriously down Emigration Canyon and out onto a prominence with a view of the valley of the Great Salt Lake. This pioneer company, as it began its journey, nearly 1,800 miles to the east, consisted of 143 men, three women, two children, seventy-three wagons, ninety-three horses, fifty-two mules, sixty-six oxen, nineteen cows, seventeen dogs, and an unidentified number of chickens.[1] It was the advance company of a migration unparalleled in the history of the American West, and one which changed the face of the Great Basin, of Utah, and of Box Elder forever. All 147 members of that weary entourage were Mormons, members of a seventeen-year-old religious movement founded by Joseph Smith in 1830.

Only sixteen days after the first pioneer company arrived in the valley of the Great Salt Lake, an exploring party was sent north to Cache Valley. The first company of Mormons to visit the Box Elder area consisted of four men, under the leadership of Jesse C. Little. Little recorded in his journal:

> On Monday, August 9, 1847, I started north with a little exploring company. . . . At Weber River we found a fort of Mr. Goodyear which consists of some log buildings and corrals stockaded in with pickets. This man had a herd of cattle, horses and goats. He had a small garden of vegetables, also a few stalks of corn, and although it had been neglected, it looks well, which proved to us that with proper cultivation it would do well. We continued north to Bear River. Here we parted with the captain's [James Brown] camp and turned east into Cache Valley, which looked beautiful from the summit of the mountains. We entered the valley and passed up to the southeast thence returned through the mountains to Box Elder Creek. We then passed down this stream into the valley (Salt Lake) and followed our outward trek to the city, having been gone a week and traveled about two hundred miles.[2]

After years of conflict and violence with non-Mormon neighbors in Ohio, Missouri, and Illinois, Brigham Young and his followers had come West to be alone with only those of their own religious persuasion. The Mormon leader sought to secure the surrounding valleys and all the arable land, before outsiders could move in. Young anticipated the arrival in Utah of thousands of Latter-day Saints over the next several years and sought locations outside the Salt Lake Valley where settlements could flourish. For that reason, even amidst their poverty, and before Salt Lake Valley was properly settled, Brigham Young stepped up his colonization of a much wider area, both in the northern valleys of the Great Basin, and the long Mormon Corridor to the south. In September 1847 Peregrine Sessions moved north to found Sessions' Settlement about ten miles north of the main camp at what became Bountiful. Not long after, Hector C. Haight settled about seven miles north of Sessions' at the site of Kaysville. In January 1848, Mormon Battalion veteran Captain James Brown bought out Miles Goodyear's holdings in Weber valley at present-day Ogden, with $3,000 in California gold. By the end of 1848, several settlements were founded throughout the Salt Lake Valley including Big Cottonwood, East Mill Creek, Sugar House, Bingham, South Cottonwood, North Jordan, and West Jordan, as well as Centerville to the north between Sessions' and Haight's settlements. This expansion was fueled by the arrival of more and more Mormons from the

East. By 1848 the population of the valley had reached more than 2,500, and by the winter of 1849, there were 4,500 people living in the valley.[3]

The year 1849 saw settlement of Genua, Union, Little Cottonwood, Brighton, Granger, and Draper in the Salt Lake Valley. Brigham's worries about the influx of non-Mormons from the East (and back from California) brought settlements farther to the south, along the route of the trail to California. The first major settlement south of the Salt Lake Valley was Fort Utah, about forty miles south at what became Provo. Also in 1849 Isaac Morley led settlers eighty miles south of Provo to Sanpete Valley where they founded Manti. Hard upon the heels of the arrival of the Sanpete company, Brigham Young sent out his first major expedition to the south. The Southern Exploring Company was sent south in December 1849. The company had as its presiding officer the intrepid Parley P. Pratt.

With all the activity south of the Salt Lake Valley, the northern valleys were not ignored, and the settlement of Box Elder began in 1849 when Orrin Porter Rockwell returned to Utah from an assignment to California and homesteaded a spring surrounded by ample meadowland for his cattle at what became known as Porter Spring.

In the fall of 1850, three men, William Davis, James Brooks, and Thomas Pierce left Salt Lake City and came as far north as Box Elder Creek, three miles north of Rockwell's homestead on Porter Spring. Lyman Wells also joined the group. Rockwell, Davis, and Wells explored Box Elder Creek from the mouth of Box Elder Canyon west to the marshes, and found what they determined was the best place for a camp. They found a sizable tree-lined stream with clear flowing water. Not only was water available from the creek, there were also numerous springs along the foothills, and to the west where the alluvium met the meadowlands. Service berries, huckleberries, and choke cherries were found along the stream and in the canyon. Deer, sage hens, praire chicken, grouse, quail, ducks, and geese were plentiful and would prove a welcome supplement to pioneer diets. The three men cached a plow for the spring and returned to Salt Lake City for the winter.[4] In the spring of 1851, as soon as the roads could be traveled, the men returned with their families to Box Elder where they found:

> the whole mountain side was covered with tall bunch grass. The foothills looked like rolling meadows except for the clumps of tall sage and sunflowers growing here and there between the brush bordered streams which flowed down the hillside across the valley to the glistening lake. Only as the streams neared the lake, the brush disappeared and the stream beds widened and were bordered with tulles and cane breaks which somewhat resembled fields of waving grain. . . . The townsite of Brigham was covered with a heavy growth of bunch grass intermingled with weeds and a few sagebrush. The growth of grass extended far up the mountainside and was bordered on the south by a sagebrush growth which extended south in more or less unbroken patches until Three Mile Creek, now Perry, was reached. Here the county was covered with a heavy growth of choke cherry, oak and maple brush, there being only a narrow strip of tillable land between this brush covered section and the lake which extended east very near the western side of that little settlement. Three Mile Creek emerged from the canyon, wound in and out northward among the brush, and gradually turned to the west until it reached the swampy sections caused by the overflow of the water from the Porter Springs and the chain of springs extending southward. The brush growth continued southward past Willow Creek. Along the banks of that crystal stream grew willows of every size and variety. . . . Box Elder Creek took much the same course as now, except that it skirted the foothills farther north before it wound in and out on its way to the North lake, making here a marsh and there a meadow. Along the whole of its course the creek was bordered with large cottonwood and box-elder trees.[5]

The site chosen by Davis, Brooks, and Pierce was along Box Elder Creek, among the willows and cottonwoods which bordered the stream. It was on the alluvial gravel hill which formed a great hump beginning at the mouth of Box Elder Canyon and subsiding into the wet meadowlands on the west. There were bushes with berries; sego lilly bulbs in the spring; as well as fish, quail, sage hens, grouse, and deer. The soil was rich, and the configuration of the alluvium showed promise for establishment of a network of irrigation ditches to make the fertile soil productive. It was a good site for a settlement, and it was where the three pioneers cast their lot.

Along the banks of Box Elder Creek they felled trees, cut the limbs, stripped the bark, notched the corners, and built cabins. Their habitation, proudly named "Davis Fort," consisted of a row of adjoining log rooms, protected by a log palisade. It was located near present 7th North, between 4th and 5th West in Brigham City. The nearby grove of trees, from which many of the logs for the fort were cut, became known as "Reeder Grove."[6] The mud-chinked walls of the rooms were not high, and the resulting low-ceilinged cabins, though cramped, kept in the heat. The roofs were of poles, branches, willows, and rushes, topped with sod cut from the stream banks. Windows were small, few, and covered with oiled cotton cloth, to keep out the weather and admit a little light. The window and door openings all faced the inside of the compound, to provide as much as possible an impregnable outer perimeter to their fort, which measured about 250 feet long and about 100 feet wide. A stream of water ran through the fort.[7]

It wasn't long before the three original families were joined by others, including Simeon Carter, Jefferson Wright, Benjamin Tolman, and George Hamson. Hamson, his wife, and two children arrived on 6 October 1851; three months later on 8 December 1851 George Hamson, Jr., was born as the creek over-flowed its banks and left a foot of water in the unfinished cabin.[8]

The settlement grew quickly. By 1852 there were 1399 individuals and 39 families living at the Davis Fort. The settlers moved from the fort onto forty to eighty acre farms in the spring of 1852[9]

A second fort was built in 1853 in response to unrest among the Utes to the south which resulted in a conflict known as the Walker War.[10] Brigham City settlers were ordered by Brigham Young to move into the fort in July 1853.

The second fort was known as Box Elder Fort and was two blocks east and three blocks south of Davis Fort.[11] At over 400 feet long and 132 feet wide with a southern extention of another 300, the Box Elder Fort was much larger than the original Davis Fort. However no walls were built around the Box Elder Fort. Instead, the log cabins were built close together on the north, east, and west sides, leaving the south end exposed.[12] Water from Box Elder creek was diverted into the fort and a log school house was built in the fall of 1853 just south of the southern addition.[13] With the arrival of more settlers, another addition was built onto the fort, which eventually consisted of three adjoining squares of cabins, with open courts in the center.[14]

Box Elder settlers lived inside the expanding fort until 1855, plowing and working their fields in the spring, summer, and autumn, and spending the winter repairing harnesses, wagons, plows, and preparing for the next seasonal cycle.

A description of life in the Old Fort is given in Lydia Walker Forsgren's history:

> As the crops were gathered they were brought into the fort and stacked either on the east or west, a little distance from the inclosure and surrounded by pole corrals. While the men were busy gathering in food, the women were just as busy laying up such supplies as they could gather. Some of the girls and women went up where the cemetery is now located and burned large piles of sagebrush, then heaped the ashes in a pile. Some piled up maple limbs in the creek bed and made ashes. When these ashes were cool, they were hauled to the fort and placed in ash leeches. Water was poured over them, and, as it trickled through, the water drew out the lye from the ashes. The lye was used to make soap which was made in large iron kettles hung on cranes over bonfires built in front of the cabins.[15]

Lydia Forsgren notes that "Cooking was done in bake kettles over wood fires built in the rude fire places in the cabins, or over camp fires built in the yard." Before construction of the schoolhouse, all community activities were held either in the open quadrangle or in the cabins of the settlers and "they danced in Mr. Hutchson's house to violin music played by George F. Hamson, Sr. and Owen Jones (Blind Jones)." Even worship services and school classes were held in the tiny, cramped cabins. "On the Sabbath Day they met in the home of Bishop William Davis to praise their Maker and rejoice over their future prospects," and "during that winter, Henry Evans, one of Box Elder County's first teachers, taught school in different homes."[16]

A major change in the fortunes of Box Elder settlement came at the 1853 October conference of the Church of Jesus Christ of Latter-day Saints held in the "Old Tabernacle" on the south-west corner of the Temple Block in Salt Lake City. Lorenzo Snow, a thirty-eight-year-old member of the Quorum of Twelve Apostles, was "called" to move to Box Elder to take charge of the settlement. A contingent of fifty families was likewise "called" to assist in strengthening the settlement. They had the winter to prepare for the move to their new home on Box Elder Creek, some sixty miles to the north. The required move must not have been happy news to all those chosen. Conditions were better in the mother city than in this frontier outpost. Snow himself traveled immediately to Box Elder, but did not move his families until the next spring. When spring came in 1854, and roads dried enough for travel, Snow's families and his group of selected artisans and tradesmen made the journey to Box Elder settlement.

In December 1854 Snow's fellow apostle Wilford Woodruff traveled north to make his first visit to the northern settlements. On 4 December he recorded in his journal, "I rode to Box Elder & preached in the evening at the School House. This place contains 60 families Brother Davis Bishop. The majority of the people are welsh & Danish & mostly poor." He adds that "But little wheat raised the past year. The Bishop had 20 tons of tithing hay in hand & 15 bushels of wheat. They have no school this winter. Their fort wall is laid out 200 Rods long 100 Rods wide to be of stone 3 feet thick at the bottom 2 feet at the top 8 feet High. Is in progress of Erection."[17]

As members of Snow's company came, a few in the fall of 1853, but most over the spring of 1854, the fort was expanded to the south. A log schoolhouse, also used for worship services and community activities, was built.[18]

One of the main groups to arrive in late 1853 was a company of Scandinavians who were the first company in a large wave of LDS converts to migrate to Utah from Denmark, Sweden, and Norway during the next three decades.[19] In the spring of 1854, a second Scandinavian company came to Box Elder, as did the main body of Snow's fifty families.[20] Upon his arrival, Snow immediately took charge, and community-building began in earnest. Under the eye of territorial surveyor Jesse W. Fox, the original survey by Henry G. Sherwood was re-done.

The survey of the townsite proper, known as Plat A, commenced at the northeast corner of the plat. At that point the creek bank dropped off sharply to the north and east. It was the land to the south and west of that point which, it was determined, could be irrigated. Plat A was chosen and surveyed according to its potential for being serviced by a network of canals and ditches bringing water diverted from Box Elder Creek. According to local lore, Thomas Mathias carried the front end of the surveyor's chain, and was honored by being given the first choice of lots in Plat A. He chose Lot One, Block One.[21] Mathias erected a log cabin on his lot, most likely a cabin from Box Elder fort, dismantled and re-assembled on his city lot, as was commonly done.

Deposits of adobe clay had been discovered directly west of the center of town, in the sub-irrigated meadowland. Adobe brick were easier to handle than logs, and houses built of adobe were better insulated and could be laid up tighter than logs. The first adobe house in Plat A was built by John D. Rees on Block Four, on a lot facing one of the two main parks in the plat, Prospect Square. The Rees home was a two-room, one-story home with a lean-to kitchen off the back. The second adobe home was a much larger, two-story home, built a block west and almost directly across Prospect Square from the Rees home. This second home, with its two downstairs parlors (each with its fireplace for warmth), its lean-to kitchen, and its upstairs for sleeping quarters, was built by one of the Scandinavian immigrants, Christian Hansen, a Dane who had cared for the royal horses of the King of Denmark before becoming a Mormon and gathering to Zion.[22]

As the settlers began to move out of the fort and onto their town lots, it was thought wise—due to continued concern over problems with the Indians—to construct a stone wall around Plat A. In exchange for a building lot (chosen by drawing lots), each family was to construct fifty-six feet of the city wall.[23] However, the walls were never finished. Rock was hauled to the construction site but only parts of the north and east walls were built to the twelve-foot height. Eventually the walls were dismantled and the rock used for foundations and to construct stone buildings in the community.

The Davis and Box Elder forts were built to protect settlers from hostile Indians. A main campground for the Shoshoni Indians was along the creek northeast of the settlement; however, Indian-white relations remained peaceful.

Lorenzo Snow, somewhat of a showman, decided that, with its new beginnings, the town needed a new name. The moniker "Youngsville" (in honor of Brigham Young) was briefly used, but by 1855 the town on Box Elder Creek, with its surveyed and sparsely settled Plat A, its Big Field, and its great plans, was known as Brigham City. It was, it must not be forgotten, a Mormon town. It was one of the settlements of the Mormon Zion, and its government was really an ecclesiastical one.

As the settlements expanded north from Salt Lake City, the ecclesiastical organization expanded also. At first, Box Elder was under the jurisdiction of Weber Stake president Lorin Farr. William Davis served as Box Elder's first bishop and, after his release in 1855, Eli Harvey Pierce was called to the position.[24] After the arrival of Lorenzo Snow in 1854, Box Elder was no longer a part of the Weber Stake, and the newly created Box Elder Stake, presided over by Lorenzo Snow, extended northward into southern Idaho. Snow was a man of culture and had attended Oberlin College in his native Ohio.[25] With his background, he was not content with the primitive conditions he found in Box Elder fort upon his arrival. He recorded, "When I arrived in Box Elder County, I found the location where Brigham City now flourishes in a very unprosperous condition. Whether its change from a primitive state should be called improvement, i.e., whether it was better or worse for what had been done on the premises, would puzzle an antiquarian. Even the log meeting house, with its ground floor and earth roof, was more extensively patronized as a receptacle for bed bugs than for the assemblage of Saints." After having lived in Kirtland, Ohio, in the stately city of Nauvoo, Illinois, and in Utah's capital city, the young apostle had to suffer primitive accommodations when he first arrived at Box Elder. He continued, "At first, in locating there, I only took a portion of my family, as a small and incommodious adobie hut was the only tenement attainable."[26] It was surely with relief, and anticipation, that Snow began building a home on his lot on Brigham City's main corner. According to his own account:

> During the summer and fall I succeeded in erecting a house, one story and half in height, thirty feet by forty. It being impossible to obtain shingles, I covered the building with slabs, and for two winters the rattling of those slabs, put in motion by the canyon breezes, supplied us with music in the absence of organs and pianos. I had thus covered the roof of my house, but before my front door was in, and all my floors laid, and before any plastering was done, our house was the stopping place and the home of President Brigham Young and his company of tourists, whenever they visited these northern settlements. We sometimes entertained as many as forty at once. As soon as my house was up and partly finished, I had all of my family with me; and on the occasion of these visits of the Presidency, my family all united to make our visitors as comfortable as possible."[27]

The visits of Brigham Young, and the cultural needs of the community, did not wait until Lorenzo's house was finished. According to his sister and biographer,

> Early in the winter of 1855–6, while his recently erected dwelling house was unfinished, he converted his largest room, which was fifteen by thirty feet, into a theatrical department, by erecting a stage in one end of this not-too-capacious hall—furnishing scenery appropriate to the situation. He then organized a dramatic company; and during the long winter evenings his amateur performers drew crowded audiences of invited guests.Realizing as he did, the fact that those who have the charge and oversight of the people, without providing proper recreation, have adopted a mistaken policy, Lorenzo made an elaborate effort, in this direction, to meet the wants of the semi-progressive inhabitants of his new-born city.[28]

The theater in Snow's parlor was small, far too small to accommodate all the citizens of even a town as small as Brigham City in 1855, so several performances were held so that all could attend. Admission was at no charge, and the actors, directors, stage hands, and scenery workers also served without remuneration. It was a community effort, bringing both culture and unity to the infant metropolis. Snow watched over the productions carefully. He examined " . . . the plays before they were exhibited on the stage, and only accept[ed] such as would create innocent merriment, or inspire elevating and refining sentiment . . . not allowing anything of a demoralizing character to be presented."[29]

The first industrial building in Brigham City was the Box Elder Flouring Mill constructed at the northeast corner of the city plat and the rock wall in 1857. The reason for its location was two-fold. At that spot water diverted from the creek farther upstream could be brought to the mill-wheel, to provide power for the ponderous millstones, and the mill could serve as a kind of stronghold, or blockhouse, at the corner of the wall, in the spot closest to the Shoshoni camp (the spot considered most vulnerable). There were neither windows nor doors in the two walls of the mill which faced outward (north and east). In those walls there were only gun-slits.[30]

The flour mill was a necessary first industry. Before all else, people need flour for bread, and a grist mill was the foundation of a pioneer town. This grist mill was built under the expert guidance of Brigham Young's own mill-builder, thirty-nine-year-old Frederick Kesler. An 1840 convert to the Church of Jesus Christ of Latter-day Saints, Kesler was directed by Young to remain in the midwest as the pioneers trekked to Utah. There, Kesler built flour and saw mills. After his experiences, and his journey to the west, Kesler wanted to build a grist mill and go into private business; in fact, he wanted to build his mill in Box Elder, but Brigham Young told him his business was to be millwright for the church rather than a private businessman. Obedient to counsel, Kesler began immediately to build mills at Young's direction. After constructing several mills in and around Salt Lake City, Kesler was sent on a mission to the East to learn about the latest technology for all sorts of mills. After his return in 1854, Young directed his millwright, now armed with the latest ideas in mill building, to erect a mill for Lorenzo Snow in Box Elder, the very place where Frederick had wanted to settle and build himself a mill. The mill was owned by Young and Snow. It was finished just in time for the harvest of 1857.

The first public building built in the new town was called the Court House, but was, in reality, a multi-purpose building. It served not only as government offices and court house, but as an auditorium for church services, public meetings, and as a theater. Construction began in 1856, and after the basement story was com-

The Box Elder County Courthouse. (Box Elder County)

pleted, it was covered with slabs and used for theatrical performances.[31] The two-story building was built of adobe brick atop a stone foundation and was forty-five by sixty-two feet in size. After the two-story walls were completed, a strong wind blew them down delaying completion until late 1857.[32]

The pioneer courthouse, forty-five by sixty-five feet, still stands, forming the rear main section of the present, expanded courthouse. Thus, the Box Elder County Court House is the oldest functioning court house in the state.

Just across the street from the new courthouse, at the town's main intersection, the corner of Forest and Main streets, Lorenzo Snow built his home, ancillary structures with a rock wall surrounding his estate.

While the upper stories of the courthouse were being finished, the basement replaced Snow's parlor for the community theatrical productions. "The upper story of the building was forty-five by sixty-five feet, and was used as an assembly hall, for meetings of religious worship, concerts, lectures and dancing, until they built their large Tabernacle. After the first year, the theater was transferred from the basement to the upper story. At stage was erected in the east end, 18x45 feet, and was furnished with fine elaborate scenery and apartments, where the members of the Dramatic Association had appropriate opportunities to exercise and display genius and ability."[33] In 1875 a "Social Hall" was built, measuring thirty-three by sixty-three, to free up space in the courthouse and provide the Dramatic Association with a better-appointed home of its own. Eliza R. Snow Smith notes that it was two stories high, "the first was designed for amusement, social and dancing parties, lectures, and the assemblies of the Polysophical Association; the second for a high school or seminary of learning."[34]

We have noted that Snow had a flair for the theatrical. Besides organizing a theater company and holding theatrical productions in his own parlor, he made the periodic visits of Brigham Young and his entourage memorable events. Snow related:

> To manifest due respect, and a proper appreciation of those visits, which were productive of a vast amount of good to the Saints scattered throughout the Territory, I introduced a precedent which was widely adopted and carried into effect, until railroads superseded those lengthy carriage drives. . . .
>
> On learning the precise time when the party would arrive, I arranged a programme for the occasion. In the first place, a set of hands was detailed to put the roads in good condition for carriages, by clearing away stones, filling crevices, repairing bridges and causeways, etc. Much care and labor were devoted to organizing the escort to meet the President's long train of carriages some miles from the city. We had not the means in those early days of our history to be very elaborate in furnishing equipments as would have gratified our vanity, but what we lacked we supplied in ingenuity and enterprise, in fixing up what our means and circumstances would admit.[35]

In organizing the gala reception for the church leader and his party, Lorenzo Snow took recourse to his military training at Oberlin.

> We selected forty or fifty intelligent, interesting looking young gentlemen, dressed in gray uniforms, each carrying a lance, the top of which was pointed with shining material, from which gay ribbons floated gracefully in the breeze. These young gentlemen were mounted on our finest horses and properly instructed and disciplined for the occasion. Next, we selected sixteen or twenty fine intelligent young ladies, had them dressed in white, with corresponding decorations. These were seated in wagons, each drawn by two span of horses, properly caparisoned. All the members of the escort were carefully instructed respecting a proper manner of giving the salute on meeting the visiting party; the various branches of the escort bearing flags and beautiful banners with appropriate mottoes. All were preceded by one or two carriages occupied by the authorities and leading men of the city, the whole led by a martial band under the direction of the city marshal.
>
> In connection with the foregoing arrangement, the children, in their Sunday attire, gathered from all parts of the city, and many from adjacent settlements, were formed into line on each side of the street, and as the company entered, it was conducted through these long lines of children to my house, amid loud cheers, the ringing of bells and waving of banners.[36]

Lorenzo closes his account of the festivities by stating that "The effect of this display on President Young and party was truly thrilling. They were taken by a surprise of the most impressive character. Thus an example was set which has been extensively followed, until carriage riding has, to a great extent, yielded to that of railroads."[37]

As the fledgling town grew, and more and more houses rose from the sagebrush-covered lots, a business district began to sprout up on both sides of Main Street, stretching north and south from Lorenzo Snow's corner. Of note is the home of Samuel Smith built on Main Street, on the corner lot opposite Snow on the north side of Forest Street.

> Judge Samuel Smith lived on the west side of Main Street directly north of this square. For many years his home was the chief business center of the settlement. It was here he maintained the post office after he received his appointment in 1855. For many years a portion of the building served as a hotel. When Dr. Oliver C. Ormsby established Brigham City's first drug store, he used a room

> in Judge Smith's home. Mrs. Carrie Smith used the north part of the home as a location for the town's first millinery store. Directly north of his home Judge Smith erected a building which for many years housed a carpenter shop and a shoe shop.[38]

The development of Brigham City suffered a temporary set back in 1857 and 1858 when news that a federal army under Albert Sidney Johnston was enroute to Utah to put down an alleged "Mormon Rebellion."

As the army approached Utah, the Mormons adopted a policy of harassment and delay, buying time to weaken the army and negotiate a peace. During the standoff, Brigham Young and his followers prepared to torch their cities and flee, as their predecessors in the Book of Mormon had done, "into the wilderness." The northern settlements, in the Salt Lake Valley and northward, were abandoned, and the inhabitants moved, lock, stock and barrel, to Utah County. There was a mass meeting in Brigham City on 25 March 1858 to discuss the Move South, as soon as the roads were dry in the spring. Two months later Frederick Kesler went to Brigham City to dismantle his new flouring mill. On 26 May he writes, "This morning I had orders (from Brigham Young) to go to Boxelder & take out the machinery & forward the same to Provo." On May 28, Kesler "commenced taking [the mill] to pieces the news soon got to the Indians who were campt nearby about 40 in no. Who soon came in to see what was up." On the 29th, he notes that "I visited the city the houses were left in a very dirty state fences down & everything bears the mark of distruction." He left with his load on the 30th. By 4 June Kesler and his precious machinery had arrived in Provo, where he "visited Pst. B. Young He showed me the site where he intended building a flouring mill." It appears that had the war not been settled, the Box Elder mill machinery might have been installed in Provo. By the mid July 1858, however, a peaceful settlement had been made with the federal government and people returned to their homes. On 25 July Frederick Kesler notes in his journal, "Loaded up the Boxelder mill & Started Back for [Salt Lake] City—arrived at Home 2 ocl at night. On 31 July he notes that he "Started for Boxelder—stayed at Ogden—roasted beef on a stick in the street for supper, slept on top of Bishop's haystack." During the first six days of August, the millwright reinstalled the machinery in the mill, and on the 13th he wrote that "it performed well making beautiful flour."[39] With the opening of the sluice gates and the rumbling back to life of the two run of stones in the stolid old Box Elder Flouring Mill, life in Brigham City began rumbling back to normal. War had been averted, and life returned to Lorenzo Snow's town of Brigham City.

The Shoshoni

Indian difficulties continued even with the arrival of federal armies under Albert Sidney Johnston in 1858 and Patrick Connor in 1862. The ever-increasing numbers of emigrants and settlers and their appropriation of traditional Indian campsites and disruption of the Indian social and economic systems led to violence. Brigham Madsen records:

> As the emigrant trains continued to roll along the Oregon and California trails, resentment began to build among the Northern Shoshoni and Bannock as they watched their grasslands and game disappear. It became particularly strong when their women, children, and men were shot and killed by the white pioneers as though they were some kind of wild animals to be hunted along the way. Near Fort Hall, and especially west of Raft River and Shoshone Falls, the young men of the tribes began to strike back, raiding the wagon camps and returning with food and booty.... The several bands of the region watched with apprehension as the Mormon farmers continued to expand their holdings until the Malad, Bear Lake and Cache valleys were entirely filled with the homes, fields, and stock of the newcomers. The Indians became more and more demanding of food from the whites, understanding well the instructions the Saints had received from their prophet. The younger men in the tribes became bolder and began to raid the cattle and horse herds in Cache Valley, which invited follow-up attempts by the armed and exasperated owners of the stock. Indian leaders disposed to be friendly toward the whites came to be in the minority as the starvation of their peoples emboldened the more rash among them. By fall of 1862 the Mormon settlers discovered that when they went in pursuit of a herd of stolen horses it was no longer possible to talk to the Indian

raiders and attempt to recover the stock by peaceful means. Instead, "the Indians immediately showed fight," and the white men were forced to withdraw. [40]

Some Shoshoni, following Chief Pocatello, attacked Oregon-bound wagon trains among the rocks, boulders, and granite formations of the City of Rocks, the junction point of the Salt Lake Cutoff and the Oregon Trail. It was an ideal spot for an ambush, and a number of whites were killed in the attacks. Three separate wagon trains were attacked during the first week of August, 1862.[41] Though Brigham Madsen and other historians discount the "City of Rocks Massacre," of August 1862, others document its reality.[42]

It was "The increased travel on the Montana Trail further heightened the difficulties between Utah authorities and the Northwestern Indians [which] led to intervention by the military."[43] The culmination of hostilities was the Bear River Massacre on 29 January 1863.[44] In the fall of 1862 Colonel Patrick Edward Connor marched his seven hundred California Volunteers to Utah to protect the western mail routes from Indian attack and to keep a close watch on the Mormons.[45]

The soldiers were unhappy in Utah, and upset that they were not winning glory on the battlefields of the war against the Confederacy. They were itching for a fight. The stage was set, and the Shoshoni gave them an excuse. According to Brigham Madsen, "The Volunteers first tried to free a white boy held prisoner by the Northern Indians. The colonel sent word to Cache Valley that unless the captives were released he "would wipe every one of them out." The Indians were just as belligerent, leading most citizens of Utah to believe they were eager for a battle with the troops. This attitude was strengthened by the Volunteers' killing of four Indian hostages when some stolen horses were not returned to the white owners."[46]

Dr. Madsen tells the story of the Battle of Bear River:

> The stage was set for battle when some miners from Grasshopper Creek in Montana were killed by Indians while traveling through Cache Valley. The Utah chief justice issued a warrant for the arrest of Chiefs Bear Hunter, Sanpitch, and Sagwitch and asked the military to support the U.S. marshal! in serving the war-

> rant. Fearing that the Indians might leave their camp and deprive the soldiers of a fight, Connor marched his troops at night. On the early morning of January 29, 1863, the Volunteers attacked the entrenched Indians across the ice-choked Bear River at Battle Creek, just north of Franklin, Idaho. At first the Indians were successful in driving back the soldiers, but a flanking attack soon turned the engagement into a massacre as the troops pursued the disorganized Indians, killing men, women, and children. According to some accounts the colonel had commanded, "Kill everything—nits make lice." . . . The ruthlessness of the troops was revealed in the casualty figures: The California Volunteers suffered 22 deaths, while the number of Indians slain varied from the death count of 224 reported officially by Connor, to 255 reported by Superintendent Doty, to 368 recorded by James J. Hill and other Utah citizens who visited the battlefield the next day. The bodies of almost 90 women and children were noted. The troops also destroyed 70 tipis, captured 175 horses, and collected over 1,000 bushels of grain. Many of the articles gathered from the Indian camp obviously came from emigrant trains. . . . The scalp of Bear Hunter was hung at Camp Douglas when the troops returned to their headquarters, and the *Deseret News* thought the Volunteers had "done a larger amount of Indian killing than ever fell to the lot of any single expedition of which we have any knowledge." When a *Deseret News* correspondent visited the site of the battlefield five years later he reported, "The bleached skeletons of scores of noble red men still ornament the grounds' and expressed regret that Pocatello and his 'gang' had not also been annihilated in the massacre."[47]

Unfortunately, the Battle of Bear River may have been counterproductive. Madsen notes that "Instead of cowing the Northwestern Shoshoni into submission, as some writers suggested, there is overwhelming evidence that the reverse happened. Mormon authorities reported that the Indians were now so angry with the soldiers that they intended to 'steal and kill every white man they could find.'"[48]

Eventually, however, the Indians were brought to heel. Washakie and his band signed a treaty at Fort Bridger on 2 July 1863, and "with the help of General Connor, [Indian superintendent James Duane] Doty gathered together ten Northwestern Shoshoni bands at Box

This photograph of the Hampton Stage Stop and bridge across the Bear River at Collinston was taken by W. H. Jackson in 1872. (Box Elder County)

Elder in Utah Territory and concluded the second treaty on July 30, 1863."[49] The treaty was signed in Brigham City, the chiefs participating having gathered in the tithing yard. According to Madsen,

> The superintendent had been afraid Chief Pocatello would not be present and was relieved to have that much-feared warrior show up. In fact, Pocatello's people were so destitute and the chief was so anxious to participate that he had sent word he would give ten horses to prove his sincerity. The nine chiefs who signed the treaty were: Pocatello, Toomontso, Sanpitch, Tasowitz, Yahnoway, Weerahsoop, Pahragoosohd, Tahkwetoonah, and Omrshee. The tenth chief, Sagowitz, had been shot by a white 'fiend' while the Indian leader was under arrest by the California Volunteers and was unable to leave his 'weekeeup' but agreed to all the provisions.[50]

According to journalist Cindy Yurth, "One by one, the Shoshoni bands settled at the reservation, but a portion of the Northwestern Band held out. Being attacked by federal troops had intensified their distrust of government, and the Mormons among whom they lived could at least be counted on for the occasional gift of food and cloth. During the 1870s, several hundred surviving Shoshoni set up their tepees at their old winter camp at the mouth of Bear River . . . "[51] It was not a propitious choice. The old winter camp was directly between Brigham City and Corinne. The rag-tag group of survivors of the Battle of Bear River found themselves this time in the crossfire between gentiles in Corinne and Mormons in Brigham City. Yurth continues, "While some Mormons tried to establish a farm for the Indians to alleviate the strain on the settlers, the editor of the *Corinne Reporter* launched a tirade in print, accusing the Mormons and their 'latter-day pets' (as he called the Indians) of being in cahoots and planning to wipe out the gentiles." In their paranoia, the Corinne gentiles enlisted the help of their only allies in Utah: the United States Army. "Eventually, the pressure got so bad military commander Gen. Philip Sheridan ordered the Indians to move—just two days into their first harvest, prompting Chief Sagwitch to lament, 'What have I stolen? Who have I killed?'"[52]

"The Shoshoni were moved to a spot near Hampton's Ford, where, with the help of some Mormon missionaries, they quickly planted again. This time it was a group of apostate Mormons who became uneasy and demanded their removal to Fort Hall." This time, Mormons came to their rescue. Yurth writes that "By that time the remaining 300 or so had converted to Mormonism and preferred to remain in Utah. In 1880, the LDS Church purchased 1,700 acres for them at the site now known as Washakie."[53]

The Indian Farm was established on land in the Malad River Valley, on the west side of the river, about two miles south of Portage. The band of Northern Shoshoni settled at Washakie. It was an interesting name. Washakie himself lived in Wyoming and is buried there. The leader of the Box Elder Band was Sagwitch, the same Sagwitch who was a survivor of the Bear River Massacre and signed the Treaty of Box Elder in 1863. "Some Indians applied for homesteads, but most simply continued to farm the church-owned land. A school and LDS ward were established, and the fame of the independent Indian settlement spread throughout Utah, attracting regular visits by Salt Lake City newspaper reporters. . . . By 1882 the Washakie Ward was doing well enough to contribute $8,000 to the building of the Logan Temple."[54] The remaining band of Shoshoni at Washakie were also Mormons. Moroni Timbimboo became the first Native American bishop in the LDS church.

Patty Madsen, local Shoshoni representative, observes that today there are fewer full-blooded Shoshoni left. However, the Washakie remains the most popular burial place for members of the tribe.[55] It is the cemetery that still draws the Shoshoni to Washakie. And with good reason. The largest stone in the cemetery is for Chief Sagwitch, who led them there, and was the first to depart from the Shoshoni custom and be buried in a marked grave.

ENDNOTES

1. Russell R. Rich, *Ensign to the Nations* (Provo: Brigham Young University Publications, 1972), 101.

2. Jesse C. Little, *Journal*,. 47, MS, cited in Milton R. Hunter, *Brigham Young the Colonizer* (Salt Lake City: Deseret News Press, 1940), 34.

3. Rich, *Ensign to the Nations,* 175.

4. Veara S. Fife and Chloe N. Petersen, *Brigham City, Utah Residents,* 1850–1877 (Brigham City: Golden Spike Chapter, Utah Genealogical Association, 1976), 4.

5. Lydia Walker Forsgren, ed., *History of Box Elder County* (Brigham City: Daughters of Utah Pioneers, 1937), 3.

6. Fife and Petersen, *Brigham City,* 5. "Here, for many years," according to Fife and Petersen, "the settlers enjoyed gathering as a church group for picnics, outings, family gatherings, and out door activities of various kinds."

7. Olive H. Kotter, "Brigham City to 1900," in *Through the Years* (Brigham City: Brigham City Eighth Ward, 1953), 8.

8. Ibid.

9. Fife and Petersen, *Brigham City, Utah,* 8; and Kotter, "Brigham City to 1900" 8.

10. Kotter, "Brigham City to 1900," 8. Veara S. Fife and Chloe N. Petersen give 1852 as the year the fort was built and occupied. See Fife and Petersen, *Brigham City, Utah,* 6–7.

11. There is a marker on the west side of the old playground of Lincoln School, on Second West just south of Third South, marking one corner of Box Elder Fort, which came to be known as the "Old Fort." The original marker was placed, with due ceremonies, on 19 August 1922 (marking the 54th anniversary of Brigham Young's final public address, in Brigham City, at which time he divided the city into four wards, and reorganized the stake). On that occasion, the remaining old timers signed a statement which read as follows: "We the undersigned, veterans of the Old Fort and citizens of Brigham City, Utah, Testify that on the 18th day of Aug 1922 at 6 o'clock

in the evening we assembled in the immediate vicinity of the Old Fort and that after due consideration and discussion and carefully weighing all evidence available and presented that we unanimously located the south west corner of the Old Fort which was the beginning of the present Brigham City, and we marked the same corner with a stake located under the direction of the Officials of Brigham City." Fife and Petersen, *Brigham City, Utah,* 9.

12. Kotter, "Brigham City to 1900," 8.

13. Fife and Petersen, *Brigham City, Utah,* 8. Pioneer Lewis N. Boothe states that "There was a small stream of water running through the center of the road. The water was taken out of Box Elder Creek, near where Bott's marble mill now stands." Forsgren, *History of Box Elder County,* 257.

14. The present writer remembers a model of Box Elder Fort, constructed sometime in the 1920s, which was exhibited in the Daughters of Utah Pioneers exhibit in the lower hall of the Box Elder County Court House. By the time he became director of the Brigham City Museum-Gallery in 1977, and the exhibit was absorbed into the Museum-Gallery collections, the model had disappeared.

15. Forsgren, *History of Box Elder County,* 258.

16. Ibid.

17. Scott G. Kenney, ed., *Wilford Woodruff's Journal* (Salt Lake City: Signature Books, 1983), Vol. 4, p. 291 [27 November 1854].

18. Kotter, "Brigham City to 1900," 8.

19. Forsgren, *History of Box Elder County,* 258. Among them were several who later not only became locally prominent in their own right, but became the founders of some of the area's most prominent families. One of them, Peter Adolph Forsgren, bears the honor of being—according to the inscription on his tombstone—the first convert to the Church of Jesus Christ of Latter-day Saints in Scandinavia. Again the histories do not agree. Kotter writes that the Scandinavian company arrived in the fall of 1854. "Brigham City to 1900," 8. The entry from Wilford Woodruff's journal seems to agree with Kotter. See Kenney, *Wilford Woodruff's Journal,* 33 n.112.

20. Forsgren, *History of Box Elder County,* 259.

21. Though the survey was begun at the north-east corner, the lots were numbered from the southeast corner, according to a pattern given by Brigham Young.

22. See Frederick M. Huchel, "The Oldest Home in Brigham City." The Rees home was demolished sometime in the first couple of decades of the twentieth century, leaving the Hansen home as the oldest adobe home standing in town. It is located at 13 North 2nd East. For a differing view concerning the second house and the first two-story, see Forsgren, *History of Box Elder County,* 260.

23. See Frederick M. Huchel, "The Box Elder Flouring Mill," *Utah Historical Quarterly,* 56 (Winter 1988): 76. See also Forsgren, *History of Box Elder County,* 259–60.

24. Kotter, "Brigham City to 1900," 8. Apparently, events surrounding the release of Bishop Davis were a bit more complex. On 28 February 1855, Weber Stake president Lorin Farr and his counselor, Abram Palmer came to Box Elder to hear complaints concerning Bishop Davis. About two-thirds of the people of Box Elder were not in good fellowship with Bishop Davis, because of complaints they had about his conduct. Among other things, he had apparently refused to allow the Welsh settlers to use the meetinghouse to conduct worship services in the Welsh language, and concealed the key by subterfuge, and harbored ill-feelings toward the Welsh. It was also alleged that Mrs. Davis was meddling in her husband's business and "trying to run the ward." After hearing the charges, and airing the complaints, President Farr arose and stated "that he thought Mrs. Davis was basically a good woman, [but] warned her to stay out of her husband's business and stop trying to run the ward. He testified to the audience that he knew the bishop to be a good man, but by following too closely the wishes of his family, especially his wife, he had been led to err." He had also been accused of "harboring gentiles in his house." President Farr stated to the congregation that "In the matter of sheltering gentiles under his roof, maybe Bishop Davis was strong enough to withstand their arguments against the church, but his family certainly were not, and unless he wanted to see the havoc such a practice would cause, he ought to stop at once." Finally, "At the close of the meeting, the greatest majority voted to sustain the bishop, with a few opposing votes." The matter, however, was referred by President Farr to the church authorities in Salt Lake City, and it was "voted [at the church general conference on 7 April 1855] to drop William Davis as bishop, and to ordain in his stead Elder Eli Harvey Pierce." See Vaughn S. Nielsen, *The History of Box Elder Stake* (Brigham City: Box Elder Stake, 1977), 6–7. Most of Nielsen's material is taken from Box Elder Stake records.

25. Eliza R. Snow Smith, *Biography and Family Record of Lorenzo Snow, One of the Twelve Apostles of the Church of Jesus Christ of Latter-day Saints* (Salt Lake City: Deseret News Company, 1884), 3–6.

26. Ibid., 261.

27. Ibid., 262.

28. Ibid., 267.

29. Ibid., 268.

30. Huchel, "The Box Elder Flouring Mill," 76, 80.

31. Kotter, "Brigham City to 1900," 9.

32. Smith, *Biography and Family Record of Lorenzo Snow,* 268.

33. Ibid., 269–270. During a remodeling in the Box Elder Court House basement some years ago, painted scenery from productions of Snow's old Dramatic Association were found painted on the east wall.

34. Ibid., 271.

35. Ibid., 262.

36. Ibid., 262–63.

37. Ibid., 263.

38. Forsgren, *History of Box Elder County,* 260.

39. See specific dates in Frederick Kesler Daybook microfilm of holograph (original in Huntington Library, San Marino, California). The book is titled on the flyleaf: "Oil Mill Sugar Works by F. Kesler." The records begin in April 1855. See also Huchel, "The Box Elder Flouring Mill," 83.

40. Brigham D. Madsen, *The Northern Shoshoni* (Caldwell, Idaho: Caxton Printers, Ltd., 1980), 34–35, citing *Deseret News,* 8 October 1862.

41. Brigham D. Madsen, *Chief Pocatello: the "White Plume* (Salt Lake City: University of Utah Press, 1986), 45 ff

42. Kent Hale and Kathleen Hedberg, unpublished typescript documenting the City of Rocks Massacre, 1998, copy in my possession . I am indebted to Kathleen Hedberg, for allowing me access to her research. Among Hale and Hedberg's sources is Charles S. Walgamott's reminiscent work, *Six Decades Back: A Series of Historical Sketches of Early Days in Idaho* (Caxton Printers, 1936). Walgamott's reminiscences were first serialized in the *Idaho Citizen,* in Twin Falls, then published in book form as *Reminiscences of Early Days: A Series of Historical Sketches and Happenings in the Early Days of Snake River Valley.* Volume I appeared in 1926, and Volume II in 1927. Madsen's criticism of the City of Rocks Massacre stories is found in his article "The Almo Massacre Revisited" in *Idaho Yesterdays.* Hale and Hedberg have located information in the family history of Chester Loveland of Brigham City who met the survivors of the City of Rocks Massacre and returned to Almo creek with Mormon militiamen to rescue the survivors. They also found an article in the 17 September 1862, *Deseret News* documenting the massacre.

43. Madsen, *The Northern Shoshoni* , 35.

44. Brigham D. Madsen: The Shoshoni Frontier and the Bear River Massacre (Salt Lake City: University of Utah Press, 1985).

45. Madsen, *The Northern Shoshoni,* 35.

46. Ibid., 36.

47. Ibid.

48. Ibid.

49. Ibid., 37.

50. Ibid.

51. Cindy Yurth, "Vanishing tribe: Time, fate take toll on Shoshoni band," Logan *Herald Journal,* 3 May 1998, 12.

52. Ibid.

53. Ibid.

54. Ibid.

55. Ibid.

CHAPTER 5

THE COOPERATIVE AND UNITED ORDER MOVEMENT

Nineteenth-century Mormonism was, in many respects, communitarian. Founder Joseph Smith sought both a religious and economic utopia that he called Zion—a place where people would be of one heart and one mind, live together in righteousness, and be free of poverty. Brigham Young and Lorenzo Snow embraced this outlook, and once the initial phase of settlement was over they sought to bring the dream of cooperation and unity closer to Zion through what became known as the United Order Movement. Brigham City proved to be an ideal beginning point for the movement that spread throughout Utah and surrounding territories and lasted until well after the death of Brigham Young in 1877.

Leonard Arrington tells of the inception of the Brigham City cooperative: "With a city of almost 1,600 inhabitants to provide for, Apostle Snow supervised the organization in 1864 of a cooperative general store. It was his intention to use this mercantile cooperative as the basis for the organization of the entire economic life of the community and the development of the industries needed to make the community self-sufficient."[1]

Lorenzo Snow. (Utah State Historical Society)

When Brigham Young formally began the United Order movement, he established a number of differing types of cooperative organizations, from the totally communal order at Orderville, in Kane County, to the Brigham City Cooperative, which was on the other end of the spectrum. In Orderville all lived in a communal state, having all things in common, eating at a common table, and sharing all duties.[2] The Brigham City order was an order in which private enterprise was the model. Professor Arrington notes that the Brigham City cooperative, as it originated, "was nothing more than a joint-stock enterprise to which Snow and three others subscribed $3,000."[3] Success brought other stockholders, and within six years Lorenzo Snow was ready to expand from a mercantile store to a mercantile and manufacturing association. The association began building its first manufacturing enterprise in the fall of 1866.[4] After four years, and an expenditure of $10,000, the Brigham City Tannery began business as the flagship of the manufacturing enterprise.[5] The tannery was constructed adjacent to Box Elder Creek (where water was available to power the machinery) in the block between Box Elder Street and Pleasant Street, just north of Columbia Street.[6] When built, the tannery was at the far north edge of Brigham City. A mill race was constructed from the mouth of Box Elder Canyon to the tannery site to provide water for the tanning process and power for the tannery and other projected industrial enterprises.

Most of the labor and materials were obtained in exchange for capital stock. To supervise construction of the tannery, procure the machinery, hire the workers, and obtain supplies, Lorenzo Snow selected as director of the operation Abraham Hillam who had practicted the tanning trade in England, Cincinnati, and Salt Lake City.[7] The tannery was successful with an annual production of $10,000 worth of goods which were reported to "equal in quality to the best Eastern oaked tanned leather."[8]

The abundant supply of high-quality leather in 1870 made possible, indeed, necessitated the development of the boot, shoe, saddle, and harness division. Soon the boot and shoe shop was turning out $770 worth of footwear per week, produced by thirty workers.[9] The leather department produced all the goods the community could use, and the surplus was sold for cash in Logan, Ogden, and Salt Lake City, and some to the Zion's Cooperative Mercantile Institution.It was at this juncture, 1870, that the growing enterprise was incorporated as the "Brigham City Mercantile and Manufacturing Association."[10]

After the leather industry was under way, the next enterprise was a woolen factory. The building was erected during 1870 and 1871,

Brigham City Woolen Mills. (Box Elder County)

utilizing—as was necessary in those agricultural-based times—the labor of those who were unemployed during the season between harvest and seedtime.

The woolen factory was built a little farther up the millrace from the tannery and the grist mill. The building was 44 by 88 feet, the bottom story being rock and the upper walls of brick. Building the structure and outfitting it with machinery procured from the East cost $35,000.[11] The machinery alone cost $7,000.[12] The cash was carried to the eastern market by Alanson Norton, the mechanic in charge of setting up the equipment in the mill, in a specially-made belt, made by tailor Ola N. Stohl of Brigham City Tannery leather.[13]

Equipment installed in the building included a spinning jack with two hundred spindles, four broad looms "calculated to weave cloth three yards wide," three narrow looms, three 48-inch carding machines "besides a double one and a picker." There was "also a complete set of cloth dressing machinery" and equipment for washing, drying, and dyeing. Even with all that, there was space and power available for expansion.[14]

The mill was built at the crest of the creek bank, on the millrace, to provide water power. A report states that the machinery in the

Woolen Factory "is propelled by a turbine wheel 26 inches with 24 feet head, equal to a 50-horse power, perfectly able to run another set of machinery equal to what the building now contains, for which also plenty of room is left in the building."[15]

By early February 1871 the new Brigham City Mercantile and Manufacturing Association Woolen Factory was operable. The machinery was set in motion on 4 February, with impressive ceremonies.

Not only was the woolen mill an expensive enterprise, it took some time to get the operation running smoothly, even with experts like Alanson Norton, James Pett, and James Buckley.[16] Lorenzo Snow wrote to Brigham Young that "Owing in part, perhaps, to a lack of knowledge and experience, the first year we made but small profits in the woolen factory."[17]

Because one of the goals of the Mercantile and Manufacturing Association—and of the larger United Order Movement—was self-sufficiency, a cooperative sheep herd was started to provide wool for vats and looms. The initial herd was 1,500 head.[18] As with labor on the mill, sheep were contributed in exchange for capital stock in the association.[19] Farmland was secured on Bear River and near the present town of Mantua and was used to produce crops to sustain the sheep in the winter. Snow explained the method of building the sheep herd to Young: "We are endeavoring to improve our wool, and retain the increase of our sheep till we have sufficient to supply our factory."[20] By 1873 Snow reported the herd at 2,500 head. By 1879 the herd had grown to 10,000.[21]

To provide a locally-controlled source of cotton for warp, the Brigham City cooperative acquired 125 acres for a cotton farm on the Virgin river over 350 miles to the south of Brigham City.[22] The camp was located on the northwest bank of the Virgin, about five miles above the town of Washington in the shadow of the Harrisville anticline. About a dozen young men under superintendent James May were called to a two year mission to the Dixie Cotton Farm, with others replacing them at the end of their mission. They established Camp Lorenzo and began construction of an imposing two-story rock dormitory.[23] The Virgin River holdings were increased and farm products grown which were not grown in the harsher climate of the Bear River Valley.

Superintendent May sent a glowing report of the progress at Camp Lorenzo:

> We are five miles east of Washington on the Virgin River. We have about 100 acres of land on the west side of the river, and 300 on the east side. We have dug a ditch one and a half miles long, three feet wide, blasted through a point of rocks 55 feet long, five feet wide; 11 feet deep; built a dam across the river, 150 feet long, 40 feet wide, 4-feet high; cleared the brush off fifty acres of land, plowed thirty acres, put out 625 grape vines and 1800 grape cuttings, planted 100 peach trees; and are all well at this time. The Lord has blessed us in all our labors, for which we feel truly thankful. There has been no swearing in camp. I have not heard an oath since I left home. We have no smoking, chewing, or card playing, but we have plenty of books and quite a variety, so we need not get lonesome for the want of amusements. Is not this a good showing for thirteen young men? We expect to plant 35 acres of cotton, 10 of corn, and 5 of Lucern.[24]

The first year's crop of cotton produced about 70,000 yards of warp. The second year's crop was double the first. The produce farm provided food for the inhabitants of Camp Lorenzo and also grapes for wine and raisins and cane for sugar, to be transported back to Brigham City.[25]

Lorenzo Snow was so pleased with the products of the association that he took occasion to show off the results of the work of the woolen factory and the tailor department during his mission to Europe.

> I engaged a suit of clothes last fall (1872) of a tailor in Brigham City, the material of which was made at our woolen factory. I wore this as a traveling suit through Europe and Palestine, and felt rather proud in exhibiting it as a specimen of "Mormon" industry, amid the vales of the Great West. While in France we had an interview with President Thiers and his cabinet; this was at Versailles, and it so happened I then was dressed in this home made suit, my aristocratic one being locked in my trunk at Paris, twelve miles distant.

> It was agreed by our party that I looked sufficiently respectable in my home-made product, boots and suit, to appear with them in the presence of the president of the French Republic. I respected their judgment and honored their decision. I was received by the President as cordially, and I believe he shook hands with me as warmly and fervently as though I had been arrayed in superb broadcloth.
>
> In several other instances, in our interviews with consuls and American Ministers, and other men of rank and station, my reserved suit was not come-atable, so I had an opportunity of showing a specimen of what we are doing here in the mountains, which was an occasion of both surprise and commendation.
>
> On my return to London, this suit was nearly as good as when I left Brigham City (nearly eight months before.) made a present of it to President Wells' son, (Junius) one of our missionaries now preaching in London. Permit me to say, that this suit I now wear, is not imported broadcloth, as you probably imagine, but was made and manufactured in Brigham City, and the boots I have on are those worn through my Palestine tour, and nearly as good as when first put on in Brigham City nearly a year ago.[26]

The woolen mill became one of the mainstays of the Brigham City Mercantile and Manufacturing Association, producing yarn, blankets, cloth, underwear, and men's and women's wear, among other things.

As the Brigham City cooperative reached its stride, the national economy slipped into the "Panic of 1873," a depression which deeply affected the national economy and the non-Mormon business community in Utah.

In contrast to much of Utah and most of the nation, Brigham City withstood the Panic of 1873 and, in fact, experienced its greatest year of expansion. Brigham City "enjoyed a certain amount of notoriety. Newspaper reporters visited the area and reported such interesting features as the manner in which homes were built for the poor and widows; how a department was set up to provide labor for tramps and benefit from feeding them; how the co-operators planned to locate their shops and factories on a twelve-acre square around the center of town and run street cars from the square to various parts of the town; and how they maintained their own monetary and banking system."[27]

Other Utah communities were not as fortunate and Brigham Young used the success of the Brigham City cooperative as a model for achieving economic self-sufficiency in other Mormon communities. In St. George, where drought, floods, grasshoppers and the impact of the Panic of 1873 had left hundreds underemployed, Brigham Young urged the establishment of a united order patterned after the one in Brigham City. Soon the United Order movement spread throughout the Utah Territory.

By 1874 the Brigham City cooperative, officially known as the Brigham City Mercantile and Manufacturing Association, grew to fifteen departments then burgeoned to forty.[28]

One department, the Co-op Dairy, was located in a mountain dell at the north tip of Wellsville Mountain, the northern end of the Wasatch Range and twenty miles north of Brigham City. The dairy was supervised by Christian Hansen, a Danish convert to Mormonism who had at one time served as a bodyguard to the King of Denmark during the Holstein war and cared for the royal horses. However, it was actually Christian's wife, Elizabeth Ericksen Hansen, who had first-hand experience with the dairy industry in their native Denmark.[29]

The dairy operation began in 1871, with construction of a large rock building against a hill from which issued a large spring of cold, fresh mountain water. In the era before mechanical refrigeration, the location of the spring dictated the placement of the dairy. The cold spring water cooled the stone floor in which depressions were built to cool the cans of milk overnight while the cream rose to the top. On the main floor was the main work area, and the top floor, beneath the long gabled roof, served as a dormitory.[30] A resident force of young women worked as milk maids, serving a herd of five hundred cows.[31] Each girl was assigned twenty cows, to be milked night and morning.[32] The cows came from Box Elder County, Cache Valley, and as far away as Malad City to the north and the Hot Springs in Weber County to the south. The cows wore a rope or strap around their necks to which a block of wood was attached that bore the number of the cow.[33] The milk produced by each cow as carefully recorded and its owners paid in butter and cheese.[34]

Each of the eight cheese presses could produce one forty-five pound cheese a day. The cheese-making process began with pouring milk into warming vats to which Rennet was added. Girls stirred the milk to help form curds, and when the whey was ready the excess water was drained off and the curd pressed into cheese.[35] In 1875 the dairy produced 40,000 pounds of cheese, and two years later in 1877 the output was 50,000 pounds.[36]

The dairy was a business enterprise, but social and religious life was not neglected. A Brother Fridal, who loved to play his violin, was employed at the dairy. "In the evening when the day was finished, the girls' bedrolls were often laid aside in the long bedroom and the whole crowd enjoyed an evening of dancing but when 9:30 approached, the music stopped and all must be retired and lights out by 10 P.M., so each one might be refreshed at their jobs at 4 A.M." [37] Sunday mornings the girls were transported by wagon to Sunday school in Beaver Dam.

The dairy maintained a herd of hogs to consume the by-products of cheese production, and to supplement the pioneers' staple diet of beef. A butcher department was added to the Co-op to provide the community with beef, pork and mutton.[38] Several "molasses mills (producing sorghum molasses) were operated, providing food for both man and milk cow."[39]

A number of farms were developed under the co-op banner, including a "dry-farm" at Portage.[40] One of the unique features of the Brigham City Mercantile and Manufacturing Association was the "Indian Farm." Taking note of the native Shoshoni, Mormons were mindful of dispossessing the Indians from their ancestral lands, and interested in bettering the state of their subsistence living by introducing them to the arts of modern agriculture. It was with this in mind that the Indian Farm became a teaching institution for the Shoshoni.[41]

Other departments of the Brigham City Mercantile and Manufacturing Association included one to plant and care for flowers, shrubs, and orchards; one for the manufacture and repair of farm machinery; one to produce hats and caps from fur, wool, and straw; a tailor shop; a shingle, lath, and picket mill; a furniture and cabinet shop; three sawmills; brick and adobe shops; blacksmith shop; a tin shop; a wagon and carriage repair shop; a rope factory; a pottery shop; a broom factory; a brush factory; a cooperage; and a lime kiln.[42]

Formal education was carried on under the banner of the co-op, with schools and a seminary for religious instruction. There was even a "Tramp Department" to supervise itinerant labor, such as those who chopped wood and performed other odd jobs.[43]

From 1864 until 1877, the Brigham City Mercantile and Manufacturing Association was eminently successful. Perhaps as a portent of things to come, disaster struck the co-op on the shortest, darkest day of the year Brigham Young died. On 21 December 1877, John Laird, the spinner at the woolen factory, was awakened in the night by smoke. The woolen factory had caught fire. The cause was never determined. The night guard "ran through town and cried fire, while City marshal C C. Loveland arose and ran to the Court House and rang the bell before dressing himself."[44] Lorenzo Snow reported that "in less than thirty minutes the whole establishment, with its entire contents of machinery, wool, warps and cloth lay in ashes."[45] It was two days before Joseph Smith's birthday, five days before Christmas, and a raging solstice fire had consumed the largest and most expensive of the industries of the Mercantile and Manufacturing Association.

A meeting of the directors was held the next day, and it was decided to rebuild, and to have the building ready for operation by July 4th of the next year.[46] It seemed an impossible task. Even the optimistic Lorenzo Snow was daunted, but not defeated. With help from all quarters, the woolen factory rose, phoenix-like, from its own ashes. On 4 July 1878, a gala celebration opened a new, enlarged, improved woolen factory, with a sturdy, new brick second story arising above the indestructible rock walls of the original structure, topped by a magnificent belvedere from which the entire city could be surveyed.[47] It seemed like an auspicious new beginning. It was, however, only the beginning of the end. Rebuilding the woolen mill and purchasing all new machinery and materials was a severe drain on the resources of the co-op. Lorenzo Snow's sister and biographer, Eliza R. Snow Smith, explains:

> After the heavy loss the association suffered by the burning of their woolen factory, estimated at thirty thousand dollars in cash, being in great need of funds to liquidate cash indebtedness incurred in rebuilding their factory, purchasing new machinery, etc., they took a large contract on the Utah Northern Railroad, then in progress of construction through Idaho, to furnish supplies of timber, ties, shingles and lumber, to meet demands. It was a gigantic contract, and they immediately shaped their plans to meet emergencies, They purchased a saw mill and shingle mill in Marsh Valley, Idaho, and moved to that place their steam saw mill from Box Elder County. They employed about one hundred men in the various departments of labor, also a number of women, who assisted as cooks.[48]

In addition to the indebtedness incurred for rebuilding the woolen mill, other problems arose. A questionable tax was levied by the federal government on the scrip used as currency by the co-op.[49] The cutting of timber was declared illegal and the sawmill was shut down.[50] Ultimately, a portion of the tax debt broke the back of the co-op. In an 1879 letter to church official Franklin D. Richards, Lorenzo listed some of the association's losses:

Crops destroyed by grasshoppers	$4,000
Crops destroyed by drought	$3,000
Burning of woolen mills	$30,000
Losses in Idaho	$6,000
By assessment on scrip	$10,200[51]

With all the losses, the association could no longer carry all the mills and factories as well as the mercantile department. One by one the factories were closed or transferred to private ownership. Usually those who had charge of the enterprises under the co-operative association purchased the operations.

Many of the smaller operations were simply terminated or became cottage industries, operated out of homes. The woolen mill was sold to manager James Baron and remained in the Baron family until 1981. The tannery was sold to three men from Salt Lake City and used for a wool pulling business.[52] Charles Kelly, who had managed the tannery, opened his own boot and shoe shop.[53] The tannery building was used as an armory during World War I, and then, owned by the Call family, it was used as a warehouse. The structure deteriorated and, although still structurally sound, was demolished in 1970.[54]

The cabinet shop passed into the hands of the Merrell family, which operated it, in connection with a lumber and hardware business on Main Street, until 1982, when the downtown business was closed and the property sold for construction of a bank and law offices.[55] The mill also remained in the Merrell family and finally ceased operation in the late 1980s. The building, at this writing, stands empty and neglected, though still houses invaluable pieces of the original water-power equipment, some unique in the state of Utah.

The only major industrial enterprise of pioneer Brigham City never absorbed into the co-op was the grist mill, the Box Elder Flouring Mill. The mill remained under the control of Lorenzo Snow and Samuel Smith, even through the period of the Brigham City Mercantile and Manufacturing Association, or co-op, while the planing mill, tannery, and woolen mill were acquired by the cooperative association. This was not unusual. It seems to have been the custom of the presiding authority in a settlement to keep an independent source of income so that he could work as overseer of the co-op without compensation and would not be open to criticism for profiting from the co-op's enterprises.[56]

By the 1880s, demand exceeded the capacity of the water-powered grist mill. The Brigham City Flouring Mills Co., under Snow and Smith, built a new mill at the mouth of the canyon, abandoning the old burr mill. The building and the entire city block on which it stood were purchased in 1890 by John H Bott, an English convert to Mormonism, who had learned the stone cutting trade working on the great granite temple in Salt Lake City. The cost of the mill and land was $300. The final payment was a large headstone for Samuel Smith, with Judge Smith's life story hand-carved by Bott into its marble surface.[57] The mill has continued in the Bott family, operated by descendants of John H. Bott, until the present day. With the demise of the Elias Morris and Sons stoneworks in Salt Lake City, it became the oldest stone monument business in the state.

Bott's Monument in 1920. The original building was the Lorenzo Snow flour mill built in 1855–56. (Box Elder County)

Descendants of Mads Christian Jensen, the miller brought to Brigham City to operate the original flouring mill, built a new mill in 1909 near the Oregon Short Line railroad station. Some of their descendants are still (1998) involved in operating the business.

The cooperative movement in Brigham City, which began with a suggestion made by Brigham Young to Lorenzo Snow, grew into the Brigham City Mercantile and Manufacturing Association, a thriving cooperative organization that spread its benefits and effects throughout Box Elder County. The cooperative affected the entire territory, with its operations in Washington County and its being the impetus and the model for Brigham Young's organizing united orders throughout Utah.

ENDNOTES

1. Leonard J. Arrington, "Cooperative Community in the North: Brigham City, Utah," *Utah Historical Quarterly* 33 (Summer 1965): 200.

2. Leonard J. Arrington, *Great Basin Kingdom* (Lincoln: University of Nebraska Press, 1958), 333 ff.

3. Arrington, "Cooperative Community in the North," 201.

4. Ibid.

5. Ibid.; and Frederick M. Huchel, *The Brigham City Tannery: An Historical Sketch,* (Brigham City, Ut: Frederick M. Huchel, 1988), 1–2.

6. Now Third North, between First East and Second East Streets.

7. Arrington, "Cooperative Community in the North;" and Huchel, *The Brigham City Tannery,* 1 .

8. "History of Box Elder Stake," 12 July 1872, quoted in Leonard J. Arrington, "Coöperative Community in the North: Brigham City, Utah," *Utah Historical Quarterly,* Volume 33, Number 3 [Summer 1965], 202.

9. Arrington, "Cooperative Community in the North," 202.

10. Ibid.

11. Ibid.

12. Lydia Walker Forsgren, ed., *History of Box Elder County* (Brigham City, UT: Daughters of Utah Pioneers, 1937), 105.

13. Ibid.

14. *Deseret Evening News,* 4 April 1871, copied into Journal History" 3 April 1871. LDS Church Historical Department Archives.

15. Ibid.

16. Frederick M. Huchel, *A History of The Brigham City Woolen Factory—Baron Woolen Mills* (Brigham City, UT: Frederick M. Huchel, 1997), 10.

17. Lorenzo Snow to Brigham Young, in Forsgren ed., *History of Box Elder County,* 106.

18. Forsgren, ed., *History of Box Elder County,* 107; Leonard J. Arrington, Feramorz Y. Fox and Dean L. May, *Building the City of God* (Salt Lake City: Deseret Book Company, 1976), 114–15; Mark Riddle, "Lorenzo Snow and the Brigham City Cooperative," typescript, 18, copy in my possession.

19. Lorenzo Snow to Brigham Young, in Forsgren, *History of Box Elder County,* 106.

20. Ibid.

21. Forsgren, *History of Box Elder County,* 107, 114.

22. Arrington, Fox, and May, *Building the City of God,* 115.

23. Andrew Karl Larson, *The Red Hills of November* (Salt Lake City: Deseret News Press, 1957), 79. On this page is a photograph of the ruins of

the building. It stood, virtually in the same condition as in the photograph reproduced in Larson, at the time of my visit in September, 1981.

24. Arrington, Fox, and May, *Building the City of God,* 16.

25. Ibid.

26. Thomas C. Romney, *The Life of Lorenzo Snow* (Salt Lake City: S. U. P. Memorial Foundation, 1955), 311–12.

27. Arrington, *Great Basin Kingdom,* 325.

28. Arrington, "Cooperative Community in the North," 203.

29. Adolph M. Reeder, untitled typescript history of the Brigham City United Order dairy, 2. Author's interview with Robert E. Jensen, great-grandson of Christian Hansen, 2 April 1997. Mr. Jensen tells the poignant story of Elizabeth's life. She buried two children in Denmark before emigrating to Utah, the latter in a borrowed cemetery amid persecution from former co-religionists. A third child was born in Echo Canyon on the way to Utah, and buried a month later. A son, Willard, was born in the house facing Prospect Square, the adobes for which she molded by hand in the months before he was born. She was carrying another child when they abandoned their new home, with its precious window-panes of glass hauled across the plains by ox-team, their garden, and the all they had in their new land, in 1858. When, under edict from President James Buchanan, Johnston's Army was sent to Utah, All Brigham City was abandoned, with a small contingent left behind to put all improvements, including Christian and Elizabeth's new home, to the torch, leaving only scorched earth behind. Christian and Elizabeth joined the rest of the Brighamites on a hundred-mile trek to Provo in May 1858, to return only two months later when peace was forged between the Mormons and the United States. Providencial rains during their absence watered the neglected crops and allowed them to realize a successful harvest in 1858.

30. Reeder, untitled typescript history of the Brigham City United Order dairy, 2.

31. Arrington, "Cooperative Community in the North," 204; Reeder, untitled typescript history of the Brigham City United Order dairy, 2; Robert E. Jensen (interview, 2 April 1997) recalls being told that the three oldest sons of Willard S. Hansen, son of Christian Hansen, were assigned the task of milking the "kickers," cows too difficult for the girls to handle.

32. "First Dairy of Its Size In The State Of Utah," undated, unattributed newspaper clipping, in the collection of Robert E. Jensen.

33. Adolph M. Reeder, untitled typescript history of the Brigham City United Order dairy, 2.

34. Essie Peterson, "Beaver Dam Monument To Be Dedicated," undated

newspaper with no publication information, from the collection of Robert E. Jensen.

35. "First Dairy of Its Size In The State Of Utah."

36. Arrington, "Cooperative Community in the North," 204.

37. Adolph M. Reeder, untitled typescript history of the Brigham City United Order dairy, 4.

38. Arrington, "Cooperative Community in the North," 204.

39. Ibid.

40. Ibid.

41. The United Order Indian Farm became the LDS church-owned Washakie Indian Reservation.

42. Arrington, "Cooperative Community in the North," 204.

43. Ibid., 206.

44. *Deseret News,* 21 December 1877.

45. Eliza R. Snow Smith, *Biography and Family Record of Lorenzo Snow, One of the Twelve Apostles of the Church of Jesus Christ of Latter-day Saints* (Salt Lake City: Deseret News Company, 1884), 307.

46. Riddle, "Lorenzo Snow and the Brigham City Cooperative," 19.

47. Huchel, *A History of the Brigham City Woolen Factory,* 22.

48. Smith, *Biography and Family Record of Lorenzo Snow,* 302.

49. Arrington, "Cooperative Community in the North," 210, 216.

50. Smith, *Biography and Family Record of Lorenzo Snow,* 303; Huchel, *A History of the Brigham City Woolen Factory,* 24.

51. Smith, *Biography and Family Record of Lorenzo Snow,* 308.

52. Olive H. Kotter, "Brigham City to 1900" in *Through the Years* (Brigham City, UT: Brigham City Eighth Ward, 1953), 12; Huchel, *The Brigham City Tannery,* 6.

53. Forsgren, ed., *History of Box Elder County,*111; *Ogden Daily Herald,* 26 January 1882.

54. *Box Elder Journal,* 18 June 1970. In the late 1960s,and early 1970s, it became the rage for Brigham City to compete for national city beautification awards. Beautification in Brigham City in those years consisted more of tearing down old 'eyesores' than anything else. Photographs were taken, and scrapbooks submitted for national competition. Under this program, championed by Mayor Olaf Zundel and city beautification chair Anita Burt, the Tannery (still structurally sound) was bulldozed on 17 June 1970 and replaced by a vacant lot. As a memorial, a sign stood at the west end of the tannery site for some years denoting the weed-choked lot as a Brigham City historic landmark. Some of the timbers from the tannery (the rest of the

debris was buried on the site) remain piled just south of the site of the tannery to mark the spot where the first industrial enterprise of the Brigham City Mercantile and Manufacturing stood for just about a hundred years. Huchel, *The Brigham City Tannery*, 6–7.

55. Conversation with Zion's Bank Brigham City branch manager Charlie Starr, 2 April 1997.

56. Frederick M. Huchel, "The Box Elder Flouring Mill," *Utah Historical Quarterly*, Volume 56, Number I (Winter 1988), 83 ; Book A of Abstracts, 155, Box Elder County Recorder's Office, Box Elder County Courthouse, Brigham City; Leonard J. Arrington, "Cooperative Community in the North," 207.

57. Frederick M. Huchel, "The Box Elder Flouring Mill," 85.

Chapter 6

The Transcontinental Railroad

Box Elder County has the distinction of being home of the Golden Spike National Historic Site which honors the completion of the transcontinental railroad at Promontory Summit on 10 May 1869. However, before officials of the Union Pacific and Central Pacific drove the symbolic golden spike thirty miles west of Brigham City, and the nation celebrated one of the most significant accomplishments in America's history, thousands of construction workers—mostly Irish, Chinese, and Mormons—toiled to open a passage through the high crags, peaks, and defiles of the Rocky and Sierra ranges of mountains, cross countless streams and rivers, build a grade, and lay nearly eighteen hundred miles of rail.

As Brigham Young and the vanguard of Mormon pioneers journeyed west in 1847, the vision of a transcontinental railroad was in the mind of the nation. Mormons welcomed the transportation revolution that the railroad would bring even though it threatened the isolation they sought. During the 1850s five major transcontinental railroad surveys were authorized by Congress and the questions became *when* and *where* the Atlantic and Pacific coasts would be tied together by rail. In 1861 the Central Pacific Railroad Company was organized to build east from California. Company officials included Leland Stanford, president; Collis Potter Huntington, vice president; Mark Hopkins, treasurer; Charles Crocker, superintendent of construction; and Theodore Judah, chief engineer. The Union Pacific Railroad Company was organized in 1862 with John Dix, president; Thomas Clark Durant, vice president and general manager; Samuel B. Reed, construction superintendent; and Grenville M. Dodge, chief engineer. The Civil War delayed construction of the railroad, but once the war ended in 1865 an army of former soldiers and new immigrants, coupled with generous subsidies and land grants from the federal government and a determination to complete the long discussed project, pushed both companies onward. As the two railroads approached each other, Congress set the meeting place approximately midway between the two ends-of-track. The place set was Promontory Summit.

Not only did the two railroad lines meet in Box Elder County, the grading for both companies through Box Elder County (as well as through other parts of the route through Utah) was done by local labor. Brigham Young, with an eye to bringing the railroad to completion, as well as providing cash-labor opportunities for Mormons, saw to it that Mormon firms got contracts for grading on both the Union Pacific and the Central Pacific. Companies with the names Sharp & Young (Bishop John Sharp and several of Brigham's sons) and Benson, Farr & West (Apostle Ezra T. Benson, Weber Stake president Lorin Farr, and Bishop Chauncey W. West) were the grading subcontractors.

The grand culmination of the transcontinental railroad project with the meeting of the two lines and the driving of ceremonial spikes was arguably the most noted historical event ever to take place in Utah—and it happened in Box Elder County. The great importance of that event merits discussion in some detail.

Driving the Golden Spike

The date: 10 May 1869; the place, Promontory Summit, Utah; the event, completion of the first railroad to span the North American continent.

A wagon train meets a Central Pacific train powered by the locomotive "Jupiter" at Monument Point on the northern tip of the Great Salt Lake in 1869. (Box Elder County)

Promontory Summit is the high point of a valley in the Promontory range of mountains in northern Utah. It lies at an elevation of approximately 5,000 feet, that is, about 800 feet above the level of Great Salt Lake. The valley, about seventy miles northwest of Salt Lake City, is shallow, roughly circular, remote, and dusty—or muddy—depending on the weather, and carpeted with sage and rabbit June grass, and a few scrub juniper. The landscape has changed little in one hundred thirty years.

The morning of 10 May 1869 was cold, and a chilling mist engulfed the valley. It had been raining for three days and Promontory dawned miserable. It was so cold that a thin crust of ice had formed on the puddles which dotted the valley.

As the rising sun began to burn off the mist and melt the chill in the air, a Central Pacific construction train came chugging in from the west to extend the C.P. spur into a siding and thus establish claim to Promontory Station as a Central Pacific terminal. This race for time and territory had driven the Central Pacific and Union Pacific railroads from Sacramento and Omaha east and west in a monumental feat of railroad construction, to be completed this day—an amazing six years ahead of the time scheduled by Congress. As the

C.P. train pulled in, laden with material and workmen, it was met by a lusty cheer from Union Pacific workmen who had reached Promontory Station after a full night's work under the supervision of Union Pacific's chief engineer Grenville M. Dodge and construction contractor Jack Casement. The Central Pacific crews could but concede and take solace in the fact that in this race they had set the track laying record, having put down ten miles in a day on 28 April, a record they still hold.[1]

At 7:00 A.M. F. L. Van Denburgh raised the flag of the United States of America to the top of a telegraph pole opposite the point where the last two rails would join east and west.[2]

At 8:45 the Central Pacific special train arrived at Promontory. It was pulled by C. P. locomotive number 60 named *Jupiter* a 4–4–0 built by Schenectady in 1868, and in use on the C.P. only six weeks.[3] The use of *Jupiter* to pull the special train was not as originally planned. When the Promontory bound train left Sacramento on 5 May, it was drawn by locomotive *Antelope*, number 29, a 4–4–0 built by McKay & Aldus in 1867. Behind the *Antelope* was a new "subsistence car" or "tender," built in April in the C.P. shops. It had the exterior appearance of a baggage car, but inside was replete with compartments, water tanks, ice bins, and all the appurtenances of a large and well stocked pantry, to cater to the needs of the dignitaries on their long journey. Behind this car was the private car of Central Pacific's president, former governor of California Leland Stanford. At one end the car had a combination dining room and office, and at the other quarters for ten passengers. Stanford's party included California's Chief Justice S. William Sanderson and Dr. J. D. B. Stillman, San Francisco County coroner and friend of Mark Hopkins. Also along were three railroad commissioners appointed by the federal government to receive the railroad, James W. Haines, William G. Sherman (brother of General Sherman), and Fred A. Tritle, who was also a candidate for governor of Nevada; Edgar Mills of Sacramento and of the Bank of California, and son of Darius Ogden Mills; Anson P. K. Safford, newly appointed governor of the territory of Arizona, on his way to take his new position; and Dr. Harvey W. Harkness, of Sacramento, scientist, educator, and publisher of the *Sacramento Press*. Also on board were a polished wood ceremonial tie, three precious metal spikes, and other ceremonial trappings for the Promontory festivities. All went well for the Stanford special until it was descending the Truckee River valley past Truckee, on the way to Reno. There a crew of Chinese were cutting logs. They saw the regular train pass and knew nothing of the following special. One of the logs, over fifty feet long and more than three feet in girth scooted down the mountain side and landed in the railroad cut with its end across one of the rails. Minutes later the special rounded the bend, and there was neither time nor track to stop the lumbering locomotive and its load. Sixty-three-year-old Harkness was riding on the pilot, wrapped in a buffalo robe and enjoying the mountain scenery. Not any too soon, Dr. Harkness leaped to the ground and locomotive and log collided. The pilot of the *Antelope* was torn off, one side of the engine was damaged, and the cars lost their steps. Harkness was bruised, but not seriously injured, although somewhat shaken. The train was able to limp into Reno, where a telegram was sent to Wadsworth to hold the regular train. There the regular was augmented with the two extra cars and the train, pulled by *Jupiter* continued east to its destination at Elko. When the special left Elko, it carried a water car as it set out across the Nevada and Utah deserts.[4]

When the dignitaries arrived at Promontory on the 7th, fully expecting the ceremony to be held on the 8th as previously scheduled, they were informed that the U.P. special was delayed due to storm damage to trackage in Weber Canyon.[5] The ceremony was delayed until the 10th. On the 8th the C.P. delegation became the guests of U.P. on an inspection tour of the line east of Ogden.[6] On the 9th Stanford's train pulled back about thirty miles to Monument Point—where there was a spectacular view of the Lake—and waited.[7]

When the special returned to Promontory on the morning of 10 May, the end of the mainline track was still occupied by Superintendent J. H. Strobridge's construction train. The Strobridge train, drawn by locomotive number 62, *Whirlwind,* backed up, and Stanford's train pulled up on the main line to a point near the end of the track. From the west all was ready and they impatiently awaited the arrival of the Union Pacific train from Ogden. At last, at 10:00 A.M., the U.P. special came into view, pulled by U.P. number 119, a 4–4–0 built in 1868, by Rogers locomotive & machine works, which consisted of four cars. Behind were four more trains full of army personnel of the Twenty-First infantry on the way to the Presidio at San Francisco.[8]

Heading the Union Pacific delegation was Vice-President and General Manager Thomas C. Durant, and U. P. directors Sidney Dillon and John Duff, chief engineer Major General Grenville M. Dodge, construction superintendent Samuel B. Reed, Contractors Jack & Dan Casement, and Durant's sidekick, consulting engineer Silas Seymour. Also on board was the Reverend Dr. John Todd of Pittsfield, Massachusetts, representing the *Boston Congregationalist.* Reverend Todd was a friend of John Duff. The Union Pacific train also carried the delegation from Utah, including Bishop John Sharp of the Church of Jesus Christ of Latter-day Saints, and of the contracting firm of Sharp & Young. The other half of the firm was made up of three of Brigham Young's sons, Brigham Jr., John W., and Joseph A., who held contracts with the Union Pacific for grading through Utah. Lorin Farr, mayor of Ogden and president of the LDS church Weber Stake, Apostle Ezra T. Benson, and Chauncey W. West represented the contracting company of Benson, Farr, and West, which had contracted with the Central Pacific for grading. The delegation represented Brigham Young, who was in southern Utah on business.[9]

At 11:15 the two trains faced each other across the gap in the tracks and Stanford led his delegation over to meet the U.P. officials. For the next hour, Grenville Dodge of U.P. and Edgar Mills, representing C.P., conferred in vain, arguing over details of the ceremony, no plans having been made in advance. Dodge wanted to have his own ceremony rather than a joint program. The two men could come to no agreement. Finally the ranking members of the two delegations, Stanford and Durant, settled the problems and five minutes later the ceremony began. During the official hour-long impasse, the workmen were busy. Since 10:30, Chinese workmen had been grading the space between the two ends of track, laying ties, and making all preparations for the last two rails. Not to be forgotten was the transcontinental telegraph, which had been built alongside the railroad. F. L. Van Denburgh, superintendent of telegraphy for Central Pacific, and W. B. Hibbard, superintendent of the Western Union

The Union Pacific's "Big Trestle" east of Promontory Summit. (Box Elder County)

Telegraph Company, were in charge of the telegraph line, and Amos L. Bowsher, construction chief for C.P. telegraph, ran the lines from east and west to a small deal table near the point of Junction and connected them to a special operator's kit. He also had wires from the telegraph line connected to a regular spike and an ordinary maul for use in the ceremony. Telegraph operators on duty were Howard Sigler and Louis Jacobs of Central Pacific and W. R. Fredricks and W. N. Shilling of Western Union's Ogden office.[10]

A crowd had gathered—a motley group of dignitaries, trainloads of soldiers, excursionists from Salt Lake City, and citizens from surrounding towns and farms. The twenty-first infantry's band assembled near the gap in the rails, as did the band of the LDS church Tenth Ward from Salt Lake City, replete with new uniforms and $1,200 worth of new instruments from London.[11]

Major Milton Cogswell, commander of the twenty-first infantry, marched a double row of soldiers to a position between the two locomotives on the south side of the track to keep back the approximately six hundred people who pushed in to get a look at the proceedings.

As the noon hour approached, the weather was becoming ideal for the day's events. The sun was shining brightly in an almost cloudless sky. The thermometer on the shaded side of the Central Pacific telegraph car showed that the day had warmed to 69 degrees and a breeze was blowing as it nearly always does across the sagebrush covered valley at Promontory Summit.[12] Mrs. Strobridge, the C. P. superintendent's wife, a Mrs. Ryan, and several children were taken to positions on the front row, and General Jack Casement asked repeatedly for the crowd to move back to give more people a chance to see the proceedings. Representatives of the press later complained that they had been pushed to the rear, and some stated that only about twenty persons got a clear view of the ceremony. One of those fortunate ones was Amos Bowsher, perched part way up the nearest telegraph pole—in case of wire troubles.

A crew of Chinese, decked out in clean blue frocks, with their boss H. H. Minkler and a crew of Irish workers under a man by the name of Guilford brought the last two rails into place and spiked them to the ties all except near the end of the South rail. There the spikes were only partially driven, and one tie was left out. At 12:20 P.M., Utah time, the Western Union network was notified that in about twenty minutes the last spike would be driven. James Gamble, Western Union's chief, had ordered top priority for news from Promontory that day, and all lines were cleared so that all across the nation people could receive almost at the same time the great news from Utah in what was the first national network broadcast in history. In almost every telegraph office crowds had assembled to get the news as soon as it came in.[13]

Then Superintendent James H. Strobridge of Central Pacific and his counterpart from Union Pacific, Samuel B. Reed, pushed through the crowd carrying from Stanford's car a ceremonial last tie of polished California laurel wood and slid it into place in the bed that had been left for it at the rail junction. The last tie was presented by West Evans, tie contractor for the Central Pacific. The tie was about the size of a regular tie and had been prepared and polished by Strahle and Hughes, San Francisco billiard-table manufacturers. Auger holes had been drilled in proper positions for four spikes and in the center on top was a silver plate bearing the following inscription:

> The last tie laid on the completion of the Pacific railroad, May 1869.

Also on the plate was a list of the C P. officers, the name of the makers, and that of the donor.[14]

With the laurel tie in place, master of ceremonies Edgar Mills (or according to some accounts General Dodge) stepped forward and called for order. As he explained the proceedings, the telegraph sent this following message to the nation:

> TO EVERYBODY. KEEP QUIET. WHEN THE LAST SPIKE IS DRIVEN AT PROMONTORY POINT, WE WILL SAY "DONE!" DON'T BREAK THE CIRCUIT, BUT WATCH FOR THE SIGNALS OF THE BLOWS OF THE HAMMER.[15]

While this message was being sent, Mills (or Dodge) had introduced the Reverend Dr. John Todd of Pittsfield Massachusetts, representing the *Boston Congregationalist* and the New York Evangelist, who would offer the prayer. The telegrapher followed his first message with this one:

> ALMOST READY, HATS OFF: PRAYER IS BEING OFFERED.

Reverend Todd prayed,

> Our Father and God, and our father's God, God of Creation and God of Providence, thou has created the heavens and the earth, the valleys and the hills; Thou art also the God of all mercies and blessings. We rejoice that thou hast created the human mind with its powers of invention, its capacity of expansion, and its guerdon of success. We have assembled here this day, upon the height of the continent, to do homage to thy wonderful name, in that Thou hast brought this mighty enterprise, combining the commerce of the East with the gold of the West to so glorious a completion. And now we ask thee that this great work, so auspiciously begun and so magnificently completed, may remain a monument of our faith and of our good works. We here consecrate this great highway for the good of thy people. O God, we implore thy blessings upon it, and upon those who may direct its operation.

> O Father, God of our fathers, we desire to acknowledge thy hand in this great work, and ask thy blessings upon us here assembled, upon the rulers of our government, and upon thy people everywhere, that peace may flow unto them as a gentle stream, and that this mighty enterprise may be unto us as the Atlantic of thy strength and the Pacific of thy love, through Jesus, the Redeemer, Amen.[16]

Some accounts state that, as a matter of protocol and courtesy, Bishop Sharp, representing the Mormon church, was asked to offer a prayer, which he briefly did.[17] It was then approximately 12:30. Iron spikes were driven by two United States railroad commissioners, J. W. Haines of Nevada and William G. Sherman of San Francisco, and by Henry Nottingham, president of the Michigan (Southern) Central and Lake Shore Railroad, and perhaps by some other guests.[18] A fishplate was bolted on, joining the last two rails, some say by Commissioner Haines. It was 12:40. The telegrapher notified the East:

> WE HAVE GOT DONE PRAYING: THE SPIKE IS ABOUT TO BE PRESENTED.[19]

Then came the presentation of the ceremonial spikes. Governor Safford had an intricately engraved spike from the people of Arizona. He read the inscription: "Ribbed with iron, clad in silver and crowned with gold Arizona presents her offering to the enterprise that has banded a continent, dictated a pathway to commerce."[20]

Commissioner Tritle, candidate for Nevada's governorship, produced a spike of silver from the Comstock Lode, on behalf of the people of the Silver State. In presenting it, he said, "To the iron of the East and the gold of the West, Nevada adds her link of silver to span the continent and wed the oceans."[21]

Harkness recovered from his mishap, presented two spikes of gold from California. One was inscribed, "With this spike the San Francisco News Letter offers its homage to the great work which has joined the Atlantic and Pacific Oceans. This month—May 1869."[22]

It had been given to President Stanford by the *News Letter*'s proprietor, Frank Marriot. The other gold spike is the spike which is famous today as the "Golden Spike." It was 5/8 inches in overall

Looking east from the Central Pacific Locomotive "Jupiter" at Promontory Summit, 10 May 1869. (Box Elder County)

length, weighed 14.13 ounces, and was made of twenty-dollar gold pieces by Schultz, Fischer, & Mohrig, of San Francisco. Inscriptions on the sides were as follows:

> "The Pacific Railroad: Ground Broken January 8, 1863; Completed May 8, 1869"
>
> "Officers. Hon. Leland Stanford, Pres'dt. C. P. Huntington. Vice Pres'dt. E. B. Crocker, Atty. Mark Hopkins, Tres. Chas Crocker, Gen. Supt. E. H. Miller, Jr. Secty. S. S. Montague, Chief Eng'r."
>
> "Directors of the C. P. R. R. of Cal. Hon. Leland Stanford C. P. Huntington E. B. Crocker Mark Hopkins A.P. Stanford E. H. Miller, Jr."
>
> "May God continue the unity of our country as this railroad unites

> the two great Oceans of the World. Presented by David Hewes, San Francisco"

The head of the spike bears the famous inscription, "The Last Spike."[23]

It was Dr. Harkness's turn to speak:

> Gentlemen of the Pacific Railroad, the last rail needed to complete the greatest railroad enterprise of the world is about to be laid; the last spike needed to unite the Atlantic and the Pacific by a new line of trade and commerce is about to be driven to its place. To perform these acts the East and West have come together. Never since history commenced her record of human events has man been called upon to meet the completion of a work so magnificent in contemplation and so marvelous in execution. California, within whose borders and by whose citizens the Pacific Railroad was inaugurated, desires to express her appreciation of the vast importance to her and her Sister states of the great enterprise which by (your) joint action is about to be consummated; from her mines (of gold) she has (had) forged a spike, from her laurel woods she has hewn a tie, and by the hands of her citizens she offers them to become a part of the great highway which is about to unite her in closer fellowship with her sisters of the Atlantic. From her bosom was taken the first soil, let hers be the last tie and the last spike, and with them accept the hopes and wishes of her people that the success or your enterprise will not stop short of its brightest promise.[24]

As they were presented, "Governor" Stanford and Dr. Durant placed the spikes in the auger holes in the laurel tie. About that time Durant, suffering from a severe headache, retired to his private car to rest. While he was indisposed, Stanford responded on behalf of the Central Pacific Railroad:

> Gentlemen, the Pacific Railroad companies accept with pride and satisfaction these golden and silver tokens of your appreciation of the importance of our enterprise to the material interest of the whole country, east and west north and south. These gifts shall receive a fitting place in the superstructure of our road, and before laying the tie and driving the spikes in completion of the Pacific Railway allow me to express the hope that the great importance which you are pleased to attach to our undertaking may be in all

> respects fully realized. This line of rails connecting the Atlantic and Pacific and affording to commerce a new transit, will prove, we trust, a speedy forerunner of increased facilities. The Pacific Railroad will, as soon as commerce shall begin fully to realize its advantages, demonstrate the necessity of rich improvements in railroading so as to render practicable the transportation of freight at much less rates than are now possible under any system which has been thus far anywhere adopted. The day is not far distant when three tracks will be found necessary to accommodate the commerce and travel which will seek a transit across the continent. Freight will then move only one way on each track, and at rates of speed that will answer the demands of cheapness and time. Cars and engines will be light or heavy depending on the speed required and the weight to be transported. In conclusion I will say that we hope to do ultimately what is now impossible on long lines—transport coarse, heavy and cheap products all distances at a living rate to the trade. Now, Gentlemen, with your assistance we will proceed to lay the last tie and last rail and drive the last spike.[25]

In the absence of Durant, the Union Pacific was represented by chief engineer General Grenville M. Dodge. His remarks were terse, but fraught with historical portent:

> Gentlemen, the great Benton proposed that someday a giant statue of Columbus be erected on the highest peak of the Rocky Mountains, pointing westward, denoting that as the great route across the continent. You have made that prophecy today a fact. This is the way to India![26]

At that, wild cheering broke out, then increased. They cheered General Dodge, they cheered Stanford, Durant, the engineers, the superintendents, the workmen, the financiers, the two railroads, and the flag of the United States. When the cheering had died down a bit, the master of ceremonies, Edgar Mills, made a few remarks and then introduced Mr. L. W. Coe, president of the Pacific Union Express Company, who in behalf of that company presented a silver-plated spike maul to Leland Stanford. The head of the maul was 6¾ inches in overall length. The base part was three inches long, and the pointed end was 1¾ inches long. The point was one inch in diameter and the head was 1¾ inches in diameter. It was described as a maul or sledge, "the kind used in driving railroad spikes." The ceremonial maul was made of iron by Conroy & O'Conner, of San Francisco, whose corporate name was stamped on the side of the maul. It was silver plated by Vanderslice & Co. also of San Francisco.[27] After being presented the silver maul, Stanford made a ceremonial tap on the heads of the spikes in the laurel tie.

It was then time for the ultimate combination of the Pacific railroad companies' routes into one road. The last spike was an ordinary iron railroad spike, the head of which had been polished, and which was wired to one side of the national telegraph hookup. The telegraph wire was fastened to a sheet of copper which, in turn, was wired to the head of a regular spike maul. The wire was twisted around the handle of the maul and connected to the Central Pacific side of the telegraph line. In this way, the spike was connected to the Western Union line, according to C. P. telegraph construction chief Bowsher. This telegraph connection was in addition to the Western Union operator's key manned by Mr. Shilling.[28]

The last spike was partially driven in an ordinary tie adjacent to the laurel tie. The moment of culmination had arrived Telegrapher Shilling wired the waiting East:

> ALL READY NOW, THE SPIKE, WILL SOON BE DRIVEN. THE SIGNAL WILL BE THREE DOTS FOR THE COMMENCEMENT OF THE BLOWS.[29]

It was about 12:45. Leland Stanford stepped forward and took the spike maul that was connected by wire to the entire American nation. Momentous as was this occasion, Stanford was plainly nervous, and the cumbersome wires dangling from the spike maul made it no easier. Those who were able to see him focused their eyes on the maul as he raised it and then slammed it down. The telegrapher sent three dots east as a signal. Stanford's blow had not made a click on the telegraph; he had missed the spike and hit the rail. The circuit had not been completed. Unknown to those "listening in" by telegraph, at Promontory everyone was yelling with glee at President Stanford's poor marksmanship. Stanford proffered the maul to Durant, who, for some reason, courteous or otherwise, also missed the head of the spike. Pride probably caused them to try again and hit the spike, before calling in reinforcements. Superintendents Strobridge and Reed, with un-wired mauls, drove the last spike into place and the transcontinental railroad was completed.[30] After more cheers, the crowd was again asked to retire, and photographers Russell, Savage, Sedgwick and Hart preserved likenesses of the event on large glass photographic plates for generations to come.

With the first of the three dots, a magnetic ball fell in the dome of the national Capitol. In New York a hundred-gun salute was fired. The choir at Trinity Church chanted the *Te Deum,* and then the steeple bells chimed "Old Hundred." In Philadelphia, the Liberty Bell rang once again. At the War Department, General Sherman and some others received the news over the army telegraph, and the time of completion was set at 2:47, making it 12:47, runtime, at Promontory.[31]

All over the country there were celebrations. In Salt Lake City, Mormons and gentiles met together in the great tabernacle to celebrate the victory of the railroads. At Promontory, Shilling followed his dots for all the blows on the last spike with one word: DONE. With the two trains touching pilots, champagne or wine from the East and West was exchanged and then broken over the joint of the rails. To complete the ceremony, *Jupiter* backed up with its train and *119* pulled its train over the junction point and then retired while the C. P. train crossed the point of union.[32]

While crews were replacing the ceremonial tie and spikes with ordinary ones, the railroad officials sent the following telegram to Washington, D.C., with a copy to the Associated Press in New York:

> PROMONTORY SUMMIT, UTAH MAY 10, 1869
>
> THE LAST RAIL IS LAID. THE LAST SPIKE IS DRIVEN. THE PACIFIC RAILROAD IS COMPLETED. THE POINT OF JUNCTION IS 1,086 MILES WEST OF THE MISSOURI RIVER AND 690 MILES EAST OF SACRAMENTO CITY.
>
> LELAND STANFORD
> CENTRAL PACIFIC RAILROAD
> T. C. DURANT,
> SIDNEY DILLON,
> JOHN DUFF,
> UNION PACIFIC RAILROAD[33]

At the invitation of Thomas Durant, the officials of both companies retired to Durant's private palace car to receive the telegrams of congratulations coming in from East and West, and to toast the railroad's completion. After the toasts, they all retired to Stanford's private car for more toasts and a sumptuous luncheon from the stocks of the pantry car.[34]

James Strobridge, meanwhile, gave a dinner in his car to the bosses and foreman of the Chinese crews who had done the work on the Central Pacific. Superintendent Strobridge then took the Chinese foreman of all his tracklayers to Stanford's car and introduced him to the group of officials. They gave him a standing ovation in tribute to the monumental construction feat of the Chinese crews of Central Pacific.[35]

The celebrating over, the brass rolled away in their plush private cars, and were on their way back to Omaha and Sacramento by 5:00 P.M. Promontory began to go quiet, and the railroad, one now, was ready to go to work—a steel artery coursing across the great North American nation. The United States of America was spanned by rail.

The driving of the Golden Spike was more of a beginning than an end for Brigham Young, the LDS church, and the people of Box Elder County. Brigham Young collected unpaid debts from the Union Pacific in the form of rail and rolling stock and other supplies and equipment, with which he began his own empire of connecting lines. First came the Utah Central, built from the terminus at Ogden south to connect the transcontinental line with the capital city.[36] The Utah Northern was built north from Ogden through Brigham City, around the northern tip of Wellsville Mountain and east into Cache Valley, then north to Franklin, Idaho. Even the building of this railroad was an outgrowth of the concept of Zion. In contrast to the crass business venture of the transcontinental, the Utah Northern broke first ground at a religiously directed dedication ceremony held at Brigham City on 26 August 1871.[37] As the railroad pushed north—reaching nearly to Cache Valley by the beginning of July 1872—it began to have the desired impact on the gentile enclave at Corinne.[38] It also provided access to a quarry (opened, apparently, during construction of the Utah Northern), which provided the bulk of the stone used in construction of the Box Elder Stake Tabernacle.

The Utah Northern brought Brigham City and the larger county into rail contact with both San Francisco and New York. Immigrant converts to the LDS faith could come by rail. A Union Pacific broadside of the time proclaimed that one could travel from Omaha to San Francisco "in less than four days, avoiding the dangers of the sea."[39] The railroad was of immediate benefit to the Mercantile and Manufacturing Association, as well. Heavy equipment, such as that for the tannery and woolen mill, could be shipped from the east in a few days by rail, instead of the long, dusty, dangerous route formerly requiring many wagons, teamsters, and animals.

ENDNOTES

1. George Kraus, *High Road to Promontory* (Palo Alto, CA: American West Publishing Company, 1969), 270.

2. James McCague, *Moguls and Iron Men* (New York: Harper & Row, 1964), 304–11; *The Last Spike Is Driven* (Golden Spike Centennial Celebration Commission, 1969), 91. The flag he raised had in its field twenty stars. The official flag of the Nation in 1869, had thirty-seven. The U.S. flag officially had twenty stars from 4 July 1818 to 4 July 1819. Why he raised that flag we do not know, but that was the flag he raised.

3. *The Last Spike Is Driven,* 73.

4. Ibid. 79–87; McCague. *Moguls and Iron Men,* 318–19.

5. Kraus, *High Road to Promontory,* 267.

6. McCague, *Moguls and Iron Men,* 322.

7. Gerald M. Best, *Iron Horses to Promontory* (San Marino, CA: Golden West Books, 1969), 49–50.

8. *The Last Spike Is Driven,* 73; Best, *Iron Horses to Promontory,* 50.

9. Best, *Iron Horses to Promontory,* 51.

10. *The Last Spike Is Driven,* 88–89, 94.

11. John J. Stewart, *The Iron Trail to the Golden Spike* (Salt Lake City: Deseret Book Company, 1969), 223.

12. Golden Spike National Historic Site locomotive engineer Bob Dowty, who has spent twenty May 10ths at Promontory Summit, disputes the accuracy of the temperature reported. On not one May 10th has the temperature risen to 69 degrees in the shade by noon. With ice on the puddles at dawn and a stiff wind blowing from the north, Mr. Dowty says the temperature couldn't have been that high.

13. *The Last Spike is Driven,* 95; McCague, *Moguls and Iron Men,* 326.

14. *The Last Spike Is Driven,* 87.

15. Kraus, *High Road to Promontory,* 273.

16. Ibid., 273–74.

17. McCague, *Moguls and Iron Men,* 328; Stewart, *The Iron Trail to the Golden Spike,* 222.

18. Stewart, *The Iron Trail to the Golden Spike,,* 225; Kraus, *High Road to Promontory,* 274.

19. *The Last Spike Is Driven,* 95.

20. Kraus, *High Road to Promontory,* 278.

21. Ibid. The spike, when it was presented, was rough-forged, with the marks of the smith's hammer. It was later polished, and the words of Tritle's presentation engraved on its surface.

22. *The Last Spike Is Driven,* 80.

23. *Ibid.,* 79; Best, *Iron Horses to Promontory,* 58.

24. *The Last Spike Is Driven,* 80. Words in parentheses indicate variants according to the differing accounts of the ceremony. The speeches are given here as they were given to the newspaper previous to 10 May, hence the inconsistencies.

25. *Ibid.,* 275–79.

26. McCague, *Moguls and Iron Men,* 328.

27. *The Last Spike Is Driven,* 86–87.

28. Kraus, *High Road to Promontory,* 73.

29. Ibid., 279.

30. *The Last Spike Is Driven* 93.

31. *Ibid.,* 89–90.

32. McCague, *Moguls and Iron Men,* 329–331.

33. Kraus, *High Road to Promontory,* 282.

34. Ibid., 284.

35. *The Last Spike Is Driven,* 100; Best, *Iron Horses to Promontory,* 55.

36. See Leonard J. Arrington, *Great Basin Kingdom* (Lincoln: University of Nebraska Press, 1958),270–75.

37. *Deseret News,* 27 August 1871, cited in Leonard J. Arrington, *Brigham Young: American Moses* (New York: Alfred A. Knopf, 1985), 284.

38. Arrington, *Great Basin Kingdom,* 284.

39. "Great Event" poster, copy in my possession.

Chapter 7

Corinne: City of the Ungodly

The coming of the railroad greatly affected the population of Utah and Box Elder County with the influx of a significant number of non-Mormons among the previously isolated members of the LDS faith. From the point of view of the Mormons, this was not a particularly sought-for situation. They had, because of their religious beliefs, clannish nature, political solidarity, and problems with some elements of the frontier American culture, been forced to flee New York, Missouri, Ohio, and Illinois. The had come to the shores of Great Salt Lake to be alone and apart—to practice their religion without interference, and without pressures to conform to the norms of the surrounding society, which they considered un-godly, degenerate, and corrupt.

From the point of view of those whom the railroad brought, this was a country and a continent of manifest destiny. A great railroad linked the raw riches of the American West with the industrial might of the East, and the rest of the United States, Europe, Asia, and the Far East beckoned.

As the tracks approached Bear River, the hungry eyes of those who came along with the rails saw the location for their Utah beachhead. The spot where the railroad crossed the Bear would be the perfect place for a town, an "American" town, a new town, free from Brigham Young's power. It was almost the northernmost point the tracks would reach in this part of Utah, and would be an ideal junction for the great trade roads coming south from the mines of Montana. Ore could be brought by wagon to the Bear River and be loaded on the railroad for shipment to the smelters. Supplies could be taken from the railroad cars and shipped to Montana. Not only that, but there was the Bear River. A fleet of steamships could be built to ply the waters of Great Salt Lake, and ore from the mines being developed south of the lake could be brought across the lake and up the Bear River to the rail junction. It was a perfect location.

In actuality, it was one of three sites under consideration by the railroad for a division point. The other contenders were Ogden and Bonneville. Odds were against the Bear River site, known at the time of its conception simply as "Bear River." Wags referred to it as "The Burg on the Bear," and in the journal of Jacob Zollinger—who passed through in 1868—by the inglorious moniker "Tough Creek."

Ogden, an already-established city, was a Mormon town, and it was not conceived and laid out with a railroad in mind. Bonneville, five miles west of Ogden, was located on the railroad, and was free of Mormon influence. The Union Pacific favored the site for a time, but it was in a rather isolated location.

The site on the Bear River had several advantages. Its location on the river provided "the only pure water in any abundance between the Wasatch and Humboldt Mountains" and the river made possible the irrigation and cultivation of hundreds of acres of rich soil in the Bear River Valley.[1] The river was conceivably navigable, making possible more commerce for the railroad and, of course, the town. It was the best location along the Union Pacific for trade with Montana, being but a few miles from the Montana wagon road established twenty years before by Captain Howard Stansbury.

On 18 February 1869, John Hanson Beadle, vehemently anti-Mormon writer, editor of the *Salt Lake Reporter,* and author of dime novels visited the budding community and found the town composed of fifteen houses and a hundred and fifty residents. Although

Staff of the *Daily Reporter* in front of their office at Corinne in 1869. (Utah State Historical Society)

Green and Alexander had by then completed their hotel, Beadle was not over-awed. He wrote, "there is no newstand, post office, or barber shop. The citizens wash in the river and comb their hair by crawling through the sagebrush. A private stage is run from this place (Brigham City) to Promontory, passing through Connor. The proprietor calls it a tri-weekley, that is, it goes out one week and *tries* to get back the next."[2]

Something caused the sarcastic Beadle to gain more confidence in the burg of Connor, for in March he returned to the banks of Bear River in company with Colonel C. A. Reynolds, Major F. Meacham, Lieutenant A. E. Woodson, General J. A. Williamson, Captain E. B. Zabriskie, Captain John O'Niel, Messrs. M. T. Burgess, S. S. Walker, M. H. Walker, N. S. Ranshoff, N. Boukofsky, and J. M. Worley. Beadle and his largely military entourage lunched on the grassy bank of the river, just below the crossing, and had quite a drinking bout. The next day most of the hung-over party located claims as near as possible to the crossing on even sections of land, in hopes of the choice of this as the junction city.[3]

Tiring of the sluggish workings of railroad and government decision-making machinery in choosing the junction city, the merchants of Corinne induced the Union Pacific to survey the site in trade for alternate lots in the new city. The survey was made during February and March of 1869 by John O'Neil, Union Pacific construction engineer, under the direction of J. E. House, the railroad land agent. The townsite, laid out west of the river, was selected in preference to the site of Bonneville, surveyed at the same time. Evidently, Mr. House was empowered to choose between the two locations.[4]

Corinne was not, like the wild and rowdy end-of-track railroad camps, just another mushroom sprung up in the night. It was a city whose conception had been planned and whose birth was anticipated. Historian Brigham D. Madsen has noted that "With . . . speculations by the eastern press about the impact the Pacific road would have, and while the Mormon people resolutely prepared to stand off the influx of Gentiles, some far-seeing men began to wonder about the possible founding of a 'Great Central City' that would control trade to vast areas of the Intermountain West."[5] These speculations took form in a report by J. H. Beadle to an Ohio newspaper in 1868. Beadle wrote that "Somewhere, then, between the mouth of Weber Cañon and the northern end of the lake, at the most convenient spot for staging and freighting to Montana, Idaho, Oregon and Washington, is to be a city of permanent importance, and numerous speculators are watching the point with interest. But the location is still in doubt."[6] Beadle saw that the new city would challenge the Mormon capital; "at no very distant day Salt Lake City will have a rapidly-growing rival here. It will be a Gentile city, and will make the first great trial between Mormon institutions and outsiders."[7] Beadle went on to predict that "It will have its period of violence, disruption, and crime, . . . before it becomes a permanent, well-governed city."[8]

From the very beginning, it was to be a great metropolis. The city was not laid out square-with-the-world, as were most Utah towns, but rather was platted with the streets running parallel to the railroad tracks, from southeast to northwest, with the Bear River as the eastern boundary. The plans for the city were magnificent, and the city plat mirrored the grandiose scheme in the minds of the founding fathers. The grand plat of the city encompassed an area of three square miles, extending much farther than the city ever reached, indicating the hopes and plans of the visionaries who built the town, in anticipation of a huge growth.

The city blocks were generally 264 by 280 feet, and the first eight blocks running west from the river, facing the tracks, were each divided into twelve lots of twenty-two feet each. Moving away from the railroad, the next row of blocks on each side were laid out in the same manner, and the rest of the blocks contained six lots (of double size) each. Through the center of each block ran a sixteen-foot alley. Each block was 132 feet deep. One whole block was set aside for a university, another for a Catholic church.[9]

Lots were put on sale 25 March 1869 by J. A. Williamson, a railroad land agent.[10] On the first day, some three hundred lots were sold at prices ranging from $5 to $1,000 each, reaching a total of from $21,000 to $30,000. Within two weeks, five hundred frame buildings and tents had sprung up, almost like mushrooms in the night. By summer the sale of lots totaled $70,000. It has been estimated that the Union Pacific held interest to a sum of $100,000 in the new metropolis.[11]

J. A. Williamson, the first "mayor" before the town was incorporated on 19 February 1870, is given credit for naming the city.[12] Some reports have it that Williamson named the town for a famous actress of the day, named Corinne LaVaunt. After an exhaustive search of records of the time, Rue Corbett Johnson found no record of an actress of that name.[13] That Corinne LaVaunt is perhaps a fictional actress in a French novel is made a subject of consideration by J. H. Beadle, who in mentioning the name, states that Corinne is "not without pleasing association in itself for people acquainted with modern French literature, it being the name of one of madame De Stael's most fascinating books." There are also claims that the city Corinne was named for Corinne Williamson, daughter of J. A. Williamson. There is ample evidence that Williamson's daughter was named before the city, as witnessed by Beadle, who in his *Utah Daily Reporter* states that the city was named for the general's "beautiful and accomplished daughter—Miss Corinne Williamson." Later, dur-

Corinne c. 1870. (Utah State Historical Society)

ing a fund drive, it was reported that "General Williamson led off with a handsome decoration for himself and 'ten dollars for the young lady after whom this city was named'—Miss Corinne Williamson."[14]

At its founding, Corinne City and her founders had almost the whole valley to themselves, as there were only two other settlements within any proximity: Brigham City, bastion of polygamy and the United Order five miles away, and—about an equal distance to the north—a tiny settlement now known as Bear River City. A description of the valley in 1869 comes from the pen of J. H. Beadle:

> Corinne is sixty miles north and twleve west of Salt Lake City, occupying the same relative place on Bear River as the other does on the Jordan. It is at the railroad crossing of Bear River, midway between the Wasatch Mountains and the spur known as Promontory, some eight miles from the lake, and in the center and richest section of Bear River Valley. The western half of this valley, unoccupied except by one small village of three hundred Mormons, contains half a million acres of the finest farming land; of this one-fourth is cultivable without irrigation and the rest

> would be made fruitful by moderate watering, while an extensive stock range of the richest kind extends westward and northward. The elevation is 4,300 feet above sea-level; 1,000 feet less than that of Denver; 2,000 feet less than Cheyenne; 3,300 greater than Omaha; surrounded north, east and west by lofty mountain ranges, and on the south by the Great Salt Lake. It is thus the central point of a beautiful valley, fifteen miles in extent with a location unsurpassed for natural beauty.[15]

After the gold, silver, and iron spikes were driven, and the coal and wood smoke and steam had cleared away, the wild tent city, known as "Hell on Wheels," that followed the construction gangs from Omaha to Promontory did not evaporate, as did the smoke and steam. Instead, the saloons, gambling houses, brothels, and other dens of iniquity found what was hoped to be a permanent home in Corinne.[16]

So it was that Corinne welcomed and gathered to her breast any and all who would come; not only the railroad workers, gamblers, store keepers, hawkers, transients, but also men of business and industry, the gentile merchants of Salt Lake City and Ogden, who were fleeing economic disaster at the hands of Brigham Young and Zion's Cooperative Mercantile Institution.

Corinne was wild, a result of the last big push to Promontory by the Union Pacific, born in a boom, and subject to all the ills of such. Alexander Toponce said of the camps just east of Promontory, "It seemed for a while as if all the toughs in the West had gathered there. Every form of vice was in evidence. Drunkenness and gambling were the mildest things they did. It was not uncommon for two or three men to be shot or knifed in a night."[17] When those same elements coalesced at Corinne, it was every bit as bad.

In the background of all this was a more stable, respectable population, which remained after the transients either moved on or took up residence in the town's boot hill. It was the efforts of these men of commerce that brought Corinne to the measure of glory that she enjoyed and the success she achieved for a time.[18]

These men realized that, for their city to succeed, it needed structure, law and order. As soon as lots were put on sale and settlement began in earnest, a city organization was set up. General Williamson was chosen as mayor. A city council was organized, a city marshall appointed, and a city attorney named.[19]

The city was not incorporated and granted a charter by the Utah Territorial Legislature until a year later, on 18 February 1870.[20] A municipal election in Corinne, on 3 March 1870, resulted in the selection of J. Malsh as mayor over W. H. Munro, by a plurality of 112 to 100 votes. There were charges that some had voted illegally, and the election was called a tie. The winner was chosen by drawing lots, resulting in the "election" of Munro as the first real mayor of Corinne. A new city council moved quickly to appoint a city attorney, and passed ordinances against the erection of tents or canvas-roofed houses on and around Montana Street between Second and Seventh streets, prohibited polygamy forever within the city limits, and designated the *Utah Reporter* (under the editorship of John H. Beadle) as the official city newspaper.[21]

The hopes of the founders of Corinne were high—that in this town, free from the Mormon influence, a new order might be established, and, supported by the vast throngs of the Gentile element, surging westward because of the railroad. Corinne might become not only the Queen City of the Great Basin, but the capital of Utah.[22]

Corinne was the first money center of Box Elder County, and it remained such for a number of years. The city's first bank was opened by Hussey, Dahler & Co., the name later being changed to Warren, Hussey & Co. In the summer of 1874, J. W. Guthrie and Company opened a bank, which became a private bank operated by Guthrie. Other banks included the Bank of Corinne.

Perhaps the jewel of Montana street was the Central Hotel built in 1874 by Hiram House at the corner of Montana and Sixth streets. It was a substantial two-story brick building. Hiram House built the first Corinne municipal water system. House, who was wounded by Indian arrows on his journey west in 1862, became a life-long resident and promoter of Corinne. The water system, installed in 1869, used a steam-operated pump to draw water from the Bear River into a large wooden settling tank. It was then sent through the central portion of the city in a wooden pipeline. The system was discontinued in 1876, and water from the river sold from door to door at twenty cents a barrel. In 1891 the old system was cleaned, repaired, and put back into operation, serving until 1912.[23] Among House's Corinne enterprises was a cigar factory. He also operated the ferry across the Bear in 1870, and helped build the bridge a few years later.[24] It was House who purchased the city bell, for use in case of fire, emergency, or celebrations. According to old documents, a Mr. House (probably Hiram) constructed a steam-powered sawmill on the banks of the Bear River just east of Corinne. Logs were floated down the river to the mill from the timber country to the north until the supply ran out. The mill was then moved to Marsh Valley, Idaho.[25] When the old water system was finally replaced in the early years of the twentieth century, one of its promoters was William F. House, son of Hiram, who was also instrumental in bringing electricity and telephones to Corinne. Henry House, Hiram's brother, who served as a scout on the plains and was a rider for the Pony Express, also lived in Corinne, and is buried in the city cemetery.[26]

The infrastructure in place, the business enterprises of Corinne could grow. Those enterprises of Corinne reached far and wide. With the help and support of the gentile merchants of Corinne, trade was opened to the vast territory of southern Montana, Idaho, and western Wyoming, allowing the products of Utah to be exported to those areas.[27]

During its peak, the freight trade in and from Corinne was tremendous, and was boosted by many of Corinne's prominent citizens. About four hundred mules and eighty heavy wagons operated night and day. The six-hundred-mile (one-way) trip to Montana took ten days and nights. If ox teams instead of horses drew the wagons, a trip to Helena, Montana, sometimes took six months. Rates from Corinne to Helena—or any other point along the way—were $7 per hundred pounds; passenger fare was $75 one way.[28] As many as five hundred freight outfits assembled at Corinne at one time. Mormon men came from the surrounding areas in large numbers as teamsters or guards on the freight lines.[29] The chief commodity shipped south from Montana to Corinne was ore. Food and other supplies made the trip in the other direction. One of the notable Corinne businessmen, John W. Guthrie, shipped produce (principally eggs and butter) from Corinne and the surrounding area to the West on the Central Pacific Railroad. His business was of such proportions as to require a warehouse-store 132 feet long and 22 feet wide, with a cellar running the whole length.[30] During this time Guthrie forwarded 240,000 pounds of powder and 125,000 pounds of case goods.[31] He did much of his trade in Cache Valley, where he bought large amounts of produce. It is said that he bought eggs for fifteen cents a dozen and sold them for fifty cents; butter for twenty and twenty-five cents, and sold it for twice as much. During Guthrie's long career in Corinne, he not only operated his shipping enterprise and his bank, but served for a long while as mayor.[32]

Another of the colorful characters of early Corinne, who deserves more than passing mention, is Alexander Toponce. Born in France in 1839 and emigrating to America in 1846, Toponce rode with Russell, Majors and Wadell before taking a job as a teamster with Johnston's army. A brother-in-law of Hiram and Henry House, Toponce gravitated to Corinne and operated a merchant freight line to the north. After he retired from active business on the line, he rented wagons and teams to traders. In his reminiscences he mentioned prices of some of the goods as follows: sugar, $1 per pound; flour, $30 or $40 to $125 per hundred; pork, $1 per pound; and eggs, $2 per dozen.[33] Toponce was a "commission man" for the meat shipping business, which grew up around the large slaughter house built by an eastern company, which drew to Corinne the livestock and dairy business of the surrounding area. By use of the railroad refrigerator system, the business became quite large.[34] In 1873 Toponce organized a company to build a canal from Sulfur Creek to Corinne, about sixteen miles, for purposes of irrigation and power. In 1874 he built a grist mill and operated it until 1883, when it was incorporated into a larger company. Toponce also served as mayor of Corinne. He tells of one of the more unusual parts of the job in his reminiscences:

> Everybody that had any grief of any kind brought it to me to fix up. Sometimes I could fix it up with masonic funds, sometimes I could use the Odd Fellows' money and at other times what little funds the city had in the treasury. Corinne was the first station out of Ogden on the Central Pacific and when people tried to beat their way to California, the conductor put them off at Corinne. The first thing the first man they met would say to them was, "Go see the mayor." Very rarely I could get help for these people from

> the county. And very often, I could arrange with the railroad for cheap rates to get the people to California or to some other point whre they had friends or relatives.
>
> Sometimes I had to go out on the street and take up a collection. I recall one occasion when a woman and her four children were put off the train because of some defect in her ticket. She was promptly advised to call on the mayor. By consulting with the local agent, I found that it would take fifty dollars to get the woman and her children to California. So I went out and raised the money while they waited. I would go into a saloon and step up to the bar and throw down a dollar for the barkeeper and say, "Everybody come up and have a drink with the mayor." Then men in the saloon would all line up and order their choice and when they had tucked it under their belts, I would then tell them about the woman and four children. Then I would say, "Now, boys, it is up to the City of Corinne. How much will each one of you chip in?" I would pass the hat and take up a collection and go to the next saloon and repeat the program. Very few of the men would refuse to donate, after having had a drink with the mayor, and some of them would "chip in" liberally because they were in town to spend their money. In an hour's time I had raised the money for the tickets and the woman and her four children left on the next train.[35]

Not only did Corinne have the freighting trade with the north, but the railhead also brought the farmers of the local area to the town. The farmers of Cache Valley, Marsh Valley, Gentile Valley, Malad Valley, Bear River Valley, and surrounding areas braved the long drive and thick choking road-dust, traveling day and night to reach the gentile railroad city with their heavily-loaded wagons of grain. Business was so good and the area from which the railroad drew so vast (it was the *only* railroad crossing the continent) that long lines of wagons waited for hours, days, and sometimes weeks to unload. The farmers were generally paid from twenty-five cents to thirty-five cents a bushel for their wheat at Corinne.[36] Several companies were active in the freight trade from Corinne. Among them were names which are well-known to historians and laymen like Creighton & Monroe, Fred J. Kiesel, Wells-Fargo, Auerbach, the Walker brothers, and the Bambergers.

Corinne was also, for a time, the home of General Patrick E.

Connor, the arch-enemy of Brigham Young and the Mormons. Connor (born O'Connor) had come to Utah in 1862, and established Camp Douglas (later Fort Douglas) on the foothills overlooking Salt Lake City. Because of Young's efforts to stop mining and Connor's belief that mining would be the most effective way to populate the territory with non-Mormons, he encouraged it with every means within his power including giving soldiers under his command leave to prospect. His efforts brought him the title "the father of Utah mining."

Patrick Connor built a smelter on the banks of the Bear River at Corinne for processing ore brought by freight wagons from the mining areas of Montana. Later, when valuable ores were discovered in the Oquirrh Mountains, the ore was shipped across the Great Salt Lake to the Corinne smelter, leading promoters to proclaim Corinne, the "Chicago of the West." Corinne had the distinction of being the only city in modern times whose streets were literally paved with gold. Due to the crude smelting methods used in early days, there was much of value left in the hugh slag piles which accumulated around the smelter. Evidently some enterprising citizen, exasperated beyond endurance at having to wade through the thick clay mud which made quagmires of the streets and sidewalks in which pedestrians sank to their ankles and the heavy freight wagons sank to their axles during the spring and fall rains, conceived the idea of crushing the useless slag and spreading it on the streets and those sidewalks which were not made of boards, to help keep the traffic from sinking out of sight while plying the thoroughfares of town. Many tons of the slag were used to improve the streets and more was dumped behind the abutments of the new bridge over the Bear River; enough slag was left to keep the streets in good repair for years. In the 1880s improved methods of smelting caused mining experts to come browsing through the slag piles and smelters of Utah. Those of Corinne came under inspection, and were found to contain $20 worth of gold to the ton, even though the ore had been smelted once. Some twenty railroad cars filled with Corinne slag were hauled away to smelters employing the newer, more efficient methods. Now the only remains of the immense slag piles are behind the abutments of the now-abandoned bridge on the old road at the east end of Montana street, and beneath the now-paved streets of Corinne.[37]

The ambitious men who founded Corinne did not wish to settle only for trade on the railroad, especially when valuable minerals were found in the Oquirrh Mountains on the southern tip of Great Salt Lake. A new phase of shipping was opened in Utah with the beginning of trade by steamboat on the Great Salt Lake. The first of the lake's fleet of steamboats were built by Patrick Connor to haul telegraph poles and ties for the Central Pacific in 1868 and 1869. They were the *Kate Connor,* the *Pioneer,* and the *Pluribathah* or *Pluribustah.* Connor realized that a great deal of time and money could be saved if steamboats could connect the mines with the railhead, and Corinne, with its smelter built by Connor and location on the transcontinental main line, was the logical connection.

The choice of Corinne was bolstered by a report that the Bear River was eighteen feet deep and three hundred feet wide at Corinne.[38] During the years 1868–72, the Great Salt Lake was rising, and the mouth of the Bear River was deep enough for navigation by boat from the lake, even though in 1843 John C. Fremont found it blocked by sand bars. The one obstacle to navigation of the Bear River was its meandering course through the marshes near its mouth. The distance from Corinne to the lake is about six miles as the crow flies, but by the river, according to C. A. Dahl, first captain of the grand steamship *City of Corinne,* "the distance seemed more like thirty-five miles which took several hours to navigate from Corinne to the Bear River Bay of the Great Salt Lake."[39]

A discussion of the possibilities of Corinne as an ore transfer port to the railroad appeared in the *Utah Tri-Weekly Reporter* in May 1870: the use of Corinne as a river port was strongly supported by the editor and further momentum was given to the proposal by the support of the miners on the lake's southern shore.[40]

One of the first commercial voyages to Corinne by a lake vessel was made on 4 November 1869 by Connor & McNassar's ninety-ton schooner bringing laths from the mills at Black Rock on the southeastern end of the Great Salt Lake.. About a week later a load of silver ore came to Corinne from Stockton in Tooele County via Black Rock aboard the *Pluribustah.*[41] The *Pluribustah* or *Buster,* a schooner with a load capacity of 100 tons, was built in the spring of 1869, by General Connor. A ship named the *Viola* was built on the south shore for use in the lake trade.

In June 1870 the *Kate Connor* was refitted as a side-wheeler. The *Pluribustah* was also converted to haul ore in June 1870.

This great boom in the lake trade aroused the citizens of Corinne, who wanted to have a ship of their own plying the waters of the great inland sea. Public interest was mobilized in 1870, with the help of three men, promoter Wells Spicer, Judge Dennis Toohy, and coal-mine operator Fox Diefendorf. The *City of Corinne* as the ship was to be called, was to be one hundred thirty feet long and was to have three decks, and a seven-foot-deep hold capable of carrying three hundred tons. Propulsion was to be by means of rear-mounted paddle-wheel. Launching was tentatively set for the end of March 1871. Of the $40,000 needed for the project, $4,000 was raised by appeals to the public from soap-box pulpits by the light of coal-oil lanterns and bonfires. The remainder was provided by private investors, Fox Diefendorf being chief among them.

A siding was built from the railroad's main line to a dock near the crossing of rails and river at the east end of the city, and the grand steamship began to take shape. Captain C. A. Dahl, one-time proprietor of the Valley House in Salt Lake City, became the skipper of the City of Corinne. He was sent to San Francisco to meet the new ship's engines which had been ordered from marine engine makers who served the Great Lakes trade, Girard B. Allen and Company of St. Louis and Chicago. The engines reached San Francisco via the long route around Cape Horn. California redwood was used for the hull and beams of the ship.

Though work was progressing, the projected launch date came and passed before the engines arrived on 8 April. The machinery was proudly exhibited in Corinne. On 20 April the boilers were installed, followed by the wheel shaft, the decks, and the cabin stanchions. A site on Clinton's Island on the lake's south side was chosen for the wharf, and work commenced to construct the necessary docks.

Launching of the *City of Corinne* was set for 23 May, and all Utah took notice. The *Kate Connor* left the Jordan Landing on 20 May at noon, to be present for the launch of her rival. Arrangements were

The steamer *City of Corinne* which was built and launched in 1871. (Box Elder County)

made with the railroads for a special train to carry visitors from Salt Lake City. People came from Ogden and Kelton, as well as from other points on the railroad line and from surrounding communities. Hundreds attended the ceremony when they commenced at 11:00 A.M.

The vessel was christened with a bottle of wine by Miss Jennie Black, daughter of a justice of the peace. The fastenings were hewn away, and the new ship began to glide down the ways accompanied by the cheers of the crowd. After moving about twenty feet, the vessel stopped. The ways near the water's edge had sunk into the mud. The crowds dispersed throughout the city while builders and crew went to work to free the ship. After about seven hours, the wild chiming of the bell in the Presbyterian church's tower announced to all that the "Queen of the Western Waters," the great sternwheel steamship *City of Corinne* was afloat. The celebrants, many of whom had spent much of the day in the saloons, flocked back to the river for a look at the great ship. The ship duly launched, the throng returned to town for a "remarkable" ball in the Opera House, which lasted most of the night.

The ship made a trial run on 9 June 1871, with an entourage of fifty guests, while soundings were taken in the riverbed in preparation for the maiden voyage of the proud vessel. The *City of Corinne* left for Lake Point on 12 June 1871, its first commercial voyage, with a load of lumber, a few orders of goods for the mines, and wire for the Western Union Telegraph Company's line to the Oquirrh mining town of Ophir. The vessel returned on 14 June with forty-five tons of ore in 1,150 sacks for the Alger smelter in Corinne. The Alger works were not, however, prepared to begin refining ore.

The day after the *City of Corinne* returned to its berth on the Bear River, a schedule of regular trips was announced, to begin 19 June. There were to be three trips a week, leaving Corinne for Lake Point on Monday, Wednesday, and Friday. Return trips were to be on Tuesday, Thursday, and Saturday. The ship's arrival in Corinne was timed to meet the Central Pacific's westbound passenger train. The schedule was followed until late July, when it was adjusted to once a week. In the middle of August, regular trips were canceled, and the ship waited for business.

During the summer of 1871, the *City of Corinne* and the *Kate Connor* competed for the scarce business. That summer marked the peak of lake freighting and passenger travel. Even though it was reported in September that the great sternwheeler's chief stockholder, Fox Diefendorf, was disenchanted and planned to sell the ship, both boats wintered in Corinne, where they were cleaned and overhauled for the season ahead.

In February 1872 the *City of Corinne* was sold to H. S. Jacobs and Company of Salt Lake City which had ties to the Lehigh and Utah Mining Company of Mauchunk, Pennsylvania. The company planned to use the vessel for trade connecting Corinne, Lake Point, the Lakeside Mining District, and the islands. However, it came to be used for private shipping between Jacobs's smelter at the south end of the Great Salt Lake and Corinne, as well as carrying excursion parties.

The fluctuating inland sea was, during this period, in the rising portion of her cycle. Eventually high, sluggish backwaters caused by the high lake level left sand bars at the mouth of the Bear River, and in about 1873 the *City of Corinne* was marooned out in the lake, far from the city for whose glory she had been built.[42] The ship's base of operations moved to Promontory Point, Monument Point, and then to a point on the lake below Kaysville, the nearest point on the lake to Salt Lake City. From there, the ship carried excursions for another ten years, and the port became known as Lake Side. When the railroad was finished around the south end of Great Salt Lake, the steamship's dock was moved to Lake Point.

In 1880, when James Abram Garfield, candidate for president of the United States, visited Utah, he took a ride on the great ship. In the emotion of the moment, the vessel was re-named the *Garfield*—the name *City of Corinne* having no meaning any more. Later the name was also given to a bathing beach and smelter nearby. The *Garfield* was moored to the bathing pier and became the restaurant and hotel for the resort. The final blow to her tarnished dignity came when her proud banners and tall smoke stacks were removed. She was only a floating building. When fire destroyed the resort in the late 1880s, the ship burned to the water line. Its charred and rotting skeleton was visible there for many years.[43]

The *Kate Connor* was sold to Christopher Layton of Kaysville, along with "some flat-bottomed scows" probably towed behind the boat to haul ore. Legend has it that she eventually sank, and was left to rot where she went down. Somewhere on one of the old river channels in the Bear River marshes lies the rotting hulk of the *Pluribustah.*

When the lake trade folded, the promoters of Corinne turned their attention back to the city's first love, the railroad. They conceived the idea of building a railroad from Corinne to the shipping points of the north and organized the Portland, Dalles, and Salt Lake Railway. The route was surveyed as far as Malad, Idaho, a distance of fifty miles, and ten miles were graded, but many difficulties, most of them apparently financial, brought the project to early abandonment.[44]

From there, it was downhill for Corinne's grand hopes. A study of its history reveals at least three reasons for the decline of the "Gentile Capital of Utah."

First, the drifting away of railroad construction crews and traders after the transcontinental railroad was completed in May 1869.

Corinne began as a construction camp, and was the last permanent settlement along the Union Pacific line. As such, it attracted railroad workers who sought diversion from their labor. When that segment of the population eventually moved on, Corinne lost its appeal to a certain element, and became a little quieter.

Second, moving the railroad junction or transfer point between the Union Pacific and Central Pacific railroads to Ogden was a severe blow to Corinne. Though the tracks met at Promontory, it was isolated in a high desert valley, far from established roads, from population centers, and did not have an adequate supply of water for a large community. Because of its location on Bear River, and near the route to Montana, Corinne's founders thought it the ideal spot, and promoted their town with almost religious fervor. Still Corinne did not prevail. In the words of S. H. Goodwin,

> Although the two railroads selected Promontory as the junction point, Fate, and Brigham appear to have picked Ogden. Seven days after the celebration at Promontory, Brigham turned the first shovel of dirt at Ogden for what was to be the Utah Central Railway connecting Salt Lake and Ogden, and this line was completed and open for travel January 12, 1870. Some time late in the summer or early fall the disputed point as to where the junction of the C. P. and U. P. Should be, was settled in favor of Ogden, when the former purchased the interest of the U. P. In fifty miles of the line from Promontory toward Ogden, for $3,000,000 and leased the remaining six miles. Upon the completion of this transaction, papers unfriendly to the "Only Gentile City in Utah," published articles under such headings as "Promontory Being Abated," and in which occurred such expressions as "Poor Promontory! And poor Corinne!"[45]

Third, the Utah Northern Railroad built north from Ogden. Even after the moving of the transcontinental terminal to Ogden, Corinne still had its huge freighting business with the vast territory to the north, which kept the city very much alive. In 1871 the idea was conceived to build a narrow-gauge railroad north from Ogden through Weber, Box Elder, and Cache counties, and on into Idaho. The Utah and Northern Railway was organized on 23 August 1871, and ground was broken in September. The tracks reached Franklin, Idaho, in early 1872.[46] The goal was to extend the line to Montana and take over the team-and-wagon freight business which belonged to Corinne.

The Corinnethians, undaunted, built a branch line in June 1873 to connect it with the Utah and Northern at Brigham City. For a while the pendulum of success seemed to swing in her direction. The Mormon church was not a railroad giant, and "as the tracks moved farther north, crews [Mormons locally available for building] became fewer and fewer in number. Construction problems, plus the depression brought on by the Panic of 1873, caused the church to reconsider railroad building."[47] Mormon church leaders sold the line to the moguls of the Union Pacific, including Jay Gould and Sidney Dillon. The renamed Utah & Northern was built to Preston, through Red Rock Pass, up Marsh Valley, along the Portneuf River, and up the canyon at Inkom. The tracks extended to Pocatello, joining the old Gold Route (the freight road), north to Ross Fork, site of the Fort Hall Agency, and then to the Blackfoot River, sowing the seeds of the town of Blackfoot. From there, the Utah & Northern laid its track to Eagle Rock, coming upon Matt Taylor's bridge, built over the Snake River in 1863. Eagle Rock had been a prosperous stage and train station, but its fortunes changed when the Utah & Northern shops were moved to Pocatello. Pocatello became the railroad town, and Eagle Rock became the Mormon town of Idaho Falls. In the spring of 1880, the Utah & Northern railroad tracks crossed into Montana through Monida Pass. From then on, the freighting days of Corinne were at an end, and the huge freighting wagons became relics of a past glory. Corinne's old freight mogul, Alex Toponce, penned the description of Corinne as a dowager: "The buildings were without paint, stores and dwellings stood vacant. Many of them were torn down or moved out on farms. People lived in houses rent free. Corinne men were found all over the west. The few who remained lived on the hope of what would happen when the irrigation water was brought on the broad valley.[48]

The railroad, which Corinne's founders thought would put the sword of victory into their hands, proved to be double-edged. Corinne was eventually severed from the silver rails which had been her crown. Perhaps Corinne's epitaph was penned by the fire-breath-

Corinne looking east from 5th Street about 1870. (Utah State Historical Society)

ing newspaper editor of her glory days, J. H. Beadle: "The history of Corinne is the history of something near a thousand towns in the 'glorious, free, and boundless west.' In a new country, when the first towns are laid out, everybody speculates, one makes money and nineteen come to grief."[49]

Alexander Toponce, in his reminiscences, wrote: "It was one story that Brigham Young had pronounced a curse on Corinne as a 'wicked Gentile city' and predicted that grass should grow in the streets. Some grass certainly did grow on some streets."[50] Adolf Reeder said that Young pronounced his curse when he visited Brigham City to reorganize the stake in August 1877. It was also on that occasion that the Great Colonizer delivered his final public address, only ten days before he died. According to Reeder, Young said that the city would go down and never regain its former size, grass would grow in the streets, the buildings would be torn down and barns would be built of the materials, and the Bear River would go dry.[51]

The population of the city declined. Many of the old business buildings were torn down. The Central Hotel was dismantled, and its materials used to build a substantial brick barn which still stands (1998) on a farm west of Corinne.

The grand Corinne Opera House, in which Tom Thumb, William Jennings Bryan, and Maude Adams performed, and where innumerable Shakespearean plays, science lectures, minstrel and medicine shows, lectures were held, was sold in 1884 to J. W. Guthrie for $300. It eventually became the meetinghouse for the Corinne Ward of the Church of Jesus Christ of Latter-day Saints.

ENDNOTES

1. John Hanson Beadle, "Scrapbook containing editorials and dispatches from the *Salt Lake Daily Reporter* (and other newspapers), October, 1868—August, 1869," Microfilm in Utah State Historical Society Library.

2. Ibid.

3. Frederick M. Huchel "Corinne: The Ghost of a Queen," paper submitted to Dr. Larry C. Porter, Brigham Young University, 23 May 1969, 36.

4. Brigham D. And Betty M. Madsen, "Corinne, the Fair: Gateway to Montana Mines," *Utah Historical Quarterly,* 37 (1969), 105.

5. Brigham D. Madsen, *Corinne: The Gentile Capital of Utah* (Salt Lake City: Utah State Historical Society, 1980), 5.

6. *Cincinnati Commercial,* 17 October 1868.

7. Ibid.

8. *Ibid.,* cited in Brigham D. Madsen, *Corinne,* 5.

9. Original plat may of corinne, Utah, copy in my possession.

10. Ray M. Reeder, "A History of the Founding, Rise and Decline of Corinne, Utah," M.A. thesis, Utah State Agricultural College, 1939, 11.

11. Madsen and Madsen, "Corinne, the Fair," 108; .S. H. Goodwin and Committee, *Freemasonry in Utah* (Salt Lake City: Corinne and Corinne Lodge No. 5, F. & A. M., 1926); Bernice Gibbs Anderson, "The Gentile City of Corinne," *Utah Historical Quarterly,* 9 (1941), 141; .John Hanson Beadle, *Life in Utah, or The Mysteries and Crimes of Mormonism* (Philadelphia: National Publishing Company, 1870), 509.

12. Anderson, "The Gentile City," 142.

13. Rue Corbett Johnson, "The History of the Drama in Corinne and Brigham City, Utah, 1855–1905," M.A. Thesis, Brigham Young University, 1954, 6–7.

14. Madsen and Madsen, "Corinne," 106, quoting Beadle "Scrapbook," 15 March 1969; *Utah Daily Reporter,* 5 November 1870 and 3 April 1871.

15. Beadle, *Life in Utah,* 509.

16. Anderson, "The Gentile City," 145.

17. Alexander Toponce, *Reminiscences of Alexander Toponce, Pioneer* (Ogden: 1923), 176. Born in France, Toponce fortunately commited his colorful life to his memoirs in 1919. They were originally published in Ogden by his widow and some Masonic friends shortly after his death in 1923, at age 83. A later edition was printed by the University of Oklahoma Press in 1971.

18. Alexander Toponce, *Reminiscences of Alexander Toponce, Pioneer* (Norman: University of Oklahoma Press, 1971), 146.

19. *Salt Lake Telegraph,* 13 April 1869.

20. That was due to the fact that no cities were granted their charters in Utah until 1870. Until then, all Utahns were, in effect, squatters. The coming of the railroad brought a formal survey and the granting of charters and deeds by the United States. Corinne's charter and Brigham City's (Brigham City was founded in the early 1850s) came in the same year,

21. Madsen and Madsen, "Corinne," 113.

22. Anderson, "The Gentile City" 144.

23. Anderson, *Corinne,*" 17–18.

24. Ibid., 18.

25. Forsgren, ed., *History of Box Elder County* (Brigham City: Daughters of Utah Pioneers, 1937), 127.

26. Anderson, *Corinne,* 18.

27. Anderson, "The Gentile City," 144.

28. Anderson, *Corinne,* 10–11; Anderson, "The Gentile City,," 146–147; John C. Hunsaker, "Corinne in 'Boom' Days," in Adolph M. Reeder, ed., *Box Elder Lore of the Nineteenth Century* (Brigham City: Sons of Utah Pioneers, 1951), 114.

29. Anderson, *Corinne,* 11.

30. Edward Tullidge, *Tullidge's Histories* (Salt Lake City: 1889), 245.

31. Anderson, "The Gentile City," 146.

32. Edward Tullidge, *Tullidge's Histories,* 243.

33. Anderson, *Corinne,* 11.

34. Hunsaker, "Corinne in 'Boom' Days," 114.

35. Toponce, *Reminiscences,* 228–31.

36. Hunsaker, "Corinne in 'Boom' Days," 115.

37. Anderson, "The Gentile City of Corinne," 147; Anderson, *Corinne,* 5.

38. Bernice Gibbs Anderson and Jesse H. Jameson, "The Saga of the Good Ship City of Corinne," *S. U. P. News,* April-May 1959, 13, 35–36.

39. Huchel "Corinne: The Ghost of a Queen," 60–61.

40. Anderson and Jameson, "The Saga of the Good Ship City of Corinne," 35–36.

41. Ibid.

42. Anderson, *Corinne,* 6.

43. Anderson and Jameson, "The Saga of the Good Ship City of Corinne," 35–36.

44. Anderson, "The Gentile City of Corinne," 149.

45. S. H. Goodwin and Committee, *Freemasonry in Utah* (Salt Lake City: Corinne and Corinne Lodge No. 5, F. & A. M., 1926), 8.

46. Hubert Howe Bancroft, *History of Utah, 1540–1886* (San Francisco: 1889), 757.

47. Betty Derig, *Roadside History of Idaho* (Missoula, MT: Mountain Press Publishing Company, 1996), 15.

48. Toponce, *Reminiscences,* 233.

49. Frederick M. Huchel "Corinne: The Ghost of a Queen," 95.

50. Toponce, *Reminiscences,* 231.

51. Frederick M. Huchel interview with Adolph Reeder, February 1969.

CHAPTER 8

THE BOX ELDER TABERNACLE

When William Davis, James Brooks, and Thomas Pierce came to Box Elder to locate a settlement, they chose a site on the alluvial fan formed by the larger predecessor of Box Elder Creek. The alluvium lifts the townsite above the lakebed plain to the west. The old Indian trail, which became the Gold Road, crossed the Box Elder Creek alluvium from south to north. When the main street of Brigham City was laid out, it followed the already-existing trail, from the south side of the alluvium at 11th South to the north side near 9th North.

Plat A was laid out with reference to the land which was most easily served by the millrace canal and a network of gravity-fed irrigation ditches. That placed the main intersection, the courthouse, and the business section of town in the center of Plat A. As city building got underway, Brigham Young, as was his custom, came to inspect, to approve, to reassure the settlers, and to give his counsel to the brethren in charge. On one of those early visits, he discussed with Lorenzo Snow the building of a tabernacle.

A Mormon tabernacle is a structure for large community reli-

The Box Elder Stake Tabernacle. (Craig Law)

gious gatherings. The first Utah tabernacle was built in Salt Lake City, on the Temple Block, to replace the pole-and-brush "boweries" which provided some shade and little comfort in the summer, and were unuseable in the winter. The "Old Tabernacle" was finished and dedicated in 1852, and served until the "New Tabernacle" replaced it in 1868.[1]

Brigham Young told Lorenzo Snow that a temple would someday be built on the gravel eminence just east of the city cemetery.[2] He also directed the building of a tabernacle for the Saints of Box Elder. A site was chosen across Forest Street north from Snow's compound, which was surrounded by a wall as Young's was in Salt Lake City. Excavation began and preparations made for the laying of cornerstones. Young passed through Brigham City on 4 May 1865, on his way to Cache Valley to lay the cornerstones for a tabernacle in Logan. When he was shown the excavation at Brigham City's main intersection, Brigham Young shook his bearded head and told the brethren that they had chosen the wrong spot. This will become the center of the business district, he told them. This is a commercial center, it is not the spot for your tabernacle. He led them two blocks south, to a place called Sage Brush Square, just outside the platted city. "This is the spot for the tabernacle; it is the backbone of the city, the highest spot along Main Street Look at the ditches. The water flows in three directions from this place, north, south, and west. The spot will be well-drained, and someday be the center of the city. A tabernacle built here, like a light on a hill, can be seen from afar."[3] By the time President Young returned from his trip to Cache Valley, the new site had been excavated and prepared. According to one report, "Brigham Young himself laid the cornerstones for the tabernacle on May 9, 1865."[4] A correspondent reported to the *Deseret News* that " . . . preparations [were] made for erecting tabernacles at Logan, Wellsville, Mendon and Brigham City, foundations being in part excavated, rock hauled to commence the work, and a spirit manifested to have them speedily completed."[5]

The rock foundation of the tabernacle was complete by 1868, work no doubt being prosecuted during the agricultural off-season, between harvest and seedtime, when labor was available. About that same time, the local brethren took grading contracts on the transcontinental railroad, being built north from Ogden, through Box Elder west of Brigham City, west across the marshes past Little Mountain, and up the steep grades of the Promontory. Not only was the Union Pacific building west, but the Central Pacific was building grade east through Box Elder. The provisions of the Pacific Railroad Act allotted land and money grants for miles of *track laid*, not grade built. Thus the surveyors and graders of the the two companies met and passed each other, in a mad rush to get the most track in place before the meeting point was reached. The two companies surveyed and partially built 225 miles of parallel grades, from the mouth of Weber Canyon to Humboldt Wells, Nevada, before Congress fixed the meeting point at Promontory Summit. The men of Box Elder hired out, under subcontractors Sharp & Young and Benson, Farr & West, to grade for the transcontinental railroad in order to get the road built for converts to come more speedily to Zion, as well as to get the cash wages offered by the railroads.[6] Construction of the great railroad took temporary precedence, and construction of the Box Elder Tabernacle waited.

Work on the transcontinental railroad, construction of the Utah Northern Railroad, expansion of the Brigham City Mercantile and Manufacturing Association enterprises and other community-building enterprises delayed construction of the tabernacle.

Actual construction of the tabernacle walls got under way in 1876. The thick walls, built of locally-available quartzite, were rising above the foundation when Brigham Young made his last visit to the city which bore his name. Young traveled throughout Utah, setting in order the stakes of Zion and reorganizing the church's priesthood structure.[7] The graying Lion of the Lord came to Brigham City and presided at a conference held under the bowery on lower Locust Street on 19 August 1876. At that meeting the town was divided into four wards and Lorenzo Snow's son, Oliver G., was called to preside over the re-organized, re-ordered Box Elder Stake of Zion, to serve under his father's guiding hand.[8]

Work on the tabernacle moved ahead with vigor. At the first quarterly conference of the reorganized Box Elder Stake, two months after Brigham Young's visit, the tabernacle was a matter of discussion. Speaking on 28 October 1877, Lorenzo Snow regretted that "the congregation consisted of the priesthood only, the reason . . . was, that the house was too small to accommodate others, and the tabernacle, which was nearing completion, not being finished, they were under the necessity of turning the conference into what might more strictly be termed a priesthood meeting."[9]

By the time construction of the tabernacle got under way in earnest, the economy of Brigham City was booming. The industries of the Brigham City Mercantile and Manufacturing Association were fully developed and providing support, materials, and craftsmanship for the tabernacle project.

All labor on the tabernacle was donated. The Scandinavian and Welsh craftsmen, who made up the majority of Brigham City's citizenry, were used to their best advantage to build a beautiful house of worship. Not only was labor donated, but also produce, which was sold to raise cash for materials such as glass, which had to be imported. Money raised from the sale of "Sunday eggs" was donated to construction of the tabernacle.

The Box Elder Stake Tabernacle was built using native materials—limestone from the mountains, lime from the United Order lime kiln north of town, mortar sand from the alluvium, lumber cut from the foothills and canyons, sawed by the association's steam sawmill, rough-finished for joists, beams and rafters, finished by the craftsman's loving hand for benches and pulpit.

Efforts to complete the tabernacle met with difficulties. The fire on 21 December 1877 which destroyed the woolen factory, seizure of the Brigham City Mercantile and Manufacturing Association's sawmill, agents of the federal government, the levying of a tax of $10,200 on the scrip of the association, as well as poor crops because of drought and grasshoppers brought loss and discouragement to the community.[10]

Lorenzo Snow, ever the optimist and savvy leader of men and women, realized that the best way to lift community spirits was work and a cause behind which all could rally. And just such a cause was before them: completing the magnificent Tabernacle. At a conference held Sunday, 26 January 1879, the call for re-commitment came and: "The people voted to sustain the tabernacle committee in erecting that building."[11] Within six months the building was completed enough that a meeting could be held within its walls.[12] It took two more years of hard work and sacrifice, however, before the tabernacle's dome dome was shingled, its benches in place, and its pulpit painted and ready for use.

The entry in the Manuscript History of Box Elder Stake for Sunday, 24 April 1881, reads, "On this and the preceding day the 14th quarterly conference of the Box Elder Stake was held in the new tabernacle in Brigham City."[13] It had been nearly sixteen years since Brigham Young selected the spot and laid the cornerstones. Finally the hopes, the sweat and the tears of the Saints of the Box Elder Stake of Zion had brought forth out of the gravel soil of Sage Brush Square a tabernacle, its gothic-arched windows letting in the light of heaven.

The building was finished enough for worship, and was used for conferences, monthly fast meetings, and weekly sacrament meetings. Improvements came as the people had time and means. In 1887 a new organ was acquired, and, gradually, finishing touches were added.[14] Even so, it was piecemeal. As the years passed, a desire grew to make the tabernacle into a more elegant, well-appointed house of worship. At the Forty-eighth quarterly conference of the Box Elder Stake, on Sunday, 27 October 1889, "It was moved and carried that the tabernacle be completed."[15] A subsequent conference dwelt at length upon "sacrifice, tithing, offerings," and stake president Rudger Clawson "was pleased at the generous response made to furnish means to finish our tabernacle, which would not be dedicated until all expenses were paid." After exhorting the Saints, he noted happily that "Work on the galleries would commence tomorrow."[16] Three months later a scheduled quarterly conference was postponed, "On account of the unfinished condition of the tabernacle in Brigham City, no Conference was held in April."[17]

By the second week in May, construction was basically completed. The building, as it stood in 1890, was ninety-eight feet long by fifty-eight feet wide, built of local limestone and quartzite with sandstone trim around the doors and windows.[18] Brick buttresses capped with pinnacles were added along the side walls between the windows and across the back during the 1889–90 phase of construction, as was the balcony or gallery, and the vestry or east stone addition. The pulpit was in the east end of the building with the choir loft behind. [19] The tower, added during this "completion" phase was a small, squat structure, which was apparently neither graceful nor attractive.[20] A stake conference was held on Monday, 12 May 1890, after the completion of the improvements. The *Deseret News* reported that "This is the first conference here, and the meeting was the first held in the Stake Tabernacle since the galleries were put in and the other improvements made, at cost of nearly $6000. The building is now furnished, and is commodious and handsome."[21]

By the middle of July, any remaining finishing touches and financial obligations were taken care of, and after twenty-five years of off-and-on construction, the tabernacle was ready for dedication. An article in the *Brigham Bugler* on 19 July titled "Ready for Worship" reported,

> The tabernacle is completed. The large force employed on the brick, carpenter and painting work was discharged Wednesday evening. But a few men are left to clean up and apply the finishing touches. Between $5,000 and $6,000 have been expended in the completion of this building. Every stroke of the work seems to have been put to good account with the exception of that on the tower. This will undoubtedly be improved later on. The erection of the tower, sixteen pilasters, and a large front step and an entire repainting has been done on the outside; the construction of two long galleries; and enlargement of the choir; a marked improvement of the painter's work and several other changes and improvements cover the main work in the interior. By the aid of the new galleries, the seating capacity is enlarged 400. The Tabernacle ought now to seat between 1,200 and 1,500. After the Stake Conference, 27th and 28th, the regular afternoon Sunday services will be held at this place.[22]

At the Fifty-first quarterly conference of the Box Elder Stake, held on 27 and 28 October 1890, the tabernacle was dedicated. It was a time of fulfillment, of completion, of rejoicing. It was a benchmark in Brigham City's history. The conference was at once solemn and joyful. Even Wilford Woodruff, president of the LDS church, was in attendance to offer the prayer of dedication. "The Choir commenced the afternoon services by singing the dedicatory hymn. President Woodruff offered the dedicatory prayer, after which the Sacrament was administered by the Bishopric of the Third Ward."[23] The *Bugler* report adds the following:

> Sunday afternoon, the Brigham City Tabernacle was dedicated to the Lord by President Wilford Woodruff, leader of the church of Jesus Christ of Latter-day Saints.
>
> People came in from all the surrounding settlements to attend Conference. Each meeting was unusually well attended.
>
> Wilford Woodruff, President of the Church; Lorenzo Snow, President of the Twelve Apostles; Apostle Franklin D. Richards, and A. H. Cannon, of Salt Lake Stake, were among the speakers at the Quarterly Conference.
>
> The largest congregation which ever assembled at the Tabernacle was that which met last Sunday afternoon. The main room and gallery were jammed; many were obliged to stand and scores were nable to gain admittance. This shows the necessity of a huge Stake Tabernacle being erected at Brigham City in the near future.[24]

At the conclusion of the conference, Brigham City's own Lorenzo Snow, now president of the Quorum of Twelve Apostles of the LDS church, stood and looked out over the congregation, the people he had led and guided for over three decades.

> President Snow proposed that, after singing, the congregation should give the sacred shout of hosanna to God and the Lamb as the closing exercises of the conference.
>
> The singing over, all stood up and joined in the glorious shout with oneness of heart, "Hosanna! Hosanna! Hosanna! to God and the Lamb. Amen! Amen! Amen!"[25]

It was a grand building, perched at the apex of Main Street, visible for miles. Assistant LDS Church Historian Andrew Jenson wrote in 1891, "The Stake Tabernacle, occupying a beautiful site on one of the most elevated spots in Brigham City, is one of the finest Stake houses of its size in Utah."[26]

Improvements continued to be made including the addition of a furnace in late fall 1891. A large, stone basement room was built beneath the east vestry in anticipation of the installation of a furnace to replace the stoves which had provided uneaven heating at best during the tabernacle's first decade. The furnace installation was explained in an article in the *Brigham City Bugler:*

> The Tabernacle is to be heated by hot air. The pipes are now being laid and the furnace placed in position. The system may not be ready for operation by tomorrow, but will be entirely completed by Tuesday and consequently in perfect working order by the following Sunday. Three registers are being placed on each side of the main room, one on the choir stand and two in the vestry, making nine in all. This number will comfortably warm the entire building. The use of an evaporating pan, to be placed in the furnace, will give the necessary moisture to the otherwise rather dry air.
>
> The idea of putting this hot-air system in the Tabernacle was conceived by President Clawson, proposed and accepted by unanimous vote of the Congregation last Sunday afternoon and in less than ten days rushed through to completion.
>
> President Clawson is to be congratulated for his energy and so are the people who are stepping so promptly forward with their generous donations to secure this very essential modern appliance for their house of worship.[27]

The new furnace was not without problems as hot and cold days brought complaints from the congregation. Then on 9 February 1896, as the people were assembling for church services,[28] someone smelled smoke. John Baird and Lars Mortensen rushed outside, opened the doors to the basement, and discovered the source of the smoke. The furnace had flamed. The flames had entered the main building through the large heat duct through which heat entered the building to be dispersed by convection. The duct was of wood, and it provided a ready conduit for the flames. Already the timbers directly beneath the pulpit were on fire.

The cry of "Fire!" was raised, and the building evacuated of the few people who had gathered. Fortunately the fire occurred before the building filled with its usual 1,000 Sunday morning worshipers.

The alarm was raised in town, and as soon as possible the fire department was on the scene. The fire was beyond the scope of their equipment. The *Bugler* notes that "They were handicapped from lack of hose and shortage of water. But the fire had already got such a headway that work as they did, like young Trojans, they could not

The Box Elder Stake Tabernacle after the fire in 1896. (Box Elder County)

cope with the rapidly spreading flames."[29] The *Bugler* account continued with an eyewitness of the conflagration:

> In less than an hour from when the fire was discovered, the main building was a mass of furious, crackling flames, and the fire had eaten its way through the roof and leaped upward into the inflammable tower. At 2:30 P.M., there was little left of the noble structure excepting the bare walls, now blackened, cracked and stripped of every square foot of wood; even the plaster was completely skinned off.
>
> Excepting chairs, benches, etc., rescued from the vestry in the rear, nothing was saved.
>
> A heavy south wind was blowing all during the conflagration. Burning cinders were carried a quarter of a mile into the northern part of the city. Several structures were thus set on fire, but the flames were promptly extinguished.[30]

The tabernacle fire rivaled the spectacular nighttime fire at the Woolen Factory nineteen years before, but, being daytime, and Sunday, a crowd of 2500 to 3,000 people gathered to watch. The grief of the community was put into words by the editor of the *Brigham City Bugler:*

> So Brigham City's splendid tabernacle is no more. It was a substantial brick and stone structure that might have bid defiance to the ravaging hand of time for hundreds of years to come. It is the last building in town one would have imagined would catch fire and burn to the ground. The foundation of the structure was laid some thirty years ago—broad, deep and strong. This was built up several feet from the ground, in which condition it stood for years. Some fifteen years ago the people took hold of the building again with admirable ardor; completed the walls; constructed the roof and in time had the structure so nearly completed that services could be held in it. About six years ago the building was greatly improved and by the addition of galleries nearly doubled the seating capacity. At least $5,000 was spent on the structure at this time. The seating was about 1,200. The cost of the building is variously estimated from $20,000 to $25,000.
>
> In addition to the building, which was a total loss, an $800 pipe organ, $300 worth of sheet music, etc., and an old and valuable solid silver sacrament service, worth over $200 were entirely destroyed. No insurance on anything.[31]

A meeting was convened, almost before the embers cooled. The question was not *whether* to rebuild, only *how.* The town and the stake had grown since 1865, when the building was originally laid out, and some consideration was given to razing the still-standing rock walls and building a larger, more commodious tabernacle. After inspection, the verdict was announced by stake president Rudger Clawson: "Excepting the tower, the walls and pilasters of the burned Tabernacle are injured little, if any. Bishop Hansen tells me the building could be restored for about $12,000. The cost of tearing down the walls to put up a larger structure would be enormous."[32] The decision was made within two days, as the ashes were being cleaned away, to build again on the flame-cleansed stone walls.

It was not an opportune time for such an expensive project. Brigham City and Box Elder County had not recovered from the financial losses which brought about the collapse of the Co-op, exacerbated by the great national financial depression of 1893. It was a time of trial. President Clawson and his two counselors, Adolphus Madsen and Charles Kelly, went to Salt Lake to consult with the presidency of the church. They explained their situation, discussed options, and finally requested financial help from church headquarters. The brethren sympathized but said that they were in a financial pinch as well. They could not help as much as they might like.[33] The stake leaders appealed to the people of the church at large through newspaper articles from the *Bugler* and and the *Deseret News.* The First Presidency of the church sent out a circular letter to all presiding authorities and members of the church in the Stakes in Zion

> requesting donations, and stating that "notwithstanding every discouragement, vigorous and active measures are being taken by the Presiding brethren of Box Elder Stake to repair the damage done and restore the Tabernacle to its former condition of beauty and usefulness. The undertaking is of such magnitude the Saints of Box Elder—few in numbers and limited in means as thy are—cannot meet it alone, and it is thought the members of the Church generally will be disposed to assist them. We think so, and feel that any assistance thus rendered them in the hour of dire calamity would be praiseworthy. We commend this matter to the favorable attention of the Latter-day Saints.[34]

The letter was signed by Wilford Woodruff, George Q. Cannon, and Joseph F. Smith.

Loss of the tabernacle made necessary the suspension of stake conferences as there was "no meeting house in the Stake large enough to accommodate the people or even half the people who would wish to attend."[35] John B. McMaster was honorably released from a mission in Scotland to return to Brigham City to supervise the rebuilding of the tabernacle.[36] Within a year, work on the rebuilt Box Elder Stake Tabernacle was nearing completion. The *Bugler* reported on 16 January 1897 that choir director S. N. Lee was rehearsing the choir for the upcoming quarterly conference after having gone to considerable trouble and expense to replace song books and sheet music destroyed by the fire.[37] In actuality, the conference was postponed, because the earlier estimates of the time required to finish the building were unduly optimistic. By the first of March, however, the end was in sight. It was determined to dedicate the new Tabernacle on 21 March 1897. On the 20th, a report in the *Bugler* revealed the details of the new building:

> Tomorrow our handsome new Tabernacle will be dedicated to the worship of God. It will be a great day of thanksgiving to the many devout souls, who, for over a year past, have had no general place for holding Sunday services, conferences, etc.
>
> One day this week a BUGLER reporter went in and examined this new building. The last time he was inside the tabernacle was last spring, when with kodak in hand he took a picture of the interior after the fire. What a marvelous change since then! Willing hands and generous hearts have completed such a beautiful and commodious place of worship as will inspire even the careless with the knowledge that they are in the house of the Lord. What on the day of the great fire appeared a calamity, will tomorrow be looked upon as a great blessing—there is really no comparison between the old and the new.
>
> It is a strictly up to date building with a seating capacity of about 1,400 people and standing room for probably 200 more. All the seats in the house will be "good seats," as the pulpit is so nicely in harmony with the auditorium that all will be able to see as well as hear. The eyes help the hearing and understanding more than most people imagine.
>
> The vestry is so arranged that on occasion the folding doors between this and the main room may convert the two into one. The upstairs vestry is finished in pure white: chairs, desk and all. The main building is finished in oak. The graining and panneling are indeed very handsome and give the interior an elegant appearance. The pulpit and choir are now in the west end of the building.
>
> The tabernacle is lighted with electricity and heated with steam. In various parts of the building are large radiators, while under each pew and in any other necessary part of the building pass the steam pipes. The city water-works are also connected with the building.
>
> In the vestibule there is a handsome onyx wash bowl. The onyx is from Box Elder County and is of most beautiful coloring and quality. This is indeed a credit to Box Elder county resources and to home skill in manipulation.

> The choir stand, with its pretty oak chairs, will seat nearly seventy singers.
>
> The gallery has a very sloping floor and no doubt will be as pleasant as the lower floor. There are four stairways.
>
> One of the attractive features of this "so-as-by-fire" tabernacle is the fact that all space is so conveniently utilized. Cunning little cupboards and roomy cloak rooms, closets, etc., are tucked away in very convenient but quite unexpected places.
>
> Yes, the interior of the building is very much handsomer than the exterior. This has been merely restored. It is substantial and not aggressively plain, but the tower smacks a little of the city hall in style of architecture. The interior, though is that of a modern church. Attractive to the eye, comfortable and convenient, it cannot fail to please all who have helped to contribute to its restoration.
>
> Out of the $13,000 which the tabernacle has cost, $10,000 has been contributed by Box Elder county; The people have been nobly generous in donating their money and the stake officers have been untiring in their efforts to give their spiritual flock a commodious fold.
>
> A year ago many said the tabernacle could not be rebuilt without working hardship to the people. It is ready for use and we fully believe none complain.
>
> Now we have a tabernacle again, which no doubt is already insured against fire, will the mischievous boys and girls who take delight in defacing the beautiful, keep their destructive pocket knives and pencils in their pockets or, safer yet, leave them at home?
>
> The building burned on that eventful Sunday afternoon, February 9, 1896. Its rebuilding has taken but little more than one year.
>
> Yes, tomorrow will be a day of general rejoicing among the Latter-day Saints of Box Elder County.[38]

At the dedication, not only the people of Brigham City and surrounding communities were present, but the stand was graced with the presence of distinguished visitors from church headquarters, including "President George Q. Cannon, Elders Lorenzo Snow, Franklin D. Richards, Bishop William B. Preston, Elders Seymour B.

Young, Hiram B. Clawson, C. F. Middleton of Ogden, the presidency and High council of the Box Elder Stake, and the Bishops of the various wards."[39] In a fitting tribute to the pioneer Saints who built the first tabernacle, the opening prayer was offered by pioneer patriarch Alvin Nichols. Ninety-year-old church president Wilford Woodruff, who had been planning to offer the dedicatory prayer, was forced by illness to remain at home in Salt Lake City, and his place was taken by his first counselor, George Q. Cannon. Reconstruction of the Box Elder Tabernacle had cost $15, 117.04.[40]

The second life of the Box Elder Tabernacle began with celebration and dedication. As the *Bugler* rightly said, the fire had proved, after all was said and done, a blessing. "What on the day of the great fire appeared a calamity, will tomorrow be looked upon as a great blessing—there is really no comparison between the old and the new."[41] Over the years changes came in the natural course of events. In 1947 outdoor lighting was installed to illuminate the sturdy rock walls and soaring Gothic Revival tower at night.[42] In 1951 a campaign was raised to purchase a new pipe organ for the tabernacle. The people were offered, for their donations, a certificate, indicating "ownership" of a pipe or pipes, depending upon the amount of the donation. The new organ was installed in a case built behind the pulpit against the west wall of the choir loft in 1951. The great windstorm of May 1954 knocked one of the sheet-metal pinnacles off one of the brick buttresses, installed during the 1889–90 finishing phase of the tabernacle, and caused worried leaders to reinforce the soaring tower.

The history of the tabernacle from the 1920s until the late 1980s was basically one of maintenance, of neglect, and of decline. In the 1970s some stake presidents began to question the value of the building, suggesting it was out-of-date and that Brigham City was not keeping up with the rest of the church. Other stakes had fine, new stake centers with classrooms, kitchens, basketball hoops, and electric pulpits which went up and down at the touch of a button. Some called for the old tabernacle to be torn down and replaced by a new, up-to-date structure. Fortunately, Boyd K. Packer, a Brigham City native and member of the Quorum of Twelve Apostles, came to the defense of the tabernacle. When the rumblings of razing the historic Box Elder Stake Tabernacle reached his ears, the word came down from church headquarters, "Just what's *wrong* with the Brigham City Tabernacle?" Upon inspection, it turned out that several minor things *were* wrong. The sound-amplification system was woefully outdated and on its last legs. The restrooms did not conform to disability access laws, and it was discovered that the old wiring had nearly caused another disastrous fire. It was decided to renovate the tabernacle. The project began in 1983, with the selection of the architectural firm of Wallace N. Cooper and his associate, Allen Roberts. Seasoned historical architects, they ran interference, deftly deflecting recommendations to cover the ceiling with acoustical tile and hang a cluster of speakers—and other historically insensitive suggestions.

The entire electrical, plumbing, and mechanical infrastructure of the building was replaced. A new roof was put on, the window glass was replaced, and the building painted more in keeping with its historic architectural style. Originally, the native softwood benches and woodwork had been "grained" to simulate oak. The "dark old" graining had been painted over in the 1930s. In the renovation, all the woodwork was grained, similar to its original appearance, by master grainers Charles James and Ron Wheat, and a crew of helpers and apprentices. Gold-leaf highlights were added to finials and pulpit, and the pillars supporting the gallery were painstakingly painted to resemble dark green marble.

On the evening of 12 April 1987, the tabernacle was filled past capacity with townspeople, now proud of their newly-renovated tabernacle. The crowd was so large that the proceedings were broadcast by closed-circuit television to other church buildings in Brigham City.

The dedicatory prayer was offered by Elder Boyd K. Packer, whose watchful eye over Brigham City has proven a fit successor to those of his predecessors, Lorenzo Snow and Rudger Clawson.

The Box Elder Stake Tabernacle—a monument to stalwart pioneers, a relic of a more pastoral era, a reminder of the faith and devotion of our ancestors, and a necessary monument in an age of prefabricated construction and disposable plastic—remains the focal point of Brigham City's Main Street. Surrounded by its green sward, it still crowns the alluvial fan upon which the city rests, strong, dignified, and graceful—a living testimony to all that is good among the Latter-day Saints.

The sturdy, stone Box Elder Tabernacle remains the focal point of Brigham City from the freeway. It is an icon, but also an anachronism. In truth, it has neither kitchen, nor classrooms, nor a basketball hoop. It is a symbol, but in reality a symbol of that earlier time, the time of not only yearning for, but building, Zion. Most of Brigham City's stake conferences are held in stake centers. The tabernacle, as of 1998, has been largely turned over to the community at-large, for interfaith meetings and productions. The centennial of the dedication of the tabernacle, rebuilt after the great fire was forgotten—21 March 1997—passed uncommemorated, unnoticed. Still, the tabernacle is a worthy Brigham City landmark and a favorite building to visit and photograph for travelers through northern Utah.

ENDNOTES

1. James E. Talmage, *The House of the Lord* (Salt Lake City: Bookcraft, 1962), 202–203.

2. Much of the information for this chapter comes from Frederick M. Huchel, *History of the Box Elder Tabernacle,* (Brigham City: author, 1997).

3. Ibid.

4. "Church News" section, *Deseret News,* 23 March 1968.

5. E. L. Sloan, "President B. Young's Trip to Cache Valley," *Deseret News,* 17 May 1865; Huchel, *History of the Box Elder Tabernacle,* 4.

6. See Robert G. Athearn, "Contracting the Union Pacific," *Utah Historical Quarterly,* V37 (Winter 1969) 16–40; John J. Stewart, *The Iron Trail to the Golden Spike* (Salt Lake City: Deseret Book Company, 1969), 175 ff.

7. See also B. H. Roberts, *A Comprehensive History of the Church of Jesus Christ of Latter-day Saints - Century I,* (Provo: Brigham Young University Press, 1965), 5:507–509; Russell R. Rich, *A History of the Church from 1846 to the Present,* (Provo: Brigham Young University Publications, 1972), 355–357; Discourse by President John Taylor, Ogden, Utah, 21 October 1877, in *Journal of Discourses,* 19:146.

8. Brigham Young died 29 August 1877, in Salt Lake City. There is a monument to the visit of President Young to Brigham City for the stake reorganization on the site of the conference, where the pioneer bowery

stood, originally known as the Public Square (where government handouts were doled to local Indians), known in the early years of the twentieth century as Chatauqua Square (because it was the site of traveling shows and circuses) and now called Brigham Young Park.

9. "Manuscript History of Box Elder Stake," Sunday, 28 October 1877, located in the LDS Church Historical Department Archives.

10. Eliza R. Snow Smith, *Biography and Family Record of Lorenzo Snow, One of the Twelve Apostles of the Church of Jesus Christ of Latter-day Saints* (Salt Lake City: Deseret News Company, 1884), 308.

11. "Manuscript History of Box Elder Stake," 26 January 1879.

12. Vaughn Nielsen, in his *The History of Box Elder Stake* (Brigham City: Brigham City, Utah Box Elder Stake, 1977, p. 41) states that "the tabernacle was used for the first time (27 July 1879), though it was not quite finished"

13. "Manuscript History of Box Elder Stake," 30 January 1881.

14. "Journal History of the Church," 4 September 1887 LDS Church Historical Department.

15. *Deseret News,* 39:622, copied into Manuscript History of Box Elder Stake, Sunday, 26 October 1889.

16. *Deseret News,* 40:275, copied into Manuscript History of Box Elder Stake, Sunday, 26 January 1890.

17. "Manuscript History of Box Elder Stake," April 1890.

18. "Description of the Box Elder Tabernacle," n. p., n. d., LDS Church Historical Department.

19. Olive H. Kotter, "Brigham City to 1900" in *Through the Years,* (Brigham City: Brigham City Eighth Ward, 1953), 11; *The Brigham Bugler,* 19 July 1890) 1: and LaPreal Wight, "The Tabernacle, Brigham City, Utah," 2, typescript, copy in my possession. I am indebted to Dr. Wynn S. Andersen for his good offices in regard to Miss Wight's tabernacle history.

20. *The Brigham Bugler,* 19 July, 1890 1. A recently rediscovered painting, by C. Eiseley, shows the tabernacle as part of a panoramic view of Brigham City. The painting was done in 1893, between the "finishing" of the tabernacle and the fire. The painting was donated by the owner, Lewis H. Jones, Jr., to the LDS church. After cleaning and restoration, the painting was placed in display in the Museum of Church History and Art.

21. . *Deseret News,* 41:232, copied into Manuscript History of Box Elder Stake under the date 27 July 1890.

22. *The Brigham Bugler* 19 July 1890, 1.

23. *Deseret News,* 41:653, copied into Manuscript History of Box Elder Stake under the date 27 October 1890.

24. *The Brigham Bugler,* 1 November 1890, 1.

25. *Deseret News* 41:653, copied into "Manuscript History of Box Elder Stake," 27 October 1890.

26. "Description of the Box Elder Tabernacle,."

27. *Brigham City Bugler,* 21 November 1891, 3.

28. It might be mentioned here that, in early Mormondom, the meeting system was not as it is today. At first, only a sacrament meeting was held on Sunday. Priesthood meetings were held on weekdays, as were the children's Primary (organized in 1878), the Young Ladies Department of the Cooperative Retrenchment Association (later Young Women), organized in 1869, and the Young Men's Mutual Improvement Association (Young Men) in 1875. The Sunday school began as a children's organization. It was not until 1906 that adults attended Sunday School. Monthly fast meetings were held on Thursdays until the turn of the twentieth century, when business replaced agriculture as the mainstay of the Mormon economy. After the division of Brigham City into four wards by Brigham Young in 1877, the four Brigham City wards came together at the tabernacle for Sunday afternoon sacrament meetings. This continued until after the new tabernacle was dedicated in 1897.

29. *Brigham City Bugler,* 15 February 1896, 1.

30. Ibid. The *Bugler* noted, in the verbose prose of the time, that "One old lady fainted in the Tabernacle when it was announced to the few present that the building was on fire. Had the fire occurred but half an hour later, when 1,000 people would have been seated in the building, there would have been a rush, crush and trampling down of scores. Many old people would have sunk down in faints and when the crowd had cooled down sufficiently to return to rescue the prostrated, the sufficating [sic] smoke would have driven them back and a terrible holocaust would have been the result."

31. Ibid.

32. Ibid.

33. "Journal History of the Church," Wednesday, 19 February 1896.

34. Wilford Woodruff letterbook No. 1352, Vol. 17, 226–27, LDS Church Historical Department.

35. *Brigham City Bugler,* 25 April 1896.

36. Ibid., *2 May 1896.*

37. Ibid., 16 January 1897.

38. Ibid., 20 March 1897.

39. Ibid., 27 March 1897; *Deseret News,* 54:468, copied into the "Manuscript History of Box Elder Stake,"21 March 1897.

40. *Brigham City Bugler,* 27 March 1897.

41. Ibid.

42. Interview with former stake president Glen M. Bennion by Frederick M. Huchel, 11 December 1981. Because the city owned the hydroelectric power plant at the mouth of Box Elder Canyon, the tabernacle was the architectural jewel of the city, and the majority of Brighamites were Mormons, the city did not charge for the electricity. When criticism was voiced in the 1980s of a similar arrangement in St. George, concerning lighting the temple there at night, Brigham City and the LDS church terminated their arrangement.

CHAPTER 9

NON-LDS CHURCHES IN BOX ELDER COUNTY

Completion of the transcontinental railroad at Promontory Summit in May 1869 also signaled the arrival of a permanent non-LDS presence in Box Elder County, with Corinne as its early focal point.[1] It is that small rural community, once a railroad boomtown, which boasts the oldest Protestant church building now standing in Utah now "converted" to the Corinne Historical Society Museum in 1995 through an agreement between the local organization and the Methodist church.

Many hopeful entrepreneurs predicted that Corinne would grow to be a large city, one with a university, many churches, and possibly becoming Utah's capitol city. In 1869 a thousand eager souls had moved into Corinne, and they were mostly unchurched, a fact which brought representatives of several major religions to the area.

They were not welcomed by all. Reverend George Foote, rector of St. Mark's Episcopal Church in Salt Lake City, preached one of the first sermons on 6 June 1869 to six persons in the city hall. The service was so disturbed by the boisterous element of the town outside its doors that it was many months before Foote would consent to come back.[2]

Presbyterian Churches

Presbyterians were among the first to arrive. On 11 June 1869, a month and a day after completion of the transcontinental railroad, Reverend Malanchton Hughes stepped off the Union Pacific train in Corinne. Despite poor health, he had accepted a three-month call in answer to the request of the Reverend Sheldon Jackson, newly appointed missionary for the opening west.[3]

Hughes held the first Presbyterian service in Utah in the Corinne City Hall on the first Sunday following his arrival, 13 June 1869. Sheldon Jackson paid his first visit in August and conducted a service in which trustees were elected. Hughes was replaced by the Reverend Edward E. Bayliss in April 1870, and in a few weeks a manse (pastor's residence) had been built and a building leased for services. On 10 July the church was officially organized with ten members and one elder.

Plans were made immediately for the building of a church, and $1,543 were raised for the purpose. Another $4,000 were secured from church boards and individual churches, and the church was built. It was dedicated on 20 November 1870 with Reverend Jackson among those in attendance.[4]

Meanwhile a Methodist church had been built and a school opened, and Mr. Bayliss saw the need for a school of higher grades and left in 1891 to secure funds in the East for that purpose. Falling in that, he decided not to return and resigned. Following his departure, the church was vacant except for a short time in 1972 until the arrival of its next pastor.

In 1874 Reverend Samuel L. Gillespie, who also served the church at Evanston, Wyoming, arrived in Corinne. He had been a missionary in Africa and was described by a colleague as a man "chosen of God for the work in Utah." Under his leadership, church membership grew to twenty-one and the Sunday school had seventy-five enrolled. The town, however, was rapidly declining due to Mormon opposition, the development of Ogden as a rail center, and building of a rail line to the north which by-passed Corinne.[5]

A larger town, Brigham City, was chosen as a more profitable location for his ministry. This was a wise move on Gillespie's part, although it was not readily accepted by the community, but it laid the cornerstone for the only Protestant church which has remained a continuous presence in Box Elder County from that period.

Gillespie had delivered the first Protestant sermon in Brigham City on 3 April 1876 from the steps of the county courthouse, which also served as an LDS meeting place. He was asked by a deputy sheriff by what authority he was there, and he is said to have answered: "by the authority of the Lord Jesus Christ, and exercising the rights of an American Citizen."

Although he met with considerable opposition, this Civil War veteran and former missionary to Africa was finally able to purchase lots at 71 and 77 North Main for the sum of $750 in 1878. He began holding services in the adobe home located on the property in February 1878, and moved his family there in June of the same year.[6]

The small frame church in Corinne, which boasted a fine bell in its tower, was damaged in a severe wind storm in March 1894. A small congregation was served by visiting ministers, including Gillespie, in Corinne until it was closed in 1915.[7] The church bell currently occupies a place of honor on a pedestal in the park next to the Corinne City Hall.

Construction on the Brigham City church building began the summer of 1878, with Watkins and Carson contracted as builders. It was not an easy year. Stones were thrown on the manse, doors kicked in, and family provisions had to be freighted from Corinne since the local Mormon cooperative had been cautioned not to trade with the family.[8]

However, a little community of followers did grow and help support one another. There were twenty-seven students in Sunday school, twenty-nine in the young people's group, ten members of a ladies missionary society, in addition to the Sunday worship services. Reverend Gillespie opened a free school in September 1878, bringing educated young women (including his sister) as teachers. An early church report lists eighteen teachers as having served the school.[9]

Although services were carried on from 1878 to 1890, it was not until that year that the Brigham City Church was formally organized.

By that time the Gillespies were well accepted in the community. The church building was sometimes used for public meetings and functions by the community, as indicated in various notices in the town's newspapers of the period.

When Samuel Gillespie left Brigham City in 1895, he and his wife Mattie had become respected members of the community. He was replaced by another Civil War veteran, Reverend Arthur Rankin, who had operated a station on the "underground railroad" which helped slaves escape. During Rankin's ministry, 1896–1907, the name of the church was changed from Box Elder to Brigham Mission.[10]

Newspaper reports indicate that Reverend Rankin was well-liked in the community, and served as a member of the city's military band. The *Box Elder News* of 8 August 1907 reports that the church was being repaired, walls and ceilings were being retinted in attractive colors, a new floor laid, woodwork and furniture stained.[11]

A succession of pastors has served the church through the years, with a constant and faithful congregation keeping the little mission church alive and vital. A new manse was built next to the church in the fall of 1914 at a cost of $3,000. Memorial stained glass windows were installed at the front of the church at approximately the same time.

Often the only Protestant church in the city, the body is still known as Community Presbyterian Church and serves people of many denominational backgrounds. It grew as Brigham City brought in different elements of population with Bushnell Hospital, Intermountain Indian School, Thiokol, and other businesses.

During the Intermountain Indian School period, the congregation had outgrown the little 1878 church on North Main, and in 1954 purchased the old LDS First-Sixth Ward building on the corner of Second East and Third South and the Old Rock School around the corner. The two stained glass windows, placed in the old church in 1914 in memory of Reverend Gillespie and Reverend Rankin, were placed in the rear of the "new" church as a link to the past. The manse was moved to the lot directly south of the church.[12]

The northwest corner of the large lot at 100 East and 300 South was purchased by Amity Lodge 23, Free and Accepted Masons, who acquired the old frame chapel and moved it onto the lot. It has since been covered with brick and still serves as headquarters for Amity Lodge.

Again in the 1960s the church was bursting at the seams with Thiokol employees and their families, and a new educational building was dedicated on 29 April 1964, named Gillespie Hall in honor of the church's pioneer founder. It has provided quarters for Girl Scouts, Boy Scouts, a migrant day care center, soup kitchen, and preschool in fulfilling some of the church's motto: "At the heart of the community, with the community at head."

Corinne Methodist Church

Corinne Methodist church is not only the first Methodist church but the first Protestant church to be dedicated in Utah. The first Methodist preaching in Corinne was on 25 June 1870 by Reverend G. M. Pierce. During the next few months Methodist worship services were held at various places until a church could be built. On the morning of 17 July, Bishop E. R. Ames preached in the Opera House and that evening Chaplain C.C. McCabe preached.[13]

After the evening service a subscription list for a church was started and $1,100 were subscribed and on the following day another $400 were obtained. Events continued to move rapidly, and the church was dedicated on 20 September 1870—the first regular Methodist church dedicated in Utah. The building cost more than $4,000, of which some was paid by the Church Extension Society.[14]

Records of the church from 1870 to 1892 are sketchy, but there is evidence of the church's decline in the fact that ministers were also assigned to such places as Ogden and Tooele.[15] Minutes of the Utah Annual Conference of 1879 mentioned the possibility of selling church property.

The church had suffered twelve years of decline when Pastor G.O. Streets arrived in 1888 and raised $350 to put the church in good repair, organized a Sunday school of sixty-five members and preached to a larger congregation every Sunday.

Through the years repairs and additions were made to the church: cement coping, a frame vestibule, electric lights, new windows, etc. It continued to served the congregation until 1957, when it was decided to discontinue regular services. Ministers from

Tremonton and later from Brigham City visited the few members still living in Corinne.

The Corinne Methodist church was used sporadically for special events, such as Christmas Eve services, and Methodists from throughout Utah gathered there in 1970 for a centennial celebration of their presence in Utah.

In 1994–95 the Corinne Historical Society and Methodist Church in Utah entered into an agreement and the building houses a "living" museum. The chapel area has been restored and is used for community events, weddings, and other functions, and a small museum of Corinne and church memorabilia is located in the rear of the chapel.

Scandinavian Methodist Church

An interesting aspect of Methodism was found in Brigham City briefly. The LDS church had many Scandinavian Methodist converts, but it was reported that about one-third left the LDS church after arriving in Utah. Methodists saw this as an opportunity to evangelize and Americanize these people. About 1885 the Scandinavian Methodist Church of Brigham City was founded. At first it was associated with the Logan-Hyrum circuit, later with North Ogden, Corinne (1897), and Tremonton (1909).[16]

A debt-free parsonage and church located on the 100 South block of 100 East was reported in 1903, with good attendance at services and Sunday school. During the next years, however, a rapid decline set in. *The Box Elder News* reported on 9 January 1908, "There will be services at the Methodist church on Sunday Jan 12, at 8 P.M. in the Danish language, conducted by the Rev. H.I. Hansen of Salt Lake City. The pastor, C. J. Mekkelsen, will also speak at the same hour, in English."[17]

In 1909 only one member was reported—still under the pastorate of Mekkelson's Corinne-Tremonton circuit. In 1918 the buildings were sold.[18] The church was converted to a home, which still has a dated cornerstone at its southwest corner. It and the former manse can be distinguished by a shared driveway.

Tremonton Methodist Church

In 1897 the Reverend Eugene H. Snow of the Corinne Methodist church visited families of new settlers arriving in Bear River Valley from the Midwest, some of whom lived in Corinne until they could build houses on their newly acquired farms. His successor, Reverend A. W. Hartshorn, held meetings in a little frame schoolhouse the settlers had built on the road called the "Iowa String" which ran north from Corinne. Following pastors also served in this manner.

Settlers in the area founded the town of Tremont in the spring of 1903, naming it for the town in Illinois from which several had come. The name was later changed to Tremonton. Before no more than three buildings had been erected in the new town; the Methodists had bought two lots. For two years the congregation met in the Wilson Lumber Company and Odd Fellows Lodge. In 1905 an abandoned church building from Cache Valley was made available, carefully taken apart, and rebuilt on a corner lot. It was dedicated in December 1906 by Bishop David M. Moore. A parsonage was built in 1914–15, and the church building was raised on a basement built under it in 1938. The church remained active for many years, serving several generations of Methodists.

With its membership dwindling, the Tremonton Methodist church finally closed its doors in the late 1980s. Since that time the building has housed Catholic services, until a Catholic church was built in Tremonton, and in 1998 was being rented by a Baptist congregation.

Aldersgate United Methodist Church

In 1998 Brigham City is home to the only Methodist congregation in Box Elder County. It had its beginning on 17 March 1963 when a group of twenty interested persons met with the Superintendent of the Utah-Western District and the Reverend Gerald F. Makepeace, pastor, Community Methodist Church, Tremonton. The meeting was held in the basement of the Masonic Lodge—the old Presbyterian church building.

Thiokol brought a number of Methodists to the community, and they were interested in forming a congregation of their own. A survey conducted in 1963 showed a potential membership of 106.

Meanwhile Sunday evening services were being conducted by Reverend Makepeace. On Easter Sunday 1963, fifty-four persons attended a service in the park bowery, and on 5 May regular Sunday services were begun at Lincoln Elementary School.

By 14 May 1963 a charter was presented to Aldersgate Methodist church with thirty-eight charter members present. A house at 482 Camaren Drive was purchased, the basement finished as a sanctuary, and upstairs rooms for Sunday school, pastor's study, and nursery. Consecration services occurred on 29 March 1964. The old pump organ, the pulpit, and communion set from the Corinne church were used for some time by the Aldersgate church. Later the home became the parsonage and Methodists arranged to meet in St. Michael's Episcopal Church.

In the late 1980s Aldersgate United Methodist Church purchased the old Bushnell Hospital-Intermountain School chapel which had been converted to classrooms, and remodeled it to its original use as a house of worship. A later addition was completed which includes a kitchen and dining area, Sunday school rooms, nursery, and pastor's office.

Episcopal Churches

Although the Episcopal church's first attempt in Corinne did not go well, it did not take long for the church to establish a presence in 1870. The Reverend Foote did return, purchased a lot, and raised about $1,000 which was supplemented by a gift of $1,500, and was building a modest church building when the community was visited by Episcopal Bishop Daniel S. Tuttle in 1870.

Bishop Daniel S. Tuttle, in reminiscences of 1869–70 wrote: "We built a church of adobe, mainly from a gift of fifteen hundred dollars sent by Mrs. Mintum of New York in memory of her late husband. By her request it was called 'The Church of the Good Samaritan.'"

The church declined as did the city: "Yet the event followed not the line of our forecast. Corinne now has two hundred and fifty inhabitants, and Salt Lake City fifty thousand . . . ," said Tuttle in 1886. As membership waned, the church was closed and the closest congregations were in Ogden and Logan.

St. Michael's Episcopal Church

In 1857 Brigham City boasted a population of about 6,000 people. The Rt. Reverend Richard S. Watson, Episcopal Bishop of Utah, recognized a lack of missionary work in northern Utah and especially at Intermountain Indian School. He directed the Reverend William J. Hannifin, vicar of St. John's in Logan, to assess the spiritual needs of students and staff. Father Hannifin found that approximately 250 Intermountain Indian School students had been raised in the Anglican faith on the reservation, and that year conducted the first celebration of the Holy Eucharist for these students. It was also in 1957 that Thiokol came to Brigham City, and a surge of non-Mormon people was expected.

St. Michael's Episcopal Church was established on 17 October 1957 when members of several newly arrived Thiokol families and other Brigham City residents met with Father Hannifin to define the new mission in the Utah Diocese. The first order of business was to find a place of worship. Community Presbyterian Church offered the use of that congregation's building. In April 1959 Sunday Eucharist services were moved to the Protestant Student Center at 435 East 700 South, which was located close enough to the Intermountain Indian School to be convenient for Indian students.

Father Hannifin was commuting from St. John's providing services for Brigham City and Intermountain School religious classes. In order to facilitate his move to Brigham City, a suitable vicarage was needed. A lot was purchased north of the corner of 600 South and First East in 1959, at which time Mr. and Mrs. John Higginson bought and donated adjacent lots to extend the church's holdings to the corner.

A drive to build the church got underway with dinner and festivities celebrating the burning of the vicarage mortgage on 12 April 1962. The building was completed for a total cost of approximately $59,000 and was dedicated by Bishop Watson on 17 November 1963. Almost every member of the small church was involved in the construction or the interior furnishings. After ten years of scrimping, St. Michael's paid off its loan. With all of the debts taken care of, St. Michael's Church was consecrated on 18 November 1973.

Buddhist Churches

Box Elder County has a longtime Buddhist presence, established by a population of Japanese workers who came from Japan early in the twentieth century, as well as from the West Coast, for employment in the mines, farms, and railroads. The Issie Buddhist pioneers who settled in the northern Uta area, though small in number, retained their religious heritage with much devotion.

The first Buddhist group began meeting in Honeyville in 1912. Spiritual leadership was provided by ministers from Ogden and Salt Lake City, commuting for regular services once a month.

The present two-story brick church building on about five acres of land was purchased in 1931 from Utah-Idaho Sugar Company for $4,000. It has been used for many purposes by the Japanese community, including a Japanese language school for youth. During World War II it was partitioned off into apartments to help house evacuees from the West Coast. The Issei women had a very active Fujinkai from 1946–70, when they temporarily disbanded and then reactivated in 1971. The members assist in preparing and serving refreshments and whatever necessary for church activities.

In 1970 the Honeyville Buddhist Church became a branch church of the newly established Buddhist Temple of Utah-Idaho which was formerly known as the Ogden Buddhist Church. The Honeyville church became independent on 1 April 1970. A Sunday school was established in 1953 and a Young Buddhist Association in 1973. For many years the church hosted the popular Buddhist Bazaar as a fundraiser, bringing people from all over northern Utah to enjoy oriental good, games, and prizes.

The Corinne Buddhist Church building was constructed in the spring of 1944 under the leadership of Jutaro Taura, Tsunekichi Ishidia, and Takematsue Tawatari, and property donated by Mr. and Mrs. Sataro Shiotani. With Yuki Kondo as supervisor, the Corinne Japanese community pitched in to shovel dirt, haul lumber, pour cement, and carry out other tasks to create this center for religious services and social functions. As with the Honeyville church, a minister from Ogden conducted services.

In 1954 the church was remodeled and enlarged, and a new

Obutsudan was purchased in 1961. The church throughout its history has received support and cooperation from the Young Buddhist Association and the Fujinkai. Today, with only a few Issei members remaining, the Young Buddhist Members have taken over administration of the church. A minister from Ogden conducts services for the small congregation once a month.[19]

The Molokan Russian Settlement

A unique chapter in Box Elder County's religious history involves a group of Russians, members of the Molokan faith, who settled near Park Valley and tried to create a religious colony from 1914–17. The experiment failed, leaving two graves enclosed in a picket fence as a lasting memorial to their adversity.

Molokan history goes back three centuries to Russia when revisions in Orthodox church rituals caused dissident groups to break away, including a group of peasants who felt led by the Holy Spirit to a simpler form of worship. With laws forbidding all non-Orthodox religions, Molokans were persecuted through the years. From 1904 to 1912, approximately 3,500 Molokans migrated to America, many of them settling in the Los Angeles area.[20]

As the modern world began to close in and impose civil law, the Molokans looked for a place where they could create a community of their own.

In Utah the Pacific Land and Water Company led by James H. Patterson, C.N. Strevell, F.A. Druehi, Harold A. LaFaunt, W. Mont Ferry, Ed D. Woodruff, and Robert LaFaunt had bought 136,949 acres of railroad land in Park Valley. In 1911 they published a brochure extolling the virtues of this land, featuring photographs of profitable farm and orchard lands.[21]

Need and opportunism meshed, and the move was on. The group's arrival was announced in the *Salt Lake Tribune* and reprinted in the 9 April 1914 issue of the *Box Elder News:* "More than 100 Russians, who for some time past have been members of the Russian colony near Los Angeles, Calif., left the southern California metropolis yesterday for Box Elder county, Utah. Another large contingent, it is said, will follow in a few weeks."[22]

The article noted that the group was traveling on a special train of four cars—two baggage cars and two passenger coaches. From the railroad stop in Kelton, they traveled by wagon to the dry sagebrush flats along the lower part of Dove Creek. They built wooden plank houses, dug wells and root cellars, and cleared land for their crops.

Tragedy struck almost immediately, as group leader Andrew Kalpakoff's wife was killed in a shooting accident as he cleaned his gun. The incident was reported on 7 May 1914 in the Box Elder News. Life went on, as a writer noted in a *Box Elder News* article of 6 August 1914: "The colony of Russians who recently located out there are building up a commonwealth after the pattern of the [LDS] United Order that was established in the city in the early years. They work together and have everything in common."[23]

Whether the colony's finances were communal, or the people were simply cooperative in their farming efforts, is not known by descendants. However, some families owned horses and some did not. Local residents who were children in Park Valley at the time recall that the women wore long black dresses and veils or scarves over their heads.[24]

Twenty family names appear on the county's delinquent tax list of 9 December 1915. These taxes were on improvements or personal property. There is no listing of change of land ownership in the Box Elder County Recorder's office, so either the land was leased or the land company failed to record a sale. By 1918 there was only one Russian name remaining on the tax list.

In April 1915 the *Box Elder News* reported that the Pacific Land and Water Company issued a deed for two acres for a school site. School board minutes of August 1915 indicate projected populations at the Russian colony were twenty boys and twenty girls. By November the superintendent reported the school had hardly enough students to justify its continuance. The next year the few children were bused to Rosette, for the town was almost empty.

Where did they go? Research and family contacts indicate most returned to California, including the Kalpakoff family. Period photographs taken by the Kalpakoff family provide a valuable visual record of clothing and structures, and this family also played a significant role in keeping the Russian Colony presence known.

Anna M. Kalpakoff was originally buried in the Park Valley

Cemetery. Later, when her sister-in-law Mary M. Kalpakoff died in childbirth in February 1915, she was buried on her husband's land, and it was decided to remove Anna from the Mormon cemetery and bury her beside her relative.[25]

Paul Kalpakoff, a child of Mary Kalpakoff, decided in 1948 to search for his mother's grave and brought his family with him to Park Valley where area residents helped them find two small wooden markers with Russian inscriptions. In 1966 they returned to place new headstones on the graves.

After Paul Kalpakoff's death in 1989, his son returned in 1990 after correspondence with a local writer who was researching the colony. At approximately the same time, other descendants of colonists and a few survivors who were children in 1914–17 also responded to the researcher's letter placed in a Molokan newsletter and shared memories and information to help create a clearer picture of the Russian settlement.[26]

The colony probably would have been forgotten if it were not for those two grave markers, which stir the curiosity of visitors. They, along with rapidly disappearing pits and a few small wooden structures, a scattering of rusted cans and pieces of broken china, and a crumbling schoolhouse foundation, remain the only visible signs of the courage and this short-lived religious experiment.

Apostolic Christian Church

As noted, Tremonton was somewhat unusual in Box Elder County in that it was colonized neither by Mormons nor as a railroad town, but was settled by Protestant Midwesterners with early Methodists and Baptists soon joined by a group from the Christian Apostolic Church. Since most of the families were of German heritage, they were referred to as the German Colony by local residents.

Settlers were lured to the area by land agents who promised cheap land with adequate potential for farming. Most of the families arrived in Tremonton between 1901–1904, most of them coming from Tremont, Illinois, and later joined by families from Ohio and Kansas. The early settlers came to improve themselves financially, but found primitive conditions when they arrived in Utah—living in shacks and drinking canal water until springs were found.[27]

A congregation was quickly established with Samuel Imthurn, Henry Baer, and Gideon Winzeler serving as ministers. The congregation built a small church on a farm in the Salt Creek area near Tremonton. After a larger church was built on the western edge of Tremonton, the church (which looked like a small schoolhouse) was moved and attached to it for use as a Sunday school. The congregation grew to as many as eighteen families. In 1906–1908 baptisms were held in a ditch near the church. There was a sense of brotherhood as the members got together for Sunday afternoon meals.[28]

The Philip and Bertha Getz family arrived in 1901 and built a two-story home in time for the birth of their fourth child, Ruth, in 1902. Ruth later recalled, "Our people were known to be industrious and hard working with well-kept homes and outbuildings."[29]

The families prospered, as noted in the 3 December 1907 edition of the *Tremont Times:* "To show what can be done in six years in the Bear River Valley, one has only to ride out to the farms of the German settlers west and southwest of Tremonton. Here he can see beautiful homes with fine orchards and gardens and hundreds of acres of oats and wheat and alfalfa where six years ago was a wilderness of sagebrush. . . ."[30]

A church schism, which manifested itself in churches in the East in 1906–1907, came to divide the unity of the community. The brethren at Tremonton were drawn into the dispute and a new church, under the direction of ministers Gideon Winzeler and Henry Baer, was formed. Because Winzeler had donated the land for the church, the group kept the church building, leaving the four remaining families, including Samuel Imthurn, without a place of worship.[31]

According to Getz, " Henry Baer was our new minister. He also preached in German. Our church sermons were in German, we sang German hymns, and Sunday School was in German. We more or less grew up to think you had to speak German to get into Heaven."[32]

Following the division, several families returned to the Midwest and the Apostolic Christian Church in Tremonton was all but dissolved. Over the years the Winzeler-Baer church began to decline and was eventually closed, although some families remained in the area.[33]

Today the only link to the church's brief past is a cemetery located near Salt Creek, southwest of Tremonton. The names reflect the German and Swiss heritage of its members: Funk, Bassner, Eggli, Meister, Getz, Kleinknecht, Woerner, and Baer. The Apostolic Christian Church and the Apostolic Christian Church (Nazarene) collectively provide funds for its upkeep, and during the summer of 1998 sent a mission group from the Midwest to the area to clean the grounds and repair the fence.

The Roman Catholic Church

The presence of the Roman Catholic church in Box Elder County dates back to the coming of the Transcontinental Railroad.[34] General Patrick Connor, one of the founders of Corinne, was an Irish Catholic, and had maintained connections with leaders of his faith from the time he came to Utah with the California Volunteers in 1862.

In May 1869 Catholic Bishop The Very Reverend Joseph Projectus Machebeuf appointed Father Honore Bourion to oversee Catholic interests in Utah. Father Bourion arrived in Corinne later in the year. He offered the first mass of record in Corinne and in Ogden, but remained only a few weeks.

Father Bourion was succeeded by Father John Foley. Though it was expected that Father Foley would make Corinne his headquarters, he stayed there only from his arrival in September to December, at which time he moved to Salt Lake City, and ministered to the Catholic population of Corinne from the capital city.

In 1871 Utah was removed from the territory of Bishop Machebeuf in Colorado and assigned to Archbishop Alemany of San Francisco. With more resources, Archbishop Alemany sent Father Patrick Walsh to Utah. At the time of dedication of a building for Catholic services in Salt Lake City, Archbishop Alemany, who had come from San Francisco for the event, stopped over in Corinne on Wednesday morning, 29 November 1871. The Archbishop offered mass in the Corinne Opera House, and met with members of the Catholic community in Corinne. The visit apparently made an impression on Archbishop Alemany. After returning to San Francisco, he appointed Father Patrick Dowling to a pastorate in Corinne. The Corinne parish served not only the Corinnethians, but Catholics living along the route of the Transcontinental Railroad from Ogden west, including Kelton. Father Dowling arrived in early January 1872. The large Catholic population expected to gather in Corinne did not materialize, and by June 1872 Father Dowling was reassigned to Salt Lake City.

It was not until Corinne's agricultural boom in 1892 that Bishop Lawrence Scanlan sent another priest to erect a church in Corinne. That attempt in establishing Catholicism in Corinne also came to naught. From that time, until the establishment of the St. Thomas Aquinas parish in Logan, Box Elder County Catholics were served from St. Joseph's parish in Ogden.

With the agricultural growth in Box Elder County subsequent to the coming of the canal system and the sugar company, the Catholic population of the county surged, especially with the arrival of a number of Mexican families in Garland to work in the sugar beet fields. Father Patrick Kennedy and Father Francis J. Sloan traveled from St. Joseph's in Ogden to Corinne to teach catechism in the homes of the Mendez and the Sunder Singh families. After establishment of St. Thomas Aquinas in Logan, pastors traveled to Corinne to offer mass in the city hall and later in the old Methodist church building.

With the establishment of Bushnell Hospital, Bishop Duane G. Hunt established St. Henry's Mission in Brigham City in 1943. At the end of the war, there were about sixty Catholics among the 6,000 residents of Box Elder's county seat. Traveling priests offered mass in the American Legion hall on east Forest Street. In 1950, as the Bushnell Hospital buildings became the Intermountain Indian School, St. Henry's was raised from a mission to a parish, which was given jurisdiction over Box Elder County. A home was purchased and remodeled into a chapel.

In 1952 Jesuit priests took charge of the parish. The priests kept a heavy schedule in the mid-1950s. Sunday masses were offered in the little chapel, at Intermountain Indian School, and at Little Valley, around the end of Promontory Point, where the new earth-fill railroad causeway was being constructed. Children were bussed to St. Joseph's in Ogden for school, and a house was purchased for a convent to house four nuns. The sisters remained in Brigham City until 1983.

In 1957 property was purchased for a new church and convent, on the corner of Second East and Fourth South. Father Joseph Clark successfully entered a bid on a surplus chapel at the Utah General Depot in Ogden. The building was sawed in half and moved to the site in Brigham City. Plans were made for a school, and property acquired on at Eighth West and Tenth South. Property was purchased for a new convent building and a site was secured for a Catholic Center near the Indian School. A house was purchased near the new Box Elder High School and remodeled into the Sacred Heart Center to be used for a released-time religious education program. With lay-offs at Thiokol, the Catholic population in Brigham City dwindled, and the school, the new convent, and the Catholic Center were not built at that time.

In 1976 Father John G. Ferguson came to Brigham City. Mass was then held in Spanish on a regular basis. Under Father Ferguson's direction, the new convent was built, a new rectory and other additions were added to the church, and the Indian Center was erected. Property was acquired in Tremonton for erection of a church there.

Through subsequent years, the parish has continued to serve the Roman Catholic community of Brigham City and Box Elder County.

Intermountain Indian School

Several Protestant denominations had their beginnings in Brigham City as a result of missionary work to Native American students attending Intermountain Indian School. A cooperative effort among mainline churches shared the already-existing campus chapel at first, but in the early 1950s a building known as the Protestant Student Center was constructed at 435 East 700 South, across the street from the campus. It was financed by the Presbyterian Board of National Missions.

Reverend August Jackley was director of activities for the students, assisted by lay persons and young people in the Brethren Volunteer Service and by Christian Reformed, Baptist, Presbyterian and Episcopal ministers.[35]

These clergymen, as well as school teachers and employees, formed the nucleus of what have continued to be local religious institutions. Another factor which spurred church growth was the change of government policies concerning students and religion. At first, students were to designate a religious affiliation and expected to attend services. Then it was decided religious institutions were to be off-campus. A glance at the "religious map" of Brigham City shows Christian Reformed, Episcopal, Bible Church, Baptist, LDS Indian Branch, Assembly of God Church, Protestant Student Center and Catholic Student Center are (or were) located within a couple blocks of the campus.

Christian Reformed

One of the most active denominations in the missionary field was the Christian Reformed Church. When the local church was formed in 1954, over 300 students had indicated a preference for the Christian Reformed Church. Reverend Cornelius Kuipers was called as the first pastor. Services were first held in the basement of the pastor's home. In 1960 a church was built at 636 South 300 East, primarily serving a Native American student population.[36] In 1964 Reverend Al Mulder became pastor.

The arrival of Thiokol personnel and the changes in government policy toward religious activity brought about significant change in the congregation's makeup. After Intermountain Indian School closed, the focus was further placed on building a strong local membership. In the early 1990s the congregation outgrew its small chapel and moved in to a downtown "storefront" church known as Living Hope Christian Reformed Church.

Baptist

Although a report in the *Ogden Herald* of 12 April 1887 states "the Baptist group was probably small and insignificant, but planned to build a Baptist University . . ."[37] No official accounts of Baptist activity are evident and no Baptist Church was erected. A Baptist church was built in Tremonton in 1908.[38] Old timers indicated this church had services for several years but gradually dwindled in membership. There was little or no Baptist activity again until the 1950s.

Reverend Delbert Fann and Reverend William Harris were among Southern Baptist clergy working with Native American students at Intermountain Indian School and saw the need for a church to serve the entire community, especially as Thiokol also appeared on the scene. In March 1958 an organizational meeting was held and the church was formed by Harris and Fann, along with Ralph and Barbara Davis, Frank and Roberta Edwards. The first pastor called to serve was Cecil Morgan.

The church purchased a home and half-completed chicken coop on the corner of 500 South and 600 West, with the pastor living in the house and the chicken coop rebuilt into a church with chapel, office, classrooms, fellowship hall and kitchen at 617 West 500 South. In 1971 the house was torn down and in 1991 a new education building was erected west of the church.[39]

First Baptist Church also had an Indian mission chapel built closer to the Indian School. After its closure the church operated a Spanish-speaking mission in the building. In addition, the church has established outreach missions in the Tremonton area.

Bible Church

In 1955 the Reverend James F. Cook joined the Evangelical Protestant Group working with Navajo students at Intermountain School and in September 1956 the Reverend Ira T. Ransom was called to work with him in that mission as well as in establishing a local congregation.

A church building was begun in September 1957 at 634 South 200 East and was dedicated in March 1958 with Reverend Ransom as pastor. Church membership was a mix of Native American students and local residents with Thiokol's arrival swelling the latter. A parsonage was added nearby in 1963, with both of these edifices still in use in the 1990s.[40]

Holy Cross Lutheran

Prior to Thiokol establishing its facility in Box Elder County, there was no Lutheran Church active in the area. When Thiokol employees began settling in Brigham City, there were enough Lutherans to establish a mission congregation. The first meeting of Lutherans was held in October 1958 to consider forming a congregation, and in November a steering committee was formed. Members were Gary Broman, Don Brelsford, Dan Carroll, Jack Dieter, Charles and Martha Shoun.

1959 was a significant year for Holy Cross Lutheran Church. In February the first Lutheran worship was held at the War Memorial Home, Pastor Donald Ranstrom was called in June, a parsonage completed in August, and the first official organization came in November. Services were held in the Protestant Student Center and Lincoln School until the group had its own building, with groundbreaking for the church at 750 East 100 South held in August 1960. The building was completed in March 1961 and still serves the congregation.[41]

Church of Christ

The Church of Christ was another group founded by Thiokol employees who attended services in Ogden and in Logan until they formed a local congregation in September 1961. Reverend J. K. Bentley was called as the first pastor. Services were held in a day care center located near 800 North Main until 1964 when a church building was completed at 207 South 600 West.[42]

Assembly of God

First Assembly of God was established in Brigham City in 1970 as the result of an earlier Bible Study group. Dan Legon was the first pastor and soon after its establishment, a church was built at 535 East 700 South. Victory Assembly of God Church, serving a Hispanic congregation, began as a mission in 1972 with a congregation formed from participants of a Bible study beginning in 1969 at the home of Henry and Maria Hernandez. The first pastor was Thomas Romero. The group met at Gillespie Hall, then purchased a building as 23 South 100 East, and later moved into the Presbyterian fellowship hall, with Tom Perea as pastor of a growing congregation. The two Assemblies combined as Victory First Assembly of God in June 1995 and hold services in the church building on Seventh South.

Cooperative Ministry Council

Brigham City churches formed a unique ministry beginning in 1968 as Community Presbyterian, Aldersgate Methodist, and Holy Cross Lutheran (later joined by St. Michael's Episcopal and the Christian Reformed churches) formed the Cooperative Ministry Council which conducted a weekday religious education program for children, combined youth activities, adult study programs, published a newsletter and directory, sponsored a Boy Scout group and held occasional joint worship services. This formal affiliation continued to some degree over 20 years.

ENDNOTES

1. This chapter was written by Sarah S. Yates.

2. A. Walton Roth, *A Century of Service in Utah, 1869–1969* (Salt Lake City: Presbytery of Utah, 1969), 3.

3. Ibid., 2.

4. Ibid., 4

5. Ibid., 4–5.

6. Sarah Yates, *A Centennial History of the Community Presbyterian Church of Brigham City, Ut, 1878–1978* (Brigham City: n.p., 1978), 1–2.

7. Roth, *A Century of Service*, 6.

8. Yates, *Community Presbyterian Church*, 2–3.

9. Ibid., 3

10. Ellen Baker, "History of Community Presbyterian Church of Brigham City," unpublished manuscript, 1944.

11. *Box Elder News*, 8 August 1907.

12. Yates, *Community Presbyterian Church*, 11–12.

13. *The First Century of the Methodist Church in Utah* (Salt Lake City: United Methodist Church, 1970), 7–8.

14. Ibid., 8.

15. Jennie M. Adney, unpublished manuscript, 1946.

16. *First Century of the Methodist Church in Utah*, 57.

17. *Box Elder News*, 9 January 1908.

18. *First Century of Methodist Church in Utah*, 57.

19. *Buddhist Churches of America: 75 Year History, 1899–1974* (Chicago: Nobart, Inc., 1974).

20. Harry J. Shubin, "History of the Russian Molokan Spiritual Jumpers Faith," *The Russian Molokan Directory.*

21. The pamphlet was published by the Pacific Land and Water Company in 1911 under the title, *Invest Dimes and Reap Dollars in Park Valley, Utah.*

22. *Box Elder News*, 6 April 1914.

23. *Box Elder News*, 6 August 1914.

24. Interviews by Sarah Yates with Lawrence Carter, Dorothy Goodlife Jensen, and Elizabeth Goodlife Hirschi.

25. Edwin Kalpakoff correspondence to Sarah S. Yates, 1989–90.

26. Correspondence from Rogoff, Nazaroff, Chernabaeff, Dalmatovov, Kalpakoff, to Sarah Yates, 1989–91.

27. Perry A. Klopfenstein, *Marching to Zion: A History of the Apostolic Christian Church of America: 1847–1982* (Fort Scott, Kan.: n.p., 1984), 305.

28. Ibid., 306.

29. Diana Hunsaker Myers, "Tremonton: A town born of diverse beliefs," in *The Leader,* 24 September 1997.

30. Ibid.

31. Klopenstein, *Marching to Zion,* 306.

32. Myers, "Tremonton: a town born of diverse beliefs."

33. Klopenstein, *Marching to Zion,* 306–7.

34. This section was compiled and excerpted from materials generously provided by Vicenta Singh.

35. Yates, *Community Presbyterian Church,* 15.

36. *Box Elder News,* 12 March 1978.

37. *Ogden Herald,* 12 April 1887.

38. Forsgren, *History of Box Elder County,* 324.

39. Mac Edwards interview by Sarah Yates, 13 March 1999.

40. Ira Ransom interview by Sarah Yates, 13 March 1999.

41. Charles Shoun, "Summary History of Lutheran Presence in Brigham City."

42. Helen Money interview by Sarah Yates, 13 March 1999.

Chapter 10

Into the Twentieth Century

With Utah firmly in the matrix of the national economy, the Panic of 1893 hit. It caught Utah full force, and Box Elder County as well, bringing unemployment and a depressed economy. The Brigham City Mercantile and Manufacturing Association folded like a crumpled paper box, and Box Elder County, along with the rest of Utah, suffered as the economic crisis swept throughout the United States. The economic order of Zion was swept away, as Utah came, for better or worse, into the economic and political mainstream of the United States of America. With the significant changes to the economy, social structure, and the political kingdom of God, and with provision in its constitution forever banning polygamy within its borders, Utah was granted statehood in 1896.

And what a time for statehood. The Gilded Age was in full swing. It was the Gay Nineties, a celebration of the coming-of-age of the United States. Just as Utah had become a full-fledged member of the Union, the United States of America had taken her place as a full partner in the community of nations. Once the Panic of 1893 was over, the economy was on the upswing, and it was a time when the

The Box Elder County Courthouse in 1896. (Box Elder County)

technology of the Industrial Age had brought power, money, and glory to the United States. Utah lagged behind many other states in its economic development. It had not had the benefit of the years of financial growth and cooperation with the other states that most had had. It had just come from under crushing political and economic sanctions, but it was a state, "Columbia's Newest Star" the people of Utah sang, and they were grateful.

The Coming of Statehood in Box Elder County

When statehood for Utah became a fact on 4 January 1896, the Corinne bell was borrowed by Brigham City, placed in the county courthouse tower, and rung so hard it cracked.[1]

Statehood did not bring an end to polygamy. There were those, laymen and LDS officials, who believed the practice would continue to be sanctioned in spite of the Woodruff Manifesto. Lorenzo Snow's successor to the LDS presidency, Joseph F. Smith, found it necessary to issue an additional manifesto, in 1904, after the brouhaha over the seating of Mormon apostle and U.S. Senator Reed Smoot disclosed that polygamy had not ceased; it had only gone underground, and another manifesto in 1910, after Utah's anti-Mormon newspaper, the *Salt Lake Tribune,* had indulged in a bit of what today we call "investigative journalism" and discovered that plural marriage had *still* not gone away.[2]

It took a president of the LDS church who had become an implacable foe of plural marriage, a man of the stature and power of Heber J. Grant, to make those who sought to enter polygamy outcasts from Mormonism.[3]

From this milieu developed a group of Mormon "fundamentalists" who coalesced into the equivalent of a "church in exile." They flourished in the Salt Lake Valley, and throughout Mormondom.[4] There were even a couple of "cells" of fundamentalist activity in Box Elder County, in Brigham City, Perry, Willard, and Beaver Dam.[5]

It was in that milieu that Box Elder County had its share of "dream mines." During the 1910s and 1920s there were a number of accounts, nowadays relegated to the realm of Mormon folklore, of sources of mineral wealth revealed by divine messengers or inspired dreams to faithful Mormons. The most famous is the "Dream Mine" of LDS bishop John Koyle on the mountain east of Salem in Utah County.[6] The dream mines seem to go hand-in-hand with fundamentalist Mormon beliefs, though not always. Reports of at least three different gold mines located in the mountains east of the Brigham City area circulated from the Dream Mine epoch including one mine associated with one of the Box Elder fundamentalist groups.[7] The mines were also a manifestation of the millenialist fervor and its anticipation of Christ's second coming carried over from nineteenth-century Mormonism.

While the people of Box Elder County listened to their church leaders, they also gave attention to the events of the nation and the economy around them. They followed the campaigns for president of the United States of William Jennings Bryan, and read his 1896 "Cross of Gold" speech, Bryan's panacea for the lingering effects of the Panic of 1893. It was not lost on them that though the Box Elder cooperative had collapsed, the church's finances had been saved during the panic, largely through the instrumentality of LDS apostle and later president Heber J. Grant.[8]

As the new century progressed, they felt the omnipresence of the LDS ecclesiastical influence less and less, and saw less and less of the apostles and prophets. Lorenzo Snow left Brigham City upon assuming the presidency at the death of Wilford Woodruff in 1898. President Snow, the patron saint of Box Elder, died in 1901. Though Joseph F. Smith visited Brigham City, and made one of his greatest doctrinal pronouncements from the pulpit of the Box Elder Tabernacle, he did not have the attachment to Box Elder that Lorenzo Snow had. It was not like the days when Lorenzo Snow became the very first president of the great temple in Salt Lake City when it was dedicated in 1893, and President Snow brought all the temple workers, along with the apostles and President Woodruff himself, to Box Elder on the train, for an excursion. They dined on Mantua strawberries and danced in the Opera House. Wilford Woodruff, too, spoke one of his most significant prophecies from the pulpit of the Box Elder Tabernacle. But those days faded. Heber J. Grant even deeded away the temple site, chosen by Brigham Young, on the point of the gravel bench above Brigham City now known as "Reservoir Hill."[9] We can only imagine what Brigham City would have been like, especially that part of town, if the temple had been built.

The turn of the twentieth century was a time of transition for Box Elder County, for Utah, and for the nation. Lorenzo Snow died in 1901, as did his first counselor, George Q. Cannon, one of Mormonism's brightest minds. At the death of George Q. Cannon, Lorenzo Snow, who had brought Rudger Clawson from prison, where he had been incarcerated for unlawful cohabitation, to Box Elder, had made him stake president, and then had raised him to the apostleship upon Lorenzo's rise to the presidency and nominated him to be his new counselor in the First Presidency. Though Rudger was sustained in the general conference, ailing President Snow died four days later, and Clawson never served in the First Presidency.

Two years after Utah's statehood, the United States found itself at war with Spain over Cuba. During the 1898 Spanish American War, Utah Mormons were divided over the issue of military service. Some leaders insisted that as Mormons they were not justified in joining the conflict. Other leaders felt that military service was a test of loyalty to the United States and as recent recipients of statehood they should serve in the military. The later view prevailed, and as a consequence military service as a patriotic duty became a tenet of twentieth-century Mormonism.[10]

All this was witnessed by the residents of Box Elder County, who were by now as affected by national events as were people in other parts of the country.They saw automobiles come to the dusty, rutted roads of Box Elder, about the same time that a major change came to the route of the transcontinental railroad.

The Lucin Cut-Off

When the railroad came through in 1869, the two rival companies, the Union Pacific and the Central Pacific, built their tracks around the north end of Great Salt Lake, because the lake was in a high cycle, and technology was not up to the task of bridging the lake. In 1898 Edward Henry Harriman acquired control of the Union Pacific Railroad, and three years later in 1901 he gained control of the Southern Pacific—successor to the Central Pacific. His modernization of the line included a technological feat of magnificent proportions.

The cost of helper engines and their facilities for pushing trains over the Promontory range were high, and Harriman decided it was time to revisit the possibility of building a bridge or causeway across the Great Salt Lake as "Traffic had increased to such a point that operation over the steep and crooked old line was becoming constantly more and more vexatious and difficult."[11] Financial and engineering heads came together, and the result was the great Lucin Cut-Off. The Lucin Cut-Off was 102 miles in length, from Ogden to Lucin, including thirteen miles of fill and nearly twelve miles of trestle across Great Salt Lake. Forty-four miles were saved in length, and hundreds of feet in grade. The project required the labor of 3,000 men, took one and one-half years of actual construction, and cost over $8 million.[12] The cutoff saved considerable time and expense. Two difficult stretches were eliminated—the seven hundred foot climb in eleven miles across the Promontory Summit and the 500

The trestle under construction across the Great Salt Lake in 1903. (Box Elder County)

feet crossing in five and a half miles of a spur of the Hogback Mountains near Kelton.

It was a herculean project. Not only did a mountain of earth and rock have to be blasted, excavated, loaded, hauled, and dumped along the twenty-two mile length of the causeway, a huge forest of trees had to be located, cut, planed, hauled, and driven into the bed of the lake in its deepest part—nearly twelve miles of it—by steam-operated pile-drivers. A temporary trestle had to be built to support the dump-cars for the fill portion. A 1906 account described the complex project in the following manner:

> In the construction of that trestle, piling one hundred and twenty-five feet long was to be used. In the main roadway bents were to be of five piles, at sidings of nine. These bents are fifteen feet apart, so that something like twenty-five thousand of these huge piles had to be obtained. They were mostly Oregon fir, and cost, delivered at the lakeside, about sixty dollars apiece. But there was also a temporary trestle to be built—many miles of it. In constructing the fill, a trestle was first made, on which a track was laid. Over this track trains loaded with rock and gravel for the fill were run out and dumped. In the shallower places this temporary trestle was of forty-foot piles, but in the deeper water approaching the

> permanent trestle seventy-foot piles were used. In the temporary trestle only four piles were driven in a bent, but the bents were the same distance apart as in the permanent trestle. Thus for the two trestles a perfect forest of piles was needed. The agents of the Southern Pacific scoured the great timber districts of the country, and train-load after train-load of the huge timbers was headed toward the Great Salt Lake.
>
> And piling was far from all. There were the big stringers and caps for both permanent and temporary trestles, and besides all the res, though a bagatelle compared with it, timber for stations, boarding-houses, and sidings, guard-rails, and even a steamboat.[13]

In all, "38,256 trees were cut down to make piles for the treat trestle. A forest of two square miles was transplanted into Great Salt Lake."[14] In addition 2 million board feet of redwood decking were used for the actual railbed.[15] Just the portion of the trestle above the waterline contained enough wood to lay a board-walk four feet wide from Boston to Buffalo, or from Snowville to St. George.

The railroad company ordered twenty-five steam pile-drivers, which were built in San Francisco while the timber cutters were doing their work. Rock and gravel pits were opened at Little Mountain, Promontory Point, Lakeside, and at the southern end of the Hogup mountains. In the car shops, 400 special steel side-dump cars were built, each with a capacity of fifty-five tons. These were supplemented by other dump cars and flat cars for a combined total of nearly 1,000 cars used in the project. Eighty locomotives of various sizes moved the thousand cars. Eight great steam-shovels with five cubic yard buckets capacity dug the material out of the banks and loaded it into the dump-cars. A 127-foot long, 22-foot wide steamer, *The Promontory,* carried supplies and assisted with construction work on the lake.

Construction occurred simultaneously at both sides of the lake and both sides of Promontory Point in the middle of the lake.

The pile drivers were the workhorses of the trestle. "As fast as the pile-drivers were ready, they were set to work. A station was erected at each mile-end of the projected road. There two pile-drivers went to work back to back, driving away from each other. Five bents of five piles each, or seventy-five in all, was a good day's work."[16]

It was hard work, and life in the construction camps was not glamorous. "At each station a boarding-house was built on a platform raised on piles well out of the way of storm-waves. There the men lived until their work was finished. The company furnished supplies and cooks, and the men paid four dollars a week for their board. They worked in ten-hour shifts, day and night, Sundays and holidays."[17] Nor were there many distractions for the workers.

> There was not much to do but work and sleep, and there was no place to spend money. No liquor was allowed. All stores and all packages coming out to workmen were carefully searched, and any liquor found was promptly confiscated. From first to last two carloads were taken in this way. The company was in a hurry, and it could not afford to have the work interrupted by drunkenness or sprees, to say nothing of the rows and fights inevitable if liquor were in camp. It was not so easy to keep it out on the fills as on the trestles. Two or three times squatters came down on government land adjoining parts of the right of way and set up groggeries. Usually it was not much trouble to drive them away, but one fellow who set up shop near Hogup determined to brazen it out. However, when one of the engineers took a gang of men to his place and began to drill holes under his shanty preparatory to blowing it up with giant-powder, his courage oozed, and he fled.[18]

Workers were allowed to bring wives and children with them. They were housed in box cars called "out-fit" cars placed on temporary sidings. Some, such as a line of more than forty cars near the Lakeside quarry, were dangerously close to the construction work. At Lakeside, "sometimes, when blasts were unusually heavy, pieces flew uncomfortably near the outfit cars. So it was ordered that at the cry of 'Blast!' all the women and children should come out of their wheeled houses and crawl under them for safety."[19]

The construction work was dangerous and minor accidents such as broken bones and smashed fingers and hands occurred. A car load of dynamite exploded and several men fell into the lake and were nearly strangled by the heavy salt water. The company maintained a hospital, staffed by a surgeon, near the work site.

The bottom surface of the lake bed ranged in hardness from gypsum-crusted sections "so hard that the huge hammers of the pile-drivers could not force a timber through, and it had to be cut out with a steam-jet."[20] In other places the bottom was more than fifty feet of soft mud where single piles disappeared out of sight and had to be spliced, lashed, and braced together in order to hold. The rock fill across these soft spots could also settle and had to be rebuilt. On 24 March 1903 a trial run was attempted by a train across the Old Bear River bed. Without warning the embankment settled. The engine, still on its rails but now in two feet of water, had to be pulled out with a cable.

In spite of these set backs, work progressed steadily. When all the bents were driven, braced, and capped, twelve-inch stringers were laid, and three-inch-thick redwood planks were laid as a deck. Atop the planking, three inches of asphalt roofing were applied, and that capped with fourteen inches of gravel and rock ballast.

Freight trains began using the cutoff on 6 March 1904 and passenger trains began crossing the cutoff six months later on 18 September 1904. The benefits were immediate:

> With six hundred thousand tons of through freight annually, and that amount increasing, the old road had reached its limit. It took three locomotives to handle nine hundred and fifty tons, and often required from thirty to thirty-six hours. Over the cut-off a single engine has hauled two thousand three hundred and sixty tons in less than nine hours. Passenger-trains that used to go in two or three sections, each with two locomotives, now run from fourteen to seventeen coaches with one engine.[21]

The building of the Lucin Cut-Off, while a blessing to through passengers and freight, and a plus to the fortunes and the timetables of the railroad, was not a boon to Box Elder County. Though most of the tracks of the new cut-off ran through Box Elder County, the benefits went to Ogden, strategically located near the eastern end of the cut-off. The Lucin Cut-Off spelled the doom of the towns and sidings which had sprung up along the old line around the north end of the Great Salt Lake. The old Promontory line became a branch line, and traffic declined from three trains a week to two a week then one a week.

By the late 1930s, the line was almost unused. The railroad tried to abandon the line, but met with strong opposition from farmers, cattlemen, and the Box Elder Chamber of Commerce.[22] Then came World War II and the old route was declared surplus. There was a cry for steel for the war, and the railroad decided that the 120 miles of rails from Corinne to Lucin could be spared. On 8 September 1942, the ceremonial "un-driving" of the Golden Spike took place at Promontory Summit, and work trains began to salvage the rails.[23]

The towns of Terrace and Kelton became ghost towns as did the grain-loading sidings and water stops along the line. Names like Wyben, Dathol, Lampo, Surban, Rozel, Metataurus, Kosmo, Zias, Peplin, Ombey, Matlin, Watercress, Medea, and Umbria faded into dust.[24]

Roads & Highways

The history of highways in Box Elder county may be said to begin with the travel of the prehistoric bands of nomadic hunter-gatherers who plied the Bear and Malad Rivers, the county's first, natural "highways." Trails along the banks of the rivers and streams and through mountain passes, such as the old trail from Cache Valley over Wellsville Mountain through Flatbottom Canyon east of Brigham City, were opened by those who summered in Cache Valley and further northward and wintered in the caves on Promontory and further west in the Great Salt Lake Desert.

The exploration of Jesse C. Little in 1847 may count as the first "survey" for a highway in Box Elder County. The establishment of the Salt Lake Cutoff in 1848 by Captain Samuel Hensley and the returning crew of Mormon Battalion veterans opened the first major east-west route across the county and around the north end of Great Salt Lake.

The trail along the base of the Wasatch Range was widened by the wagon tires and the countless hooves of horses and cattle belonging to the California gold rushers in 1849-1850. It was that tide which made of Brigham City's main street a major thoroughfare.

It was, however, the settlers themselves who first opened roads and trails for common use as they explored and settled the farms and communities of Box Elder County.

Lydia Walker Forsgren in a chapter on road building in the 1937

History of Box Elder County provides a good summary of early road construction.

> During territorial days in Utah, from 1850 to 1896, road building was left in the hands of county officials, in fact, in many cases the matter was handled entirely by precinct supervisors. . . . The difficulties encountered by those pioneer road builders were many. Roads, generally speaking, followed the trails made by animals and early day explorers and trappers. When these trails skirted the foothills, there was the danger of rock and gravel slides and avalanches; when they entered and crossed the valleys, there were bogs and marshes with which to contend, and in the canyons the underbrush formed an obstruction . . . they cut the brush, hauled off the loose rocks, and filled in the marshes and swamps. Occasionally they graveled the roads and thus laid a solid foundation upon which the roads of the future could be built.
>
> In a very early period of road building particular attention was paid to canyon roads. . . . The saw mills were located in the nearby canyons—Willard, Three Mile, and Box Elder—and passable roads were necessary in order that logs and lumber might be hauled to and from these mills. Posts and poles for the building of fences and corrals were also hauled over these roads, and in the fall of the year the highways were lined with men and teams going to the canyons for wood, at that time the only fuel obtainable.[25]

Road building, along with all other community development was abruptly arrested when the inhabitants relocated to Provo during the "Move South," in 1858, but after settlers returned to their homes, farms, and businesses, road building resumed with even greater attention.

A major expansion of territorial highway building occurred from 1860 to 1870. According to Ezra C. Knowlton, funds were appropriated:

> . . . to start opening new wagon road gateways—these included the northern outlet of San Pitch Valley from Fairview to Spanish Fork Canyon; Box Elder Canyon from Brigham City to Wellsville; Ogden easterly to Huntsville and over the mountain to Bear Lake Valley; the important Logan Canyon road connecting Cache and Rich counties; the appropriations for roads connecting the upper

virgin River settlements with the lower Washington county towns; from Washington County easterly to Kane County; thence northerly from Kanab to Piute County; and the over the mountain crossing from the upper Sevier River to Iron County."[26]

One of the reasons for the noticeable increase of road-building was a supply of non-Mormon, non-agricultural labor. According to Lydia Walker Forsgren, " . . . this was just three years prior to the commencement of the Civil War; and in anticipation of warfare, many men from both North and South came West to avoid enlistment in the service. Many of these men found their way into Utah, and during their short stay here they were willing to accept any kind of work."[27] They were hired for a variety of activities including road construction. During one summer Mathew W. Dalton and Alfred Cardon kept a dozen of these men at work on a road in Willard Canyon.

Brigham City provides an example of the problems in building roads. Only to the south was road building relatively easy, following the old Indian and Gold-Rush road toward Ogden. To the east was the obstacle of the narrow defile of rock-and-brush-filled Box Elder Canyon. To the West was a swamp between the town and the railroad station on Forest Street—the main east-west thoroughfare. Old-timers recalled that "travel to and from the railroad station demanded that the swamp on West Forest Street be drained and filled. It took years of work and many tons of gravel to make the street what it is today."[28]

To the north, it was as bad as to the west: "North Main Street of Brigham City was a veritable quagmire from near Seventh North to some distance north of city limits. This, too, was graded and made passable."[29] To the north-west, it was the same. The "Watery Lane" road was built "through the bogs and marshes which were caused by the overflow waters from Box Elder Creek. Many hundred tons of gravel and rock were hauled by team from southeast of Brigham to be used in making a road bed. The work was slow because the gravel was loaded with a hand shovel. Year after year more gravel was added until finally a solid foundation was laid."[30]

Out further in the county there were other problems in linking the far-flung communities together by road. In the "easy" places, roads were surveyed, and then marked out for the builders. In locating the route from Grouse Creek to the Utah-Idaho border, "Lorenzo Jensen of Brigham City plowed a furrow much of the way to mark where the county road was to be."[31] The road built in 1885 between Grouse Creek and Terrace required a mile-long hand-built dugway.

Early fords over creeks and rivers (the most famous of which are Hampton's Ford on the Bear and Rocky ford through the Malad) were eventually replaced by bridges.[32] The first bridges were built by individuals, who were granted the privilege of charging a toll for use of the span, such as Ben Hampton's bridge over the Bear, and Hiram House's bridge over the same stream at Corinne. Eventually, those bridges passed into county ownership.[33]

As towns grew, especially after the "second tier" of settlements were established around the turn of the twentieth century, road building grew apace. The construction required a massive infusion of resources. One source of funding was a poll tax.

The very first paved "macadamized" road in Box Elder County was laid between Willard and Utah Hot Springs at the Box Elder-Weber county line. Construction was carried out by an experimental gang of "convict labor."[34] According to Ezra Knowlton, "the first concrete pavement placed on the rural roads of Utah" was "1.2 miles of single-lane pavement . . . placed in Box Elder County in 1912."[35] By 1919 there was "with a few minor gaps" paved road from Brigham City to Spanish Fork. In 1941 a four-lane high way stretched from Springville on the south to Brigham City on the north.[36]

Many histories chronicle the epic of the construction of the well-known "Lincoln Highway" through Utah, but there was another such project which directly impacted Box Elder County.

> An unusual and interesting action of the 1913 legislative session was its designation of the so-called Midland Trail all the way across Utah, the route intended extending westerly from the Colorado line by way of Cisco, Green River, Price, Colton, Spanish Fork, Salt Lake City, Brigham City, and around the north end of the Lake to the Nevada line. This 1913 Midland Trail activity was the first in Utah or other similar efforts, which during the next dozen years were destined to rise, and all of which had as an object the

> improvement of connecting links in the interstate routes across the country. These promotional efforts were chiefly directed at the less populous states which lay across the natural path of the important transcontinental routes . . . ."[37]

In 1926 there were approximately 1,600 miles of roads in Box Elder County of which 1,350 miles were supervised by the county commission and 250 miles by the by the state road commission.[38]

Early hard-surfaced roads were paved either with concrete or simply oiled. Oiling a dirt road really did not add a hard surface, it mostly kept down the dust and shed some water.Box Elder County was the site of an experimental project to build roads using oil mixed with gravel or crushed stone. In 1927 a ten-mile-long experimental section of the new paving was laid between Brigham City and Logan. After the tests, it was discovered that the "California method" was superior to the "Oregon method" and better suited to the alluvial gravel available in Utah.[39] The Oregon method utilized crushed stone.

Over the years since the period of colonization and expansion of towns in Box Elder, the roads have, of course, been upgraded, given new surfaces, and many have been widened.The most notable road construction projects in the county in recent years have been the construction through the county, first of Interstate 15, then Interstate 84. As the Interstate project approached reality in the 1960s some county residents resisted seeking to postpone construction and to have the highway go as far west of town as possible. The Interstate, it was said, would take travelers whizzing past town away from main street and their dollars away from local businesses. That concern was an important reason that when the Interstate was built, there was no Forest Street interchange. The logic was that people would get off the Interstate at one end of town, and would have to go down the entire length of Main Street, thus giving all businesses an equal chance at the travelers' dollars. It was another three decades before Brigham City got its Forest Street interchange in December 1996.

After the Thiokol plant was built between Corinne and the Golden Spike Monument, that road was widened and strengthened to bear not only the heavy commuter traffic incident to the facility,

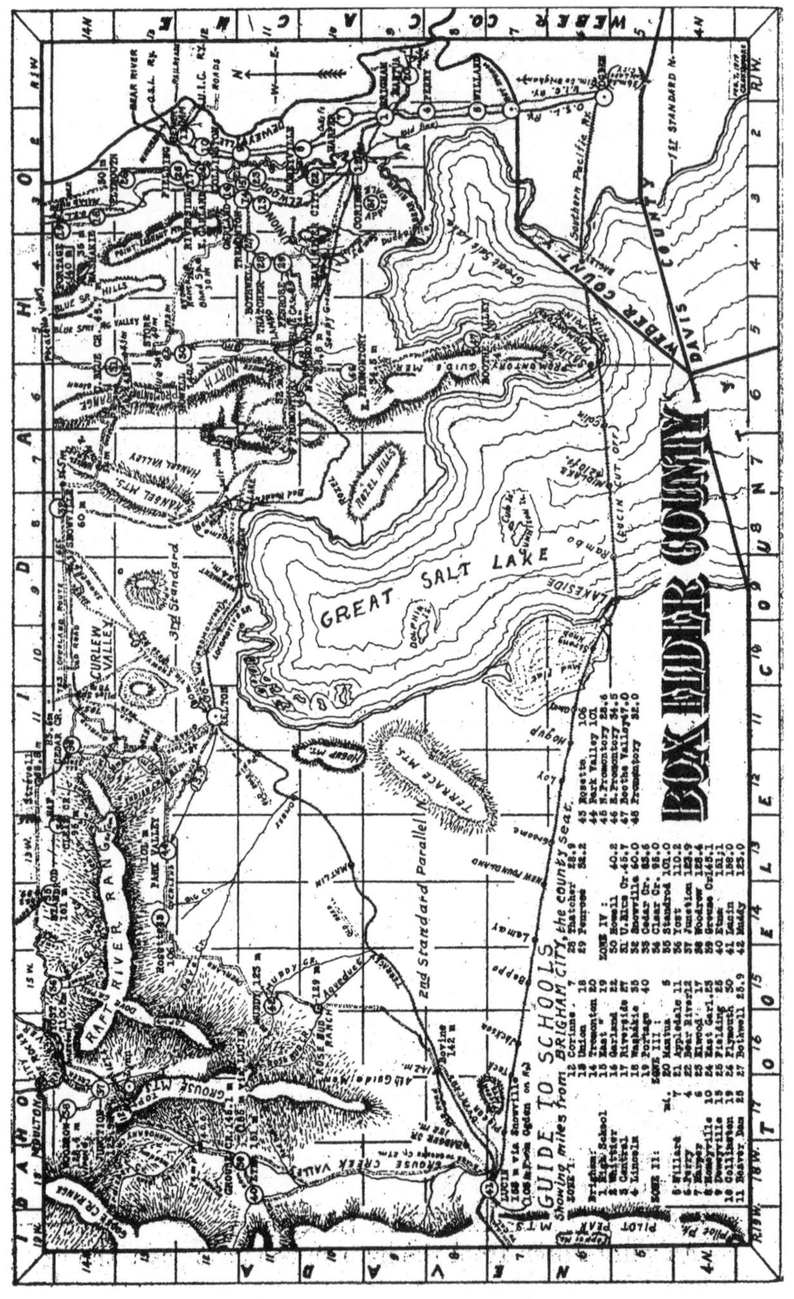

Map of the Box Elder County School Districts. Printed in Charles H. Skidmore, *Administration and Supervision in the Box Elder School District*, 1921.

but large trucks carrying heavy industrial loads, such as booster engines for the Space Shuttle.

Schools in Box Elder County

Though schools existed in Box Elder from the beginning of its settlement by Mormon pioneers, the development of an organized school system was some time in coming. According to Lydia Forsgren:

> During the winter of 1852–53, Henry M. Thatcher, an emigrant enroute to California, stopped over and taught school in the newly erected Willard [North Willow Creek][40] school house. He instructed twenty pupils who ranged in age from five to eighteen or twenty years. The tuition was three dollars a month per capita paid in produce and articles the teacher could use. The course consisted of spelling, reading, and a little arithmetic and writing. The texts used were the blue-backed Elementary Speller and a few readers which had been brought across the plains as treasured keepsakes from. childhood homes. The writing was done with pencil and slate.[41]

In Box Elder settlement private instruction preceded public school. According to Simeon Carter, Jr., "every day his mother, a well educated English lady, would call her children in from play and teach them to read and spell, using the Bible as their main text book. This no doubt was the custom in many homes in this community."[42] Some of the families in the Box Elder Fort provided and educational experience for their children by arranging with Henry Evans, "Brigham City's first teacher" who "taught during the winter of 1853-1854 in the homes of the people who lived in the "Old Fort."[43]

As the number of families in Box Elder Settlement increased, so did the dimensions and facilities of the Fort. According to an account written when many of the old-timers were still alive, "In 1854 the people erected a long log school house just outside of the Fort limits. If it were standing today, it would be located almost in the center of the street east of the Third Ward L. D. S. Chapel."[44] During the school's first season, 1854-1855, George Bramwell was the teacher. During the next school-year, and for a number of subsequent sessions, the teacher was Jonathan Calkins Wright (who later became a counselor to Box Elder's presiding officer, Lorenzo Snow.)

After the fort was broken up and the city plat established and homes built in town, school was held in the basement of the Court House, at least after 1861. According Lydia Forsgren's account of schools and school buildings:

> The school hours were from nine to twelve and from one to four, with a recess morning and afternoon. The curriculum consisted of reading, writing, spelling, and grammar. Night school was conducted for the benefit of the older people, and many men spent their evenings there, learning to write and getting a knowledge of the four basic processes in arithmetic.
>
> At that time there were no graded schools and children of all ages were in the same room. Try to imagine sixty pupils, ranging in age from six to eighteen years, seated on long slabs without backs-say six or eight on a seat, no desks and no particular order of arrangement each studying from any kind of book he could get, and each reciting his lesson when learned. When one lesson was completed, another was assigned him for the next day.
>
> At intervals a number of boys who were in about the same place in arithmetic would be called up before the small blackboard to recite. At the same time Miss Susan [Watkins] (later Mrs. L. P. Johnson of Brigham City), would be teaching the letters to a group of little people.
>
> Whenever the writing period came, the grown boys and girls would surround the long table which stood in the center of the room and there try to imitate, with bluing ink and all sorts of pens, the copy which was 'set them' by the teacher. Mrs. Johnson says she well remembers seeing her father spend hours in the evening "setting copies" by the light of a tallow candle, and then next morning setting off to school with an arm full of "fools cap paper." Many of these copies were taken from the National Blue-Backed Speller
>
> For all this work Mr. Watkins received about three dollars a quarter per capita and that was paid in anything from eggs to cedar posts.
>
> The conditions under which he worked were not conducive of results; yet he left a lasting impression for good on the life of every boy or girl who attended his school.[45]

Gradually the quality of the educational experience of Box Elder's students increased. Louis Frederick Moench came to Brigham City in about 1871, after having taught at the University of Deseret in Salt Lake City. Mr. Moench was an educated man, having passed his high school grade in his native land, Germany, and taken advanced work at Bryant and Straton's College in Chicago. He was an expert penman, and aside from his store of knowledge, Mr. Moench was a real educator. His discipline, methods of presentation, and the general atmosphere of his room were far above the average.[46]

Louis F. Moench went on to become principal of Ogden's Central School, and, as his heroic bronze statue attests, became the "father" of what began as Weber Stake Academy and is now Weber State University.[47]

The work of Professor Moench and his assistant, E. A. Box brought such honor upon their students that Lorenzo Snow "considered the work so meritorious that . . . he gave the school the title of 'Academy.'"[48]

The first school building in the county was built in North Willow Creek in 1852. The structure at Box Elder Fort had been used not only for school classes, but for church and community meetings as well. The North Willow Creek school was "a one-room log building twenty by sixteen feet, with a fireplace in the south end. There were two small glass windows in the west side, and the door in the north was made from boards carried across the plains by ox teams. The roof was made of rough slabs hewed from logs with an ax, and the whole was covered with dirt."[49] The first brick school in the county was built in Three Mile Creek in 1874.

In Brigham City each of the four wards had a school, usually in or adjacent to the ward chapel.[50] Following the lead of Salt Lake City in consolidating its schools in 1890, "Brigham City consolidated its schools on Sept. 28, 1896."[51] Consolidation of Brigham City's schools was only the beginning. According to Charles Skidmore, "The Box Elder School district was conceived on May 10, 1907 when more than forty progressive citizens petitioned the Board of County Commissioners to consolidate the county schools."[52] The consolidation became a reality on 20 June 1907.

Steady growth followed consolidation and the creation of the

School District. A building for the Box Elder Stake Academy was built on a block of the United Order or Brigham City Mercantile and Manufacturing Association property, on east Forest Street. It was succeeded by Box Elder High School, which "had its beginning in 1894-5 when J. S. Bingham was hired by the twelve trustees of the four Brigham City school districts to teach a high school in the old Academy Building on East Forest Street."[53] A large, brick, high school, with then-stylish Norman features, was built in 1912 on the site of the old Academy building. An addition was built a few years later in 1918. According to Superintendent Skidmore, "The congestion in the elementary schools of Brigham City was very much relieved at the opening of the school year 1918-1919, when the 7th and 8th grades moved from the Whittier to the new $40,000.00 addition that had been erected on the east side of the Box Elder High School."[54]

A high school serving the farming areas around Tremonton and Garland began in 1916 when "Bear River High School was founded in the Elementary School building at Garland."[55] The main building of the present campus was erected in 1921 with an auditorium and gymnasium added in 1924. The new high school campus was located midway between Tremonton and Garland so it would be only a twenty-minute walk from either town.[56]

Additions to both high schools were made during the 1930s utilizing labor and assistance from Franklin D. Roosevelt's New Deal programs. Bear River High School gained new classrooms and a mechanical arts department. Box Elder High School got a large new south wing and a free-standing gymnasium across Forest Street to the north, on the site of the old Brigham City Mercantile and Manufacturing Association's Boot, Shoe, Hat, Broom, and Harness factory. In the early 1960s a new Box Elder High School was built in the south-west part of town, and the old High School was demolished in 1969 to construct a newer junior high building.

Brigham City's four "ward" schools were consolidated into two large, brick elementary schools. The Central School, built on the west half of "Sagebrush Square" across Main Street west from the Tabernacle, was erected in the late 1890s. It served the students who lived south of Forest Street and who had attended the First Ward school[57] and the Second Ward School (later the Whittier). In 1912 the

The first Collinston School. (Courtesy Sonja Secrist Shelton)

Lincoln School was built on the site of the old Box Elder Fort between First and Second West and between Second and Third North. When it was ready for classes, the students of the old Third Ward school were ceremoniously marched from their old building south to Second South, east two blocks to First West, and then north a block to the doors and stairs of their huge new school building.[58]

The next major milestone was World War I. On 22 May 1917 U. S. Commissioner P. P. Claxton said: 'When the war is over there will be such demands upon this country for men and women of scientific knowledge, technical skill and general culture as have never ,come to any country. The world must be rebuilt.'"[59] Superintendent Skidmore noted that:

> On the 18th of January, 1918 President Woodrow Wilson expressed his very urgent concern 'that none of the educational processes of the country should be interrupted any more than is absolutely unavoidable during the war.'
>
> Such information was not only advantageous in determining

> the value of education when put to the crucible test, but also was influential in declining the wishes of certain large local organizations of Box Elder District that seemed determined to close the schools, or reduce the length of term to a minimum for war purposes. The result was that the schools continued to increase during the worlds war and became very helpful in carrying on many a war drive through the schools, rightly called the 'second great line of defense.' The teachers of Box Elder District went over the top 100 per cent strong in purchasing their quota of war saving stamps and liberty bonds. Captain Henry D. Moyle published the fact that the Box Elder schools led the schools of the State in 1919 W. S. S. campaign besides averaging more than $20 per pupil for W. S. S. and Liberty Bonds. The pupils were enthusiastic in conserving food and clothing, planting war gardens, gathering peach pits, furnishing needful war articles such as towels, covers, bed shirts, wash clothes and gun wipers. They dreamed many times of how they had really whipped the Kaiser.[60]

In 1921 there were 48 schools in Box Elder County. Four schools were in Brigham City: Box Elder High School, Whittier, Central, and Lincoln, comprising Zone I. In Zone II, were schools at Willard, Perry, Harper, Honeyville, Deweyville, Collinston, Beaver Dam, Corinne, Union, Tremonton, East Tremonton, Garland, Riverside, Washakie, and Portage. Zone III schools included Mantua, Appledale, Bear River, Elwood, East Garland, Fielding, Plymouth, Bothwell, Thatcher, and Penrose. The schools in Zone IV were Howell, Blue Creek, Snowville, Cedar Creek, Clear Creek, Standrod, Yost, Junction, Woodrow (in Junction Valley north of Junction and west of Yost), Grouse Creek, Etna, Lucin, Muddy (on Muddy Creek at the foot of the Muddy Range north of the Rosebud Ranch), Rosette, Park Valley, North Promontory, East Promontory, Booth Valley (about half-way along the Promontory between the East Promontory school and Promontory Point), and Promontory. It is interesting to note that there were four schools strung out along the Promontory.

The number of small, rural schools was necessitated by the lack of rapid transportation and the primitive condition of many of the county's roads. Superintendent Skidmore noted in 1921 regarding the construction of the new Bear River High School building, that "As soon as good roads will permit the 7th and 8th grades from most of the nearby surrounding schools will be transferred to this center to participate in the great advantages it affords."[61]

Over the years most of the rural schools have been closed and the students transported on busses to larger schools in the cities and towns of the county. Growth has brought more and more of those centrally-located schools. The Central and Lincoln schools, for example, served Brigham City for nearly fifty years without rivals.[62] The coming of Thiokol with its influx of scientists, laborers, and other support personnel brought not only a new Box Elder High School, but several elementary schools and a new Junior High. Other Box Elder communities saw growth and change in proportion.

In the 1970s the Board of Education offices moved from the County Courthouse to the old Second Ward Chapel, just west of the still-vacant site of the old Whittier School, when the Second Ward building was declared surplus by the L. D. S. church.

In 1999 Box Elder County schools are fully the equal of any in the state, and continue to provide a quality education for the children of the county.

Religious and Secular Conflict During the Early Years of the Twentieth Century

An example of the birth pains of a new social order was the controversy over the Brigham City Opera House that began in early 1903 and lasted for over eighteen months. The affair was covered extensively in the Salt Lake City daily newspapers and received some national attention as well.[63]

When the Opera House came on the market as part of an estate sale, it was purchased by one of the four Brigham City LDS wards. The other three wards then purchased shares in the building. Plans for the building included a variety of church-related activities, with church-sponsored dances the primary purpose. Church leaders in charge of the dances anticipated keeping the Opera House Orchestra, but reducing its size and lowering the musicians pay. Chris Christiansen and Christian O. Anderson, leaders of the Opera House Orchestra, elected not to play and made plans to build a privately owned, open-air dance pavilion that threatened competition with church-sponsored dances in the Opera House.

In an effort to address potential problems before the pavilion was constructed, Christiansen and Anderson met with the Box Elder Stake Presidency and High Council to outline their plans. The church leaders advised the men not to open the competing pavilion, and when the two men went ahead with the project, LDS members were strongly encouraged not to patronize the pavilion and were threatened with a loss of church membership if they did.[64]

Apparently the accusations of Christiansen and Anderson were not without foundation. In a meeting of the First Ward Relief Society officers, the bishop:

> Spoke a little about the new dancing floor . . . said it had been built against counsel. Said the authorities had bought the opera house for the amusement of our youth and we don't want our people to patronize the other place, advised the teachers to use an influence with the people against it. Said we don't want to injure anyone, but we should strive to do our duty. Spoke how we should shun discord and disunion, and how we should sustain those placed over us . . .[65]

Critics castigated church leaders for interfering with how individuals made a living and for being unjust and dictatorial.[66] Christiansen and Anderson offered the pavilion to the local wards with the stipulation that they be hired as musicians. The local bishops felt the Opera House was the only dance facility that was needed and the stake high council concurred, recommending that the "said pavilion be removed and the material in its construction be disposed of."[67]

The demand by the high council that the building be demolished galvanized the position of the musicians, and the pavilion was opened in June 1903 with some 300 couples attending the pavilion dance while, according to the *Salt Lake Tribune,* only twelve couples attended the church-sponsored dance at the Opera House.[68]

Perhaps the stake presidency was surprised at the mass disobedience. Perhaps they were awakened to the fact that they no longer could control the people by the sheer force of edict. Perhaps they received word from their superiors in Salt Lake City that controlling the dancing lives of the citizens of Brigham City was not worth the bad publicity the controversy was generating across the nation. In any event, reconciliation was sought. LDS church leaders withdrew objections to members patronizing the pavilion as long as proper order and conduct were maintained. Christensen and Anderson admitted that church opposition to the pavilion may have been justified.[69] It was an uneasy truce and problems resurfaced shortly after Christiansen built and opened the Box Elder Academy of Music and Dancing in March 1904. A letter published in the *Box Elder Report* placed the blame squarely on Box Elder Stake president Charles Kelly.

> There is ample evidence to show that the men who opposed Kelly in civil and business matters were made to suffer business loss, degradation from church offices, and the loss of standing among their associates. This, be it observed was not for any violation of religious obligations but for . . . daring to start an Academy of Music against Kelly's wishes.[70]

A formal complaint against Kelly was filed and outside LDS church leaders negotiated a new agreement that turned control of both the dance pavilion and Box Elder Academy of Music and Dancing to the stake amusement committee of which the president of the academy's board of directors was made a member. Beneath the façade of cooperation and tranquility, hostility and resentment simmered. [71]

Stake president Charles Kelly came under criticism again in the spring of 1904 for his opposition to the establishment of a municipal electric plant. Kelly held stock in a private power company which he promoted to provide electrical power to Brigham City. Rumors circulated that the stake president threatened supporters of the municipal plant with church action. However, the municipal power plant was established and local church leaders took one more step away from open participation in political affairs.[72]

Peach Days

Brigham City's first Peach Day Celebration was held in September 1904 under the organization of local LDS church leaders and city officials. Fruit displays were set up on the courthouse lawn and other activities were held on the school grounds. The first celebration did not have concessions or a parade, but after the Box Elder Commercial Club was organized in May 1905, these activities were included and the celebration drew visitors from throughout Utah and southern Idaho as the commercial club advertized the event in newspapers and highway billboards and extended special invitations to commercial clubs in other Utah cities. By 1927 the Peach Days parade was held on both Friday and Saturday and had become an elaborate affair with, in addition to the marching bands, twelve different divisions consisting of chamber of commerce, city, county, church, and school officials; the colors, national guard, and fire department; clubs and organizations; schools; businesses; industries; community floats; livestock; decorated automobiles; display automobiles; children's decorated vehicles, bicycles, tricycles, scooters, express wagons, and doll buggies; and children in costume—fairies, elves, clowns, animal representations, and other characters.[73]

Peach Days was both a celebration and a part of the promotion to attract settlers and investors to the county. Local newspapers championed Box Elder's prospects as did the following editorial from the *Box Elder Journal* in 1914.

> There is not a better place in the world to live than in Box Elder county. This is not thought much of by the average citizen of our big county but is strikingly true. . . .
>
> The truth about the county remains the same however and we can boast of being able to produce as great a variety of products as all the rest of the state. Anything in the line of grasses and grains that will grow in a temperate climate is found in the county if it is profitable. In grains we have anything from corn and wheat to barley in the one extreme and Jerusalem corn in the other. We produce all kinds of temperate fruits both pitted and seeded. We have all kinds of root crops, vegetables etc. and one of the growing industries is the growing of fine nuts. English walnuts that are grown in this section are far better than the imported article. They have a firmer and better meat and will compare favorably in size. Young trees that are properly cultivated will bear heavily in a few years and they are also the best to be had for shade. almonds and hazel nuts are also grown here and their uality is also the very best.

> Home seekers from all over the world can find room here for a good home. The climate is good and the schools are the best that can behad anywhere in the world. Truely Utah is a great state and Box Elder is the greatest county in it.[74]

Dams, Canals, Sugar, and Land

In the beginning, agriculture in Box Elder was restricted to the land below the mouths of canyons and adjacent to streams, where water could be diverted and irrigation ditches dug to water gardens, orchards, and crops. The settlers prayed that the snow-pack lasted until harvest, or nearly so, to provide flowing water for the food which was their subsistence.

The next step was to build dams across the streams in the mountain defiles, to preserve the water, and hold it in reservoirs, so it would last throughout the season. On land that could not be irrigated, dry farming was undertaken.

Dry farming proved successful and Box Elder County became the largest wheat-producing area of the state. Cattle and sheep herds fed, grew, and multiplied over the hundreds of square miles of grazing land within the county. A number of large ranches grew up in Box Elder County, besides the grand operation of Alexander Toponce and John Kerr. One of the earliest was that of Central Pacific Railroad magnate Charles Crocker. The old Crocker ranch utilized sections of land granted to the Central Pacific as a perquisite of construction of the Transcontinental Railroad. The Crocker ranch house was a landmark in Promontory valley. The names of other large land and livestock operations are familiar to Box Elder County old-timers. The Rose Ranch, the Promontory Ranch, the Adams Ranch, the Browning Ranch, and the Lindsay Land and Livestock Company.[75] In recent years, the sheep operations of D. H. Adams and the legendary Nick Chournos, and the presennt-day sheep empire of Malcolm Young and his sons are an integral part of the agricultural life of Box Elder county.

Dry farming depends upon the moisture trapped in the soil during the winter. If there is enough water in the soil-layer, seeds planted in the spring will germinate and grow. Later-season growth and ripening depends upon the moisture which falls during the summer.

This earth-filled coffer dam on the Bear River was built east of the Cache–Box Elder County line in 1889–1890. (Box Elder County)

In Box Elder County the chief dry-farm crop has always been wheat. Abraham Hunsaker reportedly raised the first crop of dry farm grain in the vicinity of Honeyville in 1863. The harvest yielded between 300–400 bushels of wheat.[76]

There were hundreds of acres of fertile soil which could be planted, if water could be brought to them. The Bear River had plenty of water, and under the leadership of Alexander Toponce and others, the water was brought to once inaccessible areas of the Bear River Valley.

Alexander Toponce was born in Belfort, France, in 1839. He came to America with his family when he was seven. Three years later he ran away from an unhappy home, and by age fifteen he headed West as a bull wacker and stage coach driver. In 1858, at age eighteen, he reached Utah with Johnstons Army as an assistant wagon boss.[77]

Toponce remained in the West in the freighting business, and in 1863 he made a trip from Virginia City to Salt Lake City and noted that Call's Fort in Box Elder County "was the first house we had seen since leaving Virginia City. It was just a cabin or two surrounded by a stone wall. Brigham City was only a 'string town' settlement, very slow going, with one store." He noted, however, that "There were some settlers on Three Mile Creek. At Willard we found the liveliest town north of Salt Lake City."[78] The enterprising Toponce bought produce in Utah and sold it to the miners in Montana. He developed many friendships in Utah, including Porter Rockwell, Brigham Young, and Lorenzo Snow.[79]

After 1869 he became a leading citizen of Corinne, serving as mayor for a time and engaging in a number of financial ventures including land and water development. According to Toponce, "In 1873, Sam Howe, George Butterball, Dr. J. W. Graham and myself took out a canal on the west side of the Malad River about sixteen miles up from Corinne. We brought out the canal both for irrigation and power purposes. It took about a year to build it down to Corinne."[80] The earthen dam was two hundred feet long, ninety feet thick at the base, twenty feet across at the top, and thirty-one feet high while the canal was fifteen feet wide, six feet deep and ten and a half miles long.[81]

Another businessman, John W. Kerr, purchased land in Bear River Canyon that included a prospective dam site. Kerr made surveys and attempted construction of a dam and canal but, at first, met with little success. Then he became involved with Alexander Toponce. According to Toponce:

> John W. Kerr had gone to California in 1881 and bought a lot of sheep that he trailed across Nevada to Utah. He had part of these sheep left and he wanted to come in on this land deal. So I let him in on the ground floor and he put in his sheep into a company . . . we purchased more land back on the hills to the north and west at from forty-seven to fifty cents an acre, until we had a total of 90,000 acres. We had all the railroad land on both sides of about twelve miles of track. . . . [We] formed a joint stock company, known as the Corinne Mill, Canal and Stock Company, with 120,000 shares of stock of the par value of $5 each. We put in the 90,000 [acres], Kerr's sheep, my grist mill at Corinne [operated by water power from the canal], with the canal and water power; also my ranch above Garland and the live stock on the ranch.[82]

Toponce was a fair-minded businessman, and in his "contract with the [railroad] company, I had agreed to treat the settlers the same as the railroad company had agreed in their pamphlet."[83] His mistake was in allowing Mr. Kerr to be president of the company. According to Toponce :

> We began to make some money. The mill was running and doing well. A few settlers were coming to Bear River Valley and buying our best land at good prices. We had herds of sheep and cattle and plenty of pasture for them, and we were able to make our payments on the land and pay interest. At one time we had 5,000 head of cattle and 26,00 sheep; also, about 1,000 horses and mules.
>
> I had to go once a year down to San Francisco to settle up with the railroad company on our contract and when I went down in 1886, I took my wife with me. She was taken ill, and we stayed there for some time.
>
> While I was gone the president of the company, my good old partner, John W. Kerr, called a meeting, notwithstanding that Mr. Spencer, who had gone to Chicago, and I were both absent. The two Fowlers and Kerr, as directors, constituted a majority of the board.
>
> They passed a resolution selling the stock in the treasury, 19,983 shares, to John W. Kerr at 10 cents a share, and the stock was at once issued to him and he paid $1,998.30 into the treasury. That fixed that. We had been offered one dollar a share for the stock.
>
> Then they voted to levy an assessment of one dollar a share on the outstanding stock, 120,000 shares, which was allowable under our by-laws.
>
> The train I returned to Corinne on, got in about 5 o'clock in the afternoon. The first man I saw when I stopped off the train said, "Come over here, Alex."
>
> Then he showed me a notice tacked up on the station house to the effect that my stock in the Corinne Mill, Canal and Stock Company would be sold the next day at 12 o'clock noon, to pay this delinquent assessment and that was the first I had heard of any assessment.
>
> I talked with my wife and she decided to remain in Corinne, but I got back on the train and went on to Ogden and then down to Salt Lake to raise $50,000, to pay my assessment. By the next morning at 11 o'clock I had the money raised.
>
> I got the money from George A. Lowe, H. S. Eldridge, presi-

> dent of the Deseret National Bank; Samuel Teasdale and others. I then wired Kerr and Fowler not to sell my stock and that the money would be up on the afternoon train, but they went ahead and sold it anyway and that left me without so much as a saddle horse, as everything I had in the shape of livestock, or anything else, was in the company.[84]

Toponce sued for recovery of his stock. The district court decided in his favor. Kerr and partners appealed, and the case ended up in the U.S. Supreme Court. When the verdict was finally rendered in favor of Toponce, both he and the Kerr group were broke: "all I could collect was a bond of $20,000 they had put up in court."[85] Alex Toponce notes that "John W. Kerr took sick about this time; in fact, I think he was a sick man when he put over the deal."[86] Both men were loosers as "much of the company's land was disposed of before either partner was able to realize his anticipated profits."[87]

As Kerr and Toponce fought in the courts, Kerr made arrangements for another irrigation promoter, John R. Bothwell, to come to Utah to construct a canal on the west side of Bear River to irrigate public land.[88]

In Bothwell's favor, Toponce writes that he "was one of the best promoters I ever saw." Bothwell "filed on the water to be diverted from the Bear River where it came through the canyon in the Wasatch range." He then "went to Kerr and got a contract with our company that when he brought out the water, our lands were to be sold and the company was to keep $4 an acre to cover its investment up to date and all received above that amount was to be divided equally between Bothwell and the company." Bothwell's plan was not small in scope. Toponce records that "we went down to Ogden and proposed to buy the city waterworks for a nominal sum. [Bothwell] surveyed a route for a canal down the east side of Bear River to bring the water of the Bear along the foothills to the Ogden River just above Farr's mill."[89]

> After a long and tedious wait, Mr. Bothwell succeeded in interesting the Jarvis and Conklin Mortgage Trust Company in the enterprise. The took hold of the work and proceeded to put the proposition into shape.

> The first act of Jarvis and Conklin was to incorporate a company under the name of the Bear Lake and River Water Works and Irrigation Company, with a capital of $2,100,000.00.[90]

On the evening of 16 August 1888, a cannon was fired at Brigham City to salute the signing of the contract by the contractors. Most of the work was completed by the spring of 1892 at a cost of $2 million.

When the work was completed, Garland was owed $89,550.[91] When he was not paid, he filed a lien on the entire canal system, on 24 December 1890.[92] The reason Garland could not be paid, is that Bothwell, Jarvis, and Conklin, who provided Bothwell with capital, had used the money from the bonds to buy land.[93] Gale Welling writes that there were other difficulties.

"Another problem was that the government land in the valley had been filed on through an Act of Congress of 1820, which allowed the people to purchase the public land, and the Act of Congress of 1862 when the people could homestead the public lands. The land owners refused to buy the water, waiting for the value of the land to raise. Three years after the canal was started not one acre in fifty was being irrigated by the original entry men."[94]

Litigation went on for years, and the canal was managed by a receiver. Finally, the United States Supreme Court ruled in favor of Mr. Garland. The canal system was put up for sale but when no one offered a bid, the U.S. Marshal turned it over to Mr. Garland for the amount of the lien."[95]

Gale Welling explains that "In 1898 Garland sold that part of the canal covered by his lien at public auction to David Evans and John E. Dooley for $250,000. These two formed the Bear River Water Co., with a capital of $250,000. The complete system had cost about $2.25 million. Now the old company was broken into three parts."[96] Evans and Dooley's company owned most of the canal system. The Roweville part of the system (named for William H. Rowe, the receiver during the Garland lien litigation) was owned by the Bear River Irrigation and Ogden Water Work Co.—the company set up to run a canal as far as Ogden, and which purchased the Ogden waterworks. The third was the land owned by the old Corinne Mill Canal and Stock Co. That was the company taken away from Toponce by J. K. Fowler, and owned by him, C. W. Bennett, and the Pitt brothers, whose mother, Toponce believed, pushed Fowler into shutting out Toponce, for the benefit of her sons.[97]

The cofferdam was built in 1889–90, the same years that the Box Elder Tabernacle was being completed. The massive project required fifty-two car loads of giant powder and 500 car loads of cement and employed some 7,000 men for over a year. The dam, completed in 1889, was seventeen and one half feet high, thirty-eight feet wide at the base, and 375 feet along from one abutment to the other.[98] In 1891, two years after completion, the dam developed a leak that required extensive repairs. A.C. True described the developments:

> In laying the foundation, solid rock was found about two-thirds of the distance across the bed, and the mudsills were securely anchored to bedrock. . . . Over the balance of the bed the mudsills were laid on clay, and upon the completion of the dam and the rise of the water in the forebay, it spr[a]ng a leak through the clay underneath the mudsills. This leak was small at first, but soon increased and finally the wh[o]le river, carrying over 20,000 cubic feet per second, passed beneath the crib. The timber crib, being anchored into the rock, remained intact, and when the spring floods subsided a concrete wall 4 feet thick and 15 feet high was built under the dam where the foundation had washed out. This wall rested upon bedrock and was tied into the upper toe of the dam. The balance of the excavation caused by the escaping water was filled with rock. For the past 20 years it had given entire satisfaction.[99]

Legal problems surfaced when farmers along the Bear River in western Cache Valley protested the inundation of land in the vicinity of Cache Junction by waters from the dam. A settlement was reached that set the elevation of water above the dam. "In order to meet this condition the top of the original dam was cut off and a system of steel flash boards was installed, so arranged as to permit the lowering of the dam crest during the flood period. This made it possible to maintain the forebay water surface elevation at the maximum agreed point during the entire year."[100]

The "system of flash boards" was, in reality, the Wheelon col-

The Wheelon Collapsible Dam on the Bear River which could be raised or lowered to control the amount of water stored. (Box Elder County)

lapsible dam. J. C. Wheelon was hired as engineer for the project. His ingenious Collapsible Dam was issued a patent by the United States Patent Office. Built between 1899 and 1901, by 135 men, the system of collapsible sections was built atop the old cofferdam at a cost of $7,750, to replace the portion removed in the agreement with the Cache Valley land owners.[101]

Water was turned into the canals in 1892. Just as the system was put in operation, the Panic of 1893 hit. The situation was made worse by the purchase of land by Kansas City financiers Samuel Jarvis and Roland Conklin and the ongoing battle between Toponce and Kerr. Money for construction of the system ran out, but bondholders advanced additional funds which were used "on the West Side Canal and on the Corinne Canal, and probably the Central Canal."[102]

Gale Welling explains that "Water rights for only about 14,000 acres were sold during the first two years, and many of the farmers used the water without making payment. In 1894 the canal was reorganized under the name of Bear River Irrigation and Ogden Water Works Company."[103] This company still intended to extend the East Side Canal south to Ogden. It was this company, with W. H. Rowe as president, and $125,000 of new capital from the bondholders, which constructed the Roweville section of the canal.[104]

Land promoters organized companies, outlined projects, and printed attractive brouchures such as one by The Bear River Land, Orchard and Beet Sugar Company which boasted that the canal system:

> Is by far the best and most complete system for irrigation in the United States. It heads in the Bear River Canyon in Cache County, Utah. A dam across the river eighteen feet high, two hundred and seventy-five feet wide and one hundred feet thick, with a splendidly constructed set of steel head-gates prepares the entrance to the Canals. There are two branches of the Canal starting from the dam, viz.: The East Side Canal and the West Side Canal. The west Side Canal was constructed purposely for the irrigation of the land belonging to the Bear River Land, Orchard and Beet Sugar Company and other lands in the Bear River Valley and lying on the West side of Bear River. The East Side Canal is not completed yet, but it was contemplated to furnish water on all the land lying on the East side of Bear River from Collinston Station to Brigham City and thence on to Ogden, a distance of fifty miles on an air line. Both East Side and West Side Canals are models of workmanship, showing the energy and pluck of the capitalists in putting money into them, and the daring and skill of the contractors in completing a work of such magnitude, as they are blasted out of the solid rock for two and a half miles on each side of the river, with between two and three thousand feet of tunnels, beautiful masonry, head-gates of steel and spillways for the safety of the Canal. The finished Canal of ninety miles, supplemented by sixty miles of laterals or side canals, now form a perfect system of water supply to the fertile valley lands. The carrying capacity of the Canal is sufficient to carry ample water during the irrigation season, and which will be almost twice the amount per acre irrigated than any other canal system in America gives.[105]

The Bear River Land, Orchard and Beet Sugar Company, owned by Fowler, Bennett, and the Pitt brothers, was promoted by the Union Pacific, the Oregon Short Line, and the Chicago and North-Western railroads. It was not the only project to be organized and promoted to bring water to the land and people and their money to the valley of Bear River.

Another heavily promoted project was Appledale west of Corinne. Appledale was set up as a model agricultural community, with acres of orchards. The water brought to the land, however, leached the alkali salts to the surface, the trees died, and the project failed. It waited for the Corinne drainage project, spearheaded by Clarence G. Adney, to place miles of drain tiles beneath the land, leach out the salts, and make the land productive again.[106] In 1901 the canal system was purchased by the Utah Sugar Company (which in 1907 became the Utah-Idaho Sugar Company), for a reported $300,000.

In 1904 James T. Hammond, Datus R. Hammond, and Lionel Hammond, construction engineers from Logan, began a project to build a canal on the east side of the Bear River Gorge. The East Side Canal was built from Collinston at the mouth of the gorge to the vicinity of Harper Spring. The East Side Canal, sometimes known as the Hammond Canal, was originally part of the irrigation plans developed by John R. Bothwell, and was surveyed at the same time as the West Side or Bear River Canal. In July 1907 a flume which spanned Happy Hollow, only a short distance north of Collinston, washed out. Several attempts at repair failed, and the canal was of no use that year. That fall the canal went into receivership. The receiver repaired the flume, and the canal was put back into operation. In 1919 the entire canal system was purchased by the Utah-Idaho Sugar Company, and operated by a subsidiary—the Hammond Canal Company. Eventually "the Utah-Idaho Sugar Company sold their power plant to the Utah Power and Light Company, [and] the power company guaranteed to furnish them 900 second feet of water at the intake of the Bear River Canal. That guarantee was backed by an immense body of water in the Bear Lake. Five large pumps, capable of lifting 2,000 second feet of water into a gravity canal connected with the Bear River in Idaho were installed in 1919."[107] In 1998 a total of 64,000 acres were irrigated by the canal system.

Electric Power Development

As irrigation canals were constructed and more and more acres of Box Elder farm land brought under cultivation, another use for the precious Bear River water became apparent—the generation of electrical power. A short time after the Utah Sugar Company acquired the coffer dam, Bear River Canal system company officials negotiated a contract to supply electrical power to the Utah Light and Railway Company at Ogden.

Construction of a hydroelectric power generating plant was begun some distance below the cofferdam. The work was directed by Utah Light and Railway Company engineer R. F. Haywood and J. C. Wheelon, an employee of the Utah Sugar Company for whom the power plant and community were named.

The power plant was built on the east bank of the Bear River, and within ten years the capacity of the plant grew from 2,700 horsepower to 9,500 horsepower in 1912. Primary users were the Utah Sugar Company Factory at Garland and the Utah Light and Railway Company at Ogden. The power plant was acquired by Utah Power and Light Company in 1914. Utah Power and Light initiated an aggressive program to fully utilize the power potential of Bear River at the mouth of the gorge for the generation of electricity. Poles were erected and lines run to Fielding to provide electricity to that community in 1917. Two years later, in 1919, five large pumps with a lifting capacity of 2,000 second feet of water were installed on the Bear River in Idaho to bring water into a gravity canal for power generation.[108]

In the early 1920s Utah Power and Light decided to replace the entire dam and generating system with a new, modern concrete dam and up-to-date generators. The project began with the assessment of Warren Swendsen and G. F. McGonagle in 1923. The project was underway by 1925.[109] The new dam was erected below the old cofferdam and above the old powerplant. A new powerplant was built near the old plant. Two new turbine-driven induction generators were ordered from General Electric. The company was told that there were two other generators, slightly smaller in size, which had been ordered for another project and not used, and were available. Utah Power and Light was given a good discount, and the two generators were shipped and installed in the new Cutler power plant at Wheelon, Utah. Each of the turbines generates 15,000 kilowatts, for a total of

View of Bear River Canyon with the Cutler Power Plant, reservoir, dam, pipeline, surge tank, east and west canals, and the railroad. (Box Elder County)

30,000 kilowatts or 40,200 horsepower. At the time of its completion, Cutler power plant was one of the largest hydroelectric generating plants in the United States. It is still (with the sole exception of the huge U.S. Bureau of Reclamation projects on the Green and Colorado rivers) the largest hydroelectric plant in Utah.[110]

The dam and power plant were named for Thomas R. Cutler, vice president of the Utah-Idaho Sugar Company, even though the project was initiated ten years after UP&L acquired the system from Utah-Idaho Sugar.[111] The Cutler project was one of the first hydroelectric projects built by Utah Power and Light Company. The Grace project (1904), the Oneida plant (1907), and the Bear Lake storage project (1909) were all begun by Telluride Power, which was one of 112 small power companies consolidated into Utah Power and Light Company.[112]

The new Cutler Dam inundated the old cofferdam and rock-cut canals. The East Side and West Side canals were connected to the new dam, and the power company guaranteed to furnish 900 second-feet of water at the intake of the Bear River Canal system.[113]

It is an interesting footnote on Cutler Dam that, though the dam is a hundred feet high, it is now (1999) silted up to within fifteen feet of the top. Years ago a log jammed against the sluice gate at the bottom of the dam. The log was never removed, and the gate rusted shut. It has not been used, and over the years silt from erosion in Cache Valley has all but filled Cutler Reservoir.[114]

Sugar Beets

The climate of Utah was obviously not suited to raise sugar cane, though early Utah pioneers made a useable product in backyard mills and vats from sorghum. Early in Utah's history, an attempt was made to produce sugar from sugar beets. LDS apostle John Taylor was sent to Europe and the British Isles to obtain sugar-processing equipment.[115] Unfortunately, the seller did not impart the secret of the techniques of processing beets into sugar. The sugar factory, which gave the Salt Lake borough of Sugarhouse its name, was a failure.

More than thirty years passed before Arthur Stayner, an LDS convert from England and a horticulturist, became beet sugar's advocate in Utah. After visiting a beet sugar plant in Alvarado, Kansas, Stayner campaigned until he overcame the reluctance of the leaders of the LDS church to invest in another sugar enterprise. The Utah Sugar Company was incorporated on 5 September 1889.[116]

The Utah territorial legislature subsidized the growing of sugar beets, and a contract was let to E. H. Dyer to built a sugar factory in Lehi. Among the major stockholders were Lehi merchants Thomas R. and John C. Cutler.[117]

As the Lehi factory sought larger quantities of beets, several Lehi farmers located on lands in Bear River Valley. It soon became evident that the Bear River beets were of a superior quality in yield and percent of sugar. The emerging interest in sugar beets led to the organization of the Bear River Land, Orchard and Beet Sugar Company in the late 1890s. Sugar beets quickly became a staple of Box Elder's agrarian economy. In 1901 the Bear River Land, Orchard and Beet Sugar Company was acquired by the Utah Sugar Company, and the sugar beet industry in Box Elder County stood on the threshold of even greater possibilities.

According to Leonard J. Arrington, "The Utah Sugar Company purchases of Bear River properties broke the legal impasse which had stymied previous efforts and provided precisely the right catalyst for the valley's development."[118] Utah sugar provided the money to bail out the canal system, a crop for the farmers to grow, and reason for settlers to come, purchase the land, irrigate it, and farm the rich valley of the Bear River. It is only fitting that Thomas R. Cutler's name should grace the dam which stands as a symbol of the miles and miles of irrigated fields in Bear River Valley.

The Utah Sugar Company was able to do what previous promoters and consortia had failed to do. Arrington notes:

> The most significant immediate action of Utah Sugar was the initiation of plans to extend the canal on the east side of Bear River. Although $450,000 had been expended on this canal by the original promoters, it had never been completed to the point of usefulness. Landowners, tho pressed for the completion, agreed to purchase enough water to justify the extension as far south as Willard—a distance of about 30 miles from the Divide. Cost of this construction was estimated at $375,000. Because of the heavy flow, it was proposed that the canal be 6 feet deep and 50 feet wide to a point five miles south of Collinston, 30 feet wide from there to the north boundary of Brigham City, and 20 feet wide from Brigham City to Willard. Completion of the canal would make possible the irrigation of 20,700 acres of land. Utah sugar completed the canal to a point near Collinston in 1902 and let a contract to J. T. Hammond and the Hammond Brothers construction Company in 1903, which completed the canal to Harper Springs ("Call Fort"), immediately north of Brigham City, in 1905. This permitted the irrigation of 8,500 acres.[119]

Expansion continued with the construction of a sixteen-mile branch railroad line by the Oregon Short Line from the main line at Corinne to Garland in 1903. The railroad was used to deliver materials and machinery for construction of the Garland Sugar Factory which was completed later in the year.[120]

The factory cost approximately $500,000 and had a capacity of

The Brigham City Sugar Factory was built in 1916 and operated until 1937. It was demolished in 1944. (Box Elder County)

600 tons a day. Periodic expansions were made until 1966 when the factory could process 2,500 tons of beets a day. Most of the beets were grown in Box Elder County, but some were shipped to Garland from Southern Idaho and Davis County.

Around the factory there developed a company town, to house the workers and serve the needs of the sugar factory. It engulfed the tiny settlement begun in the early 1890s as Mormons moved from elsewhere to new land. According to Arrington,

> The factory was located at Sunset, later Garland, and a site was acquired for a "company town" three-fourths of a mile west of the factory site, just west of the Malad River. In addition to the factory, the company built a hotel and 14 homes and other facilities for its employees. In keeping with the dominant faith of the settlers, Utah Sugar donated to the Garland Ward Ecclesiastical Corporation a block of land in the center of the town for an L.D.S. ward chapel and amusement hall. By 1906 the town had a newspaper (*The Garland Globe*), a mercantile business, a bank, and a post office. By

the 1920's there was a high school, seminary, Carnegie Library, flour mill, and lumber yard.[121]

During World War I, a sugar factory was built in Brigham City by E. H. Dyer company. It had a capacity of 500 tons, and was built at a cost of $425,000—a considerable savings made by using equipment from a cutting at Parker, Idaho.[122] The capacity of the Brigham City plant was soon increased to 650 tons before the end of World War I, and to 900 tons by the early 1920s. Arrington states that:

> During its first campaign 506 growers in the Brigham City district planted 5,613 acres, producing 70,253 tons of beets which were converted into 124,255 bags of sugar. In March 1917 the factory was sold at cost to the Amalgamated Sugar Company, which operated it during the years 1917–1919. The plant was re-acquired by U and I in 1920. The factory reached a peak production of 246,060 bags of sugar in 1923. Owing to Curly Top this dropped to only 57,362 bags in 1924. The factory was inactive in 1926, 1930–1932, and 1934–1936. After a short campaign in 1937, the factory was permanently closed. The factory was dismantled in 1943. At that time its capacity was 1,300 tons.[123]

The Garland factory continued in operation, and farmers in Bear River Valley, using water from the canal system, continued to irrigate land in the Bear River Valley and provide the factory with sugar beets, but times began to change. According to Gale Welling, "The Utah Idaho Sugar co. became aware in the 1960s that the Bear River Canal Company could not operate on the original contracts of one and two dollars per acre and needed more money for maintenance."[124]

In 1973 the rate was raised to $2.73 per acre, in 1974 to $3.17 per acre, in 1975 $4.73, in 1976 $10.89 per acre. At that point "the Bear River Water Users Association was organized. A law suit was started and a court order forced the rates back to the original contract."[125] Then the axe fell. Gale Welling remembers that "In 1979 U & I Sugar announced they were not going to operate the canals for the year of 1980. The Bear River Water Users Association fought this. As a result, Paul Holmgren was named receiver of the canal and the Bear River Water Distribution was organized. After a long tedious battle, they negotiated with U & I Sugar, and the canal was purchased April 10,

1980, for $1,750,000."[126] About that time the sugar industry in Box Elder County came to an abrupt end. The major stockholder of the Utah-Idaho Sugar Company decided that the sugar industry was no longer profitable and the stockholders' money could receive a better return by diversifying.[127]

Box Elder County's Ethnic Groups— The Chinese, Irish, Japanese, Hindus, and Mexicans

The first ethnic group to settle in Box Elder County were Scandinavian converts to the LDS Church who arrived in the 1860s. Although they became integrated with the Mormon community, elements of their heritage persisted through several generations.

The transcontinental railroad brought Chinese and Irish construction workers to Box Elder County. Chinese had crossed the Pacific Ocean to participate in the California gold rush. While many remained in the gold fields, others became residents of San Francisco. Officials of the Central Pacific Railroad Company hired all available Chinese as construction workers on the railroad.

The demand for workers on the Central Pacific required many more laborers than were available in San Francisco, so the railroad advertised in the urban areas of China. When insufficient numbers volunteered, recruiters resorted to what amounted to kidnapping.

Chinese workers did much of the tunneling, culvert-building, grade preparation, and track work on the Central Pacific. Their language, manner of dress, eating habits, and cultural differences did not lead to integration with other workers on the C. P. The Chinese had their own camps, sang their own songs, prepared their own food, played their own games, and in the evenings smoked their opium pipes in their own isolation. After the completion of the railroad, though some stayed operating laundries in Corinne and pursuing other occupations, most returned to their homeland. Even the graves of those who died during construction of the railroad were opened and the bodies returned to the soil of the Celestial Empire for final repose.

Along with the Chinese came the Irish. Many families fled the great "potato famine" in Ireland, and came to the United States. A number of Irish men served in the Civil War, and obtained employment on the Union Pacific Railroad after the war's end. After completion of the railroad, it seems that few if any remained in Box Elder County.

In addition to the Chinese and Irish, there were Mexicans also among the railroad workers. Alexander Toponce recorded that when Leland Stanford missed the last spike, "Irish, Chinese, Mexicans, and everybody yelled with delight."[128] Like other railroad construction workers, the Mexicans did not remain in Box Elder County. They did return after the sugar beet industry began to expand. The initial group was made up of sixty families and more came especially for the sugar beet harvest. A number were victims of the 1918 influenza epidemic, and in 1920 there were 276 Mexicans in Box Elder County.[129]

The workers were first housed in the Sugar Factory Hotel until single-walled, uninsulated houses were built for them near the sugar factory. In addition to work in the sugar factory, Mexican laborers worked in the sugar beet fields of the county, on the railroad tracks, as domestics in the Sugar Factory Hotel and in homes of Garland residents. During the 1920s many moved to Ogden or returned to Mexico. Others returned as migratory workers in the orchards and fields of Box Elder County.

Other agricultural workers were recruited to work in Box Elder County including a group of East Indian Hindus who reached Utah from California and Arizona in the early 1900s. Some acquired farms and remained in the county.[130]

The Japanese were the largest ethnic group to come into Box Elder County just after the turn of the century when jobs were to be had with the railroad or as a result of the coming of the sugar industry. Although those who came "included artisans, merchants, students, professionals, and bankers, almost all Japanese began their life in America by working fields or on railroad section gangs."[131] Most Japanese hoped to earn enough money to return home and buy land and other property to raise the economic status of their families. However, many remained in America and some found a new home in Box Elder County. Others established themselves in Weber and Salt Lake counties.

With good land available in Box Elder County and with the new

Box Elder County Japanese-Americans in a photograph taken 26 February 1926. (Box Elder County)

canal system to provide irrigation water, many Japanese immigrants took up land after making enough money working for others.

They soon became known for their produce, growing "the nationally acclaimed Sweetheart and Jumbo Celery and the Twentieth Century Strawberries." Although most found more freedom in Utah than they had known in Japan, still they were not always accepted on a par with other settlers.

> In 1922 the Cable Act deprived Nisei (second generation Japanese) women who had married Issei (first generation Japanese) of their citizenship. In 1931 as a result of the JACL (Japanese American Citizens' League), the 1922 Cable Act was amended, regaining citizenship for Nisei women. American citizenships were also granted to 700 World War I Veterans.
>
> In 1924 the Japanese Exclusion Act prohibited any Japanese from entering the country, but many of them swam ashore from boats, anchored in harbors or were smuggled across the Canadian and Mexican borders by compatriots.[132]

In Box Elder County the Japanese who had settled and become farmers organized a farmers' association, the "Hoshin-Kai," in 1914. They built a hall in 1916. In 1930s they organized a Japanese language school to teach their children. Even though they had settled in a new land, they retained the old Samurai ideals—"courage and loyalty to one's people, esteem for stylized politeness, courteous treatment of inferiors, and exalted respect for elders. Children were taught through the bushido code that they must do nothing that would cause others to laugh at them, or bring disgrace on their families."[133] They also experienced some of the class distinctions and social restrictions and taboos under which their ancestors had lived for generations.

In 1931 the Japanese community purchased the only structure built on the site of the uncompleted Honeyville sugar factory. The substantial two-story brick building became the Honeyville Buddhist church. As a generation passed and the children (Nisei) grew up attending school with children of neighboring families and speaking English, the wall of prejudice that too often exists between neighbors of different cultures and ethnic groups began to crack.

Prohibition and Gambling

During the 1910s most Box Elder County residents supported the prohibition of alcohol—first locally, then statewide, and finally nationally as provided with the passage of the Eighteenth Amendment to the United States Constitution in 1919. A temperance meeting was held in Tremonton on 22 February 1914. Among the speakers were Milton H. Welling, state representative and president of the Bear River Stake, and LDS apostle David O.McKay. An editorial in the *Box Elder Journal* in 1916 proclaimed, "Let us wake up, elect only men who stand for prohibition. . . . Let Utah arise in might and drive the accursed liquor traffic from our borders. Leu us clear our skirts from paltering politicians, and cunning shysters who betray the public trust."[134]

A local prohibition law was passed by Brigham City and almost immediately bootleggers were arrested for violation of the law. In November 1915 three men were jailed for smuggling whiskey into the city. Four bootleggers were arrested in March 1917 and the ring leader given a five-month jail sentence. Five bootleggers were arrested at Kelton and Lucin.[135] Gambling seemed to go hand-in-glove with the consumption of bootleg alcohol. A raid on the Elberta Club in Brigham City resulted in the arrest of the club president and a $65 fine.[136]

The First World War

On the morning of 28 June 1914, Francis Ferdinand, Archduke of Austria, was assassinated by a Serbian nationalist as he traveled in a motorcade through the city of Sarajevo. That event was the trigger which set of the First World War. After nearly three years of conflict, the United States entered the war in April 1917 as an ally of Great Britain and France. A wave of patriotism washed across the United States and engulfed Utah. It was in World War I that Utah first fielded a significant contingent of United States troops. In sharp contrast to Utah's lack of support of the Civil War and the Spanish American War, 21,000 Utahns served in WWI. It is an indicator of how far Utah had come from its pioneer immigrant beginnings that of that number, only 10 percent were of foreign birth.[137]

It was in WWI that Utah fielded its famous 145th Field Artillery, under the command of Colonel Richard W. Young, with sixty-year-old Brigham Henry Roberts as chaplain. Richard W. Young was not only a son of Brigham Young, he was a graduate of West Point and a veteran of the Spanish American War. According to J. Cecil Alter, "The One Hundred and Forty-fifth Artillery of the American Army was distinctively a Utah organization. It was the particular pride of the people of the state, as it was recruited from the farms and factories, the mines and mills, the stores and shops, from the railways, the ranches, the offices, and the schools, from all trades, occupations and professions, from every valley, village, camp and city throughout the commonwealth."[138]

At the beginning of the war, British-born Brigham H. Roberts, LDS general authority and prodigious author, convinced Utah governor Simon Bamberger to appoint him as chaplain to the First Utah Light Field Artillery which became the 145th Artillery Unit. According to his biographer, "Chaplain Roberts soon demonstrated that he did not care as much for his rank of captain as he did for action. In an intense recruiting campaign he represented the governor's staff up and down the Rocky Mountain Corridor, and soon won the honorary title of major. In his meetings and conversations Roberts motivated hundreds of young men to enlist in the military rather than wait for the draft. To anxious but committed parents Roberts said, 'You send your sons and I will be a father to them.' There were undoubtedly Box Elder County residents in attendance at a patriotic rally in the Ogden Tabernacle on 27 March 1917, when Roberts promised " . . . the fathers and mothers of Utah that if their sons go to the trenches I will go with them.' For a full three minutes the audience cheered."[139]

However B.H. Roberts was past sixty and when the 145th was called up for active duty in September 1917 his name was not included. Roberts contacted Utah senator Reed Smoot and a compromise was reached with army officials. If Roberts served, it would be as a lieutenant, not as a captain, and he would have to pass a series of written and physical tests at the Officers and Chaplains School at Camp Zachary Taylor in Louisville, Kentucky. Apparently some of the requirements thrown in his path, particularly the drop in rank, were meant to discourage him. His biographer, Truman Madsen, notes that "To the chagrin of his family, and perhaps also of the army, Roberts welcomed the appointment on these terms."[140] With a fixed determination to serve with his boys, the old man refused all compromises at the training camp, and passed. When he went to join with his men before embarking for the theater of war,

> he was offered a sedan. He chose instead a spirited horse. He rode most of the morning and as he approached the regiment [which was "on a coastal hike north of Camp Kearney in the California mountains"], he kept out of sight until he was at the head of the column. Then he galloped into view, reining his horse high on its haunches and lifting his hat to sweep the sky in a symbolic gesture that electrified the men. He had made it. Sixteen hundred men, including the officers, broke rank and cheered him. Then the chaplain left his mount, shouldered the standard sixty-pound pack, and joined his men in the hike on equal terms. In the following seven days the regiment hiked 190 miles to Santa Ana, took three days of rest, and then in six days hiked back to camp."[141]

It was in this spirit that boys from Box Elder joined the United States Army and entered the War to End All Wars.

It was not so difficult in Box Elder, where most of the people or their ancestors had come from Scandinavia or the British Isles and the few German or Austrian Americans were a small minority.

The Huchel family felt some of the same prejudice during the First World War, when the German-Americans were subjected to some of the same sort of prejudice and bigotry, though they had come from Germany forty-five years before Sarajevo. About the same time the Japanese came to Box Elder County, in the first years of the twentieth century, a number of families of first- and second-generation German ancestry came from the Midwest and settled along what is known as the Iowa String, between Tremonton and Little Mountain. As a result of the war hysteria which accompanied World War I, with its anti-German prejudice, most of those families were made so unwelcome that they left the area.

World War I was an economic benefit to Box Elder County. The demand for sugar was high, and the Brigham City sugar factory was built during World War I. The potash plant at Kosmo was built during World War I. Canneries were built, and the orchards prospered.[142] The old, abandoned Box Elder Tannery of the Brigham City Mercantile and Manufacturing Association was turned into a National Guard Armory.[143]

The Liberty Bond Drive in Box Elder County brought an outpouring of subscriptions that by 1 November 1917 totaled more than $176,000 with most county residents purchasing $50 bonds, although two individuals purchased bonds worth $2,500 and several others bonds worth $1,000.[144]

Box Elder sugar beet farmers were urged to raise more sugar beets. W.W. Armstrong, federal food administrator for Utah, explained that French soldiers received only 1/5 the amount of sugar that American soldiers received because most the country's 226 beet sugar factories were located in the war zone. Some of the factories had been destroyed and many had been damaged because of the war. In his appeal Armstrong noted that Utah was only one of four states that had fifteen more sugar beet factories but that these factories were operating at only two-thirds capacity because of the shortage of sugar beets. Armstrong concluded: "Will you carefully plan your crops for next season so that you can grow more sugar beets? It is one of the things you can do to help win the war."[145]

Some eighty Box Elder County soldiers were given a grand send off the first week of September 1917. A banquet was held in the Laurel Cafe and Hotel Boothe dining rooms on the evening of Wednesday, 1 September. The next morning at 9:00 A.M. a program was presented in the Box Elder Tabernacle. The soldiers were seated in the choir section. Musical numbers included the congregation singing "America," and several numbers sang by a quartet of soldiers. Among the speakers was Reverend A. G. Frank of the Presbyterian church who "showed how the boys were building their lives in a telling way by giving their lives for us that our civilization might go on and he assured all that our thoughts and prayers were for their safe return to us and more than ever fitted for the duties of life."[146] As the soldiers prepared to entrain for Logan on Sunday morning, 5 September 1917, a "parade was formed at the corner of Main and Forest streets which was led by the police officers. Second in line was the Brigham City Military band, then the fire department, which was followed by several hundred loyal and patriotic men, women and children on foot. . . . During the march to the O. L. & I. depot the band struck up 'The Star Spangled banner' which made the thrills of patriotism pass through the veins of those in the parade as well as those who were not."[147] At the train station "was the saddest scene possibly ever witnessed in the history of Brigham. Mothers clung to their boys and wished them well; wives could hardly stand the departing of their husbands; sweethearts, friends and relatives of the brave sons grasped their hands in the thought that they may never return again."[148]

Two young men did not depart as scheduled. Orville Merrell was delayed with an ulcerated ear, and Orlando Peterson received a severe cut while returning to Brigham City from Bear River where he had gone to visit friends and relatives before his departure. Peterson received the cut when he was riding on a motorcycle with Willis Morgan. The back tire blew out causing the motorcycle to overturn and injure the boys.[149]

Anti-German sentiment was manifest on several occasions. Judge

J.D. Call spoke against German sympathizers and spies who would receive their deserved punishment. He warned that spies were flying across the county to survey resources for the German enemy and admonished county residents that if they did not report any information about the unauthorized flights or other information about pro-German activities they would be considered traitors themselves.[150]

Louis and Earl Bowen, two brothers, enlisted together in Brigham City, although Earl was only seventeen years old at the time. By January 1918 they found themselves in France. Writing to his sister at the end of January Louis reported: "Today I received the box you sent before Christmas. The cake was alright and the nuts were good, but the candy was a little hard. We were not particular, however, bout a little thing like that." Louis went on to explain that "It is hard to write because things you would be interested in might also be of value to the enemy in case such information fell into their hands." He then went on to describe life in the army camp, the French people, their farms, and their railroad cars. Earl admitted that at times he was discouraged, but that he was not sorry he had enlisted, "for I am getting a great experience that will help me in after years." He urged his sister to "not waste anything. . . . Don't even throw away a small potato. People in this country certainly need all you can save at home. There are people in the United States that throw away enough from one meal to keep a family here a week."

Not all of the county's enlistees were able to stay together as did the Bowen brothers. Abraham (Abe)Tracy of Yost ended up as a scout for "L" Company of the 3rd Battalion, 307th Infantry of the 77th Division, which gained notority as the "Lost Battalion," in the Argonne Forest in early October 1918. The company was made up mostly of boys from New York and Tracy recalled that it was hard to tell who the real enemy was—the Germans or the New Yorkers who seemed to have little use for a Mormon cowboy from Box Elder County.[151]

One soldier, Welton Woodland, the son of Mr. and Mrs. John T. Woodland of Willard, was killed during the fighting in the Argonne Forest in October 1917. Five years after his death, his parents received a remarkable letter from a German soldier who had obtained the

Woodland's home address from the New Testament he found among Welton's possessions. Heinrich Sohn, the former German soldier, was one of twelve children and was twenty-five years old when he wrote the following account:

> It was on October 16, 1918. We were lying in the Argonne, in Grande Pre. facing the American troops. In the morning at about 10 o'clock the American division made an attack towards my division and in this battle your dear son fought very bravely.
>
> After the attack had been repelled and the Americans forced to go behind their embankments again, your son dared to come over his embankment again towards us, for what reason was unknown to us. In doing so he came under our gun fire and was killed.
>
> When it was evening and the American troops were back in their former trenches, your dear son was lying dead very close to our lines. Under the protection of the night, I, with a few of my soldiers, crept over to your son to see if he had any food on his person, because we were very much in need of food. In searching your son we found some chocolate, cakes and a piece of white bread and the new testament. What other things he had on him I do not know, as we were searching only for food.
>
> And since I belonged to the Lord Jesus Christ, and am a disciple of Him, I could not leave the testament there to be lost, therefore I took it with me and I found the name and address.[152]

The Flood of 1923

The pioneers had ignored the counsel of Brigham Young and had overgrazed both valleys and mountains. The overgrazing of cattle and sheep changed the face of the Utah landscape. Grass and browse were cropped too close, and spring runoff brought serious erosion. Streams which, in pioneer days, ran along the surface of the land, by the 1920s and 1930s ran in deep channels. More seriously, the mountain summer ranges were stripped of the erosion-resisting vegetation. It happened all over Utah, but in Box Elder County it was felt most disastrously in Willard.

Willard Basin, high up in the Wasatch range, had been overgrazed for years, and was a catastrophe waiting to happen. According to a history of Willard:

Willard after the flood of 1923. (Box Elder County)

> Beginning in the early evening hours of August 13, 1923, a heavy downpour of cloudburst proportions struck Willard and the nearby mountains. This deluge was especially heavy in the hills so that the runoff from the bare hills accumulated in the bottom of the canyon and sent a flood of water down into the settlement, causing great damage to many homes and carrying away many outbuildings. The main highway was made impassable and traffic was diverted to the fields to get around the debris. Several feet of slimy mud was deposited in some homes, and it was weeks before order was restored.[153]

Mrs. Ellen Ward, Willard town treasurer and LDS Relief Society president and wife of Alfred Ward—who had died years earlier—was drowned in the flood that also claimed the life of Mrs. Agnes M. Ward. Three others were hospitalized as a result of the flood. Sylvia Ward, age eleven, was pulled from the flood waters and mud unconscious and taken to the Dee Memorial Hospital in Ogden where she later recovered from the frightful ordeal. The terrible flood began about 8:00 P.M. when a terrific clap of thunder rocked the town. Within minutes, "a loud rumbling noise was heard." When V.M. Graser when outside to investigate, a flash of lightening revealed a wall of water and mud streaming into his house. His family miraculously escaped, although Graser complained of heart problems later in the night. Near the Glasers, Arthur Hanson, his mother, sister, and niece barely escaped with their lives by taking refuge in a nearby tree. One of the women was knocked from the tree by the rush of water, but all were rescued by several neighbors.[154]

The Willard flood caused extensive damage. Homes and barns were demolished, crops were ruined, and at least 300 acres of prime agricultural land were destroyed. The cement highway running through Willard was closed for several weeks while a crew of 250 men used equipment and dynamite to remove tons of rock, mud, trees, and other debris. The town's water supply and electricity were disrupted. A number of horses were drown or had to be shot because of broken legs or backs sustained during the flood. Members of the Utah National Guard were ordered to Willard by Governor Charles Mabey to provide assistance, and thirty Boy Scouts were assigned to burn piles of rubbish. Over $75,000 were raised statewide to aid the communities of Willard and Farmington.

Finally, in the 1930s, the Civilian Conservation Corps built a camp in Willard basin, terraced the mountainsides, built a dike and spillway at the mouth of the canyon, and saved the town below from further flooding.[155] The area was made part of the Cache National Forest and is under U.S. Forest Service supervision.

Earthquakes

On 12 March 1934 Box Elder County suffered a major earthquake—the most recent in a series of tremors that began before recorded history and continued after the settlement after the county. The first recorded report of seismic activity in Box Elder County was made by John D. Gibbs, who along with his wife, Julia Ann Tompkins, and their two boys, settled in Portage in 1868. Gibbs reported a dozen years later that "at about 120 P.M. [Portage] experienced a terrible shaking from earthquakes. There were two shocks, at an interval of three or four minutes, each shock lasting two or three seconds." Gibbs reported no damage; however, the towns folk "rushed out into the streets badly frightened for a little while, but went back to bed on finding their houses were still on their foundation."[156]

Less than five months later, the railroad village of Kelton was shaken by a stronger earthquake which was probably centered in the Hansel Valley Fault. The tremor was accompanied by a rumbling noise and set off a tital wave on the Great Salt Lake which left its mark on the surrounding mud flats.[157]

The residents of Snowville reported an earthquake in late August 1893. The people of the county seemed to have been more knowledgeable about earthquakes for it was reported in the *Deseret News* that the earthquake "passed from west to east, bearing a little North."[158]

There were a number of seismic activities in the county. The *Brigham City Bugler* reported,

> During the past two weeks the people of Corinne have actually felt twenty separate and distinct earthquake shocks. [More] tremors have been felt there than were felt [at any] other place. The town seems to be over the center of some internal disturbance.
>
> But more extraordinary than this is the authentic story that comes from Point Lookout. It seems that last June a great cloudburst and earthquake occurred near there at the same time. Now that region is marked by great fissures in the earth. Some of these cracks are a foot and a half in width. Stones can be dropped into them and they go rattling down to a depth of eighty feet.
>
> Some people attribute the numerous slight shocks recently felt at Corinne, probably ten miles to the south of Point Lookout, to the earth settling back after its upheaval at Point Lookout.[159]

Another quake, perhaps an aftershock to the October quake, occurred on 13 February 1897. The local newspaper chronicled the event:

> At about 6:15 Monday evening occurred the last (so far) of the series of quakes that have been playing hide and seek during the past few months in the bowels of the earth beneath us. This was the jumbo shock of all. In five minutes a lighter one occurred. The first stopped clocks; shook bricks from chimneys and swayed the court house tower so that it caused the town clock bell to strike five times. The walls of houses appeared to sway back and forth several inches. Strong men were so frightened that they turned pale in the face and sick at the stomach. Some of the earth motions seemed to

be directly up and down, but the main vibrations were west to east.[160]

In the 20 February 1897 issue of the *Brigham City Bugler,* the editor offered a note of counsel to local inhabitants. "More earthquake shocks Sunday morning. Well, let 'em shock and let 'em shake; it does no good to either worry or fret over them; that will neither augment nor lessen their force."[161] The report went on to analyze the series of quakes which had shaken a large area of the county over a period of several months:

> A peculiar thing about our own pet earthquakes is that they are almost entirely confined to the valley lying on the north and northeast of Great Salt Lake, the center being near the muddy mouth of Bear River, where it empties into the briny lake. They extend only about twenty or thirty miles. There are nearly always two shocks. A shock that is not considered a light one in Brigham is many times more severe near the river's mouth. A hard one in Brigham is frightful out there. One observer said the land there, during a severe shock, rose and felt like a billowy ocean. Even now slight shocks are felt there almost daily. They have so cracked up the ice in the frozen river that the dislodged cakes have floated out into the lake, leaving the river open.[162]

The earthquake may have been the cause of a mud geyser, believed by its observer Martin Rowher, to be an active volcano. Rowher, a young farmer living on a ranch west of Corinne, recounted his story to a *Brigham City Bugler* reporter in March 1897:

> Three weeks ago he saw a great column of smoke rise up into the heavens. At first he thought it must [be] a sheep camp on fire, as it came right out of the lake, or flat alkali lake lands where nothing grows. Later his wife called his attention to the same occurrence and by closely watching it he found this column of smoke shot high up into the air several times an hour. It was especially active every afternoon. The smoke would first rush up like a great smokestack several hundred feet high; then gradually sink down until it could hardly be seen. Later he could see a mound of earth in the vicinity; one never before seen there. It was undoubtedly cast up by these convulsions of nature. Mr. Rohwer is positively convinced it is an active volcano. From his ranch the position appeared

> to him in the region of the mouth of Bear River, nearly 20 miles almost due west of Brigham. At this time of the year when the snow and mud are so deep he says it would be impossible to reach the scene of this natural wonder.

Another convincing fact is that its location is near where the recent numerous earthquakes were severest. In that vicinity for weeks at a time shocks were felt daily, some of them making the ground rise and fall like a billowy ocean.[163]

By mid-March the tremors had apparently ceased, but an additional report on the "volcano" was printed:

> . . . Martin Rohwer said that since his return to his ranch west of Corinne he has seen no further eruptions. A few days after Mr. Rohwer last beheld the spouter his father was down much nearer the place; within five or six miles. In addition to the big spouter he saw two much smaller eruptions. It will no doubt be several weeks before the mud will be dried up enough to that they can go down to investigate. Mr. Rohwer has no dubiety but that he can find cinders and other marks of eruption.[164]

Other tremors were recorded seven miles north of Bear River City on 5 August 1897, at Promontory on 2 and 3 October 1898 and 9 April 1900, and at Snowville on 11 November 1905.[165]

The next major earthquake of record occurred in the first week of October 1909—"electric lamps hanging by the wire swung to and fro, water in buckets and milk in pans rocked from side to side, while windows rattled and articles on the edge of the table were thrown onto the floor." It was only the first of several shocks. "In about half an hour after the first shock, there came another just as real as the first and having about the same duration. This performance was repeated about midnight again, two quakes being felt by many persons who were awakened and arose from bed." The report concluded: "There were some scared people in Brigham all right, many being unable to sleep for fear there would be something dreadful take place."[166]

The earthquake was felt from Preston, Idaho, to American Fork, Utah. There were high waves on the Great Salt Lake, some "rolling high . . . over the [Lucin Cufoff] structure." During the same seismic incident, it rocked a moving passenger train near Logan. "Passengers on a north bound train when nearing Logan last night [5 October] at the time of the shock felt the shock on the moving train. So strong was it that the engineer brought the train to a standstill until the disturbance had ceased. It was thought that the track was shifting and an examination [of the track] was made."[167]

During this period of seismic activity, chimneys were toppled, clocks and other loose objects were thrown to the floor. During one of the earthquakes in Plymouth, "birds were shaken out of the trees and people were frightened out of their homes." In Brigham City the earthquake was sufficiently strong "to rattle dishes and spill water from wash basins. One lady was so freightened that she ran a couple of blocks to the home of a relative, clad in her night clothes only."[168]

Dr. James E. Talmage, noted professor of geology at the University of Utah and later a member of the LDS church's Quorum of Twelve Apostles, urged the installation of seismographic equipment at the University of Utah to monitor the frequency and size of area earthquakes. Shortly after the installation of the equipment and at the time of the Hansel Valley earthquake, Professor Frederick J. Pack, successor to Talmage at the University of Utah,

> hurried from his home and arrived in time to witness the recording of the last tremor, which began at 8:24 and lasted several minutes. This was the first opportunity anyone at the university has yet had of observing the instrument in action. As the second shock came on, the heavy glass cases in which the seismograph is stationed, shook violently and for a moment the needle threatened to jump from the recording sheet, so wide was its zig-zag path.[169]

Few deaths have occurred as a result of earthquakes in Utah. At least three deaths since 1900 were a result of earthquakes whose epicenters were in Box Elder County. According to a 1934 newspaper account, Rufus Tiner, an employee of the cement plant west of Brigham City, was badly burned when coal dust which had gathered in the rafters of the plant exploded when an earthquake struck on 19 November 1919. Tiner died from the effects of the burns several years later.[170]

All of the earthquakes fade into relative insignificance, however, when the great earthquake of Monday morning, 12 March 1934, shook the county. The 12 March episode was indeed a severe earthquake. The initial shock, at 8:00 A.M., registered 6.6 on the Richter scale. A second shock came three and a quarter hours later, registering 6.1. Aftershocks occurred on 15 March and 6 April. On 15 March two aftershocks, an hour and three-quarters apart, registered 5.1 and 4.8, respectively. The earthquake was felt in Burley, Mackay, Idaho Falls, Paris, and Lava Hot Spring, Idaho, and in Rock Springs and Kemmerer, Wyoming, and as far away as Elko, Nevada.[171]

The *Box Elder News* reported that the shaking lasted a full minute and, "The tremor was distinct and quite severe for this section. The motion of the earth seemed to be from east to west, and was felt in all parts of the city. Many families here were seated at the breakfast table and each person experienced quite a sensation when the dishes began to move about the table, electric light chandeliers began to swing and the windows rattle."[172]

Earl Croft, a trapper who had an old boxcar rigged up as a cabin in the center of the earthquake zone about half-way between Salt Wells and Kosmo, told Reed Bailey, a geology professor at Utah State Agricultural College: "I was in my cabin when the first shock was felt at about 8 o'clock. I ran to the doorway, and was thrown out. From my knees, I watched my car—an old touring car—roll back and forth over the rough ground as the earth rocked. It was impossible to get to my feet." Later in the day Croft, while tending to his traps, experienced an after shock. "I was kneeling on the ground setting a trap, when suddenly I felt another shock. Again I tried to rise, but was thrown violently to the ground. On both sides of me, to the east and west, water spouted out of cracks in the ground. I thought my minutes were numbered; but then, just as suddenly as they started, the shocks ceased, and the water stopped except for bubbling springs which brought black sand to the surface, forming small craters or cones." A sheepherder in the district told Bailey that so violent were the shocks that they threw his horse to the ground.[173]

Known as the Hansel Valley earthquake, it originated near Kosmo, Utah, and was felt as far north as southwestern Montana. It was one of the largest earthquakes to occur in Utah after settlement in 1847.[174]

Windows were broken at the power plant below Cutler Dam and as far away as Magna. The tremors were felt from Boise, Idaho, on the north to Rawlins, Wyoming, on the east, west in Nevada, and as far south as Delta, Utah.[175]

Closer to the county, severe damage occurred on the Utah State Agricultural College Campus in Logan where the Home Economics Building had to be abandoned. Elmer G. Peterson, president of the college, reported that the quake "split the three-story brick economics building from top to bottom. Students already assembled for eight o'clock classes fled to the campus as the chimney fell with a roar." In Preston, Idaho, the high school building was severely damaged.[176] The chimney fell off the school building in Snowville, as also occurred in Kelton, where it was reported that "after the chimney of the building had fallen, school was dismissed and the fire of the building put out."[177] Numerous other buildings were damaged, including the school house in Cove, Cache County.[178]

In Salt Lake City "furnace doors swung open, while water splashed out of Monday morning wash tubs. Late sleepers were awakened as beds were rolled out from walls and frantic house pets scurried for out-of-doors. . . . Dishes were knocked from the pantry walls and stoves jerked off balance until they fell over."[179]

Even the Angel Moroni statute atop the Salt Lake temple was in danger.

> Opinion was divided this afternoon on whether the Angel Moroni, tall golden statue on the topmost spire of the temple, had been tipped and turned slightly on his base. Officials of the Church architect's office seemed to think there had been a slight forward movement in the statue, with a slight twist to the right causing the Angel's trumpet to point a few points south by east. Bishop David A. Smith of the Presiding Bishop's office declared that the statue has not moved, but many people disagreed.[180]

In Ogden a man asleep on a bench in the Union Station "woke up to see the great station chandeliers swaying overhead and the brass cuspidor beside the bench tilting first one way and then the other. He was wide awake in a moment and leaped over the bench with a shout and headed for the door."[181]

Two deaths were attributed to the Hansel Valley quake. Charles Bitthell of Salt Lake City was crushed when a trench in which he was working collapsed. He died several days later. Ida May Venable Atkinson, of Ogden, died of a heart attack.[182]

The earthquake impacted springs and wells and left large fissures. According to the *Box Elder Journal,* "A dry well at Cosmo, drilled fifteen years ago in a vain effort to reach water, became an active flowing well Monday." It was also reported that "The flows of the springs at Locomotive were entirely shut off during the disturbance for about thirty minutes. Coming back slowly, the waters were a brilliant red in color." The *Journal* noted that "In the vicinity of Cosmo and monument, fissures and holes were made in the earth, water gushing from many of them. About forty new springs appeared."[183]

The most visible result of 1934 Hansel Valley earthquake were the fissures. They were "about a half mile apart, run almost parallel over a plateau marking the southwestern tip of Hansel valley, then down onto the alkaline and salt beds and to the shore of the Great Salt Lake. They extend nearly four miles in length."[184] Along the Hansel Valley-Locomotive Springs, the road near Cosmo separated and a two-and-one-half foot fault appeared.[185]

M. T. Shore, Southern Pacific Railroad agent at Kelton, noted at Kosmo "at least 40 gushing wells poured forth on the ground and flooded an area of several hundred feet."[186] In the *Deseret News* professors Pack and Bailey summarized the geologic effects of the quake:

> While 30 separate shocks of short duration shook the vicinity of Locomotive Springs this morning as the ground settled after Monday's slip, the geologists' tabulations showed a total of 50 mud volcanoes created by the tremor, and four huge fault scarps ranging from three-eights of a mile to three-fourths of a mile in length and with a "throw" or face of from 6 to 15 inches in height. The mud volcanoes, some of which were four feet across, with three-foot craters the fissures, the changed stream courses, the once dry pipes now flowing and the flooded flats, were all phenomena found near the center of the quake in the lower end of Hanzel valley 15 miles southeast of Kelton in Box Elder county on the north end of Great Salt Lake.[187]

Box Elder County is the home of a complex fault system, which has shaped the landscape of the county. The land remains seismically active, and many await what is referred to as the coming of "the big one."

Bear River Migratory Bird Reserve

In the early fall of 1843 the county and the area of the present-day Bear River Bay Migratory Bird Refuge was explored by the famous "pathmaker" Captain John C. Frémont. Following the Malad River (which he called the Roseaux or Reed River), Frémont accompanied by Kit Carson, Basil Lajeuaesse, and others explored the Bear River delta. At one of the campsites on the delta, he described the Bear River "bordered with a fringe of willows and canes, among which were interspersed a few plants. . . . The whole area was filled with multitudes of waterfowl, which appeared to be very wild—rising for the space of a mile round about at the sound of a gun, with a noise like distant thunder."[188]

The Bear River delta provided food and fiber for a number of Indians living in the county, Frémont identified them as members of the Digger tribe (Shoshoni). Frémont happened upon several families of Indians who were fishing in the Bear River delta using weirs and nets.

Less than a decade later, another government explorer, Howard Stansbury, reported that the Bear River delta was "covered by immense flocks of wild geese and ducks, among which were many swans." Stansbury was astonished at the number of water fowl. "I had seen large flocks of these birds before in various parts of the country, and especially on the Potomac [River], but never did I behold any thing like the immense numbers congregated together. Thousands of acres, as far as the eye could reach, seemed literally covered with them."[189]

The Bear River delta was highly productive commercially for hunters. Ducks, geese, and other water fowl were hunted prodigiously from the 1880s to the turn of the century. Dressed water fowl supplied local markets as well as markets in Chicago, Kansas City, and San Francisco. Acccording to one report, as many as 335 ducks were killed in one day in 1899 and over 5,600 ducks were killed in one season.[190]

Before being made a federal migratory bird refuge in April 1928, the area was popular for private duck clubs. Three of the important clubs were the Bear River, Duckville, and the Chesapeake. David Moore Lindsay, a renowned outdoorsman at the turn of the century, included a full chapter on duck hunting in the Bear River area in his 1912 book, *Camp Fire Reminiscences or Tales of Hunting and Fishing in Canada and the West.*

Through the efforts of Alexander Wetmore, among others, Congress authorized the Bear River Migratory Bird Refuge in 1928, and plans were developed for land purchases, river control works, road building, and other work associated with the reserve. In 1929 plans were announced to construct a marginal dike around the first three units between the marshes and the lake. The dike would be twelve miles long, five to eight feet high, and 100 feet wide at the base.[191] In September 1932 President Herbert Hoover signed a proclamation declaring the area a refuge and establishing its boundaries.

The high-water cycle that impinged upon so much lake-front property and caused extensive damage to both commercial business holdings and the dikes of the Lucin Cutoff in the mid-1980s all but destroyed the Bear River Bird Refuge. It did destroy the Refuge Headquarters and much of the dike system. At this writing, more than a decade later, the facility has not yet fully recovered.

The Depression and the New Deal

The prosperous 1920s ended abruptly in the great crash of October 1929, and the ensuing Great Depression. Box Elder fared better than many places, because it had an agricultural base. The farmers and orchardists at least had food. They raised potatoes and corn and tomatoes and peas, and had cherries and apricots and peaches and pears and plums to bottle for the winter. There were cows to milk, chickens to provide eggs and meat, and a pig to slaughter for the winter. Everyone had a relative who worked at a cannery, and sugar was made right in town (or in the next town). For those who were not farmers, it was more difficult. My mother recalls that they had little, but they always had food. My father came to Box Elder in 1930. For a dentist, life was not easy. When times get tough economically, he said, one of the first things people stop doing is having their teeth checked. I recall my sister telling me of an especially unpleasant Sunday, when there was little to eat. Her mother said, "Florence, please go next door and see if Sister Anderson will let us have a few carrots out of her garden." The little girl's timid knock and hesitantly asked question brought a quick and stern reply: "We do not dig carrots on the Sabbath." For many families, even in Box Elder, it was aptly named the Great Depression.

In 1928 the Garland factory paid local beet farmers $440,000 for approximately 65,000 tons of sugar beets. However, during the next session of the state legislature, Senator Tracy R. Welling of Box Elder County introducted a memorial to Utah's congregational delegation calling for even higher tariffs on sugar imports from Cuba, Purto Rio, and the Philippines. Senator Reed Smoot had been a longtime supporter of Utah's sugar industry and sought to give Utah sugar beet growers and sugar manufacturers an advantage with higher sugar tariffs that were included in the Smoot-Hawley Tariff passed in May 1930.[192] The sugar industry continued to be a major part of the economy during the Great Depression. In 1936 approximately $350,000 were paid for labor in the sugar beet fields and sugar factories, with an estimated production of 120,000 tons of sugar from 7,200 acres. That amount was about half of the 240,000 tons of sugar beets grown when there were 17,000 acres of sugar beets in production before the Depression began.[193]

The Great Depression brought hard times for the county's wheat growers as well. In 1930 Box Elder County produced its largest crop of wheat, one million bushels, but farmers received only 63 cents a bushel compared with as much as $1.10 a bushel in 1929 before the Depression began. Because of the low price, farmers opted to store much of the wheat in hopes that the price would increase.[194]

Responses to the economic difficulties included a closer watch on transients in the area, "Hard Times Parties," and an enthusiastic response to Franklin D. Roosevelt when he arrived in Brigham City on Sunday afternoon, 18 September during his 1932 presidential campaign. According to the Bear Valley Leader, the Roosevelt campaign train "made a brief stop at Ogden and Brigham City, where thousands had gathered to see and hear him." After brief remarks during which Roosevelt "smiled his famous smile when he told the

Brighamites that he too, was a peach grower in New York state but had made no money in that industry industry the past few years."[195] After Roosevelt's comments, the Peach Days Queen and her attendants presented Roosevelt with five cases of fresh peaches much to the delight of Roosevelt and the rest of his entourage. The train continued on to Ogden then Salt Lake City where Roosevelt spoke for forty-five minutes in the Salt Lake tabernacle. On the eve of the election, the *Box Elder Daily Journal* carried a front-page article that Mormon church president Heber J. Grant would vote for Republicans Herbert Hoover and Reed Smoot.[196] However, Utah and Box Elder County Republicans were disappointed when state and county voters chose Democratic candidates. In Box Elder County Franklin Roosevelt won over Herbert Hoover, 3,604 votes to 3,086, while Republican senator Reed Smoot, who had been a thirty-year supporter of Utah's sugar industry, lost to Elbert Thomas by 3,594 votes to 3,187. The only Republican winner in the county was Albert E. Holmgren who was elected to the Utah State Senate, defeating Tracy R. Welling by 3,474 votes to 3,240.[197]

The New Deal programs that followed the 1932 election had considerable impact in the county. Under the social security program, the county received federal funds for the benefit of the needy, old people, blind, and dependent children. Under the Bankhead Act passed in 1936, families received assistance to purchase farms. Under the Works Progress Administration and the Public Works Administration, new water systems were installed, a county jail constructed, and new roads built.[198] The most popular and best known of all the New Deal Programs was the Civilian Conservation Corps, or CCC, which hired young men to work on a wide variety of badly needed construction and conservation projects in the forests and on range land throughout the county. The men were housed in camps that were usually under the administration of the army, while the eight-hour work day was under the supervision of forest service personnel or other public land administrators. The CCC personal did everything from building roads, trails, fences, cattle guards, comfort stations, and telephone lines to developing duck marshes, laying water pipe lines, fighting forest and range fires, and undertaking erosion and flood control measures.

CCC enrollees arrived in Box Elder County from several states, including Kansas, Arkansas, Missouri, and Mississippi. Local residents sought to make them welcome. At Tremonton, Company 736 received visits from the local Lions Club which provided a banquet, entertainment, and speaker on "The Places and Resources of Utah." The Bear River High School Band and individual performers entertained at the camp. A local Mormon bishop and clergy from the Methodist church provided Sunday services, while on Mothers Day 1940 the Bear River High School cheerleaders presented a special Mother's Day program for the young men. At an open house in April 1940, several hundred people visited the camp. The highlight of the day was the evening dance "in which many prominent people from the northern part of the state were present. Plenty of girls were present from the nearby communities and due to its success, more dances will be held in the future."[199]

The CCC boys worked eight hours a day and had plenty of time in the evening for educational and recreational activities. A first-aid class was mandatory. Elementary and high school classes were offered in the camp to those who had not completed their schooling. In addition, evening classes were offered at Bear River High School in bookkeeping, typewriting, shorthand, and elementary applied art. Auto and tractor mechanics instruction were also offered along with other classes. The camp fielded a basketball team which played practice games against local LDS ward teams before competing against other CCC camps, including Kemmerer, Wyoming and Rupert, Idaho. The baseball team also competed against other CCC camp teams and played in the Box Elder Farm Bureau championship. In 1939 the six-man football team lost only one game in competition. Individual sports included swimming and boxing. The CCC boys also participated in community service projects. In cooperation with the Odd Fellows Lodge at Tremonton, members of the camp repaired and painted a truckload of Christmas toys for distribution to the needy children in the area.[200]

While the Civilian Conservation Corps continued is work in Box Elder County, the threat of war loomed near and with the Japanese attack on Pearl Harbor on 7 December 1941 the CCC members realized they would likely exchange their secure and carefree days in Utah for the uncertainties of military service and the dangers of war.

ENDNOTES

1. The bell remained in the court house tower. When the great front addition was built in 1909, and the old tower removed, the bell was lowered into the attic, and wedged among the beams. There it remained until 1995, when the 1909 roof finally needed replacing. During the work, the old bell was "discovered" (it had been seen by the present writer over twenty years before) and removed through an opening cut in the roof. It was then placed in a frame and became a county treasure during the centennial of the statehood celebration, and was finally returned to Corinne, there to repose in a museum.

2. James R. Clark, ed., *Messages of the First Presidency* (Salt Lake City: Bookcraft, 1970), 4:84–85, 216–18. For a biography of Reed Smoot, see Milton R. Merrill, *Reed Smoot: Apostle in Politics* (Logan: Utah State University Press, 1990). For Senator Smoot's journals, see Harvard S. Heath, ed., *In the World: The Diaries of Reed Smoot* (Salt Lake City: Signature Books in association with Smith Research Associates, 1997). For the U.S. Senate hearings concerning the seating of Senator Smoot, see *U.S. Senate Document N° 486* (the entire document contains 3,427 pages). See also Thomas G. Alexander, *Mormonism in Transition: A History of the Latter-day Saints, 1890–1930* (Urbana: University of Illinois Press, 1986), 60–73.

3. Besides the 1904 and 1910 "Manifestos," Joseph F. Smith issued an anti-polygamy statement on 31 January 1914. See Clark, *Messages of the First Presidency*, 4:301. Heber J. Grant found it necessary to issue condemnations of plural marriage in April 1921, 1925, 1926, 1933; see Clark, *Messages of the First Presidency*, 5:195–98, 242, 249, 292–303, 316–30. This last statement, the most strongly worded of all, was written by a lawyer, J. Reuben Clark, and seemed to settle the matter for those within the church.

4. And they continue to flourish. Despite disagreements between fundamentalist leaders, leading to schisms and factionalization, those who adhere to the "old religion" continue to grow and prosper. It was stated by LDS general authority Hartman Rector, Jr., in 1971, that at that time there were 40,000 "Fundamentalists" in the Salt Lake Valley alone, according to LDS historian Reuel M. Jones. In 1998 Utah once again received national attention because of the ongoing practice of polygamy—stemming from an incident in Box Elder county—and the role government should play in dealing with practicing polygamists.

5. One of the first "manifestos" of the fundamentalist movement was B. Harvey Allred's *A Leaf in Review* (Caldwell, ID: The Caxton Printers, Ltd.,

1933). For doctrinal diatribes against the Fundamentalist movement, see Clair L. Wyatt, "... *Some that Trouble You* ... ": *Subcultures in Mormonism* (Salt Lake City: Bookcraft, 1974); J. Max Anderson, *The Polygamy Story: Fiction and Fact* (Salt Lake City: Publishers Press, 1979); and Brian C. Hales and J. Max Anderson, *The Priesthood of Modern Polygamy: An L. D. S. Perspective* (Salt Lake City: Northwest Publishing Inc., 1992). For historical and doctrinal discussion of the Fundamentalist movement, see Martha Sonntag Bradley, *Kidnapped from That Land: The Government Raids on the Short Creek Polygamists* (Salt Lake City: University of Utah Press, 1993).

6. The story of Bishop Koyle's mine was published by Koyle disciple Norman C. Pierce, and more recently by well-known Mormon fundamentalist Ogden Kraut: *John H. Koyle's Relief Mine* (Salt Lake City: Pioneer Press, 1990). It was in response to Bishop Koyle's revelations that the LDS First Presidency issued an official statement on the subject on 2 August 1913. See Clark, *Messages of the First Presidency*, 4:284–86.

7. I had an interesting conversation with Glen M. Bennion, a stake patriarch who had been, he said, the stake president who had to threaten with church discipline the chief advocate of the mine, and tell him to stop standing up in testimony meeting and preaching about his mine.

8. According to one source, "During the Panic of 1893 and its aftermath, his eastern loan brokering and public subscriptions maintained the solvency of his church and many Utah businesses as well." Ronald W. Walker says it this way: "No doubt the panic could have been worse. Fortunately, Utah and Mormonism at the time had the good services of the young businessman and churchman Heber J. Grant. Grant, who almost thirty years later would succeed to the Mormon presidency, was able to get eastern banks to renew much of the local debt during the worst of the panic. His efforts were instrumental in keeping the two primary Mormon banks, Zion's and the State Bank of Utah, from collapse. Had they gone under, the floodgates would have been opened wide. For Utah the panic of 1893 was not simply another financial panic to be briefly endured and weathered. It left deep scars and brought profound results. The rest of the nation could speak of the 'Gay Nineties,' but the aftermath of the panic in Utah brought a depression that lasted most of the decade. These hard times, as well as Grant's eastern loans, also suggested something new about Utah itself. No longer regionally self-sufficient as per the Mormon pioneer dream, Utah was now very much a party of the national financial structure and at peril to its cycles and development." Ronald W. Walker, "The Panic of 1893," in Allan Kent Powell, ed., *Utah History Encyclopedia* (Salt Lake City: University of Utah Press, 1994), 414.

9. Box Elder County Clerk's office Book S of Abstracts, p. 476 (7 August 1928). The "Temple Lot," identified as such, is described in records in the

Box Elder County Clerk's office, Book K of Abstracts, p. 465. In Book 6 of Deeds, p. 92, the description of the parcel is given: "Com. At a pt. 640 ft E & 33 ft S of NW cor of said SW^4 of said sec [section 19, Tp. 9 N, R 1 W]—thence rung E 686 ft,—S 625 ft—W 722 ft, N 6° E, 318 ft—N 318 ft (in several subsequent entries this number is given as 308 ft) to pt of begng. Contg 10 acres."

10. Alexander, *Mormonism in Transition,* 13. See also Thomas G. Alexander, *Things in Heaven and Earth: The Life and Times of Wilford Woodruff, a Mormon Prophet* (Salt Lake City: Signature Books, 1991), 320–21.

11. Oscar King Davis, "The Lucin Cut-Off: A Remarkable Feat of Engineering across the Great Salt Lake On Embankment and Trestle," *Century* Magazine, Jan. 1906, 460. I am indebted to my friend Fred Cannon for a copy of the article. Mr. Cannon is the president of Cannon Structures, the company that is presently (1998) dismantling the trestle.

12. Ward J. Roylance, *Utah: A Guide to the State, Revised and Enlarged* (Salt Lake City: Utah Arts Council, 1982), 298.

13. Davis, "The Lucin Cut-Off," 463.

14. Lydia Walker Forsgren, ed., *History of Box Elder County* (Brigham City: Daughters of Utah Pioneers, 1937), 34.

15. "Trestlewood: High Quality Douglas Fir & Redwood Materials," brochure of Cannon Structures. According to Cannon's calculations, "The trestle contains approximately 30 million board feet of Douglas Fir material (10 million BF in timbers and 20 million BF in piling) as well as about 2 million BF of Redwood material."

16. Davis, "The Lucin Cut-Off," 465.

17. Ibid.

18. Ibid.

19. Ibid., 466.

20. Ibid., 465.

21. Ibid. 468.

22. "S. P. To Abandon Promontory Railroad Line," *Tremonton Leader,* 25 June 1942. According to a 8 May 1942 article in the *Box Elder Journal,* "A report has been received by the commissioners from George M. Mason, county attorney, to the effect that in his opinion there is little hope for the saving of the old railroad line from abandonment by the Southern Pacific. Mr. Mason attended the hearings in Salt Lake City last week relative to the tearing up of the rails. He pointed out that in the past the army has opposed the abandonment of this line which passes around the north end of Great Salt lake, but now, they insist that the rails are needed badly to build a side track for army use." Ultimately, the rails went to the navy.

23. See David H. Mann, "The Undriving of the Golden Spike," *Utah Historical Quarterly* 37 (Winter 1969): 124–34.

24. Local legend has it that when Thiokol Chemical Corporation chose its site eight miles east of Promontory Summit, and just across the road from the old grain-loading siding at Lampo, in the early 1950s, it was using old maps, which showed the railroad still running along the border of the parcel Thiokol purchased. See Frederick M. Huchel, "Ribbed with Iron, Crowned in Gold," delivered on the floor of the Utah House of Representatives, 22 Jan. 1996.

25. Forsgren, *History of Box Elder County,* 140–41.

26. Ezra C. Knowlton, *History of Highway Development in Utah* (Salt Lake City: Utah State Department of Highways, 1967), 67–68.

27. Forsgren, *History of Box Elder County,* 141.

28. Ibid., 142.

29. Ibid.

30. Ibid.

31. Ibid.

32. It is ironic that, as of this writing, Rocky Ford remains intact, as the only solid-bottom crossing for miles in either direction on the Malad. Within feet, however, of the ford, is a huge concrete structure carrying Interstate 15 high above the level of the river. The greater irony is that, within the past year, the old bridge over Bear River at Hampton's ford has been demolished. The highway has been re-routed over a new bridge some distance to the south. Now, at Hampton's Ford, the only to cross the river is by the old, gravel-bottom ford.

33. Forsgren, *History of Box Elder County,* 147–48.

34. Forsgren, *History of Box Elder County,* 142; and Knowlton, *History of Highway Development in Utah,* 153.

35. Knowlton, *History of Highway Development in Utah,* 163.

36. Ibid., 201, 291.

37. Ibid., 156.

38. Forsgren, *History of Box Elder County,* 143.

39. Ezra C. Knowlton, *History of Highway Development in Utah,* 270.

40. The settlement was not named Willard until 1859.

41. Forsgren, *History of Box Elder County,* 206.

42. Ibid.

43. Ibid.

44. Ibid.

45. Ibid., 206–208.

46. Ibid., 208.

47. See Richard C. Roberts and Richard W. Sadler, *A History of Weber County* (Salt Lake City: Utah State Historical Society, 1997), 224, 228.

48. Forsgren, *History of Box Elder County,* 210.

49. Ibid., 212.

50. Until construction of the Whittier School building, Brigham City's first actual school building, the Second Ward School was held in the old Rosenbaum Hall, located on Main Street, just south the corner of First South. When Alma Compton built his photogrpahic studio and store in the 1890s, it stood between Rosenbaum Hall and the intersection. When Rosenbaum hall was demolished, it was replaced by the Fishburn Store, and then eventually by the Roxy Theatre. When the Roxy was demolished in the early 1980s to build a Smith's Food King store, one remaining wall of the old Rosenbaum Hall was discovered, against the wall of the Compton building. A vestige of Rosenbaum Hall survived for over a hundred years, hidden between two newer buildings. At this writing, even the Compton Building has fallen, to provide space for a bank and a newer grocery superstore.

51. Charles H. Skidmore, B. L. M. A., Superintendent of Schools, Administration and *Supervision in the Box Elder School District* (Brigham City: Board of Education, 1921), p. 71. The author is grateful to Lewis H. Jones, Jr., for lending him an original copy of this rare historical treasure.

52. Ibid., 72.

53. Forsgren, *History of Box Elder County,* 214.

54. Skidmore, *Box Elder School District,* 85.

55. Forsgren, *History of Box Elder County,* 215.

56. Skidmore, *Box Elder School District,* 84.

57. The old rock structure is the only one of the original "ward" schools still standing at this writing, on the block south and east of the Tabernacle.

58. Author's interview with Mary Andersen Huchel, whose memory of this first-grade experience was long-lasting.

59. Skidmore, *Box Elder School District,* 77.

60. Ibid., 77-78.

61. Ibid., 84-85.

62. Though the Central School building burned to the ground in a spectacular fire (probably Brigham City's largest conflagration) in the summer of 1947, and was replaced by a one-level, post-war facility.

63. Abigail Omerza, "Brigham City, Utah, at the Turn of the Century: A Community in Transition," M. A. Thesis, Arizona State University, 1998, 74.

64. "Church Crisis at Brigham City Due to a Dance," *Salt Lake Tribune* 22 June 1903.

65. "Brigham City First Ward Relief Society Minutes," 5 May 1903, cited in Omerza, "Brigham City, Utah, at the Turn of the Century," 76.

66. Ibid.

67. "The Pavilion Question," *Box Elder News* 25 June 1903, cited in Omerza, "Brigham City, Utah, at the Turn of the Century,." 76

68. "Church Crisis," *Salt Lake Tribune,* 22 June 1903, 1, cited in Omerza, "Brigham City, Utah, at the Turn of the Century," 76–77.

69. "Harmony is Restored," *Box Elder News,* 6 August 1903, 1, cited in Omerza, "Brigham City, Utah, at the Turn of the Century," 77.

70. "Brigham City Trouble," *Box Elder Report,* 23 April 1904, cited in Omerza, "Brigham City, Utah, at the Turn of the Century," 78.

71. Omerza, "Brigham City, Utah, at the Turn of the Century," 78–79.

72. "A Remarkable Statement," *Box Elder News,* 17 March 1904.

73. "History of Brigham's Peach Day Festival," *The Box Elder Journal,* 1 September 1927.

74. *The Box Elder Journal,* 8 October 1914.

75. On the LL&L Co., see Clyde W. Lindsay, *Daddy Lindsay: Highlights in the Colorful Career of a Man with a Vision* (Oakland, Calif.: The Claremont Press, 1954). I am indebted to Steven G. Lindsay for a copy of this rare and valuable book.

76. Forsgren, *History of Box Elder County,* 56. For a biography of Abraham Hunsaker, one of Box Elder's prominent pioneers, see Andrew Jenson, *Latter-day Saints' Biographical Encyclopedia,* 3:415–16.

77. Alexander Toponce, *Reminiscences of Alexander Toponce* (Norman: University of Oklahoma Press, 1971) (first ed. published 1923), 3. Toponce's *Reminiscences* are well worth reading, and provide a charming, candid first-hand look at early Box Elder County.

78. Ibid., 48.

79. Ibid., 115–119, 67–68, 211–13.

80. Ibid., 157

81. Gale Welling, *Fielding: The People and the Events that Affected Their Lives* (Fielding: Gale Welling, n.d.), 70.

82. Toponce, *Reminiscences,* 185–86.

83. Ibid., 186.

84. Ibid., 187–88.

85. Ibid., 188.

86. Ibid., 189. Toponce notes that "Kerr and I, by our fighting, knocked ourselves out of a half million each" (189). He states that "he was the last man on earth that I thought would go back on me. I had the utmost confi-

dence in him" (190). He blamed Kerr's duplicity on the influence of others, especially J. K. Fowler.

87. Leonard J. Arrington, *Beet Sugar in the West* (Seattle: University of Washington Press, 1966), 42.

88. Forsgren, *History of Box Elder County,* 327; and Toponce, *Reminiscences,* 189.

89. Toponce, *Reminiscences,* 189.

90. Forsgren, *History of Box Elder County,* 327. Alvin Hess found that Jarvis and Conklin secured additional money from "Irish Capitalists in Ireland." See Welling, *Fielding,* 76. Leonard Arrington adds that the bonds, "underwritten by Jarvis-Conklin, were purchased by Quaker societies on Glasgow, Scotland; Newcastle, Ireland; and Birmingham England." See Arrington, *Beet Sugar in the West,* 43.

91. Welling, *Fielding,* 72.

92. Warren G. Swendsen and G. F. McGonagle, "Retrospective Appraisal of the Bear River Canal System as of and when Acquired by the Utah-Idaho Sugar Company, July 18th, 1907," 5. Typescript dated 1 October 1923. Copy in my possession; I am indebted to Frank Nishiguchi, director of the Bear River Water Conservancy District, for furnishing the report. McGonagle started out as a construction engineer for the Southern Pacific. Swendsen was a civil engineer, and an expert on the Bear River drainage. He had worked for the Telluride Power Company, which built the first long-distance AC transmission lines in the country. The Telluride Power Company is described by Swendsen as "predecessors in interest of the Utah Power & Light Company" (affidavit at the beginning of the Swendsen and McGonagle study). He was also involved in construction of the historically fascinating Last Chance Canal farther up on the Bear River near Soda Springs. See Max R. McCarthy, *The Last Chance Canal Company,* Charles Redd Monographs in Western History No. 16 (Provo: Charles Redd Center For Western Studies, Brigham Young University, 1987).

93. Welling, *Fielding,* 73.

94. Ibid., 74–75.

95. Forsgren, *History of Box Elder County,* 328. There is some controversy over the amount that Garland received. Forsgren gives the amount as $21,000. A 1928 study by Alvin Hess gives the figure as $125,000, and Swendsen and McGonagle give "$120,000, or the amount of his judgment plus interest." Having paid his own lien, Garland kept the canal for a year, and then, according to Forsgren, sold it to two Salt Lake City businessmen for $75.000. According to Swendsen and McGonagle, on the same date that Garland paid the lien and took possession, he "conveyed the property, including water rights, storage reservoir, filings, etc., to the Bear river Water

Company for $120,000.00." See Swendsen and McGonagle, "Retrospective Appraisal of the Bear River Canal System," 5.

96. Welling, *Fielding,* 77.

97. Toponce, *Reminiscences,* 189–90.

98. Swendsen and McGonagle, "Appraisal of the Bear River Canal System," 17.

99. A. C. True, *Bulletin No. 249,* U.S. Department of Agriculture, quoted in Swendsen and McGonagle, "Appraisal of the Bear River Canal System," 17.

100. Swendsen and McGonagle, "Appraisal of the Bear River Canal System," 18–19.

101. Welling, *Fielding,* 84–85.

102. Ibid., 72.

103. Ibid., 75

104. Ibid., 75.

105. Bear River Land, Orchard and Beet Sugar Company, Utah brochure. I am indebted to Eugene Bigler for a copy of the brochure.

106. Interview with Bernice Gibbs Anderson, 1966.

107. Forsgren, *History of Box Elder County,* 329, notes that "Thus far, the system has been constructed on the Bothwell plan, which also included a survey through Brigham City and beyond to Ogden." See also Toponce, *Reminiscences,* 189. This plan was revisited in the early 1990s when the ill-conceived "Honeyville Dam" project was under consideration. Bringing water to the foothills between Brigham City and Ogden was finally brought to pass with construction of the high-line canal from Pineview Reservoir in Huntsville, north to Brigham City. According to Utah Power and Light Hydrologic Supervisor Carly Burton, the agreement is to furnish 900 second-feet of water during the summer season—1 May to 31 October—and 250 second feet from 1 November to 30 April. Carly Burton, Hydrological Supervisor, Utah Power and Light Company (now PacificCorp), interviewed by Frederick Huchel, 1 April 1998.

108. Welling, *Fielding,* 88.

109. Interviews with Wesley Andersen who worked on the construction of Cutler Dam.

110. Carly Burton Interview.

111. Cutler had worked his way up from manager of the first successful sugar plant in the Mountain West, at Lehi, Utah, according to Arrington. See Arrington, *Beet Sugar in the West,* 44–45.

112. Carly Burton Interview.

113. Welling, *Fielding,* 88.

114. Carly Burton Interview.

115. Arrington, *Beet Sugar in the West,* 5.

116. Ibid., 6.

117. Ibid., 8–9. John C. Cutler later became governor of Utah. See Noble Warrum, *Utah Since Statehood* (Chicago & Salt Lake: The S. J. Clarke Publishing Company, 1919), 1:135–36.

118. Arrington, *Beet Sugar in the West,* 46.

119. Ibid., 47.

120. Ibid. The branch line went north from Corinne, with sidings at Dumona (just north of Corinne), Holmgren (west of the south end of Bear River City), Evans (west of the north end of Bear River City), and then turning east at Garland, and south at the sugar factory. West of Deweyville there was a siding at Haws, another at Lamb east of Elwood, almost directly west of the Madsen siding on the main OSL line north from Brigham City (Madsen was near Crystal hot springs), and Bradford west of the site of the projected sugar factory west of Honeyville. The Honeyville factory was never completed. One building was built, and machinery and supplied hauled to the site, but the project was abandoned. The building is now the Honeyville Buddhist church. (Information on the Honeyville comes from my interview with Veloy Boothe of Brigham City, whose father worked for the canal company.)

121. Ibid., 48.

122. Ibid. The Parker plant was located six miles from the main sugar factory at Sugar City, near Rexburg, Idaho. According to Arrington, "This was operated only a short time (until 1913) because of the extremely cold weather in that section."

123. Ibid., 190. The year the factory was dismantled, 1943, was the same year the old Promontory branch of the Central Pacific line was dismantled, during the scrap iron campaign waged during the height of World War II.

124. Welling, *Fielding,* 81.

125. Ibid.

126. Ibid.

127. I remember a discussion at that time with one of the principals of the Bear River Water Distribution Company. He had raised sugar beets all his life. His remarks at that time were nearly as follows: "I have raised sugar beets all my life. Every time there was an experimental project, I let them use my land to try it out. We worked to eliminate disease, and to raise a weed-free crop. Just this past year, I was *finally* able to raise a weed-free, disease-free, perfect crop of sugar beets. Then, with a stroke of his pen, N. Eldon Tanner killed the sugar beet industry in Utah. I probably know more about

raising sugar beets than any other man alive. And what the hell good does it do me now?"

128. Toponce, *Reminiscences,* 150.

129. Vicenta Singh, notes on Mexican settlement in Box Elder County. I am indebted to Mrs. Singh for assembling this material. See particularly the *Garland Globe,* 6 December 1913; *Box Elder News,* 22 January 1914. Vicenta Singh cites family reminiscences of the Sunder Singh family, especially Petra Moreno Singh and Maria Moreno Cervantes.

130. Vicenta Singh, notes on Mexican settlement in Box Elder County. Mrs. Singh cites information "Told to the Sunder Singh family by their father, Herman Singh and Hernan 'Baga' Singh."

131. "History of Japanese Life in Utah," in the Box Elder Japanese Reunion Planning Committee 1990 publication, *1990 Japanese American Reunion.* Copy provided to me by Frank Nishiguchi.

132. "History of Japanese Life in Utah."

133. Ibid.

134. *Box Elder Journal,* 13 April 1916.

135. *Ibid.,* 18 November 1915 and 8 March 1917.

136. Ibid., 19 February 1914.

137. Allan Kent Powell, "World War I and Utah," in Powell, *Utah History Encyclopedia,* 644.

138. Alter, *Utah: The Storied Domain,* 1:56.

139. Truman G. Madsen, *Defender of the Faith: The B. H. Roberts Story* (Salt Lake City: Bookcraft, 1980), 301–2.

140. Ibid., 302.

141. Ibid., 307.

142. My mother recalls contracts her father had with Eastern interests for his peaches. The children would pick, then carefully wrap each peach, and pack it for shipment on the railroad to be sold in the Eastern United States.

143. I recall as a child exploring, as children do, interesting abandoned buildings, the old Tannery, and seeing remnants of the military equipment remaining from the days of WWI.

144. *Box Elder Journal,* 1 November 1917.

145. Ibid., 4 January 1918.

146. Ibid., 9 September 1917.

147. Ibid.

148. Ibid.

149. Ibid.

150. Ibid., 9 September 1917.

151. Merlin Abe Tracy, "World's Great War Young Man from Yost: Abraham (Abe) Tracy," unpublished manuscript prepared by the son of Abraham Tracy.

152. *The Box Elder Journal,* 13 October 1923.

153. Hannah B. Nicholas, comp., *Willard Centennial, 1851–1951: A Brief History of the Past One Hundred Years* (Willard: Willard Centennial Committee, 1951), 27.

154. *Box Elder Journal,* 16 August 1923.

155. Merlene T. Braegger, "Willard," 1992 typescript in my possession, 4.

156. *Deseret News,* 19 July 1880.

157. Ibid.

158. *Deseret News,* 12 September 1893.

159. *Brigham City Bugler,* 17 October 1896.

160. Ibid., 13 February 1897.

161. Ibid., 6 March 1897.

162. Ibid., 20 February 1897.

163. Ibid., 6 March 1897.

164. *Brigham City Bugler,* 27 March 1897. Mr. Rohwer told an *Ogden Standard Examiner* reporter that, "There is a man in Penrose at the present time who can also verify my story." He declared the man to be William Miller. "He also saw the columns of smoke rising to the heavens from the center of the lake" (*Ogden Standard Examiner,* 25 March 1934). Seismologists discount the possibility of a volcano in the area, since no evidence exists, nor is the area known for volcanic action. Another possibility, however, presents itself. In that same area, near the mouth of Bear River, in the flats, eruptions of methane have been known to occur. Several of the duck-hunting clubs heated their buildings from "gas wells" for years. Within my own memory, one of the gas wells erupted, and the Bird Refuge road had to be closed for days while tons and tons of concrete were pumped into the ground to stop the spurting of flammable gas into the air. (See also *Deseret News,* 23 March 1934.) The *Ogden Standard Examiner* of 25 March 1934 reports the following: "Recent happenings near the headquarters of the Bear river migratory bird refuge indicate that what Mr. Rohwer saw in the distance coming from the lake may have been a mud geyser. In August 1931, while drilling for water at the refuge headquarters gas was struck by the drillers, which time and time again blew tons of mud and water high into the air. In fact, the well had to be abandoned. Pictures of the geyser, throwing mud 75 feet into the air, are on file at the refuge headquarters in

Brigham City. It seems possible that the quakes of 1897 opened up scarps in the lake bed, gas came up through the cracks and blew black mud high into the air, which furnished the basis of the scene beheld by Mr. Rohwer from Connor Springs."

165. *Brigham City Bugler,* 7 August 1897; *Salt Lake Tribune,* 23 March 1934; *Box Elder News,* 7 October 1909.

166. *Box Elder News,* 7 October 1909.

167. *Deseret News,* 6 October 1909, and *Salt Lake Herald-Republican,* 6 October 1909.

168. *The Journal* (Logan, Utah), 7 October 1909; *Deseret News,* 19 November 1909.

169. *Salt Lake Herald-Republican,* 6 October 1909.

170. *Ogden Standard Examiner,* 28 March 1934.

171. *Salt Lake Tribune,* 13 March 1934.

172. *Box Elder News,* 13 March 1934.

173. *Box Elder Journal,* 16 March 1934.

174. Walter J. Arabasz, et al., *Earthquake Studies in Utah, 1860 to 1938* (Salt Lake City: Department of Geology and Geophysics, University of Utah, 1979), 37.

175. *Box Elder Journal,* 13 and 15 March 1934.

176. *Box Elder Journal,* 13 March 1934. The Preston High School, "formerly Oneida stake academy revealed the intensity of the shock more than any other building [in Preston]. Several top stones were shaken loose and fell to the lawn below, weakening the roof structure of the building and allowing a slip of the main rod braces." Even so, the venerable old academy building stands, firm and strong, as of this writing.

177. *Box Elder Journal,* 15 March 1934.

178. *Deseret News,* 17 March 1934. A report in the *Deseret News* of 22 March 22, however disputed the earlier report. "Levi H. Allen, former county commissioner, representing a group of Cove residents, moved today to squelch reports that were made by Supt. J. W. Kirkbride and Building Inspector H. R. Adams of Hyrum, that the local school is unsafe. He claims that the 'cracks' have been in the building for years, even before an addition was built some time ago."

179. *Deseret News,* 12 March 1934.

180. *Ibid.*

181. *Ogden Standard Examiner,* 12 March 1934.

182. *Box Elder Journal,* 15 March 1934; *Salt Lake* Tribune, 14 March 1934; and *Deseret News,* 12 March 1934.

183. *Box Elder Journal,* 14 March 1934; *Deseret News,* 13 March 1934. Cosmo is also spelled Kosmo.

184. *Box Elder Journal,* 16 March 1934.

185. Ibid., 14 March 1934

186. *Ogden Standard Examiner,* 14 March 1934.

187. *Deseret News,* 14 March 1934.

188. John C. Frémont, *Narratives of Exploration and Adventure,* ed. Allan Nevins (New York: Longmans, Green & Co., 1956), 240.

189. Howard Stansbury, *Exploration and Survey of the Valley of the Great Salt Lake of Utah* (Philadelphia:), 100.

190. William H. Behle, *The Bird Life of Great Salt Lake* (Salt Lake City: University of Utah Press, 1958), 165.

191. *Bear River Leader,* 17 January 1929.

192. Ibid., 15 November 1928 and 24 January 1929.

193. Ibid., 17 September 1936.

194. Ibid., 10 July 1930.

195. *The Box Elder Daily Journal,* 22 September 1932.

196. Ibid., 4 November 1932.

197. Ibid., 9 November 1932.

198. *Bear River Valley Leader,* 11 July 1935, 1 October 1936, 14 October 1937, 25 August 1938, 29 December 1938, and 21 November 1940.

199. Ibid., 11 April 1940.

200. Ibid., 3 August, 1933, 12 October, 1939, 30 November 1939, 14 December, 1939, 4 January 1940, 18 January 1940, 4 February 1940, 21 March 1940, 11 April 1940, 9 May 1940, 12 September 1940, 14 November 1940, 25 December 1940, 9 January 1941, and 13 February 1941.

CHAPTER 11

BOX ELDER COUNTY IN THE LAST HALF OF THE TWENTIETH CENTURY

Box Elder entered a new era with the outbreak of World War II in 1941. The war impacted Box Elder County, in many ways, far more than it did most other Utah counties. The aftermath of the war left changes that were felt throughout the remainder of the twentieth century.

War broke across Asia and Europe at the end of the 1930s, and after the attack by Imperial Japan on the American navy at Pearl Harbor on 7 December 1941, the United States was again at war.

As with World War I, World War II brought financial benefits along with community challenges, new experiences, and, for some, great family and personal tragedy. This chapter will examine the impact of World War II on Box Elder County and look at other major developments in the last fifty years.

Bushnell Hospital

The first and largest war-spawned installation in Box Elder was the construction of an army hospital at the south end of Brigham City. As early as December 1941, local newspapers reported that

Brigham City, along with other towns in Utah and Idaho, was being considered for a military hospital. When the announcement was made of Brigham City's selection, it was the banner story in the local newspaper: "The greatest boon this city will probably ever experience is in the immediate offing, it may be safely predicted, for construction on a 1500-bed U.S. Army hospital will start here in the future, it was learned from a strictly reliable source in Washington, D.C., last night by the *News Journal*."[1] The editor of the newspaper, speaking for the progressive interests in town, sought to anticipate any opposition to the project by "Referring to citizen protest against the proposed location of Utah State Agricultural College in Brigham City 50 years earlier." At that time, "a few ultra-conservative people felt that such a move was too progressive."[2] The fears of a half century before at bringing students and professors from outside Box Elder County to interact with the citizens of Brigham City had been dampened by the passing of time and the success of the Agricultural College as an institution, and its economic benefits to Logan and Cache Valley. Later that same month, the United States War Department announced the acquisition of 235 acres of land located east of Main Street and south of 700 South.

Construction of Bushnell General Hospital began on 1 March 1942, and the first patients were admitted on 10 October 1942. When completed, the facility boasted sixty buildings and was equipped to handle 3,000 patients with neurosurgical and neuropsychiatric disorders.

The facility "was named in honor of the late colonel George E. Bushnell, who was commissioned in the Medical Corps U.S. Army, February 1881, and served until his retirement from the service in 1919. Colonel Bushnell was in internationally known specialist in tuberculosis. He died in 1924."[3] When the hospital went into operation, Colonel Robert M. Hardaway, a career army medical officer, was appointed commanding officer.

As the war casualties mounted, specialized units were established in the military hospitals. Bushnell Hospital became the West Coast center for plastic and maxillofacial surgery, neurosurgical, amputation center, penicillin therapy, neuropsychiatric center, and malaria therapy and investigation. Bushnell Hospital also served as a general hospital for soldiers from the states of Utah, Idaho, Montana, Nevada, and Arizona in meeting the army's objective to place wounded soldiers in hospitals as close to their homes as possible.

Though Bushnell was known as the hospital for amputees and psychiatric cases, "there was a large variety of number of cases with fractures and deformities involving the bones and joints. To care for these, a full time staff operated a 'brace' shop where metal appliances were fashioned to aid in function and locomotion."[4] Harry Truman, who became president of the United States after the death of Franklin D. Roosevelt in April 1945, visited Bushnell Hospital while still a United States senator from Missouri and was much impressed with the effectiveness of artificial limbs for the amputees.

Vocational therapy and recreation were important aspects of the treatment programs. Classes were offered in such areas as photography, metal and needle work, and car repairs. Film stars and other celebrities performed for the patients and made bedside visits. Outings were offered, with fishing trips being the most popular. At Snow Basin, in nearby Ogden Canyon, amputees were even taught to ski. The curbs at Brigham City's downtown intersections were fitted with wooden ramps to accommodate wheelchairs. The Idle Isle Restaurant in Brigham City offered amputees a free steak dinner the first time they walked into the restaurant using a new artificial leg. The Peace City Apartments and Bushnell Motel, across the street from the hospital, were erected to house family and other visitors to the hospital. Local residents also took in workers and visitors. Verabell Call Knudson remembered:

> Everybody did whatever they could to help get Bushnell completed. In our home across the street from the Central School, we had a little apartment. It was a duplex and everybody had to open their homes to the influx of people that came—even when they were building the place. I used to get up at five o'clock in the morning and go down and open up the store [Idle Isle Restaurant] in order to feed the workmen breakfast and then put up their lunches. We used to put up about a hundred-and-some-odd lunches every morning at the store. . . .
>
> Living in our home we had a couple of engineers and I thnk we had two girls also, so everybody that was used to sleeping in a

bed by themselves had to double up in order to give sleeping accommodations to someone else.[5]

Once patients arrived at Bushnell Hospital, the housing shortage became even more critical as family and loved ones came to visit the patients. Verabell Knudson recalled one occasion when she took a family member to Ogden at 5:00 A.M. to catch a train for San Francisco. At the Ogden station was a couple with a small child who were headed for Bushnell Hospital.

> They had a blanket over them, and he'd thrown the blanket back and he only had one leg. I said, "Are you going to see someone?" He said, "I'm a patient." They were going to amputate part of his leg and get him a new leg. He said, "We came in, and there was no way until in the morning that we could get up to Bushnell." Then there was a bus or something that was going to take them.
>
> I said, "If you want to go back to Brigham with me, I'll take you back as soon as this train leaves." So I put them in the car, and I said, "Have you got a place to stay?" He said, "Yes, they know I'm coming. I imagine that my wife and baby here can find a place to stay." I said, "I don't think there's an empty bed in Brigham City." He said, "Oh, you're kidding!" I said, "No, I'm not kidding."
>
> So when we got to Brigham—the Red Cross had a place that was in the remodeled Academy. They had put beds there for people to stay. I called the Red Cross and said, "I've got a young wife and her baby and this patient of the hospital I brought up from Ogden. What am I going to do with them?"
>
> "Well" they said, "that's your bad luck. You brought them. Now you take care of them." I said, "I can't take care of any more people. The house is full."
>
> Whoever I was talking to said, "Well, we're full. I don't know of a bed in Brigham that's vacant, and you brought them to Brigham. Now it's your responsibility."
>
> I thought, "Well, there's Dorothy's bed that she had just vacated." So I took them down to the house. I put them to bed, the three of them, in Dorothy and Marjorie's bed. Then I went back to work. . . . Dick and his wife were here for nearly two years, and they lived with us. . . . Every home was the same way.[6]

Bushnell hospital brought other things to Brigham City besides buildings, patients, and jobs. A number of young, single, school teachers in Brigham City chose husbands among the young men who came to town in some way connected with the hospital. Perhaps the first people of African-American lineage came to Brigham City in conjunction with the hospital where they worked primarily as domestic help for high-level hospital staff. During the early months of the hospital, before housing was built in the section of town near the facility, the people of Brigham City were asked to open their homes and rent rooms to doctors and other hospital staff. Kathleen Bradford writes,

> From the outset of its construction, Bushnell Hospital affected Brigham City's economy and lifestyle. Local carpenters and painters were hired to work on the project. Proprietors of a local restaurant were commissioned to cook breakfast and prepare sack lunches for more than a hundred construction workers each morning. Townspeople were asked to house the influx of hospital personnel, construction engineers, and laborers in spare rooms in their homes. . . . local residents were hired to work in such areas as the kitchen, bakery, and laundry as well as in maintenance and clerical positions.[7]

Margaret Atwood Herbert, a native of Pleasant Grove in Utah County, came to Brigham City in September 1944 to work at Bushnell Hospital. She recalled her work at the hospital.

> Every morning I would go on ward rounds with the doctor and take progress notes. After I finished transcribing my notes, one of the jobs that I was assigned was to write letters and talk with the soldiers. I had this one friend who was a quadro-amputee. He was a football player from the Seattle area, and here he was at Bushnell with no arms or legs. The psychological damage it did to him was a big problem. They were also so young.
>
> Not only was I a secretary, but I also felt like I was kind of like a psychologist, too, without any training. I just had my own gut feeling on things. I mostly just listened and gave patients the feeling that people cared and that their lives would go on in spite of their ordeals.[8]

A little-known facet of Bushnell's operation was a "prisoner of war camp" near the hospital "for German and Italian prisoners of war, some of whom were taken to work in the hospital under the close supervision of hospital personnel."[9] Margaret Atwood Herbert recalled the work and the flirting of German prisoners of war at Bushnell Hospital.

> They did the cleaning of the wards, the ramps, the hallways, and windows. Many of them worked in the mess halls. As we would walk up and down the ramps, they would always have things to say to us in their native tongue—flirting with you or whatever. They always wanted us to write our names down so they could call us by our names. The one phrase, "*Ich liebe dich,*" (I love you) in German was a common phrase they would say to us. Our instructions regarding the prisoners were that we were not to fraternize at all. I remember them washing the windows. They'd get on the outside of the window and you'd be typing and they'd be pounding on the window and waving. I can't really be angry at those guys because I thought they were victims of their situation as much as our guys were victims of their situation.[10]

German prisoners of war and American soldiers did become friends. Paul Hupfner, one of the prisoners, disclosed that one of the American soldiers insisted that Hupfner accompany him into Brigham City and even loaned him a spare American uniform to wear. Hupfner also became good friends with Frank Woods, who had lost his legs in the Pacific theater. Hupfner recalled that whenever Woods needed something, he called for his German friend, and that Woods told the German "that he loved me like a brother."[11]

German prisoners also worked for farmers in the county. A prisoner of war camp was located in Tremonton from June to December 1945 at the county fairgrounds in barracks that had been used by the Civilian Conservation Corps. The initial arrangement was for 300 prisoners of war to work from 15 May to 10 July 1945 to thin and hoe sugar beets, and pick cherries, but local farmers were so pleased with the prisoner labor that the number was increased to 440 and two extensions were made keeping the prisoners in Tremonton until 10 December 1945.[12]

As the war wound down, so did the business of Bushnell Hospital. Colonel Hardaway left, and Robert D. Smith, a medical doctor from Phoenix, Arizona, took over command for the remaining months. In the nearly four years of the hospital's operation, some 13,000 patients were served.

The Borgstrom Family

World War II brought national fame to the Alben Borgstrom family of Thatcher. Five sons enlisted in the armed services, four of whom were killed in action during the war. All four died within a six-month period between March and September 1944.[13] Clyde, the second oldest, was one of the first of the young men to join the military service after the war began, served more than three years before he was killed on 17 March 1944 on Guadalcanal in the Pacific. Le Roy, the oldest son, was killed in Italy on 22 June 1944. Twins Rolon and Rulon had joined the service together at age eighteen. Rolon went to gunnery school and became a tail gunner flying out of England. He died in England in August 1944 of injuries received in action. His twin Rulon was reported missing in action in France the next month—September 1944. He was confirmed dead a few weeks later. Rulon, an excellent marksman and boxer, had won the middleweight boxing championship of his outfit and the expert rifleman medal.

Following the death of their fourth son, the Borgstroms requested that their last son, Boyd, who had served in the Marine Corps for three and a half years including a year and a half in the Pacific, be released. The request was granted and led the Secretary of War, Henry Stimson, to announce a new policy that the sole surviving son of any family which had lost two or more sons in action would be exempted from combat duty.

The Borgstroms were featured on a nationwide radio broadcast Sunday evening 19 November 1944 which was part of the launching of the Sixth War Loan drive. Initially it was planned to make the broadcast from the Borgstoms home in Thatcher but when radio and telephone officials determined it was too far to run the special lines to their home the broadcast was made from the home of their friends Mr. and Mrs. K. H. Fridal in Tremonton.

Condolences and expressions of sympathy came from around the country. F. O. Haymond of the Bingham and Garfield Railway

Company in Magna, Utah sent a framed copy of a letter from Abraham Lincoln to a widow, Mrs. Bixby, who had lost five sons during the Civil War. The letter had hung in Haymond's office for many years. President Franklin Roosevelt also wrote to the Borgtroms on 11 October 1944:

> I have been told recently that you are listed in the records of the War and Navy Departments as the parents of Rulon J. Borgstrom, LeRoy E. Borgstrom, Rolon D. Borgstrom all of the Army of the United States, and Clyde E. Borgstrom and Boyd C. Borgstrom of the United States Marine Corps. I am distressed to learn that of these young men, three, LeRoy, Rolon, and Clyde, have died while in our armed forces.
>
> I cannot forbear to extend to you this assurance of my deepest sympathy in your loss. Their manner of passing, however, is something for which you can justly be proud and I know it had served to increase the determination of all of us to bring this war to an early and successful conclusion.
>
> I have been informed further that your son, Rulon, has been reported as missing in action. It is my earnest hope that he will be found soon in good health and that the worry which you are now sustaining in his behalf will be happily ended.
>
> As the parents of such men who have so ardently participated and contributed in service to their country, you stand as an inspiration to the parents of all soldiers and marines.
>
> Very sincerely yours,
>
> Franklin D. Roosevelt.[14]

Japanese Americans in Box Elder County During World War II

World War II impacted the lives of every Box Elder County resident, but for Japanese Americans living in the area, the war brought a unique set of problems and issues that were thrust to the forefront on 7 December 1941, a day, in the words of Franklin D. Roosevelt, "that would live in infamy"—the day the Japanese attacked the American naval base at Pearl Harbor in the Hawaiian Islands.

The Japanese who had made America their home, and their Nisei children, "were stunned by the bombing of Pearl Harbor."[15] These were people who had been in the United States for forty years or

Jim Tazoi receiving the Distinguished Service Cross for his heroism during World War II. (Box Elder County)

more. Their children knew little of Japan except the cultural elements they had been taught by their parents and grandparents.

But war brings fear; fear is the mother of bigotry, and bigotry breeds hatred. There were many in the United States who could not differentiate between soldiers of the Empire of the Rising Sun and their own American neighbors. They could not see past ethnic physical characteristics. It was a difficult time for the Japanese and their Nisei children and their Sansei grandchildren and their Yonsei great-grandchildren. In the hysteria of war, anyone of Japanese heritage or descent was suspect.

Japanese and Americans of Japanese descent were relocated from the Pacific Coast for fear that they would open a door for invasion of the United States from the Pacific Ocean. Ten internment camps, such as the Topaz Camp in Millard County, Utah, were hastily built to house 110,000 Japanese Americans from California and the Pacific Northwest. In many cases the internees were given only a few days to dispose of their property and prepare for evacuation. Those who were not interned "were to find inland locations to settle themselves. Men left their families and traveled to Mountain states, hoping for help from relatives and friends."[16] A number of the evacuees from the West Coast came to find shelter among their friends and relatives in Box Elder County. The Honeyville Buddhist church building was turned over to housing as many as could be accommodated.

It was a time of contradictions. A number of Nisei Box Elder Japanese Americans served in the war, on the side of the United States of America. Shoji Watanabe, for example, spent part of his military service at the end of the war interviewing Japanese prisoners of war, many of whom were high-ranking officers in the Japanese military. He interviewed them in broken Japanese, because he only learned the language after he enlisted in the war.[17]

Jim Tazoi, of Garland, was a member of the Nisei 442nd Regimental Combat Team.[18] It was the 442nd which rescued the "Lost Battalion" near Biffontaine, France, in October 1944.[19] PFC Tazoi received several wounds, and saved his comrades going beyond his assigned duty as a radioman during the action. He was one of fifty-two Nisei who, in the course of the work, "[were] awarded the nation's second highest military honor, the 'Distinguished Service Cross.'"[20] Private Wynn K. Jensen, another Box Elder County soldier, was a member of the "Lost Battalion" rescued by the 442nd.[21] It has been said that the war was shortened by perhaps two years because of the work of the 442nd and the Nisei who served in the United States armed forces. They were able to translate Japanese documents, interrogate prisoners, and—on the Pacific Islands—talk the Japanese soldiers holed up in caves into surrendering.

While PFC Tazoi and his Nisei comrades were fighting in France for the United States of America against the Empire of the Rising Sun, prejudice and bigotry were building in Bear River Valley. On 4 April 1944, the *Box Elder News-Journal* carried account of a meeting of "approximately 40 men at a meeting at the Bear River high school."[22] At the meeting two resolutions were presented, "the first of which urged the retention of all cultivated lands in the hands of native white Americans until the return of our men from the armed services, and the second of which urged land brokers not to handle deals for land contemplating Japanese ownership."[23] This was not a wildcat group of angry farmers. The newspaper reports that "The meeting had been called to hear the report of a committee on

Japanese land ownership in the valley which had been named at a meeting sponsored by a group representing the Tremonton Junior Chamber of Commerce two weeks previously."[24] There were apparently fears that either the Japanese Americans in Bear River Valley would buy up lands for their friends and relatives who had been evacuated from the Pacific Coast, or that the evacuees would come and buy up land in the valley. The reasons given at the meeting may have seemed reasonable at that time and place, but fifty years later, they sound like the machinations of thinly veiled bigotry. According to the article,

> Speakers before the group were Kleon and Clifton Kerr and James Walton. They emphasized the idea that racial hatred was rising at home and among the men at the front due to efforts of war propaganda groups, and that the only practical way to avoid conflict here was to see that no new Japanese were present in the valley as owners of property.[25]

The article continues its account of the meeting, and the rationale given for the resolutions:

> Efforts of a similar committee in Davis county were frequently referred to as an example of what must be done. There, not only are further Japanese land purchased being prevented, but such strong pressure is being brought to bear that Japanese are steadily disposing of title to any lands whatever, such holding now being well under 200 acres in the whole county, according to the report.
>
> The speakers freely protested that they themselves bore no ill will toward the Japanese here but left a clear impression that any ownership of land by them would be calculated to arouse violence. . . . The problem of a permanent organization to carry on the work of "education" the object of which, according to one speaker, was to "put the fear of the Lord into both groups—the prospective buyers and sellers of land"—was met by turning the responsibility back to the Junior Chamber officers. They will act as a central group to stimulate and coordinate the work of those who will be enlisted to take it up in the separate localities.[26]

It was a time of war, a time of fear, a time of rising bigotry and hatred, and the meeting at Bear River High School was not an isolated incident. Headlines from Box Elder County newspapers of the period proclaimed: "Lt Wardrop, who was at Pearl Harbor, Believes Japs Should Be Sent Back to Japan," and "Farm Group To Oppose Any Jap Land Deal: Corinne Farm Bureau Against Sale of Land to Jap Evacuees."[27] At a meeting of the Corinne Farm Bureau, "A lengthy discussion was carried on regarding the sale or lease of land to the Japanese. It was pointed out that Americans pioneered this valley and made it what it is today and that farmers wish to keep that heritage for their boys when they return from the war fronts." It was resolved that selling or leasing land in Box Elder County to Japanese evacuees was "unpatriotic and out of keeping with the community spirit." The thinly veiled threats of the Garland meeting were openly expressed in Corinne: "To those Japanese residents already established here it was stated that if they wished to retain the respect and friendship of the community it would be to their interest to refrain from buying any land for their countrymen who might wish to locate here."[28]

At the same time, other headlines announced that evacuees were being brought from relocation centers to help in the fields of Box Elder. The idea was welcomed with open arms. One headline read, "40 Japanese Imported for Crop Harvest: Will First Assist With Bean Picking; Later Other Crops." The article went on to indicate that extension and employment officials were delighted to have the much needed workers to ease the local labor shortage.[29] The war was on, the reasoning went, and our sons are gone to war, and how will we take care of our crops without them? Here is a ready supply of Japanese (in reality most were American citizens, not Japanese nationals) evacuees, living in relocation centers. Why not use them in our fields? They were not allowed to buy their own fields to work in, but they were welcomed to work in the fields of others. Even in the Corinne Farm Bureau meeting, just after the threats, was this sentiment: "The farmers present voted to accept new Japanese laborers as a patriotic duty and under supervision with the understanding that when the present war emergency is over they will return to their homes they migrated from."[30]

While they lived in Box Elder County and worked the fields of others, they were housed in labor camps. One headline reads, "Labor Camp Nearly Ready for Workers: Farmers Urged To Apply At Once

For Help This Summer."[31] The old "C.C.C. State Labor camp at Willard will, in a few days be ready to house Japanese farm laborers who will be distributed to farmers throughout the county needing assistance in producing war crops."[32] Under the headline "Beet Growers To Erect Homes for Japs," it was announced that "Jap evacuees from the west coast are gathering at Garland to work in the beet fields and the Utah Idaho Sugar company will lend financial aid to beet growers to provide houses for the workers and their families." The article added "that Japanese labor will be absolutely necessary to bring the crop to harvest."[33] Perhaps the best capsulization of the situation is this headline in the *Box Elder News-Journal:* "The Japs, Whose Cousins Cause It All, Seen As Cure To Box Elder's Labor Ills: Labor Camps May Be Established In County To Relieve Pressure Caused By War Jobs and Selective Service, During the Autumn Harvest Season."[34] The article begins, "The labor situation in Box Elder county, which has taken a shameful kicking around since Pearl Harbor and the location of the Bushnell General hospital in Brigham, may be picked up, brushed off and set on the right track at a meeting this evening, to he held in the court room at the court house." The article then explains the solution, by noting, "And with fatal irony, or perhaps it's poetic justice, it is likely that a race of small, brown-skinned men and women which brought the ill may provide the cure."[35]

Two months later it was announced in the *News-Journal* that Professor "M. Q. Rice, English professor of U. S. A. C. at Logan," had spoken at Rotary club. According to the article, "Professor Rice's topic was, 'The Japanese Question.'" The article's headline read "Insight Into The Jap Mind: U. S. A. C. Prof Tells Rotarians of Race."[36] Professor Rice's comments were not directed at the Japanese-American farmers in Box Elder County; he was attempting to enlighten his hearers about the Empire of the Sun, the impetus behind the Japanese invasion of Pearl Harbor, and the philosophy of Imperial Japan.

Fortunately, the war ended, and with the end of hostilities came cooler heads in Bear River Valley and a new era began. In 1944 Wat Misaka of Ogden, a Nisei, became a member of the University of Utah Varsity basketball team, the first Nisei to do so. In 1947 George

Shibata of Garland received an appointment to the United States Military Academy at West Point, again a first for a Nisei. Beginning in 1948 with the Evacuation Indemnity Claims Act, and continuing into recent memory, the wrongs done to loyal American citizens in the midst of the hysteria of war were addressed and healing has come. The treatment of the Japanese Americans during World War II was not our finest hour. Even so, not all participated in the war hysteria. Overruling the few who succumbed to the contagion of war hysteria were wiser, cooler heads. There were many of Bear River Valley's and Box Elder County's citizens who stood by and defended their neighbors, and finally the war ended. Healing comes, but it takes time. One distinguished Nisei, who has contributed much to Box Elder County, related that when he was slated to visit Japan with a number of other agricultural officials, he hesitated to visit the land of his ancestors saying that he didn't want to go because he hated that nation for the suffering it had caused him during the war.

The Berlin Candy Bomber

While World War II brought issues of prejudice and intolerance, it also brought opportunities for friendship and good will. The story of Gail Halversen, who became known as "The Berlin Candy Bomber," is one that reflects positively on Halversen as an individual and his Box Elder roots as well. A native of Garland, Halverson was trained as a pilot during World War II and in 1948 found himself in Germany flying supplies to Berlin during the Berlin Airlift after the Soviet Union closed land routes into Berlin from West Germany. On one of his trips to Berlin, Halversen had some time while his plane was being loaded, and as he walked around Templehof Airfield, he came upon a group of thirty children. After conversing with them in his limited German and their limited English, Halversen recalled that "It was soon obvious that these young people had been schooled and tested in a laboratory far more rigorous than any classroom situation. The lessons they had learned were deeply implanted over the scars left by the trauma of war. None had asked if I had been in one of those bombers in former times. I certainly wore the uniform they had been taught to hate; a symbol of death from the skies. Yet in none of their conversation or in their tone of voice was there a sign of resentment or hostility."[37]

As had thousands of other American service men, Halversen reached in his pocket to share whatever he had with the children. He found only two sticks of Wrigley's Doublemint gum. He broke the sticks in half and gave them to the four children who had acted as translators, but when he saw the disappointment of the others he lamented what he did not have thirty sticks of gum so that he could give each child a full stick. Halversen writes:

> Just then another C-54 swooped over our heads across the fence and landed. That plane gave me a sudden flash of inspiration. Why not drop some gum and even chocolate to these kids out of our airplane the next daylight trip to Berlin?
>
> At first their response was cautiously reserved for fear they had misunderstood. I took the opportunity to add, "I will do this thing only if the persons who catch the packets will share equally with everyone in the group."[38]

Because of the hundreds of planes that landed at the airport every day, a signal was worked out so that they would be able to recognize Halversen's plane when he wiggled the wings just before landing. Halversen persuaded two friends to add their candy ration to his, and, using handkerchiefs for parachutes, he made good on the promised delivery. When a German newspaper man was nearly hit by one of the candy bars, he wrote a story about Halversen, and the "Berlin Candy Bomber" became an instant celebrity. Donations came flowing in, and by the time "Operation Little Vittles," as the undertaking became known, was over, some twenty-two tons of candy and gum were dropped to the Berlin children.

Upon his return to Utah in early 1949, Halversen was given a two-day celebration in Garland that included dropping parachutes with candy from an airplane for local children—an activity repeated in Ogden, Salt Lake City, and several times in Berlin for the children of the children who were recipients of Halversen's generosity.

Intermountain Indian School

When Brigham City was chosen for the military hospital during World War II, the city fathers worked hard to procure a piece of land

Bushnell Hospital which became the Intermountain Indian School after World War II. (Box Elder County)

large enough for the project and close enough to town. The parcel of land chosen was largely in fruit orchards. Brigham City residents understood that army officials had given promises that the facility would continue as an army hospital long after the war. However, as soon as the war ended, the facility was shut down and the buildings left vacant. The campus of Bushnell hospital became an empty "white elephant" tacked onto the south edge of town. The question became what to do with the buildings of the old army hospital. Finally, in 1949, a proposal was offered to convert the facility into a boarding school for Navajo boys and girls, where they could be taken from their impoverished circumstances on the reservation and given the vocational training of main-stream American society.

A meeting was held in the Box Elder Tabernacle, and all interested persons were invited to attend. Word came that LDS church president George Albert Smith, who had a great interest in improving the lot of the Indians, was interested in the project. At the time of the meeting, however, it was announced that he was ill and would be unable to attend. The meeting was well underway when into the hall came the tall, thin, beloved leader of the Mormon people. The speaker immediately relinquished the pulpit to the aged patriarch, and he spoke powerfully of the plight and the need of the Indian children. He spoke of the opportunity the people of Brigham City had to help these young people and better their lot in life. Then President Smith promised that if the people of Brigham City would support the project, "I will bless you that you will prosper, and the Lord's protecting hand with rest upon this community and this people, and they will be protected and greatly blessed."[39]

The campus of Bushnell Hospital became the campus of the Intermountain Indian School in 1950.[40] The LDS church responded by building a showplace seminary and chapel across the street from the school, and sending their best teachers to teach there. The school fulfilled its purpose into the 1970s when it became an intertribal school for Indian high school students—not just Navajos. The housing of students from many different tribes in such close quarters caused a great deal of tension. Finally, the Native American nationalist movement came out in opposition to U.S. government boarding schools and the taking of Native American children away from their homes and seeking to purge them of the culture of their ancestors. The Intermountain Intertribal School closed in 1984.[41] After languishing for some time, the buildings boarded up and "mothballed" by the Bureau of Indian Affairs, the land and buildings were conveyed to Brigham City Corporation, which eventually entered into agreements with private developers to utilize the facilities. After being dormant for years, this property is being developed for commercial use, including mixed housing, ranging from single-family homes to townhouses and condominiums. Some of the original buildings are being converted for office use. Some will be demolished.

The Great Causeway

Times change, and even the new Lucin Cut-Off reached its limit after fifty years. Maintenance costs on the nearly twelve-mile-long trestle were higher than on the earthen fill portion of the "Cutoff." Furthermore, the single-track trestle restricted traffic. The new diesel locomotives could pull long, heavy trains much faster than the trestle would allow. The trestle had reached its capacity and had become a bottleneck on the main Southern Pacific line.[42] It was decided to replace the trestle with an earth-fill causeway.

The undertaking began in 1953 with the selection of a feasible route across the lake 1,500 feet to the north of, and parallel to, the old trestle. Instead of undertaking the massive construction project itself, as it had in 1901, the Southern Pacific Railroad contracted with the Morrison-Knudsen Company of Boise, Idaho, for the $49 million contract.

One of the greatest earth-moving challenges in American history, the project came none too soon. Railroad officials had long feared a fire on the trestle, and in 1956 those fears became a realilty. The trestle caught fire. More than 600 feet of the trestle burned and had to be re-built.[43] According to Southern Pacific historian Don L. Hofsommer, "For the first time in its history the trestle was out of service (for six days), and traffic normally moving over it was rerouted or annulled. For [Southern Pacific president] Russell the fire emphatically proved the wisdom of constructing the fill."[44]

The first challenge was the same as faced in the early years of the century—dealing with the soft muddy bottom of the lake. The lake bottom contained not only mud, but a thick layer of organic material, composed of the exoskeletons of countless brine shrimp, the only animal life in the lake. The material was dubbed "organic clay." Utilizing the relatively new science of soil mechanics, a solution was found. It was decided to dredge a channel in the lake bottom along the line of the new causeway. Marine dredges were acquired, the digging heads of which could go down 90 feet. As it turned out, the deepest they had to go was fifty-five feet.[45] The lake sediment was removed wide enough and deep enough to provide a firm base for the fill material.The dredges removed 16 million cubic yards of lake-bottom sediment before the channel was ready for work on the causeway proper to begin.[46]

This time there was no temporary trestle. Instead of working from the land at either end, material was moved by the Great Salt Lake navy. The company assembled the world's largest land-locked construction navy. Six bottom-dump barges, each nearly the size of a football gridiron, were built in Napa, California, and assembled at

An aerial view of Little Valley and its "sea port" which was built to provide rock and gravel fill for the railroad causeway built across the Great Salt Lake 1956–1959. (Box Elder County)

the Little Valley shipyard, on the west side of Promontory Point. There three dredges had dug out a harbor and a channel 250 feet wide into the lake. Five flat-top barges, fabricated in Provo, Utah, were brought to the shipyard and assembled. Besides the barges, there were smaller boats for construction supervisors, engineers, and other personnel, and a fleet of tugboats to haul the barges.

The construction camp town of Little Valley was built two miles from the boat harbor and shipyard and the old Lakeview mines quarry site to the south. The town boasted schools, shops, homes, dormitories, warehouses, and a supermarket for 1,000 people.[47] Six hundred men worked for the contractor, including barge and tugboat operators from the Pacific and Gulf coasts. At the Little Valley borrow pit, huge electric shovels lifted fill material into long-bed dump trucks. The trucks carried their loads to a terminal at the head of a two-mile-long conveyor belt. Working around the clock, the conveyor carried 90,000 tons per day to the barge-harbor, where two high-capacity conveyors loaded two barges simultaneously at the rate of 12,000 tons per hour. A barge could be loaded in fifteen minutes.[48]

Work progressed seven days a week, twenty-four hours a day, in three around-the-clock shifts. Besides the barges, sixty huge Euclid dump trucks worked from both ends. Not only did material come from Promontory, it came from the west end and from quarries three miles west of Lakeside. There power shovels loaded end-dump trucks for transport to the end of the causeway. The fleet of trucks logged a combined 20,000 miles per day, and each round trip averaged twenty miles.

At the peak of construction, 3.5 million tons of material were moved into the lake in a month, and 150,000 tons a day on good days. The rock had to be blasted from the mountains. In the mountains west and north of Promontory Point were the old Lakeview workings, lead-silver mines which had flourished around the time of the First World War. The abandoned tunnels of the mines honeycombed the mountain not far from Little Valley. The old mine tunnels were drilled and packed with tons of ammonium nitrate, interspersed with fifty-pound dynamite cartridges for detonators. In all, over 10 million pounds of powder was used. In the largest of the blasts—the world's largest man-made non-atomic explosion up to that time—more than some 2 million pounds of concentrated force pounded the mountain rock, taking out the entire mountainside and loosening 5.5 million tons of material. The string of barges carried the rock into place along the line of the causeway. Each barge carried as much material as a train of seventy heavily-loaded railroad dump cars.

By mid-1956, 50 million tons of material had been moved. One hundred-thirty-five thousand tons a day were moved at Promontory. The record was 160,000 tons in one day, in three round-the-clock shifts.

By late spring 1959, barging was completed as the entire length of the fill was brought above water level. During construction, and after the causeway came to full height, constant measurements were taken—every hundred feet along the entire length of the project—to check the stability of the fill. The engineers had studied the records of the turn-of-the-century project, and took all possible precautions. Sensors were placed in the lake bottom, some distance from the causeway, on either side, to detect any lateral movement.[49]

After the causeway was completed, it varied from 175 to 600 feet wide at the bottom, and in some places was 90 feet in height. At grade, the causeway was thirty-eight feet across. The entire project required 60,832,000 cubic yards of rock, sand, and gravel for the 12.68 miles of causeway.[50]

Even so, the job way not done. A communications line had to be stretched across the new causeway, necessitating excavating hundreds of holes for the wooden poles in the rugged rock rip-rap of the causeway. At the top were strung the railroad telephone lines and a "composite cable" to handle the railroad signal lines. A layer of extra-heavy rip-rap was placed along the outside surface of the causeway as a bulwark against the heavy salt water of the lake. During fierce winter storms, the heavy salt-laden waves pound and suck at the fill with more power than ordinary water.

The causeway was finished, leveled, graded smooth, and declared finished on 9 July 1959, nine months ahead of the scheduled completion date. After the double track was laid, the first train crossed the causeway on 27 July 1959.[51]

The new line was all the railroad hoped for. The parallel tracks carried freight and passenger trains at standard operating speeds, and the old bottleneck was eliminated. The total cost of the twelve-mile causeway was $50 million.[52]

The old trestle continued to be maintained for emergency use when especially fierce storms damaged the causeway and necessitated repairs. The trestle was finally abandoned after severe storm damage during the high-water cycle of the mid-1980s. The engineers of the 1950s project had counted on the lower lake level, and instead of building the causeway to the level of the trestle—4,217 feet above sea level—it was built at a lower, 4,212 level.[53]

Finally in the mid-1990s, railroad officials decided that the trestle had outlived its usefulness and Cannon Structures was contracted to dismantle the ninety-year-old trestle.

Thiokol and the Second Half of the Twentieth Century

After World War II and the Korean Conflict, Box Elder County and the nation settled down to an uneasy peace with our former World War II ally, the Soviet Union, often called by the name of its chief province, Russia. The economy always prospers during a war, and this time the politicians found a better kind of war: The Cold War. There was little fighting, hardly any soldiers were dying, but the economy of the military buildup for a *possible* war spawned the great military-industrial complex of the 1950s and beyond.

It was this world scenario which finally brought Box Elder County, a community of small agricultural settlements with a largely homogenous population, into the mainstream of both American society and the military-industrial complex. In one sense the story begins in 1926, in that period after the Great War and before the Great Depression.

Joseph C. Patrick, a chemist with a Ph.D, was working in his garage-laboratory trying to develop a new kind of antifreeze. In the course of his work, he discovered the world's first synthetic rubber, a substance which had eluded a number of scientists and experimenters for many years. Patrick named his discovery Thiokol, from the Greek words *theion* (sulfur) and *kolla* (glue). Two years later Patrick hired a salesman and continued to experiment and improve Thiokol rubber. On 5 December 1929, just after the crash of the stock market, Thiokol Chemical Corporation was incorporated. In 1935 the company moved to New Jersey, and over the next few years continued to develop its product. In 1943 the company developed the world's first (and only) synthetic liquid rubber. The "liquid polymer rubber was used extensively during the war years as an indestructible sealant for fuel tanks, gut turrets, and seams of all kinds."[54]

In 1944 Joseph W. Crosby, who had joined Thiokol in 1936, became vice president. He noticed that large quantities of Thiokol liquid rubber were being purchased by the Jet Propulsion Laboratory in Pasadena, California. Upon investigation, Crosby discovered that JPL was using the liquid polymer in a solid propellant for small rocket motors. Soon, Thiokol and JPL were collaborating "to develop and pioneer the case-bonded solid propellant rocked motor."[55] After the war, Thiokol's Crosby obtained a grant from the U.S. Army "to develop and produce a 75-lb (33.975 kilograms) infantry support rocket."[56] Production took place at a plant which was built at the army's Redstone Arsenal in Huntsville, Alabama. After years of expansion and development, Thiokol Chemical Corporation decided to go for the big-time by building a huge plant to develop and produce solid rocket motors. The principals of the company looked for a site large enough, and far enough away from any major metropolitan area, to manufacture large military-grade rocket motors. According to an official Thiokol document, "Successes with ever-larger solid propellant motors led the Company in 1956 to take a giant gamble: without a contract in hand, the Company bought acreage 25 miles west of Brigham City, and built a $3 million rocket motor plant."[57]

After looking at a number of sites across the country, they hired Brigham City Attorney Walter G. Mann to help negotiate for the purchase of a large tract of land in western Box Elder County. The site, much of which is hilly and good for nothing else, includes some good dry-farms and homesteads to the north. Local legend has it that when Thiokol first became interested in the site, they were using an old map which showed the Promontory Branch of the Central Pacific Transcontinental Line running along the western border of the tract. It is said by some that the decision to purchase was made before Thiokol fully realized that there were no tracks to haul their huge rocket motors to market. Thiokol's Utah Division, later renamed the Wasatch Division, officially opened on 17 October 1957.

Two things happened in 1958 which benefitted Thiokol. The company received the contract to build the first stage rocket motor for the Minuteman intercontinental ballistic missile which, for its time, was the largest solid rocket motor ever built. Second, on 30 April Thiokol merged with Reaction Motors, Incorporated.

Reaction Motors, Inc., or RMI began when "four enthusiastic amateur rocket experimenters of the American Rocket Society [became] convinced of the military and business possibilities of the rocket motor for use in this nation's defense efforts." They "began to explore ways of attracting the U.S. Military to the potential of the liquid propellant rocket engine." They lobbied the National Advisory Committee for Aeronautics, and organized Reaction Motors, Inc., "in the tiny upper floor room of John Shesta's brother-in-law's garage."[58] Then came the war. "In November 1941 a U.S. Navy representative witnessed a test-run of the motor (a 100-pound thrust regeneratively cooled rocked motor). The run went well. Pearl Harbor was bombed the next month and a Navy contract with Reaction Motors was signed almost immediately after the bombing. The four men received $5,000 for one liquid fuel motor to be delivered to the Navy, and a contract for $20,000 to develop and demonstrate a 100-pound-thrust motor."[59] It was Reaction Motors Incorporated which produced the 6000C-4 liquid-fueled engine for the Air Force XS-1 (C-1) made by Bell Aircraft. The first human to break the sound barrier, Chuck Yeager, accomplished the feat in the RMI-powered Bell X-1. It was RMI which developed the XLR-II engine, with a thrust of 8,000 pounds, and the newer XLR-99 (1956), with a thrust of 50,000 pounds. It was first XLR-II and then XLR-99 engines which powered the X-15 "rocket plane." The first flight of the X-15 with XLR-99 engines took place on 15 November 1960. The X-1 is considered the forerunner of the space shuttle.

In 1958 RMI's sales had risen to $24.5 million, and Thiokol's to $30 million. The two companies merged at midnight, 30 April 1958.

The RMD (Reaction Motors Division of Thiokol) developed the engines for the Douglas D-558–1 No. 2 (Skyrocket), the first aircraft to exceed double the speed of sound.

Thiokol's fortunes flowed and ebbed with the vicissitudes of the aerospace industry and the state of the cold war, including U.S. involvement in the war in Southeast Asia. The company built its Plant 78 for the air force, developed and produced motors for the Poseidon submarine-launched missile, the Peacekeeper missile, the Trident missile, and the huge segmented engines for the space shuttle. Beginning in 1969, the company "used its expertise in propellants to develop castable illuminating flares at its Utah facilities and is today the world's largest supplier of such devices for both U.S. and foreign markets."[60]

In 1982 Thiokol merged with Morton Norwich to become Morton Thiokol. The new company became a major producer of automobile airbags, which Thiokol had pioneered in 1965.

After the space shuttle *Challenger* disaster on 28 January 1986, when the entire *Challenger* crew was killed by an explosion just after liftoff from the Kennedy Space Center, Morton divested itself of Thiokol, which became Thiokol Corporation. The company continues to be one of Box Elder's foremost employers, and a partner in the county's development.

It was the coming of Thiokol in the 1950s which transformed Box Elder County. Brigham City went through the throes of being wrenched from a placid existence as a sleepy Mormon agricultural town to a city of industry and cultural diversity. And Brigham City's experience was mirrored throughout the county. The large influx of scientists, engineers, administrators, military personnel, and support staff from all over the country was a major shock to the culture of Brigham City. The way things had been done for generations was immediately challenged. There came a major cultural confrontation between the Brigham City Mormons and the outsider gentiles.

ENDNOTES

1. Sarah Yates, "Bushnell General Hospital was 'a city within a city,'" *Box Elder News Journal*, 4 August 1993, 13. Information on Bushnell Hospital is based on this article along with Kathleen Bradford's article "Bushnell General Hospital," in Allan Kent Powell, ed., *Utah History Encyclopedia* (Salt Lake City: University of Utah Press, 1994).

2. Yates, "Bushnell General Hospital," citing an editorial in the Box Elder paper on 17 January 1942.

3. Ibid.

4. Ibid.

5. "Verabell Call Knudson," in Allan Kent Powell, ed., *Utah Remembers World War II* (Logan: Utah State University Press, 1991), 177–78.

6. Ibid., 179–80.

7. Kathleen Bradford, "Bushnell General Hospital" in Powell, *Utah History Encyclopedia*, 65.

8. "Margaret Atwood Herbert," in Powell, *Utah Remembers World War II*, 173.

9. Kathleen Bradford, "Bushnell General Hospital," 65.

10. "Margaret Atwood Herbert," in Powell, *Utah Remembers World War II*, 174.

11. Allan Kent Powell, *Splinters of a Nation: German Prisoners of War in Utah* (Salt Lake City: University of Utah Press, 1989), 202.

12. Ibid., 170–71.

13. *Bear River Valley Leader,* 23 September 1943, 20 January 1944, 10 February 1944, 13 April 1944, 27 April 1944, 3 August 1944, 31 August 1944, 6 October 1944, 26 October 1944, 2 November 1944, 6 November 1944, 9 November 1944, 23 November 1944.

14. *Bear River Valley Leader,* 19 October 1944.

15. "History of Japanese Life in Utah," in Box Elder Japanese Reunion Planning Committee, *1990 Japanese American Reunion.* I am deeply indebted to Susan Sunada of Logan, Utah, for access to her voluminous archives on the Japanese Americans in Utah, and to Frank Nishiguchi for facilitating our meeting.

16. Ibid.

17. Sarah Yates, "Local resident recalls days interviewing prisoners," *Box Elder News Journal,* 22 January 1992. See also, "Shoji Watanabe," in Powell, *Utah Remembers World War II,* 233–36.

18. "Jim Tazoi," in Powell, *Utah Remembers World War II,* 228–32. See also Chester Tanaka, *Go For Broke: A Pictorial History of the Japanese American 100th Infantry Battalion and the 442nd Regimental Combat Team* (Richmond, Calif.: Gor For Broke, Inc., 1982), for a history of the 442nd, and Joseph D. Harrington, *Yankee Samurai: The secret role of Nisei in America's Pacific Victory* (Detroit, Mich.: Pettigrew Enterprises, Inc., 1979).

19. "PFC J. C. Tazoi wins D.S.C.," *Box Elder News Journal,* 22 June 1945. See also *Box Elder News Journal,* 1 June 1945.

20. "History of Japanese Life in Utah."

21. "Was member of Lost Battalion" newspaper clipping with no name or date attached, in the collection of Susan Sunada.

22. "History of Japanese Life in Utah."

23. "Resolutions Urge that Native Whites Regain Ownership of All Farm Lands in the Valley: Jap Purchases Are Seen As Conducive To Race Conflict," *Box Elder News Journal,* 4 April 1944.

24. Ibid.

25. Ibid.

26. Ibid.

27. *Box Elder News-Journal,* 21 and 27 March 1942.

28. Ibid., 27 March 1942.

29. Ibid., 27 July 1943.

30. Ibid., 27 March 1942.

31. Ibid., 11 May 1942.

32. Ibid.

33. Ibid., 7 April 1942.

34. Ibid., 21 August 1942.

35. Ibid.

36. Ibid., 23 October 1942.

37. "Gale S. Halversen," in Powell, *Utah Remembers World War II,* 261

38. Ibid.

39. Interview with Lewis H. Jones, Jr.

40. Bradford, "Bushnell General Hospital," 65.

41. Ibid.

42. Morrison-Knudsen Company, Inc., *Mariners in Hardhats,* copy in Golden Spike National Historic Site collection.

43. Ward J. Roylance, *Utah: A Guide to the State, Revised and Enlarged* (Salt Lake City: Utah Arts Council, 1982), 298. The history of the Southern Pacific gives the exact figure as 645 feet, and the date as 4 May 1956. See Don L. Hofsommer, *The Southern Pacific, 1901–1985* (College Station: Texas A&M University Press, 1986), 247.

44. Hofsommer, *The Southern Pacific,* 247.

45. *Mariners in Hardhats.*

46. Roylance, *Utah: A Guide to the State,* 298.

47. Ibid.

48. *Mariners in Hardhats.*

49. Ibid.

50. Hofsommer, *The Southern Pacific,* 247.

51. Ibid.; *Mariners in Hardhats.*

52. *Mariners in Hardhats;* and Roylance, *Utah: A Guide to the State,* 298.

53. Hofsommer, *The Southern Pacific,* 247.

54. Thiokol Corporation, *History of Thiokol Corporation,* 1, copy in my possession.

55. Ibid.

56. Ibid.

57. Ibid., 2.

58. Ibid., 1.

59. Ibid.

60. Ibid., 2.

Chapter 12

Reflections on Box Elder County at the End of the Twentieth Century

In Brigham City it is Peach Days, which lays claim to being the oldest harvest festival in the state of Utah. In the rocky alluvium of Brigham City, the honored crop in the early agricultural years was peaches. Out in "the Valley" it is Wheat and Beet days, with produce coming in from the dry farms and the sugar beet and onion fields. Then there is the County Fair. Though there are variations, taken together, they conform to the ancient pattern. The people come together once a year. Those who come in from outlying communities with their produce and their farm animals to exhibit have to stay near the fairgrounds. They have to stay, to eat, and to visit the banks. Sometimes they suffer injuries and have to go to the hospital. They meet other family members from nearby towns, and share news and family photographs. Sometimes they go to the photography booth or the caricaturist's booth, and have a family portrait done. While waiting for the judges to come by, they play cards or throw horseshoes. Sometimes they race, either on foot or on their sleek, combed horses. They go to the street dance, they walk and talk, and spend time with girlfriends or boyfriends. There is the election of the Peach Queen or

Wheat and Beet Queen, or Miss County Fair. All go to the rodeo, where brave youths, the cream of the crop, wrestle with calves or broncs or bulls, and show their athletic prowess. More than this, like the youth who fought the bulls in the Mithraic contests of ancient times, young men at the peak of their virility battle the powerful, dark bovine brute beasts, as Mithras slew the bull centuries ago. In days gone by, one of the county heroes, Sheriff Warren Hyde, rode his horse at the head of the procession through the rodeo arena. And a hero he was, a hero of thirty-some years as sheriff of one of Utah's largest counties. There were amazing tales of daring captures, and his famous battle with one of the great prizes of World War II, one of the elusive "fire balloons" sent from Japan to set fire to the cities and countryside of western America. Such is the mythic power of Peach Days, Wheat and Beet days, and the County Fair. It is these seemingly frivolous events which provide that mystic tie between the residents of Box Elder County in the 1990s with people much like themselves separated from them by thousands of miles of geography and thousands of years of time. We dress differently, and get around differently, but we, citizens of Box Elder County, are also related to people throughout the world, people who live, laugh, cry, eat, sleep, go to school and to work, read, worship, sicken, die, despair, and hope. To some degree, our history is part of theirs.

There are so many facets of our history. There is the change from church schools to public schools, and the eventual consolidation of schools and the utilization of school busses and long bus rides instead of small schools closer to home.

There is the building and re-routing of roads, from the coming of Interstate 15 and Interstate 84 to the minor re-routing of the highway from Brigham City to Corinne and I-15 to Box Elder Canyon. One of them, the building of the road west toward Corinne from the north end of Brigham City, was one of those historically significant projects brought about through Franklin D. Roosevelt's alphabet agencies during the Depression. It was build largely by hand, and the huge sections of concrete laid one at a time. Now they make an annoying bump, bump, bump, as cars speed along, but then it was a fine highway (and, even now, that construction has lasted longer than a lot of sections of new freeway). It provided employment for many

Brigham City Main Street. (Utah State Historical Society)

who survived because of it. I am acquainted with a wonderful woman, now in her nineties, who drove a team of horses in the construction of that piece of highway. Even Box Elder's concrete has its history, and its personal stories—the stories of people, individuals and families, and their own personal struggles and triumphs.

There is the story of the old Cement Plant, still a monument of ruins next to the freeway between Brigham City and Honeyville. Cement was made from the marl beds north and west of Brigham City. There was some disagreement between someone in the administration of the Cement Plant and the mayor of Brigham City, some personal thing. When the plant caught fire, the mayor, the old-timers say, wouldn't allow the city fire department to put the fire out. The Cement Plant burned. By then the new Portland Cement process had been developed, and the old plant was not rebuilt. All that is left is the ruins of the east part of the large plant, a few crumbling company houses west of the freeway, and the old "Cement Plant Pond" which served as a swimming hole before Brigham City built its municipal pool in the 1960s.[1]

There is the saga of game hunting in Box Elder County, from the plethora of duck clubs of the 1920s and 1930s, the great deer hunts and rabbit drives of the 1930s and 1940s to the pheasant and goose hunting of the present day. There is the development of private hunting reserves and the commercialization of bird hunting in western Box Elder County.

There is the coming of public utilities, including the saga of electrical power generation in Brigham City, from the first generator connected to the waterwheel at the Woolen Mill to the steam powerplant near the OSL Depot to the city-owned hydroelectric plant at the mouth of the canyon. Brigham City was so proud of its own electrical power generating facility that it made the people of the city an offer. If they would agree to leave their porch lights on all night to make the streets more safe and friendly, the city would pay for the electricity to operate the porch lights. Of course, Thiokol came, Brigham City connected up to the great power grid, and eventually the offer was withdrawn, the porchlights wired through the meters, and the streets of Brigham City became a little darker and a little less safe, and the city a little less friendly. There was the coming of the telephone lines, then finally dial telephones in the 1960s and digital switching in the 1990s. There was the coming of Mountain Fuel Supply Company's gas pipeline along the bench east of Brigham City, with its attendant scar along the mountainside. Brigham City's power company, and even the great Cutler power plant on the Bear River, became only sparks in the great power grid that served the nation, and brought brownouts and blackouts when a transformer failed hundreds of miles away.

Then there are the mines. There is Fred Holton's dream mine above the old Brigham City temple site. There is the Vipont Mine near Lucin, and there is the Baker Mine, above Harper Ward. There is the old Antimony Mine, its access road a long scar along the foothills north of Brigham City. Each has its own story.

There are the stories of the Oregon Short Line, the Utah-Idaho Northern, and the Utah-Idaho Central. There are the old streetcars which plied the streets of Brigham City. The old-timers talk about the motor-man, Tommy Slatter. Everybody knew him. They also said that the old streetcar had one wheel with a flat side, from all the clanking noise it made as it moved slowly along.

There is the story of the American Greetings plant which came to Brigham City, and then went. There is the Lazy Boy furniture factory which boosted the economy of Tremonton and Garland. There is the Morton Airbag Factory, a spinoff of the partnership of Morton and Thiokol, which took over and enlarged the American Greetings factory west of Brigham City.

There is the Box Elder Water Conservancy District, organized to protect Box Elder County's share of the water of the Bear River. It was not involved in planning of the ill-conceived Honeyville Dam, which considered finishing John R. Bothwell's grand plan to extend a canal from the Bear River to Ogden. Under the direction of former Box Elder County commissioner Frank Nishiguchi, the Water Conservancy District is pursuing a long-range plan to connect the culinary water supplies of Box Elder County's major communities and provide an adequate supply of drinking water for a majority of the citizens of Box Elder County. It favored storage of Bear River Water farther upstream, in Cache Valley, preserving the old Hampton's Ford hotel and stage coach station, which would have been inundated by the dam.[2]

Then there is the story of Box Elder County in the art world. One of the most noted artworks in the world is in Box Elder County. Most residents of the county don't even know it. Those who do, guffaw and belittle it. Even so, it is in the art texts used in universities all over the world, and (as the staff at Golden Spike National Historic Site can attest) people come from all over the United States and the world to visit it. It is the *Spiral Jetty*, a product of the "earth art" movement of the 1960s. The *Jetty* was the "crowning achievement" of James Smithson. It "is a 1,500-foot-long, 15-foot wide artwork made of 6,650 tons of black rock."[3] Smithson hired a local bulldozer operator to push the rock out into the shallow waters of Great Salt Lake, making a "Left handed spiral, which turns in on itself twice"[4] in 1970. Many of the visitors to the site are disappointed to find that the jetty was built during a low-water cycle of Great Salt Lake. Most of the time, the jetty is several feet under water. According to Mark Saal, "It has only been since 1993, after 10 years of receding water levels, that visitors could see the jetty from the shore, and its re-emergence has brought renewed interest."[5]

Not to be outdone (or to continue the legacy), Smithson's widow, Nancy Holt, had four huge concrete pipes, which resemble ten-foot-diameter concrete culverts, hauled to a remote site south of Lucin, where they were carefully placed on the alkali playa, in line with the summer and winter solstice sunrise and sunset, and holes cut in them for viewing selected constellations. She named her work of art the *Sun Tunnels* and said that their "public art"—the *Jetty* and the *Tunnels*—"went out into the world." More people visit the *Jetty* than the *Tunnels,* due to the greater exposure given the former in the art texts and its near proximity to paved roads and cities, but the *Tunnels* are a more impressive sight from the ground.[6]

In 1996 the state of Utah reached its centennial. In preparation for that event, Box Elder County clerk and recorder LuAnn Adams decided that a renewal of the old Box Elder County Courthouse was in order. An article in an anecdotal history of Cache County some year ago opined that the Cache County Courthouse was the oldest courthouse in the state still functioning as such. In reality, it is the courthouse in Box Elder County, built in the mid-1850s. Though it underwent a facelift in the 1887, and was given Italianate ornamentation, and a clocktower, and though it was extensively added to in 1909–10,[7] it still incorporates the original structure, used for church meetings and theatrical productions in the days of Brigham City's infancy. During what turned out to be a renovation, a new roof was installed to replace the roof which had served for over eighty years. The exterior was cleaned and the stonework covered with a moisture-resistant sealant. Inside the building received a new coat of paint. The old juvenile courtrooms were converted into spacious new quarters for the county commission, and the county surveyor, county inspector, FEMA office received larger quarters in the old commission chambers. The building was retrofitted to conform to the requirements of the Americans with Disabilities Act, new carpeting was installed, and the building was given a new life and a shining new face. The old pendulum clockworks, which had turned the hands of the tower clock from 1910 until the 1960s, was rebuilt and placed in a case in the main hallway, for all to see and admire. Then there is the "Jay Room," so called by those who work in the courthouse because its existence is due almost totally to the vision and persistence of County Commissioner Jay Hardy. One room in the old section of the courthouse has been restored and renovated to the period of the 1880s. It is a wonderful conference room, filled with lovingly restored (by the commissioner himself) oak furniture. It is the crowning touch of the project.

At the same time, in conjunction with this volume, historical photographs from all over the county were found and reprinted, and many of them—sponsored by companies, groups, families, and individuals—were framed and hung throughout the hallways of the renovated courthouse.[8] A book, *Box Elder County Historical Photo Tour,* was published in 1996 and contains copies of many of the priceless historical photographs, now preserved in print for future generations. A large plaque is being prepared, to honor the names of all who have served in the armed forces from Box Elder County throughout the years. A grant has been received to repair and replace the crumbling steps which grace the front of the courthouse.[9]

Then there are the rich and the famous, the local people who, over the years, have achieved the fame of "name recognition." The problem with singling any out for honor in a history is that, if they are long dead, the families of others think that *their* "famous" sons or daughters, or aunts or uncles, or fathers or grandfathers are more deserving of note. If they are living, there are their rivals who would rather the space be devoted to them. In the olden days, heroes were people who did things that were truly heroic and were widely or universally acknowledged to be heroes.

Even so, Box Elder County has produced some people who are commonly acknowledged. There is Elmer "Bear" Ward, the famous football player. There is L. Jay Sylvester, who competed in the Olympic Games. There is Keith Nuttall, of boxing fame. There is Dee Glen Smith, who built a business empire out of the old Lorenzo Smith grocery store on the corner of Fifth South and Main Street in Brigham City. There is Jay Call, who came to Brigham City and rented a modest office in the Professional Center, and eventually developed a Fortune-500 company with its headquarters in Brigham

City.[10] There is Box Elder native son Boyd Packer, son of an automobile mechanic, who took Rudger Clawson's and Lorenzo Snow's place representing Box Elder in the highest councils of the LDS church, along with a number of others who have served their church and community in high and responsible positions. They are many. Fame and notoriety come and go, but the real story of Box Elder is not in those with fame and position (who generally have to live outside Brigham City to take their positions and serve their fame), it is people like the members of the committee who provided most of the information for the histories of the individual communities in the following chapter.

There is Merlin Larsen, who has lived much of his life farming the dry hillsides of Promontory, and his wife, Doris. There is LeGrand Morris, who knows the hills and trails around Park Valley and Rosette better than just about anybody else, and his wife Dorothy who shares life and work with him. There is Keith Andersen of Bothwell, who amazes people with his knowledge of almost the entire western two-thirds of the county. There is Gale Welling of Fielding, who gave me a wonderful tour, and saved hundreds of hours of research about the canals and the dam in Bear River Canyon. There is Frank Nishiguchi, farmer, administrator, county commissioner from Riverside, who got this project going in the first place. There are the Secrists of Collinston, who were so helpful and supportive, and Merlin Tracy, who spent untold hours working out the route of the old Salt Lake Cutoff through Yost. There are those who came with the Thiokol influx, who have added depth and breadth to the matrix of culture and faith of Box Elder County. They can be exemplified by Lorna Ravenberg, who has kept the Box Elder County history project on track and, as its secretary, keeps the Box Elder County Commission running smoothly, and also serves as a pillar of her church.

Then there were those who are long gone. There were William Davis, James Brooks, and Thomas Pierce, who first came to Box Elder in 1850. There were all the unnamed souls who pioneered Brigham City, like my own grandparents and great-grandparents, who left homes in Wales and Denmark to pioneer a new land. There were those who came with the railroad, those who came with the sugar

Smoothing out a stock pond site on the Adams ranch in 1939 using a caterpillar tractor, four horse fresno, four mule fresno, and a bucket scraper pulled by two oxen. (Box Elder County)

company, the canal system, and the land boom of the turn-of-the-century. There were those who came from Russia and India, and from China and Japan. These are the people who deserve the real publicity and honor in a history of Box Elder County.

Perhaps the story of the real people of Box Elder can be told in the story of those unsung heroes, the story of "everyman." It is the story of my maternal great-grandmother, who as a girl worked in the coal mines of Wales, and who, with her sweetheart, crossed the ocean and the plains to come of Box Elder when it was a tiny, struggling settlement. It is the story of my great-grandfather, who left a hard life in Denmark to come to Utah to gather with others of his faith, to worship in the community of Zion. It is the story of the Nelsons and the Nielsens, of the Larsens and the Rasmussens, of the Andersens and the Andersons, of the Evanses and the Davises and the Bodens, of the Wellings and the Christensens. It is the story of the Wrights and the Kellys, of the Joneses and the Rosenbaums (Morris Rosenbaum was one of Lorenzo Snow's converts from Europe, and one of the first

Jewish converts to Mormonism). It is the story of the Nishiguchis and the Tazois and the Satos and the Yamasakis, who came to Utah to work for the railroad or the sugar company, or raise vegetables in the newly irrigated soil of Bear River Valley. It is the story of the Singhs and the Madsens, the Pierces and the Forsgrens (Peter Adolph Forsgren was the first person in all of Scandinavia baptized into the LDS church). Box Elder would not be Box Elder without the Wrightons (William Wrighton brought the first peach seeds to Brigham City). What would our history be without Shadrack Jones, Willard's Welsh stonemason, or John H. Bott, who learned the stonemason's trade working on the Salt Lake temple and came to Brigham City with his three wives and numerous posterity? What about the Dunns and the Barons and the Horsleys and the Merrills and the Reeders and the Valentines and all the others who came? What would Honeyville be without the Hunsakers, the Binghams, and the Tolmans? What would Beaverdam have been without the Bowens and the Busenbarks? Could there have been a Bear River City without Holmgrens, or Yost without Tracys and Tanners; and how about Park Valley without the Kimbers? These families, and hundreds like them, have made Box Elder County what it is. Then there are the Timbimboos and their kin, whose ancestors were here before any of the rest of us. And what breadth has been added to our community by those who have come since pioneer days: the Misrasis, the Kozaks, the Sholtys, the Browns, the Basses, the Wilhites, the Breitenbüchers, the Martinezes, the Savocas, the Harrises, the Ravenbergs, and so many others.

The real story of Box Elder County is the story of its people, people from many nations, people of different ethnic and cultural backgrounds, people with varied religious beliefs. It is the story of the common people more than those who have achieved notoriety. Perhaps the best summation of the people of Box Elder is the story of Adolph Olsen, whose mother carried silk-worms in a specially made pouch under her dress to keep them warm so that the Mercantile and Manufacturing Association could have silk and be self-sufficient—so that the Relief Society could present a beautiful silk dress, made entirely from home industry, to the noted Susan B. Anthony when she visited Utah.

Adolph Olsen left home, farm, and town to serve a mission for his church in the old Southern States Mission, when they were still stoning and killing and tarring and feathering and castrating Mormon missionaries. He came home older, more wise in the ways of the world, and more self-confident. He went to the coal fields of eastern Utah with the National Guard to put down a strike. He thought of home as he lay perched on the hillside above the mines and the striking unionists, wondering if he would have to kill someone. He spent most of his life in Brigham City, married to the same girl for over fifty years, farming and raising his family. He spent his later years systematically walking the streets of Brigham City in his blue-striped overalls, reading the water and power meters. He never worked for a large corporation, he probably never had his picture in the newspaper, but his story, and the stories of thousands like him, is the story of the farms and the families and the towns of Box Elder County. Let us never forget that.

Endnotes

1. That pool, which succeeded an older one at the north end of Pioneer Park Pond, wore out, in its turn, and was replaced by one of the largest and most up-to-date outdoor water-recreation facilities in Utah in the late 1990s.

2. The thing which finally put an end to the dam project was the discovery that the high-earth banks of the river channel would not stand up to a reservoir, and would continually cave in, widening the channel, eating away farmland, and rapidly filling the reservoir with silt.

3. Mark Saal, "The Spiral Jetty," Ogden *Standard Examiner,* 23 June 1996.

4. Ibid.

5. Ibid.

6. Ibid. See also, Angelika Pagael, "The Immobile Cyclone: Robert Smithson's Spiral Jetty," cited in Saal's article. Collateral articles in the same issue of the *Standard Examiner* provide more information about Smithson, construction of the jetty, and access to the site. Information and directions are also available at the visitor center at Golden Spike National Historic Site.

7. See Sarah Yates, "BE County courthouse featured in publication," *Box Elder News Journal,* 19 January 1994; and Ernest Freeman, chair, Brigham

City Eighth Ward Building Committee, *Through the Years* (Brigham City: Brigham City Eighth Ward, 1951), 25.

8. Many of the photographs come from the priceless collection of glass plates from pioneer Brigham City photographer Alma Compton, and the large-format celluloid negatives of his son, Matthew Compton. Matthew Compton's son, Glen, bequeathed the collection to the Special Collections archives of Utah State University's Merrill Library, where they are cared for and provide a resource for generations to come.

9. Interview with LuAnn Adams, 25 March 1998.

10. See Howard M. Carlisle, *Colonist Fathers, Corporate Sons: A Selected History of the Call Family* (Salt Lake City: Publishers Press, 1996).

CHAPTER 13

THE TOWNS OF BOX ELDER

The chief means through which people make their mark upon the landscape are in their farmland and cities. Before the coming of people, particularly the nineteenth-century coming of industrial-agricultural people, Box Elder County was virtually a desert land, its topography broken here and there by watercourses, springs, mountain peaks and ridges, and their attendant oases of green amid the alkali playa, grass, sagebrush, and rock of the high desert which make up the valleys, slopes, and alluvial fans of the Great Basin.

Those who settled Box Elder County at the beginning of the second half of the nineteenth century had to impound available water resources, divert the flow of the natural watercourses, and bring the precious life-giving water to bear on the virgin soil in order to raise the crops they needed for subsistence in a largely inhospitable land. Plowing, planting, ditching, and fencing of the land have resulted in the patchwork of fields which dot the arable land of Box Elder County with many-hued and multi-textured crops. In addition, those early colonists had to build settlements—places both habitable and inhabited—where water could be concentrated for gardens, mills, and other industrial and mercantile pursuits. Those settlements blossomed into the towns of Box Elder, and seeded later towns and villages which now dot the landscape.

There were two main waves of village-settling in Box Elder, coming approximately fifty years apart, and two other periods of establishment of railroad towns, sidings, and attendant settlements.

The first white settlement period is exemplified by the county's chief town and county seat, Brigham City, the first settlement in Box Elder to be explored and sited, and the first settlement of the Mormon colonization north of the Ogden River. The site for Brigham City's predecessor, Box Elder settlement, and its physical manifestations, Davis Fort and Box Elder Fort, was chosen for two main reasons. It was at the mouth of Box Elder Canyon, where the water of Box Elder Creek could be diverted to irrigate the land, and it was near a significant Shoshoni settlement and on the Shoshoni trail between Box Elder and Cache valleys. It was also bisected by the great Salt Lake Cutoff, the road to the gold fields of California

Brigham Young sent his first main colonies to settle near the major bands of Indians—the Ute, the Paiute, and the Shoshoni. Box Elder Settlement was the first settlement among the Shoshoni. With that objective gained, other settlements could be built along the streams of Box Elder. What became Brigham City was, then, one of only a handful of the most important colonies established by Brigham Young.

We have discussed the founding and development of Brigham City at some length. We have also discussed Brigham City's gentile complement and rival, the archetype of railroad towns, Corinne, the Burgh on the Bear. They are paradigms, in Box Elder County, respectively, of the first-tier agricultural settlements and the railroad towns. The third type of settlement, which we will call second-tier towns, those settled around the turn-of-the-century with the coming of Cutler Dam and the Bear River canal system—making possible more irrigated farmland, and hence more settlements—are exemplified by Tremonton and Garland on the gentile side and Thatcher and Fielding on the Mormon side. This chapter provides historical sketches, in alphabetical order, of Box Elder County communities.[1]

Bear River City

Bear River City takes its name from its proximity to the major tributary of Great Salt Lake, which flows in its deep channel east of the town, giving its name not only to the town, but to the valley through which it flows, from its passage through what were once called "the Gates" where it enters the valley, to its debouchment into the Great Salt Lake south of Corinne.[2]

Bear River City is located on State Highway 13, about eight miles south of Tremonton, about four miles north of Corinne, and about ten miles northwest from Brigham City.

The site was settled in 1866, by a group of Scandinavian immigrants who set out from Brigham City to found a colony on the Bear River. They first lived in dugouts in the river bank, just north of the old iron bridge across Bear River, which was demolished in 1998.

The settlers intended to dam the Malad River, and divert the water for their farmland. After only a year, they found it necessary to build a fort to protect themselves in case of Indian attack. The fort, on block twenty of the Bear River survey, was perched on the brow of the hill, and commanded a sweeping view. It was a number of years before the settlers dismantled their fort and built houses on town lots.

In building the dam, the settlers thought that the water from creeks near Malad, Samaria, and Portage would provide enough fresh water to make the project successful. Promoters of the project included some of Brigham City's prominent men: Judge Samuel Smith, Peter Adolph Forsgren, and Christian Hansen. Water from the Malad canal irrigated sorghum cane which was crushed in a molasses mill built southeast of the old iron bridge. Though the mill was close to the Bear River, it was high on the bluff, and its water wheel was powered by Malad River water.

As settlements were established in the Malad River Valley, farther north, water from the creeks was diverted for irrigation there, and the waters of the Malad, true to its name, became alkaline, and useless for irrigation. The settlers were discouraged, but Brigham Young encouraged them to stay and promised that they would some day use water from the Bear River.

The town was incorporated in 1885, and platted in 1888. Water was purchased from Blind Springs and Wheatley Spring, to be used for culinary purposes. It took until 1924 for sufficient funds to be raised and the project brought to completion.

Their first church-school building was replaced by a sturdy brick chapel, which was dedicated in 1899 by Lorenzo Snow, who by that time had become president of the LDS church. The first funeral held in the building was that of Bishop Carl Jensen. A later addition was made to the building, providing a recreation hall and classrooms, with additional changes being made in 1939, 1952, and 1978. The roof of the addition was taken off by a ferocious wind in the mid-1990s, and the entire building was condemned, demolished in 1996, and replaced with a much more functional and much less attractive "standard" LDS chapel.

After the damming of Bear River and construction of the canals, Bear River City was finally served by Bear River water. The now-fertile land produced canning crops, such as tomatoes, peas, corn and beans. With closure of the canneries, local fields now produce mostly hay and grain, or silage corn for beef and dairy animals.

Many local residents are employed at Thiokol, Nucor Steel, and La-z-Boy. Community growth is hampered by a limited supply of culinary water. There is only one store left in the business district, adjoining the post office.

The social life of the community centers around the church and the large city park, complete with rodeo grounds, little league ball diamond, baseball diamond, and soccer field. Each summer the community celebrates the 24th of July, with parades, a baby show, races, programs, and a rodeo. In 1900 Bear River City had a population of 390. By mid-century the population had increased slightly to 438 and in 1990 to 700. Bear River City has remained a small Mormon agricultural community.

Beaver Dam

Beaver Dam is located on Utah Highway 30 between Collinston and the Cache County line, about twenty-two miles north of the county courthouse in Brigham City. It lies north of the northern tip of the Wellsville range, just south of the canyon of the Bear River, and east of the river channel. Since completion of Interstate 15, Highway 30 has been one of the major highways to Cache Valley, and has brought increased traffic along the edge of Beaver Dam.[3]

Beaver Dam takes its name from the beaver dams found along Bear Creek when the town was first settled. Bear Creek, which runs through the town, was later named Willow Creek. The creek originates in the Wellsville Mountains, and, after quitting Beaver Dam town, empties into the Bear River west of the Union Pacific railroad tracks west of town.

In 1863 and 1864 Jonathan Bowen and Henry Busenbark into the area came looking for a place to pasture cattle. The town was settled in 1867 or 1868 by people from Providence in Cache Valley. Others came north from Deweyville. Early settlers came from the Bowen, Durfey, Miller, Dunn, and Busenbark families. The foothill and bench land around the townsite were found to be ideal for dry-farming.

They dammed Bear Creek, dug an irrigation ditch, and laid out a seventy-two acre field. As is the sad reality in many of Utah's valleys, overgrazing caused the creek to cut a deep channel along its course through town. In some places the channel is fifty feet deep, and is gouged down to bedrock.

The first school was built in 1883. The most prominent building in Beaver Dam is the outstanding rock chapel, completed in 1898, under instructions from LDS stake president Rudger Clawson. Rock for the building was cut by John H. Bott, who had learned his trade working on the Salt Lake Temple. The building, which cost between $6,500 and $7,200 was dedicated by Rudger Clawson, by then one of the twelve apostles in the LDS church.

A recreation hall, classrooms, and a relief society room were added to the chapel about 1948, and the renovated building was rededicated by Le Grande Richards. Another addition was constructed in 1987, providing a new, larger chapel. The new addition, by Cooper-Roberts architects, was sympathetic to the original structure. Though the original massing of the little chapel has been lost, the new addition is the best possible compromise.

Beaver Dam is the nearest town to Cutler Dam, about a mile north of town, and to the Brigham City Mercantile and Manufacturing Association's cheese factory, built in the canyon south of town, in the foothills of Wellsville Mountain.

The original Beaver Dam schoolhouse was replaced by the "yellow brick school"in 1905, which in turn was replaced by a larger school in neighboring Collinston in 1927. The town has had three stores, one at a time. When the Oregon Short Line was built through Bear River Canyon, the tracks passed close to Beaver Dam.

A flour mill was built in 1916, powered by electricity from the old Wheelon power plant. The mill produced good flour, but the cost of electricity was so high that the mill, which went through several owners, proved unprofitable.

The Johnson Hay Fork was an invention of Joseph S. Johnson, son of early Beaver Dam settler Jarvis Johnson. Some five hundred of the forks were produced and sold in Box Elder County, Cache Valley, and other areas.

Conrad Johnson operated a wheat puffer and produced King Kernel puffed wheat in the old rock school house behind the flour mill. Apparently the old advertisements for puffed wheat were accurate. According to Russell Johnson, "The puffing action sounded like a large cannon being fired."

The people of Beaver Dam installed a pumping plant large enough to irrigate five hundred acres of land, in 1921. The $18,000 cost of the project, plus the cost of electricity to operate the pumps made the project ultimately unprofitable.

The chief source of employment in Beaver Dam is farming, but, besides Alton Veibell's well-known gas and diesel engine rebuilding operation, Beaver Dam residents are employed at Thiokol, La-z-Boy, Autoliv, Moore's Business Machines, Utah Power and Light, and Utah State University.

Beaver Dam has never been incorporated, and community services and functions are furnished by the cooperation of the citizens. Besides Cutler Dam, and Early Park, one of the local sights is Garth and Veda Kidman's "Tractor Patch," a menagerie of old tractors and farm equipment.

Bothwell

The town of Bothwell lies 4.5 miles west of Tremonton, on Salt

Creek. Bothwell is twenty miles northwest of the county courthouse in Brigham City.[4] It covers an area 4.5 miles wide and six miles long. It has a population of approximately 400 people. The elevation is 4320 feet with 120 to 140 frost-free days each year, and eleven to fifteen inches of annual precipitation. The topography is level to slightly sloping, and the land is adaptable to raising wheat, barley, corn, oats, alfalfa, onions, beans, potatoes, peas, sugar beets, tomatoes, sunflowers, and safflower. There are few days in the summer when the temperature exceeds 100 degrees. Winter days and nights are seldom colder than 20 degrees below zero.

The earliest accounts written about the Bothwell area tell of beautiful waves of tall bunch grass covering the lower region and of tall sagebrush growing on the hills. From inscriptions found on the rocks at the head of Salt Creek and artifacts dug up on the farms adjacent to the creek, it is apparent that Indians obtained water from Salt Creek and used this area for hunting grounds and camp sites.

The first white settlers came to the Bothwell area to take advantage of the Homestead Act. They settled near Salt Creek, as it was the major source of water for the region west of the Bear River and Malad River.

The first white home in this area was built by Andrew Anderson from Bear River City. Soon others followed to take up homesteads and plant dry land wheat. They hauled water from Salt Creek.

In 1892, after several years of construction, the Bear River canal system was completed, and water flowed into the arid region in sufficient quantities to irrigate thousands of acres of land. The community was named for John R. Bothwell, the engineer and promoter of the canal system

Most settlers were members of the Church of Jesus Christ of Latter-day-Saints, and an LDS branch was organized in 1894. Joseph M. Stokes was set apart as presiding elder. In 1898 a ward was organized, and Stokes was called as bishop. He presided for fourteen years. Three LDS buildings have served the community. The present one, a beautiful red brick structure dedicated in 1948, has been remodeled twice. The church is the center of all entertainment, such as dances, drama, banquets, ball games, and socials, as well as worship services. It remains the center of all community activities.

Some of the first settlers who bought land under the Homestead Act, and became farmers in Bothwell, were of German descent and were members of the Christian Apostolic Faith. They attended church in Tremonton. These people came about the same time as the settlement of Tremonton, and shared aspects of their culture with the Tremonton settlers.

The first school was held in 1894 in a small frame building on the west banks of Salt Creek. There were about twenty pupils, who walked or were transported in wagons or sleds to the school. The second school was also frame, located a half mile west and a quarter mile north of the first school. The third school was a brick structure and was located just west of where the LDS church now stands. The bricks were made by John Sommers on the banks of Salt Creek. After a series of earthquakes in 1908, the building was condemned. In 1909 a new brick building, with four classrooms, was erected. It served elementary students until 1967, at which time the students were bussed to Tremonton.

Mail service was established in the area by James Ipsom. He would pick the mail up at Bear River City and bring it to his home in Bothwell where the residents would go to collect their mail. In 1895 Mrs. Margaret Priest was appointed the first post mistress. The post office consisted of a room in her home. In 1898 the post office was moved to the Foxley Store and was given the name of "Point Look Out Post Office." A Rural Free Route for mail delivery was established in 1909, and mail is still delivered six days a week to all RFD box holders.

The first telephone lines were extended from Tremonton to Bothwell in 1907. The first phones were the old oak crank type that were attached to the wall. Only a few lines were brought into Bothwell, so everyone who signed up to have a phone installed was on a party line. As many as twelve to fifteen homes were serviced by one line. It proved to be a very efficient method for everyone to get the local news and happenings in the community. The dial system was installed in about 1950, and the number of parties on one line was cut to five or six. Improvements were gradually made until all residents were provided a private line.

The first settlers used tallow candles to light their homes, and in

Hauling sugar beets from Appledale, now West Corinne, May 1911. (Box Elder County)

time coal oil lamps became available. Later several families had carbide light systems installed in their homes, and some bought gasoline-powered washing machines. Before World War I, attempts were made to bring electricity to Bothwell, but war scarcities made materials unavailable. Later committees were organized, and after several unsuccessful attempts electricity was finally turned on in Bothwell in April 1926. At first, people were interested in electricity only for lighting. All the comforts and conveniences of electric power came later.

When the first settlers came to Bothwell, they got their water from Salt Creek, hauling it in barrels on skids or in wagons. When the canal was completed in 1892, nearly everyone used water from it. They dipped the water, strained it through cloth into barrels, and let it settle. It was used for drinking, washing, and other purposes. Later many of the citizens dug deep wells. Most of the water from wells was too salty to be good. However, Rasmus Anderson, Fred Dienger, and Thomas Payne were able to get good water from their wells, which they shared with their neighbors for drinking.

In 1935 Eli Hawkins started work on a project to get federal funds through the PWA or WPA to pipe water from the spring east of Bothwell to supply the community with good clean culinary water. It was necessary to incorporate the area into a town so it could be bonded in order to get funds for the water project. In February 1937 Harry Drew was elected mayor. The county commissioners were approached with a petition to form a town, and it was approved for incorporation in April 1937. Work was started on the water project in the spring of 1938. By July 1940 nine miles of trenches had been dug, the pipes all laid, the water turned on, and the system accepted. The water system continues to serve the community in 1999.

Before 1960 the community was totally dependent upon agriculture for its economic base. Every farmer raised acres of sugar beets, the main cash crop. Many farmers had feed-lot cattle and raised lambs and hogs. Most farmers had small herds of dairy cattle, raising grain and alfalfa to feed all their animals. The milk from the dairy herds was picked up daily and taken to Tremonton or Cache Valley to be processed.

In the late 1930s a few of the local men tried raising large flocks of turkeys. They met with enough success that through the 1940s, 1950s and 1960s, at least one-fourth of the farmers were involved with brooding, growing, and finishing the holiday birds. Some had several flocks of over 5,000 birds in size. This proved a successful enterprise most years, but some years disease would cause severe losses. Several farmers also had chicken farms, and produced eggs for consumers in Tremonton and surrounding communities.

Bothwell is now an unincorporated area. At this writing, there are only three dairies in Bothwell and only one farmer is involved raising turkeys. The U&I Sugar Factory closed its doors in 1975, and therefore there are no sugar beets grown in the valley. There are now no egg producers. There are still a few hog producers and also some feed-lot cattle and beef cattle producers, as well as a sod farm and a large potato farm. Only half of the residents now depend on agriculture for their livelihood. Many work at nearby industries. Thiokol Corporation is located ten miles west of Bothwell, and employs many residents of the community, as does Nucor Steel, located twenty miles north, and La-Z-Boy Company in Tremonton. Some are also employed by the school system. All of these industries help to provide a healthy economy for the area. Tremonton is the business and shopping center for Bothwell, providing banking services, a hospital, and stores, which supply most of the needs of the valley.

Brigham City

Because the history of Brigham City has been extensively covered in the main body of the text, only highlights will be given in this section.

Brigham City, that is, Box Elder Creek, was a place of habitation by prehistoric Indians, who used Flatbottom Canyon as a route to and from Cache Valley. There was, when the Mormon settlers came, in the middle of the nineteenth century, a Shoshoni camping ground on the creek where John Adams Park now lies.

The area was explored by the fur trappers of the early nineteenth century, and by the government explorers who came some years later. Jesse C. Little explored the area for the Mormons shortly after the main body of pioneers arrived in 1847.

The first permanent settlers, William Davis, James Brooks, and Thomas Pierce, came in the fall of 1850, to reconnoiter, and then returned with their families in the spring of 1851. Their camp, called Davis Fort, was along the banks of the creek, in northwestern Brigham City. Rising spring runoff and vermin caused abandonment of the fort. An "Indian scare" forced construction of another fort in 1853, called Box Elder Fort, or the Old Fort.

Lorenzo Snow, an LDS apostle, was called at the October 1854 LDS general conference, to take fifty families to Box Elder. Most of them came in the spring of 1855. At that time a city plat was surveyed, and the settlers moved onto city lots.

The first industrial building was a grist mill, at the northeast corner of Plat A, overlooking the Indian camp. The first public building was the court house. Though expanded, the original portion remains in use, the oldest-functioning court house in the state.

Box Elder settlement was renamed Brigham City by Lorenzo Snow, in honor of Brigham Young. It was in Brigham City that Brigham Young delivered the final public address of his life, just ten days before his death, as he completed the reorganizations of the stakes of Zion and of the priesthood, according to a revelation he received in St. George in April 1877 at the time of the dedication of the temple in that city.

Brigham City was one of the showplaces of the Utah Zion. It was

Brigham City Main Street shortly after the dedication of the sign 19 September 1928. (Utah State Historical Society)

the cradle of the United Order movement, started by Lorenzo Snow in the 1860s. Brigham City was one of the most successful of the cooperatives established throughout the Mormon kingdom in the 1860s and 1870s. It did not breathe its last gasp until the national financial Panic of 1893.

Brigham City was founded as an agricultural community. It was bypassed by the Transcontinental Railroad, but was on the line of the Utah Northern, the Utah Idaho Central, and the Oregon Short Line.

During World War II it was the site of the Bushnell Army hospital, which closed immediately after the war ended. The hospital buildings later became a boarding school for Native American children.

In the 1950s Thiokol Chemical Corporation built its Wasatch Division plant west of Brigham City, and its coming changed the demographics, the face, and substance of the town.

Brigham City is the county seat of Box Elder County. Until 1892, when a municipal water system was constructed at a cost of $24,000, water came from three sources—irrigation ditches, open wells, and pumps. Twenty years later the system was upgraded and expanded, at a cost of $35,000.

Electric power came first about 1890. A generator was attached to the waterwheel at the old woolen mill building, but an unreliable supply of water, slippage of the belts operating the generator, and the limited capacity of the generator itself, led to abandonment of the effort.

The Knudson family spearheaded installation of a new source of electric power. A generator was installed in a small building near the OSL depot and operated by a coal-fired steam boiler. The system went into operation on 15 January 1892 with a capacity of seven hundred lamps. The steam engine was too expensive to be profitable, the generator was installed at the mouth of Box Elder Canyon and operated by water power. The plant was insufficient to meet the city's needs and voters approved a $30,000 bond on 1 September 1902 for a new power plant. The Brigham City Municipal Corporation built the one unit, 470 horsepower capacity plant in 1903–04.[5] By 1920, the plant was at capacity, and the Knudson Investment Company sold its rights to Brigham City Corporation, paving the way for a new plant. The 1,200 horsepower plant went into operation 10 January 1922.

Besides being the county seat, and the largest city in Box Elder County, Brigham City is the location of the school district offices and is, with the exception of Logan, the largest city in Utah north of Ogden. It is located almost equidistant from Logan and Ogden, and is a hub of business, industry, and commerce. In 1990 the population was 15,644 and in 1996 16,398.

Cedar Creek

Cedar Creek is one of Box Elder County's ghost towns. The site is located near the dry stream bed of Cedar Creek, as it comes down from the Raft River Mountains, eastward, into Curlew Valley. Farmers and ranchers moved into the area in the 1860s and 1870s, and by the first decade of the twentieth century a small community had developed. By the end of the twentieth century, the community had been long abandoned.

In 1889, James Alonzo Tracy and Margret Melinda Whitaker as newlyweds took up a homestead on the main stage and freight road at Cedar Creek. The Tracy family owned and operated the only store for many years. Stephen Carr recounts the history of Cedar Creek in his book, *The Historical Guide of Utah's Ghost Towns:*

> By 1900–10 some twenty to thirty families lived in town and on the surrounding farms and ranches. Some of the homes were attractively furnished, others made do with comic papers for wallpapering in the upstairs rooms. The new school marm in 1916 was so homesick she couldn't sleep. She spent the first night roaming around her attic bedroom reading the wallpaper and chuckling, which no doubt relieved the anxiety of her situation. A frame school-church house was located on the eastern edge of town, in the vicinity of a log inn and store, called the Halfway House, where freighters and travelers stopped to eat and rest along the old overland trail. Later, as the new highway system was being developed, the highway ran due west from Snowville to Cedar Creek, then southward and westward around Crystal Peak to Park Valley and beyond. The town had at that time a service station in addition to the store.
>
> Much of town activity centered in the school building, with hoedowns, home theatrics and talent shows. Bands of Indians were often seen migrating through town, making their living catching rabbits and collecting pine nuts. . . . In as much as many of the children rode horses three to four miles to school, a supply of cheese and crackers was kept on hand for the occasional times a blizzard came up and marooned them overnight. . . .
>
> The little town never felt the need for more than the tiny grocery store, as Strevell, Idaho, a somewhat larger town, was just three and a half miles northwest up the road. The folks drove over every two to four weeks to do their marketing. The mail wagon dropped off the town mail at the Tracy home, and folks came by there to pick it up instead of having a regular post office.
>
> Around 1920–25, farming became extremely hard with cold winters and ever present low water in summer. Travelers were now bypassing Cedar Creek and finally the residents all moved way. Some of the best buildings were moved to other towns, others were left to crumble away.
>
> Only a few old, weathered, fallen and falling log and frame

houses remain in an area covered with sagebrush and grass. The small but forlornly picturesque town remnants lie eight-tenths of a mile on a dirt road south off U.S. Highway 30-S five miles west of the exit of State Highway 30.[6]

Collinston

Collinston is one of the oldest communities in Box Elder County. Its center has been located in several places, and its history is closely linked to the development of transportation and industry in northern Utah.[7]

Collinston is located on Utah Highway 30 at the north end of the Wellsville range. Four miles to the east is Beaver Dam near the entrance into Cache Valley.

Approximately five miles downstream from the mouth of the canyon where the Bear River enters the Bear River Valley is located the ford where Indians, trappers, and early explorers crossed the river. John C. Frèmont probably crossed the Bear River at this location on 14 September 1843, on his way to Fort Hall. Captain Samuel J. Hensley used the ford in 1848, as he established the Salt Lake Cutoff. In 1848–49 some of the Mormon Battalion members, following Hensley's route, returned this way, from California. Captain Howard Stansbury crossed with wagons in 1848, and the Gold Rush emigrants used this crossing to go to the gold fields of California, by way of Fort Hall or the Salt Lake Cutoff.[8]

As routes became better established, more and more travelers crossed at the Bear River ford. It was a good ford, with a stable bottom, but it was not always an easy ford. The river was wide, swift, and deep, and some of those who crossed were swept down the river. Each year several lives were lost. Two early settlers, Benjamin Hampton and William S. Godbe, foresaw the need of a ferry as a safer means of moving emigrants and freighters across the river. An act approved 30 January 1852, Laws of Utah Territory, granted the right to establish a ferry across the Bear River. In 1853 Hampton and Godbe established a ferry at the Bear River Ford. Toll charges were ten cents for a horse, twenty-five cents for a wagon.

The first permanent settlers to the area came in 1860. Among them were Henry Busenbark and sons Alonzo and Monroe, who

The central area of Collinston in the early part of the 20th century. (Courtesy Sonja Secrist Shelton)

came from Providence in Cache County.[9] They were followed by the families of Henry Jemmett, Thomas Potts, Mark Bigler, John Barnard, and the Sprague family.

As travel increased through the area, traffic became too great for the ferry. In 1859 a bridge was constructed by Hampton and Godbe a few hundred feet south of the ferry crossing. It was said to be the first bridge over the Bear River. A small log building with a thatched roof was built near the bridge and became a stopping place for travelers.

On 30 June 1864 the Holladay Overland Mail and Stage Company, coming from Salt Lake City, made its first run through the territory to Virginia City, Montana, and Boise, Idaho. In 1866 Benjamin Hampton obtained a charter from the Utah Territorial Legislature to build a new bridge across the Bear River. It was built on the original piers of the first bridge.

In the same year William Godbe, Ben Hampton, Alvin Nichols, Sr., Mark Bigler, and others erected an eighteen-room, two-story rock hotel and restaurant south of the bridge.[10] Called the Stage Coach Hotel, it served as a home station for the Oliver and Connover, Ben Holladay, and Wells-Fargo stage lines. The hotel was the first overnight stop north of Salt Lake City. The trip from Salt Lake City took an entire day, and the horses were changed every ten miles. Shortly after the hotel was finished, a barn was built to accommodate the stage coaches and horses.

In 1875 James Standing and his wife Mary exchanged property they owned in Salt Lake City with Hampton and Godbe for 584 acres of land, the stone house and the bridge known as the Bear River Bridge, together with all other improvements. The place became more of a home than a business venture, but the Standing Family continued to operate the toll bridge and provide meals and lodging for travelers. Leonard W. Standing opened a store and blacksmith shop down by the bridge in 1880. School was held at the inn and Hyrum Standing was the teacher. James Standing operated the toll bridge until 1883, when he sold it to Box Elder County.

In 1864 Asenath Patton from Farmington, who had helped cook and serve meals at the old log structure that predated the hotel, married Mark Bigler. One of their sons, Jacob A. Bigler, married Agnes Standing, the youngest child of James and Mary Standing. After the death of James Standing, Jacob and Agnes Bigler acquired the home and property from the Standing estate and continued to run the hotel. The Bigler family owned and occupied the property longer than any others.

On 26 August 1871 construction began for the Utah Northern Railroad, a narrow-gauge line from Ogden through the northern Utah communities to Franklin, Idaho. The railroad passed north through Brigham City, Deweyville, and crossed the top of the hill north of the quarry above present-day Collinston and over the Mendon Divide into Cache Valley. A train station was built northeast of present-day Collinston and named Hampton Station. The Utah Northern Railroad was completed to Hampton Station in June 1872, to Mendon by 19 December 1872, and to Logan by 31 January 1873. It was completed to Franklin, Idaho, by May 1874. According to tradition, local citizens changed the name of their community to

Collinston to honor Collins Fulmer, a favorite conductor on the Utah Northern Railroad.[11]

With the building of the railroad, the importance of stage coach transportation began to diminish. Hampton's Crossing at the river remained, but the center of activity moved to the railroad east of the river. A railroad siding was established at the northern boundary of the track, and named Ukon. Not much is known about this first community located on the northwest boundary of the railroad. A post office was first established in Collinston (located at the Ukon siding) in 1881, with William S. Hansen as postmaster. Mail was sent from Brigham City to the Ukon siding on the Utah Northern Railroad for the Malad Mail Route. Records mentioning the Malad Mail Route at the Collinston post office date to 1888. The nearby Hansen Dairy shipped its products from the Ukon siding to locations to the north and south.

On 3 April 1878 the Utah Northern Railroad was sold at public auction and the name was changed to the Utah and Northern Railway. On 1 August 1889 it was consolidated with the Oregon Short Line. By that time it had become evident that the route over the northern tip of Wellsville Mountains was too steep for the narrow-gauge trains to pull through the deep snow during the harsh winters. The decision was made to widen the tracks and to change the route of the train to a location parallel to the old Utah Northern tracks, but approximately a half mile to the west. It followed a route parallel and east of the Bear River northeast through the Bear River Canyon into Cache Valley. The new Oregon Short Line route was completed through the canyon in 1890.

When the railroad route east over the Wellsville Mountains was abandoned, so was the town of Collinston at the Ukon location. The new railroad siding for Collinston was located on the new Oregon Short Line tracks, about a mile to the north and west down the hill from Ukon. A map of Collinston dated 24 March 1891 shows a detailed street plan for the town of Collinston located in the northeast quarter of Section 9. This ground belonged at that time to Monroe Busenbark. Post office records also indicate that a post office was being operated at this location in 1891, and that Eliza Jemmett was the postmistress.

This second town of Collinston did not survive long. Again the railroad was directly involved. Not long after the new railroad station was established, it became evident that the choice of locations was poor. At the north location, the tracks left the flat land and climbed toward Bear River Canyon. Just when trains should have been building up speed for the steep ascent, they had to stop at the Collinston station. Regaining speed for the climb through the canyon was difficult. The decision was made to relocate the station farther south down the tracks at the present town site. Post office records indicate that application was made on 29 September 1892 to change the site of the post office from the north location to a new site situated on the southeast quarter of Section 17. This location became the center of the new and permanent site of the town of Collinston. The town was surveyed and laid out in lots on 12 November 1892. The post office had been moved to the south location by January 1893.

Because all freight for Malad and Boise, Idaho, was unloaded at Collinston, it became as important a shipping center for points to the north and west as Hampton's Crossing had been for the stage lines, as all freight for Malad and Boise, Idaho, was unloaded at Collinston. The January 1898 issue of *The New West Magazine,* published in Brigham City by F. Will Ellis, states that in 1897 100,000 bushels of wheat were shipped from the Collinston station and that it was predicted that "not less than five carloads of alfalfa seed, besides great quantities of barley, potatoes, onions, etc." would be shipped in 1898.

During the prosperous years of the 1890s, businesses opened. John Baxter and Sons, Jed Earl, Boothe & Pierce, Evan Morgan, and Royal and Busenbark carried on mercantile businesses. Henry G. and Eliza Jemmett ran a large hotel and restaurant. In addition, Mr. Jemmett ran a livery, feed, and stage stable. Eliza Jemmett was postmistress and also a licensed physician. Timothy and Julia Bigler Covert ran a store near the hotel. Mr. Covert was also the postmaster for a time. Dr. William G. Freiday practiced medicine in Collinston around the turn of the century.

Benjamin Williams, the proprietor of the Malad and Collinston Stage Line, made daily trips between these points, a distance of thirty-five miles for a two dollar fare. Another store, owned by G. G. Sweeton, boasted a second floor which was used as a dance hall. A confectionery and barbershop was owned by Jack Standing. A. J. Jenson ran a pool hall. In addition to his duties as a local doctor, Frederick Wach ran a drugstore.

Hyrum Jensen ran a lumber yard, a hardware store, and a furniture store, and Jack White ran a blacksmith shop and store. Mr. Robertson sold Studebacker buggies to the people in the area. Dances were popular, and admission to the silent motion picture shows was twenty-five cents for adults and ten cents for children. Many of the town's young men played in the area's baseball league.

In the years from 1893 to 1905, Collinston was the rail center for the northeastern part of the valley. In 1904, because of the building of the East Hammond Canal and the railroad, Collinston reached its peak as a shipping and business community. Hogs and cattle were shipped from the stockyards located by the railroad tracks. Wheat and beets and other farm products were shipped from the town to outside markets.

In 1905 the Malad Branch of the Oregon Short Line was built through the center of the valley. Completion of the Malad Branch dealt the same kind of blow to Collinston that had been dealt by the Utah Northern Railroad to Corinne some thirty years before. Collinston began to wither as its importance as a shipping center began to wane and Tremonton started to bloom.

The post office was an important institution in Collinston, functioning continuously for over l00 years. All of the mail for the northern part of Box Elder County was distributed at one time through the Collinston Post Office. When the post office closed on 9 April 1982, a rural route was established from Brigham City.

Until 1900 Collinston had been maintained almost entirely by freighting, but at this time farming began to come into prominence. From 1889 to 1907, the East Hammond Canal was built to irrigate hundreds of acres of ground in the Bear River Valley. The area around Collinston became a rich farming district. More families moved in, building homes and planting crops. Some of the early permanent residents were the Robert A. Fryer family, the Jacob A. Bigler family, the Hyrum Jensen family, and the John M. Saunders family. Other longtime residents of the area were the T.W. Potter family, the Sterling W. Secrist family, the William Rucker family, the James A.

Peterson family, the Ormes, and the Marbles. Some members of these families still live in Collinston today.

Around the turn of the century, a one-room schoolhouse was built approximately a quarter of a mile to the south and east of the center of Collinston. In 1912 a two-room grade school was built just to the south of the first building. The number of children who attended the Collinston School dwindled over the years, and in 1962 the school was closed and the children were bussed to grade school in Fielding.

In 1914 the Ogden Rapid Transit Company consolidated with the Logan Rapid Transit Company to operate an electric railway between Ogden and Preston, Idaho, that ran on the same roadbed used by the old Utah Northern Railroad above Collinston. It was called the Utah Idaho Central and was also known as the Bamberger. The Bamberger railroad proper came north as far as Ogden, where the Utah Idaho Central, or UIC began. To the people who lived along the line, however, the entire electric interurban, north to Preston, was known as the "Bamberger" line.

In the mid 1920s the residents of Collinston put away their candles and oil lamps. Electricity lighted their homes. About that time telephone lines arrived.

When Bear River High School was built in 1921, it was not large enough to accommodate the students east of the Bear River. Many of the high school age students from Collinston traveled on the Utah Idaho Central to Box Elder High School in Brigham City. Later, when Bear River High was enlarged students from Collinston began attending high school there.

Many of the settlers in the Collinston area were members of the LDS church. In the early years Collinston members belonged to the Deweyville Ward. In 1896 the ward was divided, with Collinston and Beaver Dam (and later the residents at the Cutler Hydroelectric Plant) being joined as the Beaver Ward with Francello Durfey as bishop. In the early years church meetings were held in the little rock schoolhouse located just north of the Collinston School. Much of the social life and church activity of the early community was centered around Collinston Hall. Collinston Hall was built and used for a business. The LDS church bought the hall in about 1928, to be used for church functions. T. W. (Bill) Potter offered Saturday night "picture shows" there. During the 1950–51 remodeling and construction of the Beaver Ward building, the Collinston Hall was used quite extensively. After completion of the recreation hall at the Beaver Ward in Beaver Dam, the Collinston Hall was no longer needed by the ward. The hall was sold and was now owned for many years by LeGrande (Dick) Jensen, a life-long resident of Collinston, until his death in the early 1990s.

In 1932–33 the State of Utah planned to put a state road through the Collinston area. The new state road was built west of the county road through about two hundred acres of prime farm ground straight into the town of Collinston. The state road shed was built just north of the LeGrande Jensen home.

The residents of Collinston get their drinking water from springs or wells that they own themselves. Irrigation water comes from the East Hammond canal.

Collinston is no longer the metropolis it once was. Most of the old buildings have been taken down or destroyed by fire. The one remaining store which housed the post office is closed, as is the fertilizer plant. The old hotel still stands, and has been for many years the home of Ed and Orpha Bowers, longtime Collinston residents. The old schoolhouse has been remodeled and turned into a home. The Hyrum Jensen home, the Mark Bigler home, and the John Saunders home, all built near the turn-of-the-century, still house town residents. The only businesses that remain in operation are a sandblasting and paint shop operated by Garren Anderson, the Hampton's Ford Restaurant owned by Sherrie and Junior Goring, the Bingham Truck Wash, and Wheatland Seed Company.

As the twentieth century comes to a close, Collinston has a population of about one hundred people and is unincorporated. The center of the town is located at approximately 14600 North Highway 30. Most of those who now live in the area no longer obtain their livelihood from farming. They work at Thiokol, La-Z-Boy, NuCor and various other places around the valley. Some new homes are being built by people who have come to work in the Tremonton-Garland area or in Cache Valley, but want to raise their families in the rural atmosphere of the Collinston community.

Corinne

Corinne is located five miles west of Brigham City at the spot where the tracks of the westward-moving Union Pacific Railroad crossed the Bear River.[12] Corinne's history is unique among the towns of Box Elder County. Corinne was founded primarily as a railroad town. It was *the* railroad town of Utah, founded to be a bastion against the Mormon Kingdom of Brigham Young and his apostles. As such, its history is fascinating and colorful.

As the Union Pacific tracks entered Utah from Wyoming early in 1868, the raucous tent-town familiarly known as "Hell-on-Wheels" moved along with it, setting up at each end-of-track camp. Though the individual sites bore names like Wahsatch, Echo, and Bonneville, those "towns" were only repeated incarnations of the same group of merchants, saloon-keepers, shillers, camp-followers, and brothels, with temporary quarters, put up and torn down week after week as the tracks moved on, inexorably westward, toward the point of junction with the eastward-pushing tracks of the Central Pacific, coming over the mighty Sierra Nevada from Sacramento.

The Union Pacific came down Weber Canyon, and established a station at Ogden, but Ogden—at that time—was a Mormon town. North of Ogden was Bonneville camp. The tracks turned west before reaching Brigham City, and Corinne rose at the crossing of Bear River. West of Corinne, the tracks crossed the marshes, then began climbing more slowly the rocky east slope of the Promontory Mountains. There, Hall's Camp and Camp Dead Fall saw the erection of Hell-on-Wheels in its penultimate manifestation before its final glory at Promontory Station, serving the needs of the workers not only of the Union Pacific, but of the Central Pacific as well.

It was not long after the driving of the ceremonial spikes and the drinking of the ceremonial champagne that both railroads agreed that Promontory Summit was far too isolated to be the division point. They agreed that the Central Pacific would buy and lease the UP tracks and right-of-way as far as Ogden. Promontory Summit became only Promontory Station, one of many small towns along the CP line.

Ogden, however, was a Mormon town, and the railroad had not

yet gained ascendancy over the town and changed its culture. The only place in between suitable for a *real* railroad town was Corinne. Thus it was that the mass of Hell-on-Wheels withdrew to Corinne, to form the nucleus of a city.

Not only was this a railroad town, it was a rallying point for all those who hated, feared, or were discomforted by the Mormon culture. Colonel Patrick Connor, who had been virtually isolated at Fort Douglas on the bench east of Salt Lake City, threw in with the railroad people. Because he had been in Utah the longest, the infant settlement was named Connor, or Connor City, in his honor. The town site was surveyed in February 1869 by the Union Pacific Railroad. The railroad company received alternate city lots for its service. By 25 March the survey was complete, and a grand survey it was, three miles square. Founders hoped the city would become the capital of Utah. There was an entire block set aside for a university, and another for a Catholic church. From this bastion, the Gentiles, as the Mormons called them, would ultimately take over the state.

It was decided by the proud founding fathers that the city needed a more suitable grand name, and the name they picked was Corinne. Various stories are told about the origin of the name. It was the name of a character in a popular novel of the day; it was the name of a popular actress of the time, Corinne LaVaunt. The most likely source, however, is Corinne Williamson, daughter of General J. A. Williamson, land agent for the Union Pacific (which surveyed the town and held alternate lots). Williamson was the first temporary citizen-mayor of the city. For whom his daughter was named is not specified. Perhaps it was the actress.

Though Corinne was the city's official name, she was given many appellations. It's founders fondly called her Corinne the Fair. The Mormons called it the Burgh on the Bear, or the City of the Un-Godly.

Initially, the city took hold, and grew. It was incorporated on 18 February 1870, and eventually had a population between 3,500 and 10,000, depending upon the time of year.

Corinne was positioned to be a hub of transportation and commerce. Trains of freight wagons lumbered between Corinne and the Montana mines. Produce went north, ore came south. Before long, steamboats were plying the waters of Bear River and the Great Salt Lake, serving the mines in the area of Stockton, Tooele, and Ophir. The most famous steamboat was the *City of Corinne.* The city had banks, stores, a grist mill, a smelter, even a cigar factory. It had a grand Opera House, with a spring dance floor (underpinned by springs from box cars). It was the largest such hall north of Salt Lake City.

Corinne had a baseball team, an ice skating pond, and hotels, one of them—the Central Hotel—a fine two-story brick structure. There were, according to some reports, twenty-eight saloons and eighty "soiled doves" plying their wares among the men of the railroad and freight yards.

The law firm of Johnson and Underdunk provided a handy device which operated somewhat like a slot machine. With the insertion of a $2.50 gold piece and the pull of a handle, one had a signed, sealed, legal divorce document lacking only the names of the parties involved.

The first water system utilized steam pumps to raise water from the Bear River into settling tanks. It was then distributed in wooden pipes to homes and businesses in the community.

Corinne had a large population of Chinese, and laundries, cookeries, and other establishments were crowded into Corinne's Chinatown.

Corinne was unique in Utah for its grand celebration of Independence Day, the Fourth of July. Throughout the rest of Utah, the big summer celebration was twenty days later. To further distinguish itself, the city fathers passed an ordinance prohibiting polygamy within the city limits. There was even a petition requesting the removal of the territorial capital from Salt Lake City to Corinne. Rallies and caucuses of the Liberal Party of Utah, numbering among its supporters the likes of William S. Godbe, Elias L. T. Harrison, Edward W. Tullidge, Eli B. Kelsey, William H. Shearman, and excommunicated Mormon apostle Amasa Lyman. The Liberal party sought to bring the economic system of the rest of the United States to Utah.

After the Utah Northern was extended north through Brigham City into Idaho, Corinne began a decline. Ogden was the junction

Main Street in Corinne during the summer of 1940. (Utah State Historical Society)

city. The building of the Lucin Cutoff and rerouting of through rail traffic west over the cutoff was another blow.

Though there were spurts and gasps, one incident to the building of the Bear River Canal system, Corinne declined. Even the canal turned against Corinne. The water leached alkali salts up through the soil, and the crops and trees died. Corinne withered on the vine. It was not until Clarence G. Adney, John Craner, and others organized the Corinne drainage district and laid miles and miles of drain tiles underneath the farmland that the alkali was leached out and the ground returned to productivity.

Corinne survived as a town because of the land, not the railroad. Brigham Young had said that agriculture was to be the mainstay of Utah, and his prophecy has come to pass.

Corinne has struggled for sources of fresh water. C. G. Adney and others bought a spring on the foothills of Wellsville Mountain and built a good water system for Corinne. A. V. Smoot and others began planning a water system for West Corinne in the 1940s, before that,

"Corinne City had a water tap as a courtesy to west Corinne people. They would come sometimes several times a day (in the summer) to fill up their ten-gallon milk cans to haul out to their homes and stockyards. This happened for fifty-two years . . . "[13] More springs were added to the system in 1957 and as late as 1990.

Corinne had the first U.S. weather station in Utah, the first non-Mormon meeting house, the first water system, the first drainage system, the first export of precious metal ore to the outside, the first public school, and, of course, the first (and only) divorce vending machine.

One by one, the Catholics, the Episcopalians, the Presbyterians, and the Methodists left as Corinne withered, and Mormon farmers bought up the surrounding land. The Opera House became the LDS chapel, until it was razed to construct a "proper" chapel in 1952.

As of 1993, Corinne had a population of 635 in the city proper and 1,200 in the greater Corinne area, most of them members of the Church of Jesus Christ of Latter-day Saints . However, citizens have undertaken an important project to restore and preserve the 1870 Methodist-Episcopal Church in Corinne—the oldest non-Mormon church in Utah.

The main occupation is farming, with many employed at Thiokol, Morton (Autoliv), Hill Air Force Base, and other local businesses and industries. Corinne, with one of the most unique histories in all of Utah, is now a fairly typical small Utah town.

Elwood

Elwood is located two miles southeast of Tremonton, and fourteen miles north from the courthouse in Brigham City. The first settler in the area was a sheep and cattle rancher by the name of Davidson. He sold his interests in 1879 to Abraham and Allen Hunsaker. Later others joined them at the site. Another influx of settlers came from Bear River City in 1882. Apparently the name of early Elwood was Fairview.

When the Bothwell Canal was completed, other settlers came in 1894–95 from Mona in Juab County and from Salt Lake City. They settled about a mile north of the main settlement. The Fairview Branch became the Manila Ward on 16 December 1900.[14] As was its arbitrary custom, the U.S. Postal Service dictated a name change to avoid confusion with the Manila Voting precinct in Utah County. The town became Elwood, and the northern settlement North Elwood.

The Manila Ward Built a chapel, but was made a part of the Tremonton Ward in November 1914. For a period of time in the early years of the twentieth century, Elwood had its own school. By 1937 the children of North Elwood were bussed to Tremonton. Eventually the Elwood school was closed.

An LDS ward was later organized in Elwood, and a brick chapel built in 1928. The building was sold in the 1980s, and the people of Elwood attend church services elsewhere. The population of Elwood was 525 in 1910, but dropped to 294 in 1970 before rising to 575 by 1990 and 632 in 1996.

Etna

Etna is located five miles south and west of Grouse Creek, and is the westernmost settlement in Box Elder County. It is located on Etna and Warm creeks four miles east of the Utah-Nevada border. Etna is over a hundred miles northwest from Brigham City as the crow flies, and half that again by the nearest paved route.

According to one account, Etna was settled "in 1875 by Valison and Alma C. Tanner, and its early name was West Fork (of Grouse Creek)."[15] In fact, the two early school precincts at Etna and Grouse Creek were called East and West Forks.[16] Because a permanent name for the location was required before mail could be delivered, the mail carrier, Charlie Morris, named it Etna.[17] Etna shares its history with Grouse Creek. There are five ranches in Etna in 1999. About a mile west of the site of Etna is Etna Hot Springs, the water of which is now pumped and piped some distance to the east to provide geothermal resources for a large home built in recent years.

Fielding

Fielding is located twenty miles west of Logan and fourteen miles north of Tremonton.[18] It is bordered by the Bear River on the east and the Malad River on the west with Plymouth Peak to the north. In the past this area has been referred to as "The Flat" and "Poverty Flat."

In the 1870s John W. Hess and Isaac Zundel were called by the LDS Church as missionaries to watch over and help the Shoshoni Indians in this part of the Malad Valley (now Bear River Valley). While riding through the valley, Hess noted the springs and the growth of the grass and sage brush. He stated to Zundel that, after returning to Farmington, he intended to bring back one of his wives and some of his boys to homestead the land and use it for farming. At that time the land was being used for grazing by the larger cattle ranchers from this valley and also the ranchers of Cache Valley during the summer.

With the Hesses came others from Farmington who settled in various parts of the valley. Some of them obtained pre-emption rights from the government to homestead the even-numbered sections of land, and others laid claim to odd-numbered sections that the government had given to the railroad company as compensation for building the transcontinental railroad. Some of the people who claimed the railroad land could not show legal title to it; therefore, they lost their claims and moved on, declaring that the government did not have the right to give the land to the railroad. Some of the early homesteaders who were able to prove up on their land were: Myron J. Richards, Jed Earl, John Earl, Oliver Wood , Willard K. Welling, Joseph Pratt, Arthur Stayner, Mary T. Richards, Calvin Richards, and Ezra T. Richards.

With the building of the earthen dam across the Bear River and the Bear River Canal System in 1888–90, more people came to the valley for work. They bought land and made their homes here.

Fielding was founded in 1892, and named for the sixth president of the Church of Jesus Christ of Latter-day Saints, Joseph Fielding Smith (1838–1918), at that time second counselor in the LDS First Presidency. The settlers sought a place for a townsite to bring them together from their scattered condition throughout the "Flat." At first they considered a site to the north and east of where the townsite is today. The building of the Bear River Canal System was the deciding factor for the present site. If they had built where they first planned, they would have been above the canal, high and dry. Before the canal, the settlers raised mostly alfalfa and grain. Irrigation water made possible lawns and gardens, and they started to cultivate sugar beets.

The committee working on the townsite then negotiated with Micah Garn, Oliver Wood, and Ebenezer Wilcox for land. The first home in town was a log cabin built by Chase Petersen on his homestead. He later relinquished his holdings to a Mr. Briggs, who then passed them on to Micah Garn. Garn proved up on the land and received a U.S. patent on it. This home, along with a rock home built by Ebenezer Wilcox on land that he homesteaded, still stands in 1999. The original Garn home is at about 45 South and 200 West, and the rock house is 45 Center Street. These homes were built before the settlers brought their cabins into town. Some of the settlers who moved into town included Alice Ann Smith, Willard K. Welling, Frank Walker, Milton Earl, Lemuel Rodgers, James H. Hess, and Jed M. Hess.

Fielding was incorporated in 1914, with a population of about 300 people, and the population has remained between 350 and 420 since then.

On 18 October 1892 Micah Garn received permission from the Post Office Department to operate the first post office in Fielding. His office was at about 25 South 200 West. The town at one time also supported three stores: a meat market, a pool hall, and later a service station. Fielding has a very large facility to support the now consolidated schools. In the 1980s a community hall with a fire station was built. The town now has a volunteer fire department and a First Responder Group which also provides services to Collinston, Beaver Dam, and part of East Garland.

Agriculture has always played an important part in the economy of the community. With the coming of the Second World War, Hill Army Air Field (now Hill Air Force Base) and the Ogden Defense Depot played an important role by providing employment for local people. Now Thiokol, La-Z-Boy and Nucor Steel support a large part of the economy

The LDS Church is the predominant religion. The Fielding Ward was divided in March 1987, resulting in the people in the south end of Fielding being joined with people form the north end of Garland East Ward to form the Hampton Ford Ward.

The middle school and high school students are bussed to Bear River Middle School and Bear River High School in Garland.

Fielding has a combination service station, grocery store, and U.S. Post Office. Electricity is furnished by Utah Power and Light, natural gas comes from Mountain Fuel Supply Company (Questar), and telephone service from Continental Telephone Company. Those who do not have their own wells are serviced by the community culinary water system.

Residents usually travel to Tremonton or Logan for business, shopping, and medical services.

Garland

Garland is located about twenty miles south of the Idaho border.[19] It covers an area from the east bank of the Malad River to the foothills on the west. It is in the middle of the Bear River Valley, about twenty miles north and some west of Brigham City, and twenty-five miles west of Logan. It is enclosed by mountains on three sides.

The Bear River, which begins on the north slopes of the Uintah mountains, winds its way for 300 miles through Wyoming and Idaho, back through Cache Valley, through a rocky gorge in the Wasatch range, down through Bear River Valley and into the Great Salt Lake. It ends about eighty miles west of where it begins. The water from this river has had a profound effect on the history of Garland. Without that water, Garland would not be like it is today.

Garland lies on the bottom of the ancient bed of Lake Bonneville, and people who live here enjoy the rich soil that was deposited during the period of the lake's predominance in the area.

Most of western Utah including the territory all around the Great Salt Lake was the hunting grounds for the Fremont Indians. A great drought led to the downfall of this culture in A.D. 1300. In later times the Shoshoni Indians used northern Utah as their fishing and hunting grounds. They wintered on the foothills west of Garland, particularly at Point Lookout.

In the 1820s trappers came through this area to trap and explore. Among them were Etienne Provost, Jedediah Smith, Kit Carson, and Jim Bridger.

In 1844 Captain John C. Frémont and his party explored this area. Fremont refused to accept the idea first presented by Joseph

Redford Walker that the Great Salt Lake was actually a basin until he explored the region.

The first permanent while settlements in the Bear River Valley were along the foothills and east of Garland-Bear River City, Collinston, Fielding, and Plymouth, near springs coming from the Wasatch Mountains. These people, and others from Brigham City, grazed their livestock in the valley, and found that the soil was better and easier to cultivate where access to natural spring water was available. Some ploughing was done and water was diverted from the Malad River to irrigate the ground, but the undertaking did not prove successful and was given up.

By 1889 homesteaders were attracted to the western part of the valley. The monopoly of the Corinne Mill Canal and Stock Company was almost broken up and there were rumors of a canal to take water from the Bear River to water the entire valley. The construction of a dam was already underway.

Land could be obtained from the government merely by homesteading it—living on it for five years and making improvements, or by purchasing it from the railroad or from the Corinne Mill Canal and Livestock Company. At the time of settlement, the land was not covered heavily with sagebrush, but with rabbit brush, wheat grass, and bunch grass. Thomas E. King, one of the first permanent settlers, said: "On coming here we found this part of the country a range for grazing sheep and cattle. However, when we fenced, the land was covered with a native grass, and in June 1890, the grass waved in the breeze just like a grain field, with a bunch of rabbit brush here and there." A. R. Capener, another early settler, said that he didn't get enough sagebrush off his 160 acres to fill a wagon.

Mr. and Mrs. David E. Manning of Farmington, Utah, also came to the valley in the spring of 1889 to homestead. That spring Mr. Manning ploughed ten acres before returning to Farmington. He came back to his homestead in the fall and planted grain. After spending the winter in Farmington, the Mannings returned to their farm in the spring of 1890 to stay. They settled in what is now north Garland on one-quarter of Section 22.

Thomas E. King of Farmington, Utah, came to north Garland on 23 March 1890. The next day he settled on his homestead—the northeast quarter of Section 22, Township 12 North, Range 3 West Salt Lake Meridian. He and E. E. Manning purchased and hauled their fence posts from Washakie and shipped wire from Ogden to Collinston. They then fenced the east half of Section 22, their land consisting of adjoining quarter sections. During this summer he did "much plowing, planted a strip of corn which matured and made splendid ears, built a house and shed, harvested 25 acres of wheat, planting that fall quite an increased acreage of winter wheat." In the spring of 1891 he brought his wife and baby from Farmington and took up permanent residence on the farm.

Mr. and Mrs. W. R. Vanfleet came from Farmington to Garland in 1889. Their purpose was also to obtain land by homesteading it. They obtained 160 acres in Section 34. They brought a team and wagon so they could do farm work.

A. R. Capener was also one of the first settlers. He started to homestead in Bear River Valley on 30 November 1891. Capener obtained 160 acres, 80 of which had been ploughed. He paid $1,000 to Mr. Tommy Doman for a relinquishment. His land was included in Section 26. The deed to his farm was signed by President William McKinley. Capener brought with him six small, poor workhorses, a double A harrow which he had made, and a twelve-dollar plough. The valley at that time was very dry, and ploughing was difficult. The horses were so weak—their only food being from grazing at night—that they did well to make ten rounds a day on the mile-long farm. When they would hit a bunch of sod grass, the horses would stop dead in their tracks. Capener lived in a small shack that Doman had built. He married Mary Larelda Garn of Fielding on 12 July 1893 and built his own house.

Other early settlers were A. H. Gleason, Hyrum Rice, Walter Grover and Oscar Harris. William "Bill" Johnson settled by the spring west of Garland and fenced off 5,000 acres which he held against all comers for ten years. The railroad finally forced him to relinquish his claim. The railroad had been given every other section of ground on both sides of the railroad for twenty miles. This was done to encourage completion of the line.

During this early dry farm period, work consisted of ploughing, harrowing, drilling or broadcasting, and heading. Each settler did his own work, except during the harvesting season when they would combine forces to work on the header or thresher. A man worked nine hours a day on a header for which he received one and one-half bushels of wheat or three bushels with a team of animals. Women worked long hours doing what had to be done for which they received no pay.

Many people including the settlers had long dreamed of what could be *if only* the water from the Bear River could be diverted onto the land. Alexander Toponce, a freighter, miner, cattleman, contractor, and promoter, purchased 52,000 acres of land from the Central Pacific Railroad Company for $1.25 per acre. In 1883 he took as a partner John W. Kerr, owner of a sheep herd, and they bought more land on the hills west and north of Garland for 47 to 50 cents an acre, bring their holding up to 90,000 acres. Toponce then filed on the water rights of the Bear River.

Toponce and Kerr formed the Corinne Mill Canal and Stock Company. At one time they had 5,000 head of cattle, 26,000 sheep, and 1,000 horses and mules. Quoting Mr. Toponce: "Kerr made a contract with a man named John R. Bothwell to bring out a canal on the west side of the Bear River to water our land and the government land [by this time Kerr and Toponce had split, and their company failed]. John R. Bothwell was one of the best promoters I ever saw. He first filed on the water to be diverted from the Bear River where it came through the canyon in the Wasatch range. I held a filing on this water for 17 years and had spent thousands of dollars on surveys, but finally had to give it up." (M. J. Richards stated that there were probably eleven different surveys before the final one.) "Bothwell then went to Kerr and got a contract with our Company. Kerr and I, by our fighting, knocked ourselves out of a half a million dollars."

Just why John R. Bothwell of Kansas City came west and became interested in the irrigation possibilities of the Bear River Valley is not clear. After sizing up the situation, Bothwell returned to Kansas City to secure funds with which to carry out the enterprise. He succeeded in interesting the Jarvis-Conklin Mortgage and Trust Company, and they secured the support of Quaker societies in Glasgow, Scotland, New Castle, Ireland, and Burmingham, England. These societies bought two million dollars in bonds underwritten by Jarvis-Conklin.

A final survey was made at the cost of over $40,000. Bids were then called for, and in June 1889, the contract to build the canal was given to William Garland of Kansas City. Excavations began in September 1889 at the site of the old power plant at Wheelon. Camps extended from above the dam in Bear River Canyon to the standing bridge. A diversion dam was built in the Bear River just east of the Cache Divide. The dam was 375 feet long, 18 feet deep, and 100 feet thick. Two canals were then dug. The one on the north side of the canyon would water the land on the west side of the valley and was known as the West Canal. The other canal, the East or Hammond Canal, would take water to the east side of the valley. Each canal was 10 feet deep and 15 feet wide with a capacity of 500 second ft. of water. During the fall of 1889, about 7,000 men were working on this project. Some settlers, including Thomas E. King, worked on the canals.

When it was learned that the Bear River Valley would soon have irrigation water, interest in the area rose sharply. Land agents in the East were promoting the valley, and people from places in Utah came to settled. At first, the families settled in North Garland. They came from Farmington, Cache Valley, and even Japan. The settlement in and around Garland was called Sunset, and the first LDS. organization was the Sunset Branch. These first settlers went to the Little Green Schoolhouse in East Garland for school, church, and social functions.

Mail was delivered by horse and carriage from Hessville. Because of road conditions and poorly fed horses, the trip took two days. The people in Garland said they had "tri-weekly" service. The mail came one week and would "try" to come the next. Some of the leading citizens of Sunset met in the home of A. R. Capener in 1889 to see what they could do to get a post office. It was decided at this meeting to change the name of Sunset to Garland in honor of William Garland who was the contractor, builder, and at one time owner of the canal. Residents were also tired of hearing their town referred to as "Poverty Flats" and "Mud Flats." Plans for the new post office were approved in 1895. John Q. Leavitt built a frame building in North Garland, and A. H. Gleason was appointed as the first postmaster. Mr. Gleason would pick up the mail at Collinston and deliver it to the people. This he did until the railroad reached Garland in 1901.

The first school in Garland was built in 1889. It was one mile north of the main intersection in Garland. Eva C. Wilcox, a graduate of the University of Utah, was the teacher. She was highly respected by her students and their parents. This school building now became the center of activity for the residents of Garland.

A tithing granary was built just south of Thomas E. King (now the Lorus King) home. It was 16 feet by 18 feet and 8 feet up to the square. An LDS Relief Society granary was constructed by the David E. Manning (now Glenn Manning) home. It served from 1899 to 1918.

Walter L. Grover opened his mercantile business in North Garland. He also installed in his store the first telephone system in the valley, which was a toll telephone.

When the Sugar Factory was built in 1903, the Utah Sugar Company bought forty acres from

W. R. Vanfleet, surveyed it into town lots, and recorded it as Garland Plat B. North Garland was Plat A. The company then proceeded to build fourteen homes to house its workers. The homes were placed along Factory Street and in the blocks south of Factory Street. Grover Mercantile, the Post Office, and other businesses were soon moved into Garland proper.

By this time the canal system was owned by three different companies. There was a great need for a locally owned unifying agency whose interest was development—not just speculation. David Evans was one of the new successful owners of the Lehi Sugar Plant. He had arranged to have several Lehi farmers settle on lands in the Bear River Valley. Under his urging and along with that of George Austin, several Bear River Valley farmers, including Mr. Welling and Myron Richards, Sr., experimented with raising sugar beets. The beets they produced were yielding a higher percentage of sugar, and the tonnage per acre was much higher, than in Lehi. The Utah Sugar Company purchased large tracts of land and gained control of the canal system. The land was sold to farmers under long-term credit arrangements, with special encouragement to sugar beet growers. In 1902 this company extended the East Canal to a point near Collinston. They let a contract to J. T. Hammond and the Hammond Brothers Construction Company which, in 1903, completed the canal to Calls

Garland's business district in the early 1900s. (Utah State Historical Society)

Fort. The Utah Sugar Company then took steps leading to the construction of a railroad connecting Garland with the main line of the Union Pacific at Corinne, Utah. The Oregon Short Line (Union Pacific) completed the branch line to Garland in 1903, in time to haul the needed machinery and material for the Garland factory which was ready to process the 1903 crop of beets consisting of 2,400 acres. The building of the sugar factory had a tremendous impact on the growth of Garland. The key personnel for the plant came from Lehi. They were young, well-trained, civic-minded people. Many other people came to farm the land and to establish businesses, and Garland began to grow rapidly.

William Garland, in accordance with his contract, had built the West Canal as far as Fielding Street, east of the junction. From there, Amos Corey and his brother continued it to Corinne and thence to Thompson Ranch in 1890. The canal was built through Garland in 1890. Bishop Carl Jensen signed a contract to take the canal to a place about two miles from the middle of Thatcher. This work was completed in 1892. In 1894 William Miller, S. L. Miller, and Tony

Christensen extended the canal to Connor Springs. This completed the main line of the canal. A branch line of the canal, extending west of Garland through Tremonton and south to Appledale just west of Corinne, was built in 1896. Upon the completion of 111.5 miles of canals and main laterals and 125 miles of small laterals, about $2.5 million had been spent—$1.8 million by Garland and the Corey brothers.

After the construction of the sugar factory and the building of fourteen houses for employees, the business buildings that had been established in Plat A or north Garland were moved to Plat B or the present location of Garland. People came from many places to start businesses in the new town. The *Garland Globe* was begun on 10 February 1906 when J.A. Wixom issued the first publication—a six page weekly of which he was editor and manager. Records indicate that thirty businesses were operating in 1914. That same year the Garland library and the LDS Tabernacle were built. In 1905 a new school was built on Tabernacle Square. A new water and sewer system were built. In 1904 a town government was organized. The telephone, a toll telephone, was moved from North Garland to Boothe's store. When the Riter Brothers store was built, a telephone exchange was placed in its top story. In 1911 Garland City spent $400 to buy a chemical engine with double tanks to fight fires.

Garland grew fast. In the 1920s there were about sixty-five businesses in the town, including three livery stables, three blacksmith shops, three medical doctors, a dentist, one Japanese store, two grocery stores, and a bank. The population was just over one thousand people.

The Great Depression of 1929 started Garland on a downward trend as far as business was concerned. The Liberty Theatre closed. The number of grocery stores decreased. The bank closed its doors, one of the two pool halls failed, the Japanese store locked its doors and all businesses were affected adversely.

The routing of the freeway through Tremonton had a negative impact on business in Garland and the community became a quiet residential area. In early 1999 Garland's population was just under 1,700. There are four LDS wards in the community and in 1999 a new LDS church was under construction.

Golden

Golden was a western Box Elder County gold mining town established in 1899 and located twenty miles north from the Central Pacific Railway station at Terrace and six miles west of Park Valley. It was located just outside and south of the national forest in Century Hollow Canyon. The town was a prosperous gold and silver mining camp between 1910 and 1913 with an estimated five hundred workers.[20] During the 1890s prospectors and sheepherders Johnny Ango and Chubb Canfield located several likely claims. The largest of these became the Century Mine.

Other mines were opened in the canyon, along the creek, and in the ravine, including the Golconda, the Buffalo, and the Susannah. Several log cabins were built to house the large number of workers. Other buildings included a store, postoffice, assay office, saloons, cook kitchen, and tool sheds. One of the saloons was given the name "Hurry Back," a name given for the large number of freighters and teamsters who stopped in the area. Teamsters would haul supplies and equipment from the rail terminus and make a long hard pull up the canyon, before hurrying back to the saloon for a drink. The teamsters also hauled ore from the mines to the railroad line at Terrace.

About 1910 a five-stamp mill was built about 1,000 feet south of the original smaller mill. Hauling the equipment to the mine location from the railroad proved to be a major endeavor. Each boiler weighed over seven tons, and a large metal drive wheel that supplied power to different parts of the mill measured twelve feet in diameter. The heavy equipment was loaded onto heavy 3¾ size wagons that were built especially to haul the large machinery. Each wagon was pulled by sixteen-head of horses. About three miles from the mine, the road became too steep for wheeled wagons, so large bob sleighs were used. Each piece of machinery was transferred to the sleigh from the wagon. It took thirty head of strong work horses to pull the loaded sleigh over the rocks and up the steep hill. Whenever the sleigh would drop through the hard crusted snows onto the rocks underneath the snow, it would take very large jacks and strong men to place wood planks under the sleigh runner before the sleigh could continue.

Once the boilers were in place, coal was the principal source of fuel. It had to be hauled by wagon to the mill. In addition, hundreds and hundreds of board feet of lumber were used inside the mines and for buildings and boardwalks. All the lumber came from sawmills in the region including the Tracy Sawmill in Yost Valley and the Chadwick Sawmill on the Park Valley side of the mountains.

The mines around Golden remained prosperous for many years. About 1907 the mines began to close when it became evident that the veins were pinching out. About 1930 a new group of men under John Marshall resumed mining operations as the Century Consolidated Mining and Milling Company. With new methods and equipment, they explored above and below the old mine strata in search of profitable veins.

Some miners claim that after the 1934 earthquake, the fault in the earth slipped and concealed the veins even more. Although other prospectors have tried to find the vein, its location is still unknown. The old mill was torn down piece by piece by individuals trying to find any gold lost through the cracks.

Grouse Creek

Grouse Creek is located at the extreme west end of Box Elder County near the Nevada and Idaho borders.[21] It is a hundred miles from Brigham City as the crow flies, and well over that via the nearest paved road, Utah Highway 30, south from Interstate 15 at Curlew Junction, then north from Grouse Creek Junction on an unpaved road.

The first white settlers of Grouse Creek came in 1875 from Tooele, and settled on the West Fork. They were attracted to the area because of the many acres of natural meadows. Valison Tanner, Sr., and his brother Alma C. were the first to arrive. They brought with them co-op herds of cattle to feed on the natural meadow lands in the area. John Ferguson and Oliver Calgary came to help with the cattle. The settlement was first named Cooksville, from a family of early settlers including Benjamin Cooke who dug the first well in the area, finding good water at the sixteen foot level.[22] William (Cotton) Thomas came from Brigham City, Utah, and shortly after he arrived, he named the valley Grouse Creek, for the plentiful Sage Grouse in the valley.

In 1876 other settlers arrived on the West Fork, later called Etna. They were Richard E. Warburton, William Gallagher, Ezra Rowberry, Seth Fletcher, Henry Merrill, Elisha Hubbard, Levi Beetal, Charles Brizzee, Thomas Atkison Philemon Merrill, Ara Sabins, Charles Smith, Sr., Charles Smith, Jr., Walter Henningway, Charles Kimber, Sr., Charles Kimber Jr., William Kimber, and B. F. Cooke. They came from Rush Valley, Tooele, and Grantsville, Utah, to engage in stock raising and some farming.

During the winter of 1877, Isaac Kimball, son of Heber C. Kimball, wrote a letter to the *Deseret News* in which he described the Grouse Creek Valley as a good place to locate homes and raise livestock. This letter attracted the attention of Albert F. Richins, William C. Betteridge, Sr., Phillip P. Paskett, William P. Paskett, R. Allen Jones, and James R. Simpson of Henefer, Summit County. They decided to investigate the suitability of the location with the idea of establishing homes. It was decided the following men should make the trip as soon as weather permitted in the spring. Phillip A. Paskett, William C. Betteridge Sr., Albert F. Richins, and Robert Allen Jones started on 16 March 1877 and arrived five days later, locating claims on the East Fork. The land had not yet been surveyed, and was covered with large sage brush. Even so, the men decided to establish their claims.

The first women to come to the East Fork were Ellen Simpson, wife of James R. Simpson, and Jane Richins, wife of Albert F. Richins, from Henefer, Utah. Soon to follow were David H. Toyn, Isaac Lee, Joseph B. Lee, Danial McLaws, Thomas Davis, James W. Betteridge, and Samuel H. Kimball.

The first settlers built dugouts then later log houses with dirt roofs, then later modern homes. In 1878 the settlers on both forks cleared land and raised some wheat. There were several very dry years with very little irrigation water, but the settlers continued to clear land and build their livestock herds. They endured many hardships. The closest place to get mail, groceries, and supplies was Terrace, a railroad town twenty-five miles across the mountain or forty miles around the mountain. Later different individuals had stores in Grouse Creek. For several years the people owned a coop store, that was sold to a private owner in recent years.

Irrigation Company of the East Fork, Grouse Creek, was formed and incorporated according to the laws of Utah. In 1908 a pipeline from Buckskin Springs was built to service the community. It has been upgraded several times.

On 17 July 1879 the Grouse Creek LDS Ward was organized by Oliver G. Snow, president of the Box Elder Stake. Samuel H. Kimball was set apart as bishop, Benjamin F. Cooke, first counselor and Philip A. Paskett, second counselor. The meeting was held in the home of B. F. Cooke. Meetings were held in homes until a log social hall was built in 1891. In 1912 a new chapel of native sandstone was completed. It was a beautiful building with stained glass windows and a basement for recreation purposes. This building served the community for seventy-one years. It was torn down and a new brick chapel was built in 1983. The people hated to see the old building go but have enjoyed the new building.

In 1882 a school was started with Phillip A. Pasket as teacher. School was held in a log tithing granary. Later a building of logs was built. A four-room school house was built of native dressed sandstone. It has since been remodeled, and a gymnasium was built in 1980. The school teaches kindergarten through grade ten. Children attend grades eleven and twelve in larger communities and have to board away from home. The first mail was brought from Terrace by horseback or teams and wagon. Later the mail was picked up from the train in Lucin. Now the mail is delivered daily from Snowville. The first post office was built about 1890. Isadore H. Kimball was the first postmaster. In the early years a school and church were held on the West Fork (Etna) also but have been consolidated and held on the East Fork or Grouse Creek.

Since the area was first settled, there have been no doctors in the community, but in the early days there were two trained mid-wives: Mary Hadfield and Ellen Blanthorn who delivered babies until about 1928. There was also a male nurse, George A. Blanthorn, who assisted in times of accidents and sickness. With the coming of cars, people have gone to larger cities for medical attention. At present the community has an ambulance and some trained emergency medical technicians.

In the 1910s Grouse Creek had a brass band that played at celebrations. They also had a good dance orchestra, which provided music for almost weekly dances.

For years, at market time, cattle were trailed twenty-five miles to Lucin, and loaded on the train to be marketed in Ogden. Sometimes they were trailed fifty miles to Oakley, Idaho. Now they are trucked to market. The main occupation of Grouse Creek residents has been cattle and sheep ranching. In years past large bands of sheep grazed in the area. Electricity was brought to the community in 1952, making it possible to have modern conveniences.

Though remote, life in Grouse Creek is enjoyable.

Harper

About five miles north of Brigham City, and just south of Honeyville, is the community of Harper, with one street (Utah Highway 38) about eight miles long, running north and south along the base of the Wasatch Mountains, prompting the remark that it is the longest block in the state of Utah.[23] Homes are built on either side of the road, and the farms run from the mountains on the east to the cattails and tules on the west where the ground is fertile. Not long ago it was a rural village with Herefords and Holsteins cropping the bunch grass of large fenced pastures. Chickens and roosters pecked the dirt, their squawks and friendly crowing distinct in the country stillness.[24] The early mountain air carried the yelps of the coyote from the nearby hills, and in the evening sunset could be seen the flight of ducks and geese above the western marshes.

Today it is still rural and somewhat unchanged, but many new frame and brick homes and modern barns stand side by side with the native rock and mortar and heavy beamed original pioneer homes. Some of the pioneer rock homes have been preserved and are still inhabited; others are crumbling, half intact reminders of another era—of a basic, sturdier time when an uprooted people strived to find permanence and put down roots in a new land.

Prior to the time of the first white settlers, the area was covered with the native grasses and vegetation. The high ground was too dry for cultivation and crop production, and the lower land except for a few fertile spots was too shallow and too full of alkali. The upper slopes were covered with loose rock, sage, sumac, and cedar trees, and in the high rugged mountains on the east were found white and yellow pine trees.[25]

The community was first known as Call's Fort after Anson Call. In July 1855 Call recorded in his history that Brigham Young "... called at my farm and counseled me to build a fort to secure the people I had with me against the Indians." The people he spoke of were immigrants, brought in by the Perpetual Emigrating Fund, who needed work and provisions. Again, from Call's earlier records: "I laid the matter before President Young, and he told me to select a tract of land where I pleased and open a large farm and set as many to work as I could and teach them to farm." This was the fall of 1854. In July 1855, after Young's visit, Call commenced to build an adobe house surrounded by a stone wall three feet thick, six feet high, and 120 feet square, laid up in mortar by a good stone mason. Call's Fort was in the northernmost outpost in northern Utah until Honeyville was established in the early 1860s. Call's Fort was also the first overland stage station north of Brigham. Call kept a blacksmith shop, a tavern, and furnished general accommodations for travel.

Anson Call was not the earliest white inhabitant of the area. John Gibbs was the first to establish a homestead. He, along with George Foster, built a little shanty of rocks in the spring of 1852, and made a few other improvements. However, they moved to Brigham the following winter because of danger from the Indians. In the spring of 1853, they plowed more ground and planted, and several families moved their implements and belongings into rough log houses. This nucleus of families working their small homesteads survived the winter of 1853–54, making it the first permanent settlement in the region.[26]

In the spring of 1856, Thomas Harper was hired to manage the Call farm, and he moved onto it with his family. Over the years the area has been called by various names: Call's Fort, North String, North Ward, and Lakeside. On 6 June 1906, the name of North Ward was changed to Harper Ward in honor of Thomas Harper, who was the first LDS bishop when the ward was organized 19 August 1889.[27]

Some early settlers were group of Welsh colonists who came from Salt Lake to the Brigham area. There are indications that there must have been some friction between the Welsh and the other settlers, because they left Brigham, settled in the large area of Harper, and built some of the first homes and the first log meeting house. Their individual farms were divided into long narrow strips extending from the east mountains and westward to the alkali. They stayed for a short time, but found the ground unsuitable for providing a good livelihood. About 1869 the Welsh moved from Harper to settle in Malad and Samaria, Idaho.

To the early settlers and pioneers of Call's Fort, later named Harper, two objectives stand out. While making a living, their religion and faith on God came first, and education or search for knowledge followed. In consequence, two school houses were constructed—one at the north end and one at the south end of the community.[28] These rock buildings were completed in 1872. The Lakeside School measured 22 feet by 36 feet[29] (four walls and part of the floor of this building are still intact). The Call's Fort or North School was 22 feet by 40 feet. Most precincts found it difficult to support even one school. This community, however, was unique in that the Union Pacific Railroad had a line that ran the length of the community from north to south, and the tax from the railroad helped support the two districts. It continued to do so until 1907, when school consolidation came to Box Elder County.[30] A new building was completed and put into use in the fall of 1911, combining both schools. This was called the Lakeside School, and was located just south of the LDS ward meeting house, which was also built of stone and was in the center of the area and dedicated in 1893. This was the fourth and last school house to be constructed in Harper. It consisted of two classrooms and a furnace room providing a central heating system. The restrooms were farther out on the hill.

Originally, the students were transported in wagons or "hacks" pulled by horses. The first officially recognized hack driver was Thaddeous Wight, who served in that capacity from about 1906, into the 1920s, when Eli Pierce took over the duties.[31] Before 1925 the high school students rode the U. I. C. railroad to school in Brigham. The prospective passenger stood on the tracks as the train was coming and waved a flag or other attention-getting device, and the strain would stop.[32] One person recalls how he and his brother had to crawl out of bed at 4:30 A.M. on wintery school mornings and ride their two big work horses down the lane to the UIC tracks to break a path in the snow for those catching the street car to high school.

As in most of the early settlements, the LDS church was the governing body of the community, and so it was in Harper. The first Presiding Elder of the settlement was John Gibbs (1853–56). In 1858 the branch moved to the new fort on the Anson Call farm. At that time John Gibbs returned to the area and again assumed leadership of the Call's Fort Branch, serving until 1860. In 1860 Chester Loveland became branch leader and served until 1865. From 1865 to 1866, the branch was presided over by James May. In 1866 Thomas Harper became branch leader and served in that capacity until 19 August 1877, when he was sustained bishop of the branch. The branch became a ward in 1879, with Thomas Harper continuing as bishop. He served in that capacity until his death in 1899.[33] Bishops who followed him were Thomas Yates, Paul Hunsaker, Elbert Beecher and Jack Webster. Bishop Webster was the last bishop to serve in the original rock chapel when the building was sold in 1977. The Harper Ward now meets in the Honeyville Chapel.

The water supply for the area comes mostly from mountain springs and wells on the property of each resident or group of residents. The irrigation water also comes from springs and ponds. In later years farmers in the north end of the area have benefitted from the Hammond Canal which was put into use by the Bear River Canal Company.

Mining was also part of the early history of Harper. East of the Elbert Beecher home there were four canyons, and each canyon has a mine that was opened in the early years. Antimony Canyon opened about 1945, for the purpose of digging antimony for government use in World War II. In a canyon to the north, located high on the south side of the canyon not too far below the top of the mountain, is a mine where most of the mining was done. It was begun in the late 1800s by Henry C. Baker and others and was quite impressive in its day.

Harper was and is the kind of community with the kind of rural landscape that can be known and loved down to the last rabbit hole. In a region thick with human history, it changes according to older, seasonal rhythms: sowing and harvest, sun and cold, rain and drought. Basic human cycles also continue to matter: the joys and sorrows of family life, sickness and health, triumphs and failures, birth and death. Those who settled Harper were rugged and religious people. They struggled daily in the mud and mire of hard work and fed bread and milk to LDS apostles who came and stayed the night. They raised sheep, spun thread, wove cloth, and sewed their own clothes. They built homes, school houses and churches. They were true inhabitants with a razor sharp sense of place and purpose.

Honeyville

Honeyville is located between Harper Ward and Deweyville, on Utah Highway 38, ten miles north of Brigham City.[34] It was pioneered about 1860 by Abraham Hunsaker of Brigham City, who secured land in the area for pasture and grazing. The first man to cultivate land in the area was Lewis N. Boothe, who came with his brother, John, and rented land from Abraham Hunsaker in 1861.

It was not until 1866 that Joseph Orme of Call's Fort purchased land from Chester Loveland (later the first mayor of Brigham City) and built the first permanent dwelling. The first white child born in the new settlement was Emily Orme (Boothe), daughter of Joseph and Emily Green Orme.

In the 1860s Abraham Hunsaker moved one of his wives, Eliza Collins Hunsaker, and two of his sons, Isaac and Allen, from Brigham City to the new settlement, which was named Hunsakerville, in his honor. He was made the first bishop of the settlement. According to local legend, Bishop Hunsaker humbly declined the honor, and the people named the settlement Honeyville, in honor of the hives of bees kept by the bishop. Some believe the settlement was named by the settlers "to remind them of their location, which was like Canaan—a land flowing with milk and honey." Some local residents say that Honeyville is a contraction of Hunsakerville (Hun-eville), and that the shortening came with the Utah Northern's station.

Other settlers came to the new town from Brigham City, from England, and from Malad, Idaho. Early industries included charcoal burning, a lime kiln and brick factory, and a grist mill, built in 1867. There was a Honeyville Cooperative Institution during the period of the cooperatives established under the direction of stake president

Lorenzo Snow, and his successor and son, Oliver. Abraham Hunsaker and his family were active in establishing settlements in Carson Valley and in Northern Arizona.

In 1865 a stage coach station on the east end of the pond was built and a grist mill was built west of town on Salt Creek in 1867. A ferry was established on the Bear River just north of the town. The Ferry was brought up the Bear River from the Great Salt Lake by a man by the name of Thurston. Later a man named Empey owned it, and it was known as the "Empey Ferry" for years. It was used by emigrants going to California to cross the Bear River.[35] The stage station was moved north to Crystal Hot Springs after a short time to serve the stage line and freight road that came from the west side of Salt Creek, along the mountains to Collinston, and over the divide and on to Montana.

Honeyville Ward was established by Brigham Young with Abraham Hunsaker as bishop and Benjamin H. Tolman and Lewis N. Boothe as counselors at the time that Young reorganized the Box Elder Stake of Zion.

The first public building, a rock structure, served as both school and chapel. It was later to become the Tolman store.

In the late 1800s and early 1900s, ice was cut from the Bear River and stored by Benjamin H. Tolman and Jedediah M. Grant. It was cut in blocks about two feet by two feet square and stored in log buildings and covered with saw dust. Benjamin H. Tolman also raised sugar cane which he made into sorghum and molasses using a horse-powered mill that he built.

In May 1872 the Utah Northern Railroad Company built a narrow gauge railroad through Honeyville. John W. Young was the manager. The first engine was called the *John W.* The three other engines were called: *Utah, Idaho,* and *Wyoming.* To show the size of the engine, the story was told that a few miles south of here the engine tipped off the track. A yoke of oxen was hitched to it and pulled it on the track again.[36]

Honeyville received its town charter in 1911. The town president and board purchased some springs on the E. C. Wheatley and John Flint property, and a year later a culinary water system was put into service. According to Norma Grant Gilmore and Ray Boothe,

> July 31, 1911, a meeting was called for the purpose of calling a special election concerning the question of incurring a bonded indebtedness fo $1,200.00 to be used for the waterworks system and lighting purposes. It was voted in favor of such a bond. Judges for this first election were B. H. Tolman, D. W. Hunsaker and J. M. Grant with Enoch Hunsaker as an alternate judge. There were 56 eligible voters and 52 votes were cast; 31 "yes" votes, 20 "no" votes and one spoiled ballot.
>
> E. C. Wheatley and John K. Flint offered their rights to the water known as the Wheatley Springs for power purposes at a cost of $4,500.00 which was accepted. The springs had a three quarter foot flow per second which could be used for culinary purposes.
>
> A second election had to be held as there was not suffient water to furnish a town owned and operated electric plant. The order of voting was to be $3,500.00 for electricity and $11,500.00 for water for a total of $15,000.00. The judges elected were: B. H. Tolman, Enoch Hunsaker and J. M. Grant. The results were as follows: Bonding for the Electric System: 34 yes votes; 18 no votes with one spoiled ballot. Bonding for the water system: 36 "yes" votes; 16 "no" votes with one spoiled ballot. For some reason the electric system never materialized. The water system was established in 1912. A cement reservoir was built and has been improved upon until we have as good a water system and as pure water as can be found in the state. In 1918 more springs were purchased and added to our water system and in 1920 the water system was extended. Also a new galvanized 2 inch pipe was laid under the railroad tracks and a 3 inch pipe was laid west of Salt Creek.[37]

After installation of the water system, "It seemed too different just to turn on a tap, and the water flowed into the trough to water the animals instead of standing there working the 'pump' handle to fill the trough in the old corral. After the coming of the water, many old pumps just stood silent and abandoned."[38]

In 1912 Honeyville had two railroad stations, one with an electric train running every two hours, between Ogden, Utah, and Preston, Idaho, and the other, the Oregon Short-Line railroad, operated with four passenger trains stopping daily in Honeyville. The railroad brought mail to the Honeyville post office. Honeyville business establishments included a mercantile store, candy kitchen, butcher shop, confectionery, barber shop, a blacksmith shop, and flour mill. Recreational and educational facilities included a closed-in swimming pool, an ice-skating pond, hand sleigh riding hill, toboggan hill (Killer Hill, by name), a little red brick school house, and a sewing school where young girls and women were taught sewing.

Electric power came in 1915. About that time reports circulated that a sugar factory was to be built by the Utah-Idaho Sugar Company on a site near the Bear River west of town. A railroad spur was built from the main line to the site and a good sized hotel was built, also an office building was made ready. But the factory was not built. The hotel is now the Buddist church and recreation center, and the office was converted into a private residence.

Over the years there have been four LDS chapels in Honeyville and four school houses. Gilmore and Boothe relate the story of the schoolhouse bell:

> We had a large bell hanging in the school house belfry. We all loved to swing on the rope and ring the bell. It could be heard for miles. It had a delightful tone sounding in the crisp air. It almost became a second Liberty Bell as it was rung when peace was declared at the end of World War I. It was rung by Ray Boothe and others. It is said that they rang it for several hours until Bishop Wheatley put a stop to it.
>
> When the school house was not needed for holding school any more, the bell was torn out of the belfry and sold to the Oregon Short-Line Railroad Company and it was taken to Sun Valley, Idaho where it now resides. Shame, shame on whoever did this dastardly deed.[39]

Just north of Honeyville is one of northern Utah's best-known water resorts: Crystal Springs. The spot, known in earlier years as Madsen's Hot Springs, is reputed to be the location of the largest hot and cold springs which arise next to each other in the country, if not the world. The water is said to be quite saline and have a radioactive component, salutary to arthritis and other joint ailments.

On 8 July 1911 Honeyville was granted a town charter by the Box Elder County Commission. Israel Hunsaker was selected town board president; Elazrus Hunsaker, Orson Loveland, Abraham Wheatley and A. R. Burke members of the town board of trustees, with Abinadi Tolman as town clerk. Israel Hunsaker, Enoch Hunsaker, Leo Hunsaker, John G. Wheatley, Thomas Wheatley, John M. Boothe, Parley Hunsaker, B. Albert Bingham, Horace N. Hunsaker, H. Ross Coombs, D. Leon Gardner, Ray Boothe, Bryon E. Hunsaker, and Boyd K. Gardner all served as Presidents of the town board of trustees.

In November 1981 a general obligation bond election was held in Honeyville. The citizens voted in favor of bonds to construct a city hall and fire station.

On 22 August 1983 Utah governor Scott M. Matheson issued a proclamation declaring Honeyville a third class city. Steven B. Johnson, David L. Forsgren, Boyd K. Gardner, Abran R. Garcia, and H. Paul Orme have served as mayors of Honeyville.

In 1986 the city council passed a revenue bond to raise funds to construct water storage facilities and upgrade the city water system. In 1996 the city council again passed a revenue bond to raise additional funds to dig a well and provide a water storage facility on property given to the city by the William S. Ellis family. Currently the city has well storage facilities on the south and north ends of the community.

Howell

Howell is a farming area located just off Utah Highway 83, and about two miles south of Interstate 84, nearly thirty miles north and west of the Box Elder County courthouse.

Howell townsite was laid out in 1910. It was a project of the Promontory-Curlew Land Company of which Congressman Joseph Howell was president. In an advertisement for the project, in 1914, a grand picture was painted of the opportunities in Howell Valley:

The non-irrigated and grazing lands of western Box Elder County owned by the Promontory-Curlew Land Company of Logan, Utah, are the best cheap lands in the state. They were acquired from the Charles Crocker estate, and originally were a part of the government's land grants to the Central Pacific Railroad Company.

The towns of Snowville, Howell, and Promontory are adjacent to company holdings. Thousands of acres have been sold since 1910.[40]

Many of the first settlers of Howell did not come from afar, but from other areas in northern Utah. They included Charles E. Gunnell, Cyrus W. Bailey, and John L. Baxter of Wellsville, Nephi Nessen of Newton, Christian Fennesbeck of Logan, William Andersen of Petersboro, all of Cache County, and Thomas L. Davis and George J. Wood of Willard, Box Elder County.[41]

A two-room brick schoolhouse was constructed in 1911. A branch of the LDS church was organized on 18 July 1911, and in April 1915 a ward was created. Church services were held in the schoolhouse until completion of a chapel that was dedicated by Apostle Rudger Clawson on 24 June 1917.

Irrigation water came from Blue Creek Springs—three miles north of the townsite. The water was stored in a reservoir a mile north of the townsite, and two canals on both sides of the valley carried water to farms. Culinary water was obtained from Hillside Springs and provided to homes through a water system.

Iowa String

The Iowa String is a local designation given to an area of farms along 6800 West between Utah Highway 83 and the Box Elder County Fairgrounds in Tremonton.

The area was settled in April 1898 during Box Elder County's "Second Tier" of settlement by people from New Sharon, Iowa, who were led by Harvey Catell. After Catell journeyed to Utah for an onsite inspection with V.S. Peet, land agent for the Bear River Land & Canal Company, he returned with high praise for the project. The Utah-bound settlers loaded their cattle, horses, equipment, and possessions into railroad box cars, along with a good supply of lumber with which to build houses. Among the group were tradesmen who expected to become part of the community.

Among the early settlers were the Hazel, Vickers, Knudson, and Watland families. It was suitable for settlement, this land in the Bear River Valley, irrigated by the new canal system, but it was not paradise. "The Vickers family and most of the tradesmen became discouraged and returned home. However, the Harts and Watlands cleared the land of the huge sagebrush, plowed the ground, and planted crops which were too late to mature so were cut for hay. Next

A herd of sheep on the Iowa String in January 1928. (Box Elder County)

season they were more successful; wheat yielded sixty bushel to the acre, and oats, one hundred fifteen bushels."[42]

About two years after the Iowa group came, a group known as the German Colony came from Tremont, Illinois. Among them were the Ricker, Goder, Kickok, Bairs, Filburn, Bishop, Stone, Kniefel, Tallmarc, Croner, Winzeler, Baer, Keatly, Bennet, Vance, Brinkman, and other families.

The people of the Iowa String built a hall which served for school and church meetings in 1899. It was known as the Union School because several denominations used it for religious services. Both groups built attractive homes and substantial outbuildings. The quality of the farmland was enhanced with the coming of the drainage district for which John Somers built a tile plant near his home on the bank of Salt Creek to produce tiles for the drainage system.[43]

Kelton

The site of Kelton is located on the line of the old Promontory branch of the transcontinental railroad, north of the northernmost point reached by that line, about eight miles west of Monument Point, and some seven miles west of Locomotive Springs. Kelton is about sixty miles northwest of Brigham City and sixty-four miles from the Utah-Nevada border.

Originally known as Indian Creek for the stream flowing southward from the Raft River Mountains, the area was renamed Kelton for an early stockman in the area.[44]

The town of Kelton developed in 1869 after completion of the Central Pacific Railroad. Kelton became a stage stop and freighting point for goods shipped north to Idaho, Montana, and Oregon as well as Snowville, Yost, and Park Valley. "Kelton, at its peak, contained quite a number of buildings. One of them was a fine brick school house. It boasted several fine two story hotels, well stocked stores, comfortable homes, a whole row of saloons and gambling halls, and even a telephone exchange. The Post Office there was established on December 16, 1869."[45]

The town was severely damaged by an earthquake in 1934. Three-foot wide cracks opened in the earth, buildings and houses shook violently, and the schoolhouse had to be abandoned.

Kelton was virtually totally dependant upon the fortunes of the railroad. When the Lucin Cutoff was built in 1903, the town began to decline, and when the tracks of the Promontory Branch were removed in 1942, Kelton died. The old railyards and homesites are vacant, and only the cemetery remains to mark the spot.

Lucin

Lucin is located in far western Box Elder County seven miles from Nevada, and vies with Etna for the honor of being located nearest the Nevada border. It is one hundred miles northwest of Brigham City on a direct line and over one hundred twenty miles by road or along the old railroad line. Lucin was a creation of the railroad, and its name has achieved permanence chiefly due to its becoming the junction point of the old Promontory line of the Central Pacific and the new cutoff, built just after the turn of the twentieth century. The cutoff was given the name of the junction of the old and new lines, and became the Lucin Cutoff. It was named, according to most accounts, for a fossil bivalve mollusk, *Lucina subanta,* found in the area. Lucin's movements and reincarnations form an interesting footnote to the history of the transcontinental railroad and Box Elder County.

Apparently there was an end-of-track camp named Lucin along the Central Pacific tracks as the railroad moved east toward its meeting with the Union Pacific. Historians Anan Raymond and Richard Fike state that their "Field investigations identified remains of a siding and foundations of dugouts and other structures. Artifacts observed on the surface of the site suggest a short-lived occupation established in 1869 by Euro-Americans and Chinese."[46]

According to Raymond and Fike, "Engineering records indicate that section station called Lucin was established on July 6, 1875, at mile post 680.5."[47] Facilities were relocated from the camp site to the 1875 Lucin. Raymond and Fike note that "Railroad documents show that Lucin contained a foreman's house and train car body north of the grade and a section house and Chinamen house south of the grade. Onside investigations verified the locations of these structures. Analysis of artifacts found on the surface suggests that occupation lasted into the 20th Century."[48]

With construction of the Lucin Cutoff in 1904, the junction of the old line and the new line, just a half mile west of the end-of-track camp and 1.7 miles west of historic Lucin, became known as Umbria Junction. The nearby railroad facilities were given the name Lucin. With the transfer of the name Lucin from historic Lucin to the railroad station in 1904, "historic Lucin was renamed Grouse and finally dismantled by the railroad in 1907."[49]

Lynn

Lynn is a small ranch area located in the southern half of Junction Valley in northwestern Box Elder County. The head waters of the Cassier Creek (South Fork of upper Raft River) flow through the narrow valley which widens as the valley slopes north towards the Utah-Idaho border. Lynn is approximately 95 miles west of Tremonton, and fifty miles south of Burley, Idaho. The settlement is within a few miles of the Vipont and Lucky Guy Opportunity mines, the latter in Cotton Thomas Basin.

The name Lynn is a corruption of the surname of John Lind, who, with his half-brother, Alexander Anderson, came to the valley from Grantsville, to which they had immigrated from Sweden. Their stay in Grantsville was less than cordial and they moved to Junction Valley in 1882.

In the 1920s there was an LDS church, an elementary school, and mail service to homes in the valley. All of these services, however, have been abandoned. Raft River Rural Electric Power provides service to the valley. The roads are gravel and are maintained by the Box Elder County Road Department. This area is somewhat isolated, and the winters can be hard and long, with considerable snow and wind.

The ranchers' source of income was from the cattle and sheep that grazed on the mountain ranges in the summer and in the lower ranges in the spring and fall. Under controlled and good management, the forage is a sufficient and satisfactory feed supply for seven to eight months of the year. Supplemental feed (hay and concentrate) must be fed for four to five months during the winter, depending on the severity of the winter.

Only two families reside in Lynn year round, but four to six other ranchers spend the summer months in Lynn caring for their hay and grain crops. The irrigated crop land is generally sloping and is watered by sprinkler or flood gravity flow irrigation method. A fair water supply is available from natural creeks and springs and from the Lynn Reservoir. Under normal conditions, the rangeland has an ample stock of water available.

Mantua

Mantua is located in what was known as "The Little Valley" five miles east of Brigham City, on U.S. Highway 89. The valley was first used as a cattle "herding ground" by people from Brigham City. Abraham Hunsaker of Brigham City and Honeyville had a summer home in the area where members of his family herded cows and made butter and cheese. Mantua was settled in 1863, largely by Danish immigrants sent from Brigham City. They were sent to raise flax for the Brigham City Mercantile and Manufacturing Association, hence the early names "Flaxville" and "Little Copenhagen." At one time the settlement was also known as "Geneva." Among the names identified with Mantua are Jeppsen, Olsen, Nelsen, Nielsen, Jensen, Andersen, Sorensen, Petersen, Rasmussen, Schow, Keller, and Halling.

The town's current name derives from Mantua, Portage County, Ohio, the birthplace of Lorenzo Snow. In 1864 some of the original settlers moved to Bear Lake, but were replaced by other families from Brigham City, and the town plat was laid out. Its main street was the road leading from Brigham City to Logan, and which later became U.S. Highway 89.

The flax enterprise met with success. "Hans P. Jensen was appointed to oversee this work. In 1864, Mr. Lars Halling had less than half an acre in flax; from this he raised twenty bushels of seed. The flax was prepared for spinning by Peter Olsen Hansen, who had learned the trade in Denmark. The coarser part was spun and woven into cloth from which grain sacks were made, and the finer parts were spun into threads used for sewing purposes. For many years this work was carried on successfully by many of these settlers."[50]

Mantua was also known for producing large crops of wheat, oats, alfalfa, potatoes, and fruit, especially strawberries. After having been made the first president of the newly completed Salt Lake Temple, Lorenzo Snow organized a Temple Workers' Excursion to Brigham City, on the train. Along with the temple workers came the First Presidency and other LDS church leaders. Among other activities, they were taken on a side trip to Mantua to dine on the strawberries there.

Some of the settlers from Mantua participated in settling northern Arizona, as well as furnishing men and teams to bring immigrants from the Missouri River to Utah.

From the beginning, Mantua was considered a suburb of Brigham City and was represented by one member of the Brigham City Council until 1911. From its settlement until the reorganization of the stake by Brigham Young in 1877, Mantua was a branch of the Brigham City Ward. On 9 September 1877, Mantua Ward was organized.

Mantua received electrical service from Utah Power and Light in 1914, at a cost of $3,000.00, and its culinary water system was completed on 16 July 1921, at a cost of $20,270.97. The event was celebrated by a rally, a luncheon, and a dance.

In the 1960s, under the driving force of Brigham City mayor Ruel Eskelsen, Brigham City obtained rights to many of the springs in Mantua, in order to secure an adequate water supply for future growth in Brigham City. The county seat also purchased much of the farmland in Mantua Valley, and constructed a large reservoir for irrigation purposes in Brigham City. It was good for Brigham, and provides a spectacular view coming down from Logan, but it raised the water table so much in Mantua that the land, the homes, and future development were significantly hampered. Mount Hope, which had been named by Lorenzo Snow in 1865, became a promontory in the Mantua reservoir.

With the widening of Highway 89 in the early 1950s, the road was re-routed west of Mantua town, and bypassed the business district. Further widening of the highway in the 1990s changed accesses from the highway to the town, providing an overpass at Willowmere west of Mantua, closing the northern junction of the highway and Mantua's main street, and moving the one in the center of town.

On the eastern edge of the valley are a couple of pure, cold springs which furnish a significant flow of water, which is now being utilized by a state-operated fish hatchery that provides Bear Lake cutthroat and rainbow trout to surrounding lakes and rivers.

Mantua is also the jumping-off place for the beautiful but unpaved road leading south into the Wasatch Range to Devil's Gate Valley and on past the Willard Basin CCC Camp and the spectacular Willard Peak overlook, from which the viewer can see from Point-of-the Mountain on the south to Idaho on the north, to Logan, and into Wyoming.

The Park Valley Area

Park Valley is located one hundred miles west of Brigham City, bordered on the north by the Raft River mountains, on the south by the Hogup and Dove Creek Hills, and on the west by the Cove Creek Mountains.[51] To the east, the valley opens toward Snowville and the Hansel Mountains. To the northeast lies Black Pine mountain, and to the southeast lie glistening white salt pans, and beyond them Great Salt Lake itself. The valley itself is roughly oval in shape, about thirty miles in length east to west, and about twenty-five miles north to south.

What is now known as Park Valley includes the locations of

Rosette, Dove Creek, Muddy, Clear Creek, Rosebud, and Kelton, as well as the long-forgotten sites of Ten-Mile, Rosen Valley, Terrace, Golden, and others. Since all these areas currently belong to a homogenous community, they are known collectively as Park Valley, though the community of Park Valley proper, in the valley center, is the hub of activities and contains the church house, store, hotel, community park, and schoolhouse.

The elevation of the valley itself varies from about 4,200 feet on the Kelton flats, to just under 10,000 feet in the Raft River Mountains, which, unlike most other mountain ranges in the Basin and Range, are aligned like the Uintas, east and west. Precipitation ranges from twelve inches to thirty-five inches annually, at different locations and at varying altitudes in the valley.

Early explorers in northern Utah returned with glowing reports of bunch grass waving around their horses' knees, and occasionally nearly as high as the stirrups of the saddles. George Parsons, the second herdmaster for early Brigham City, said that "The Promontory was a mountain of waving grass when I became the flockmaster."[52] The Park Valley area was said to be the same. The abundance of good grass attracted settlers, who brought their livestock to graze. Although there were always some sagebrush and juniper, they were not predominent then. Even up to the 1920s, grass and wild flowers among the sagebrush were much more prevalent. During good years the grass was reported to be high above the sagebrush.[53] Heavy grazing resulted in a sharp decrease in grass and an increase in sagebrush and juniper trees.

The early settlers located homesteads on a series of natural springs along the foothills of the Raft River mountains. Streams fed by runoff from melting snow in the Raft River range was dammed and diverted for irrigation, and the natural meadows provided fresh green feed for livestock and hay for winter months. They also found wildlife abundant.

It is said that the name was bestowed by Cotton Thomas, the first settler, who was reminded of his native Wales, by the park-like surroundings. Another theory holds that the name came from an early settler named Parks.[54] Cotton Thomas had owned a livery stable, store, and hotel in Brigham City before he moved to Park Valley in

1869. It is said that he had probably heard of Park Valley from the railroad workers who had frequented his livery stable and hotel. Thomas was appointed Indian agent for the area. He later moved farther west, and became one of the first settlers of Grouse Creek. The Cotton Thomas Basin still bears his name.[55] In the fall of 1869, he entered into a contract to winter some 1,500 head of cattle for a dollar a head. The community at Brigham City had started the practice of combining their herds with the surrounding communities and hiring a herder to care for them. Their herds ranged across the Bear River towards Promontory and beyond to the west. It is presumed that the contract Cotton Thomas had was an extension of these efforts.

Thomas drove the cattle to the valley, and he and his family settled near Willow Creek Spring, located about six miles south of the present store and school house. The Indians killed two of the cows for food, but gave the hides to Mr. Thomas, so he could get the dollar for pasturing them. This more-or-less friendly cooperative relationship marked the interaction of the settlers and Indians from the very begining of settlement here.[56]

Most of the early non-Native settlers were Mormons, but some were railroad workers. They established themselves on natural springs and near the mountain streams. They fenced in the meadows and cleared the junipers and sagebrush, and planted crops. The lack of rainfall made dry farming impractical. Some of the early settlers were Thomas Dunn, Adam Larsen, Andrew Callahan (a railroad man), Lucinda Shipman Campbell and her sons, Christian Hirschi, Jacob Kunzler (from Tooele), James Newberry Morris, Hyrum Yates, and William Callahan. Others were Antone Olague, Jonathan Love, Joseph Fisher, Orson and Sam James, Moroni Coleman, Abraham Chadwick, Joseph Godfrey, William Mecham, Charles J. Rohwer, Andrew Rose, Absalom Yates, and Erastus Darwin Mecham. Other early settlers bore the names Nelson, Woodruff, Larrabee, Highland, Roger, Frost, and Warren.

Much of the livelihood of the inhabitants of Park Valley had come from grazing cattle and sheep. The gardens, orchards, and meadowlands provided for and necessitated the keeping of bees, which pollinated the crops and provided honey. Most families kept a hive or two of bees.

The settlers had to be self-sufficient, so far from larger towns. Blacksmithing enterprises were a necessity, until the coming of electricity, and then electric welding machines. There was a lime kiln and a grist mill at Rosebud. Among the "enterprises" of the valley were at least three stills which operated during the years of Prohibition. One was located at Hardup or Ten Mile, one at the abandoned Carter cabin in Pine Canyon, and one at Muddy.[57]

About the late 1930s, Kraft Food Company built a plant in Malta, Idaho, and contracted to buy the milk of valley ranchers. Milk from Park Valley herds was hauled to Malta for processing until the 1960s.

Mining was a significant industry in Park Valley, beginning in the 1890s. The largest mines were the Century and others along the same vein, the West Century, and the Susannah, as well as the Golconda, the Buffalo, the Deer Trail Mine, the Buffalo Mine, and others. The Susannah was developed on the westward extension of the rich ore vein on which the Century was located. Today there is hardly a canyon in the Raft River and Black Pine Mountains that does not have numerous mine dumps where prospectors once attempted their luck at striking it rich.

There were three levels to the Century Mine. The first work was done at the discovery near the top of the hill. Ore was first hauled from the second, or middle level, and from the third, or top level, down the steep hillside by teams of horses or mules and wagons. There was said to be a big room which had been dug out inside the mine where the mules were stabled.

Underground water became a problem and a continuous hindrance to mining operations. As the water problem continued, they drove a tunnel at the level of the mill and began working level one. Water continued to be a problem, especially as they began making shafts between the levels. The water was useful, however, as the mill was enlarged. Water for the large boilers in the mills and the sluicing beds was piped about half a mile down the hill from the West Century Mine and from the upper levels of the Century.

As the shafts were sunk deeper, the gold ore gave way to silver, often yielding up to 1,000 ounces to the ton. With the gold and silver, lead and copper were also found. As the mining operation increased in size, a large new five-stamp mill was built. It produced about five hundred dollars a day for its owners.[58] Then in 1906 the old mill was replaced by a new sixteen-stamp mill and concentrator, built about a thousand feet south of the original smaller mill. The new mill was powered by steam, and large boilers and much heavy equipment was installed. The boilers each weighed over seven tons, and the flywheel was over twelve feet in diameter.[59] This equipment came from the Trent Engineering and Machinery Company in Salt Lake City, and consisted of a Blake crusher, two five-stamp Trent batteries, and two three-stamp Marrall batteries, with a combined crushing capacity of fifty tons of crude ore in twenty-four hours. Below the stamps there were about 200 square feet of silver-plated copper plates. Below these plates were five Wilfley concentrating tables. Power was generated by two sixty-horsepower boilers, one thirty-horsepower boiler, and an eighty-five-horsepower Corliss engine. In addition there was a six-drill Rand compressor, a dynamo, and a switchboard for the electric lighting of the mill and mine buildings.[60]

Great difficulties were encountered in moving the heavy equipment. It was first shipped on a railroad flat car to Terrace, about fifty miles south of the mine. A special wagon was constructed, three-and-three-quarter sized, to haul the equipment to the mine. It was pulled by a team of sixteen horses. The trip was slow and laborious. About three miles from the mine, the road became too steep for the horses to pull the heavy wagon. The equipment was reloaded onto sleds, which then required thirty head of horses to pull it up the steep and rocky road. Sometimes the sleighs would drop through the snow onto the rocks underneath. The workers would have to jack up the sled and skid it on planks to get the sleigh off the rocks.[61]

When the new mill was finished, the large boilers supplied power to various parts of the mill. Coal was the principal source of fuel for the boilers, but cord wood was also used, and was cut in the surrounding area. The new equipment crushed the ore much more rapidly. The metals were separated from the waste and made in to concentrate, or bricks. Often the bricks were concealed under the seats of wagons leaving the mine. The wagons were pulled by two, four, and six teams, which also hauled coal and the mail to the mines from Terrace or Kelton. "Most any time of day" these wagon trains could be seen slowly pulling their loads of coal and supplies to the mine, and taking ore concentrate back to the railroad.[62] John Miller of Brigham City says that his father, Wilford Miller, was one of the teamsters who hauled coal from Kelton to the mine, a distance of thirty miles. He drove a six-horse team which pulled a wagon and a trailer.

In 1907 one of the first Chilean Rod Mills was installed at the Susannah Mine. The population at the time was estimated at about five hundred. At the same time, the panic of 1907 hit the mining industry as a whole, including the town of Golden. Hard money was replaced by worthless scrip. Mines closed daily, and miners were left unpaid. E. H. Jones's General Store in Golden closed its doors, and its inventory was moved to Park Valley and Rosette. Golden as a town ceased to exist.[63] By this time, however, the rich oxidized ore was also being exhausted.[64]

In 1909 the Century mine was under the supervision of T. W. Ireland, with P. W. Madsen as the general manager. By then it was staffed with a reduced work force, but was not actually in operation. The Susannah Mine, with its new mill, had quite a bit more activity. The stage was then traveling from the area to the railroad at Kelton three times each week. At the time the Century Mining Company owned a group of seventeen claims, all but three of which were patented. It owned the water rights to all the springs in the vicinity. It had also purchased two ranches in the valley below, which were used to supply hay and grain for the livestock at the mine.

The mines in the area had a brief rebirth in 1910, when several mines were reopened and lower grades of ore were worked.[65] The second boom really began, however, in 1920, when the owners of the Vipont Mine uncovered an ore body with values as high as 12,000 ounces of silver to the ton. A long tramway was built from the Vipont down the steep slopes to a new concentrating mill. Three hundred men were hired, with none being paid less that $4.50 per day, a large salary for the time. The Vipont proved to be a real treasure house of silver, and it was mined steadily until the Depression years of the 1930s. After that owners shipped some ore from it through the 1940s.[66]

The opening of the mining industry greatly added to the economy of the valley. It provided work for many of the men, as well as a nearby market for vegetables, eggs, fresh-churned butter, milk, meat, and fruit from the ranches. Some of the local men employed to freight supplies to and from the mines were James W. Palmer and his sons James and Joseph, as well as David James and his sons, and William and Amasa Callahan and their sons.[67]

The mines remained prosperous for many years, but at last they began to dwindle as the ore veins began to pinch out. It was estimated that a fault in the earth's crust had at some time slipped and hidden the main rich veins of ore away from the miners' reach. Mining activity began to decrease, until finally it stopped altogether and Golden became a true ghost town. Before that unknown millions of dollars worth of ore, chiefly gold and silver, were removed from the mines. The ghost town of Golden didn't remain empty and quiet for too long. Many of the buildings and equipment made their way to the ranches in the valley to become building material for barns and outbuildings.

In 1929 and 1930, John Marshall headed a new group which called itself the Century Consolidated Mining and Milling Company. They leased the mine holdings, opened the tunnels, and tried, with more modern machinery, to pick up the lost and elusive veins. They explored above and below the old main strata, drove new stopes and drifts, and found some smaller deposits, but were never able to locate the main vein. Because of the low content of the ore found, it was not long until it was determined to be an unprofitable venture, and again, about 1936, the workers left and the mines were abandoned. Gradually even the old mills were torn down piece by piece by individuals trying to find any gold which may have fallen among the timbers or lost in the sluicing beds.[68]

Throughout the years others have come and attempted to rework the old claims, hoping to find a few undiscovered nuggets, or even the illusive mother lode itself. One of these was John Cordon, who worked the Little May Mine in Corner Canyon during the 1930s. In recent years Al Dart and the Gillespie family has attempted to do some reworking of the mines, but so far without great success.

Mormons in Park Valley first met in the homes of the members.

The Park Valley Ward was organized 14 July 1879. After the brick school houses were built, they were used for church services as well. The meetings were held for one month in Rosette, then for the next month in Park Valley. The Rosette Ward was organized on 22 May 1910. Meetings were held in the schoolhouse until 1916. At that time the school district determined that church meetings should no longer be held in schools. Consequently, a chapel was built in Rosette, and the Park Valley Ward, organized in 1910, purchased a large hall built by Charles W. Goodliffe adjoining his store. In 1915 the wards in Park Valley were transferred from the Box Elder Stake to the newly organized Curlew Stake, headquartered in Holbrook, Idaho. During the Depression of the 1930s, many people moved from their homesteads, and the Curlew Stake was dissolved, the Park Valley wards becoming part of the Bear River Stake, organized in 1908. Further stake divisions have followed. A new chapel was built in Park Valley in 1951, and the Rosette chapel was sold and moved to Lynn.

Telephone service to Park Valley came with the formation of the Park Valley-Rosette Telephone Company on 11 April 1923. The telephones were hand-cranked and battery-operated. At the home of Will Carter was a telephone that would connect to the "outside." To call long distance, one had to go to his home, call Kelton, and then connect to the regular telephone lines. Anyone calling in from the outside called the Carter home, and the message was relayed.

When electricity was brought into the valley in 1948, the power lines made such a buzz in the phone lines that they fell into disuse. Some parts of the system continued to function beyond that time, but most ended then.

In 1953, when the road was oiled, or surfaced with asphalt, many of the old phone poles were removed, as the fence connecting them was replaced for the road right-of-way. A few can still be seen along some of the fences throughout the valley.

In the late 1960s telephone service came again, when Art Brothers, owner of the Silver Beehive Telephone Company started to install phone lines to the ranches in the valley. At first the phone lines were merely strung along the ground or along fences. Eventually the system was completed throughout the valley.[69]

Electrical service came in the 1940s. In 1940 Ferd Hirschi,

Howard Larsen, Floyd Carter, and Gordon Carter went to the Rural Electrification Association (REA) in Malta, Idaho, and asked for electric service for Park Valley. An engineer was hired and plans were nearly completed when World War II was declared. After the war work resumed, and the valley people eagerly watched the poles go up and asked one another, "Have they reached your place yet?"[70]

Local men helped build the line. It was turned on at the store at Christmas time in 1947. By early 1948 the central part of the valley had power. Then it was taken west to Chester Kunzler's ranch and on to Muddy. It was also extended east to Royal Morris's ranch and on to the Kelton ranches.

It was discovered that the poles had been placed too far apart. There were many power outages because the lines kept crossing and breaking. Then the REA put up more poles, and the reliability of electrical service improved.

Everyone welcomed the new genie and the work-saving devices it made possible. All the valley went "modern," with electric lights, appliances, irrigation pumps, and milkers for the cows.

Gordon Carter was a member of the REA board of directors from the time Park Valley joined the REA, and served for many years. LeGrand Morris was the meter reader for the valley, serving from early 1980s to the spring of 1996.

Perhaps water has played the largest part in shaping the lives and destiny of Park Valley. As the Indians frequented the valley on their annual migrations, hunting and gathering food, they left behind evidence of their passing,—arrowheads and corn grinding stones—mainly near the natural springs flowing along the foothills. As the first settlers arrived, they also made their homesteads by the springs or along the mountain streams.

When the first white settlers first arrived, the Intermountain West was in a much wetter cycle than normal. The cattlemen and sheep men stocked the range according to what the available water and annual rainfall would then allow. Within a few years, they found that they had overstocked the land and that the range was being overgrazed. When drier years set in, many families who were not fortunate enough to have settled on more permanent water sources were forced to move away or seek other means of livelihood. Many took with them shattered dreams, but left behind their contributions to the history of the valley. Some of their homesites can still be seen, in empty cabins or outlines of forgotten fields in the sagebrush. Many have been entirely forgotten as cabins were removed or traces in the sagebrush disappeared. Some, especially the Russian settlers who were lured here by false promises, found the area just too dry—even to dryfarm. For the Park Valley area, the adjustment was made fairly early, so that by the really dry years of the 1930s, when other communities such as Black Pine and Juniper, Idaho, were severely affected, the adjustment to the drier climate of Park Valley had already been largely accomplished.[71]

During the earlier history of the valley were fights, both fistfights and legal battles, over the rights to the springs and streams. Soon, however, the streams came to be controlled by organized irrigation companies, with each member having a portion of the water that comes from the canyons. The main streams used for irrigation are, starting on the east, Indian Creek, Dunn or Marble Canyon, Fisher Canyon, Rock Canyon, Pine Canyon, Big Hollow, Dove Creek, Muddy Canyon, and finally Rosebud on the west.

In Rosette the irrigation company on Pine Canyon Creek was formed in 1914. In order to control the division of water, a settling pond and head gates were constructed during 1918 and 1919. During the drought year of 1934, the company, with the help of federal agencies, laid some eight-inch concrete pipe from the mouth of the canyon, to aid in getting more late runoff water to the fields. Many of the ranchers dug additional ditches of their own to facilitate the distribution of water. In 1948 an addition was made to the pipeline.

Fisher Canyon was incorporated into an irrigation company on 28 April 1915. The company developed some springs and installed one mile of eight-inch pipe from the mouth of the canyon. In 1934 an additional three-fourths of a mile of pipe was laid to stop more of the water loss. There was still a great water loss in the ditches from the end of the pipe to the ranches farther down stream, so in 1953 a fifteen-inch concrete pipeline was installed, and the earlier one was abandoned. The cost was $40,000. Government agencies helped with the surveying and plans, and $23,000 of the amount was borrowed from the Utah Water and Power Board, on a seventeen-year loan. This pipeline was four miles in length.[72]

Dunn Canyon or Marble Creek was the first irrigation company to install a large pipeline. Many years before the amount of water that each ranch was allocated from the creek was settled in a court decision. In 1949, working together, valley residents installed almost four miles of twelve-inch concrete pipe. The cost was almost $37,000.

Many wells have been dug through the years in an attempt to obtain more water. At first, they were dug by hand and the sides were rocked in. The wells supplied drinking water for families, gardens, or stock water. Water was usually pulled to the surface with a pulley and rope attached to a bucket. Often the lot of drawing water from the well fell to the daily chore of the older children in a family.

Fred Zaugg had a horse-powered well driller that he used to drill for artesian water. The well on his place, where Fred Hirschi later lived, was over 400 feet deep. Water was found, but not enough to flow freely. Then he hand dug a well about 8 or 10 feet across and timbered it up like a log cabin. It was about 60 feet deep. A windmill was installed to pump water from the drilled well into the hand-dug well. If the wind did not blow, then a hand pump was used to provide water for the household, garden, and livestock. There was one flowing well on the Christian Hirschi place next door.

Several other people installed windmills. Though they were used for quite some time, they were undependable, and people turned to hand pumps. Some gasoline motors were used to pump water, and served until electricity arrived in the valley in 1948.

With the coming of electricity, several people tried drilling deep wells to obtain water. In Rosette, Charles Kunzler, Harold Kunzler, Roy Pugsley, and Henry Kunzler each had a well drilled. Some of these resulted in enough water for household use, but not enough for irrigation. One of Henry Kunzler's is a flowing well, but the amount of water is not significant.

The first deep well that proved successful for irrigation was drilled by Alma Fehlman in 1951, on the Kelton Flat, about two miles north of the old Conant Ranch. It is a sixteen-inch well and, when tested, pumped about 300 inches of water. Since then more wells have been drilled on the Kelton Flat, where hundreds of tons of alfalfa hay are now raised.

Other deep wells were drilled by Chester Kunzler on the old Rosevere Ranch, or E. H. Jones Ranch, and also by Roy and Max Kunzler on the Clark and Johnston Ranch on the lower Dove Creek. All of these better-producing wells are in the lower part of the valley, and it is still the only part of the valley where sufficient amounts of water for irrigation have been found.

Park Valley—with its settlements—has a rich history and, despite its remote location, is one of the most beautiful places in Box Elder County.

Penrose

Penrose is located four miles southwest of Thatcher, about nine miles southwest of Tremonton, and about seventeen miles northwest of the courthouse in Brigham City. It is an agricultural village whose existence dates to the "second tier" of settlements in Box Elder County. It owes its existence to the coming of the canal system at the turn of the twentieth century. Through the influence of Peter N. Pierce, the settlement was named for Charles W. Penrose (1832–1925), an LDS apostle in 1904, and counselor in the First Presidency after December 1911.

The Penrose Ward was organized 28 May 1911, from the Thatcher Ward, with Peter N. Pierce as bishop. Many of the settlers of Penrose came from Davis County. Until its demise, the Malad Valley branch of the Oregon Short Line had a spur from Tremonton to Penrose, to serve the farms and especially sugar-beet growers.

Perry

Perry is located three miles south of the Box Elder County courthouse, accounting for the first name given to the settlement—Three Mile Creek.[73]

The first white settler at Three Mile Creek was the noted Orrin Porter Rockwell, who settled what is now known as Porter Springs, west of Perry's main street, U.S. Highway 89, at the time of the California Gold Rush.

Rockwell made no improvements on this land, although he

claimed it for a number of years. It was the northernmost point where there was sufficient water and grass for a major emigrant stop where he hoped travelers would stop to rest and allow their animals to recover before striking off across the great desert between the Wasatch and Sierra mountains.

There was a tidy profit to be made in such an enterprise, but the business never really got started. Porter returned to Salt Lake City to serve as marshal and maintain law and order. He turned over the emigrant stop to his brother Merritt. An Indian scare forced Merritt to abandon the remote spring, and the Rockwells did not become established in northern Utah.

According to Lois Nelson, the spring was a popular place for the Native Americans for many years before the white settlers came. She writes that "The spring was a place where the Indians would come to stay in the spring while going to the lake bottoms for duck eggs. In the fall, before the ducks could fly, the Indians would go out in the swamp and kill them with a stick. They would stay at this spring for several weeks and feast on duck. There was always an abundance of feed so their ponies could find plenty to eat."[74]

The first white settlers after the Rockwells arrived in the spring of 1853. They were the Gustavus A. Perry, Orrin Perry, Henry Perry, Lorenzo Perry, William Plummer Tippetts, William Walker, and John Wakley families. They were joined by a group of Welsh families.

Lois Nelson writes that

> People from Wales began arriving in Box Elder in 1853. The Welsh people established homesteads just south of Box Elder, in the northern section of Three Mile Creek, taking their water from the north stream of Three Mile Creek. A small crop of grain was grown that year.
>
> When Indian trouble came, all those living in the Welsh Settlement went to the fort in Box Elder. Most did not build permanent homes on their land at Three Mile Creek until 1855.
>
> The women from Wales brought with them the knowledge of sheep shearing and taught the women of Three Mile Creek this art.
>
> When the call was made by Brigham Young to colonize Malad, Idaho. which was part of Box Elder at that time, many from the

Welsh Settlement left their new homes and traveled north to Malad.[75]

Among the Welsh settlers at Three Mile Creek were David Hughes Peters and his wife Laura. Of their first home at Three Mile Creek, David Peters wrote, "The first shelter, as I recall, was sort of a wickiup, built by putting two forked posts in the ground, about 16 feet apart, then a pole across the top. Small poles were placed in a slant position resting on this parallel pole, down to the ground. It was then covered with willow, cane and dirt. One end was open, the structure looked like a gable end of a house. In the structure was a table and logs to sit on."[76]

Among the Peters' children were John David Peters, a well-known educator and probate judge in Box Elder County as well as superintendent of schools, and Pearl Peters, who married Matthew Compton, son of pioneer photographer Alma Compton, and who continued the Compton legacy in Brigham City until his retirement.[77]

Another of the Welsh settlers was Thomas Mathias, who gave his name to Mathias Canyon, east of the northern boundary of Three Mile Creek.

Many other families joined those first pioneers, and made their own contributions to the community and the county.

Log cabins, made of aspen trunks, replaced the earliest shelters, like the "wickiup" described by David Peters. As in other settlements in the county, tallow candles were used for light until coal oil became available. Water was hauled from the creek, and the settlers made do with what they had, and made most of what they used.

The early interface between the Mormon settlers and the Native Americans who held the land before their coming was not always easy or comfortable. Their customs differed, as is evident from this story, as told by Lois Nelson: "The Indians had a custom of leaving the old and helpless to shift for themselves as the tribe moved on. One winter two old Indian squaws were left by their tribe to die. The Perry family took them in and cared for them. In the spring the son of 'Chenie' came looking for his mother's remains and found her well and happy living at the home of Gustavus A. Perry."[78]

The stories did not always have happy endings.

> The first real Indian skirmish in Box Elder County was caused by an immigrant train camp just south of Willow Creek. During the night a horse strayed away from the enclosed encampment and the Indians were blamed. After some delay on the part of the immigrants, an Indian was seen leading the horse to camp. One hasty settler drew his revolver, shot, and killed the Indian.
>
> The settlers who gathered at the scene of the shooting advised the train to make a hasty departure. The advice was followed, but they only reached Three Mile Creek when the Indians surrounded them where they had camped at noon on the knoll. The Indians offered to let the train go on if they would give up the man who did the shooting, but this the immigrants refused to do.
>
> The trouble occurred near the home of Lorenzo Perry, who with his wife, May W. Perry, had great influence with the Indians. Mr. Perry, William Walker, and others induced the Indians to let the company go on, which they did.[79]

Electrical power came to Perry in the 1890s, when the Perry Electric Company was organized for the purpose of purchasing excess electrical power from Brigham City. The Perry Electric Company was a private company of local men with Vinson F. Davis, Sr., as president. During the winter of 1904–05, the Perry company built their own lines, installed their own poles, did their own wiring, and in spring of 1905 electricity was brought to Perry.[80] The electric company was purchased by Perry City in 1921. A citywide culinary water system was installed in 1911, and telephones came to Perry in 1905. Natural gas service came in 1960, and a modern sewer system in 1973.

As with other Box Elder communities, Three Mile Creek had molasses mills, saw mills, and a co-op store. One of the notable enterprises in Three Mile Creek was the Barnard White creamery, established in 1893. It operated until 1909. One of the most important businesses is the Perry Canning Company, established in 1884 by Alexander Brewer and purchased by James and Alice Wilson in 1919. The cannery received and canned local produce until the early 1990s. North of the cannery there was a sugar beet dump during the 1940s and 1950s which received beets bound for the Utah-Idaho Sugar Company factory in Garland.

A second cannery and freezing plant was constructed in Perry during the Second World War. The R. D. Pringle Plant was built at 1480 West 2700 South giving job opportunities to residents during the war years. Aaron Snow was called to manage the plant.

> Because it was hard to find workers, it became a place for the dislocated Japanese citizens from the Pacific Coast to find employment. Many of the workers were living in camps in surrounding states and would come and work for the cannery when it was operating and then be taken back to the camp when the work was done. While working at the plant they would live in bunk houses to the east of the plant.[82]

That plant was later purchased by the George A. Nielsen family. It was used for apple sorting and packing. In recent years it has housed, among other enterprises, a venture making dog food out of worms.

Though the canneries have come and gone, one fruit plant remains. In 1977 several cherry farmers, including Paul Nelson and Roger Nelson of Perry, Gay Pettingill and Glenn Woodyatt of Willard and Weldon Cragun and Earl Cragun of Pleasant View, formed a co-op to process sour cherries under the name Utah Pie Cherry Co-op. The plant was acquired by Muir Roberts in 1990.[82]

One of the most interesting enterprises in the Perry area was the raising of ranch mink. It began in the 1940s, when Dr. J. L. Huchel, a Brigham City dentist, raised mink on his Three Mile Creek Mink Ranch between 1945 and 1956.

After World War II, Wes Osmond and Lawrence Molgard began raising mink in the Perry-Willard area. Later George A. Nielsen began raising mink. Mink ranching began as a money-making enterprise, but the importation of foreign mink pelts in the 1960s made raising Utah mink less profitable.

One of the locally best-known establishments in Perry was Jessie's Café. Jessie Hamson was known to make some of the best pies in the county. The secret of her flaky pie crusts, she said, was that she used a beer bottle instead of a rolling pin.

Perhaps the most famous Perry eating establishment is Maddox Ranch House. Irvin B. Maddox came to Brigham City with the

Bushnell Hospital. After the war, and the closure of the hospital, Mr. Maddox ran a little "chili-counter" in Brigham City.

> On August 11, 1949, Irvin B. and Wilma K. Maddox opened the first Maddox in Perry. It started as a little one-room log cabin kitchen, placed on skids.
>
> Fried chicken and sandwiches were served to customers by car service. By Thanksgiving a lunch counter had been added and plans were made to add a dining room.
>
> The dining room was opened for business on Mother's Day, 1950, and the following summer saw the addition of a lobby. In succeeding years, two more dining rooms were added to the main floor, and one dining room upstairs. The Maddox family living quarters were above the restaurant.
>
> Mr. Maddox's mottos were "The Best is None Too Good" and "Quest for Excellence." He and Mrs. Maddox believed in good products and good service.
>
> In the late 1950s, a feed lot was built behind the restaurant, where Mr. Maddox raised a portion of his own beef.
>
> In the 1980s, Steven K. Maddox, a son, became president and general manager. Today the entire living quarters upstairs have been converted to dining rooms. In the 90s, Maddox Ranch House has received a new face uplift. The modernized facilities have the original log cabin decor, good products and good service. The "Quest for Excellence" continues.[83]

The area between Willard and Brigham City, along U.S. Highway 89, has become known as "fruit way." The rocky ground of the foothills is ideal for fruit trees. Representative of all those who raise and market their fruit and vegetables is the enterprise started by George A. Nielsen. George Nielsen came from Sanpete County to become the chemistry teacher at Box Elder High School. In 1939 he purchased fifteen acres of ground in Perry, with a sixty-five dollar down-payment. George Nielsen and his hard-working wife, Lola expanded their land holdings and their fruitstand, and employed their children and grandchildren to help. George kept up his teaching during the school year, and spent the summers producing his famous fruit and produce. After his retirement and death, his sons continued the operation. Lola worked at the stand into her late eighties, and continued to greet old friends and customers at her accustomed post into her nineties, shortly before her death.

Perry began as part of the Box Elder Ward, "often walking to Brigham City to attend the Sunday services which were held in the Court House."[84] A branch was organized in Three Mile Creek in the 1860s, and a ward with Orrin A. Perry as bishop was organized by Brigham Young when he reorganized the stake on 19 August 1877.

A brick meetinghouse was built for the Perry ward in 1899. A central heating system was added in 1925, and a large addition constructed on the south side between 1951 and 1956. With completion of a new chapel in 1975, the old building was sold and became home to the Heritage Theater.

The town was officially renamed Perry in 1898 when a post office was established.[85] The town was incorporated in order that a municipal water system could be installed.[86]

From the days of the Gold Rush and Porter Rockwell's homestead on Porter Spring to the Welsh settlement, the fruit industry and more recent changes, Three Mile Creek became Perry, and is today one of the important towns of Box Elder.[87]

Plymouth

Plymouth lies just east of Interstate 15, twenty-six miles north and a little west of the courthouse in Brigham City, and about eight miles south of the Idaho border.

> Plymouth, for many years known as Square Town, was first settled in March, 1869 by Harman D. Person, Isaac E. Zundel, John Taylor, Joseph and William Merrill. They located on the side hill on the extreme north of the Bear River Valley. They lived in tents during the first summer, but in the fall they laid out a one-block townsite which was divided into lots. Like Israel of Old they cast lots for their portion and each set up a tent on the site he drew
>
> Because the plat was one block square, they called the settlement Square Town. According to Ella Abbot Leavitt, "Myron Abbott, his two wives and daughters, were out for a Sunday walk. On their way they passed a large lime rock. Mrs. Emily Farley Abbott remarked that the stone resembled the Old Plymouth Rock and all present agreed that Plymouth would be a good name for

> their new settlement. This was in the early seventies as the Abbotts came to Plymouth from Ogden in the early spring of 1871."[88]

The first white child born in Square Town was Solomon Zundel, son of Isaac and Elizabeth H. Zundel. Mrs. Zundel was one of only two women who remained in the infant settlement that winter.

The raising of dry farm wheat was a frustration in the early years of Plymouth settlement, due to an infestation of crickets, which devastated crops in Plymouth and in neighboring Portage. After the cricket infestation cycle had passed, dry farming was again attempted by several men who moved to Portage from Farmington in 1876–77. There efforts were successful.

The raising of cattle brought the necessity of a dairy operation: "In 1886–7 George Mason established a dairy at Mound Springs near Plymouth on land formerly owned by James Cole, a member of the Mormon Battalion. Butter and cheese were made on quite a large scale, and the dairy employed seven to eight people, mostly women."[89]

Local farmers were also successful in raising sheep. Flocks and herds increased rapidly; however, infected sheep also came into the area making the construction of a sheep dip near the Malad River a necessity. During some years as many as one million sheep were dipped and sheared at this location.[90]

To provide water for their gardens and crops, the settlers dammed the creek coming down Bishop Canyon, and used the water not only for irrigation, but to operate a vertical reciprocating saw to make lumber. The sawmill, operated by Willliam Neeley of Bear River City, produced lumber which was used in the construction of homes and Plymouth's first school house, built in 1871.[91] In the early days, the school precinct at Plymouth was known as Zarahemla, a place name from the Book of Mormon.

The people of Plymouth were, in the early days, included in the Portage Ward, which, in 1877, extended from Hampton Bridge on the south to a point a number of miles over the Idaho lines on the north.[92] Plymouth was given its own ward in 1884. The ward included Riverside and Fielding. On 27 December 1891 the Plymouth Ward was divided into two wards—Plymouth and East Plymouth or Hessville.

Besides Hessville or East Plymouth, the immediate area contains the settlement of Mound Springs, four miles north of Plymouth, which was first settled in the spring of 1874 by John Tims, James Spencer, Jarvis Mansfield, George Mason, and Charles Mangelson.[93]

In recent years the Nucor steel mill was built along the route of the Malad Valley branch of the OSL, directly west of Plymouth and west of the freeway, with its adjacent business, the David J. Joseph Company. The Nucor plant, one of the new breed of steel mills in the United States, utilizes electricity instead of open-hearth coke furnaces, and is less polluting than the old mills. It and the Joseph Company provide employment to those who live in the area.

Portage

Portage is located eight miles northwest of Plymouth, two miles south of the Idaho border, two-and-a-half miles west of I-15, and approximately thirty-four miles north and west of the county courthouse in Brigham City.[94]

Several accounts describe the Malad Valley and the early settlers of the Portage area. These accounts seem to agree that the valley was used as a herd ground. The meadows which extended to the east and west of the Malad River and north and south from Tremonton to Malad provided lush meadow grass upon which livestock could graze. Prior to 1854, there were two or three shacks which had been erected for the livestock herders to use.

One account states, "In the spring of 1854, there were five families located at the springs they named Mountain Springs. The families were: Waldrons, Dales, Barnards, Frodshams and Paynes." In another account it is stated that "The first attempt made to settle it was in 1855 when Ezra Barnard of Farmington, Utah and others (about 15 families altogether) located a settlement on the east side of the Malad River, nearly opposite the present Washakie." Another account states that "Ezra Barnard . . . Daniel Stewart, James Stewart, A. B. Hill and others (about 15 families altogether) settled in the Malad Valley in the summer of 1855. They located on the east side of the Malad River, nearly opposite the present Washakie, on Sec. 15 of Tp. 14 N. of Range 3 W. Salt Lake Meridian."

Each written account adds some interesting information about the conditions under which the settlers lived and the efforts they made to sustain themselves in this somewhat hostile environment. It is obvious that these early settlers were aware of the survey beginning at Temple Square in Salt Lake City and which extended from that point north, south, east, and west. Their settlement was established in relationship to that survey as recorded above.

These settlers built an adobe fort enclosing about an acre of ground inside of which they dug cellars and erected log houses. Here the first house in the valley was erected. It was built of sod with the grass down and roots up with a dirt roof, one door, one window, a fire place, and chimney constructed of flat rocks. For a door, they used a quilt, and a piece of white muslin for the window.

It was in this house that the Waldrons made their home. During the summer the Waldrons had a number of unwelcome and unwanted guests. They were rattlesnakes. However, the snakes cleaned the place of mice.

The wolves were many and fierce. It was dangerous to venture far without a rifle. Many wolves were killed and pelted during the first few years.

It was in this humble sod house on 9 October 1856 that the first white child, a girl, was born. A bed of straw in the corner of the room with a few blankets and quilts served as the maternity ward for this first child to be born in Malad Valley. This child, Emmeline Eliza Waldron, was the daughter of Benjamin and Emmeline Waldron.

One morning the men came out of their cabins to find that during the night a number of tepees had been pitched a short distance to the south. The Indians seemed to be more surprised to find white men with homes at these springs. Salutations by the wave of the hand were given with each group responding. They cautiously mingled together, and a strong friendship grew among them.

Among the Indians was a young man who went by the name of Tob or Toby. He became very friendly with the white people, trying to learn and speak the English language. He was very helpful to his new and apparently welcome neighbors.

Among the first settlers who arrived sometime in August 1855 were Emmeline Waldron and Amelia Frodsham, the first two, and the only two, women in the camp in the beginning. There were about thirty men and boys in the camp who arrived first. More families came in the fall of 1855 and cast their lot with the first settlers. The place did not suit a number of them, and consequently some of the first settlers moved away until there were only about seven families left to spend the winter of 1855–56 in the Malad Valley. Only part of the families spent the winter in the fort, while others camped on the outside. No attempt was made at farming in 1855.

Early in the spring of 1856, the pioneer settlers in Malad Valley went to work in earnest plowing and sowing and planting, but the grasshoppers saved them the trouble of harvesting as everything was destroyed by these pests that year.

In 1857 the settlers in Malad Valley had better success. A good crop of wheat and other cereals, as well as garden stuff were raised in the Valley.

The prospects of a good crop in 1858 were very promising when word came from the headquarters of the Mormon church for all the Saints living in the settlements north of Salt Lake City to vacate their homes because of the Johnston Army troubles. The few pioneer settlers in Malad Valley, obeying counsel, left their improvements and moved south.

Before the general move south, however, the Saints in Malad Valley were advised to vacate because of Indian troubles, the natives being very hostile at that time in the north. Joseph Parry, of Ogden, Utah, who in his connection with the Fort Limhi Mission traveled through Malad Valley, recorded, "We left Fort Limhi Dec 4, 1855, returning to Utah after provisions for our new settlement and arrived in Fort Hall on Snake River, Dec. 19, 1855. Continuing over the Bannock divide, we camped on Deep Creek on the night between Dec. 23 and 24, 1855, near the boundary line between Utah and Oregon Territory (later Idaho) with a few families of Saints who had settled here a few months previously. They were extremely poor and could not help us with any provisions. Among them was my old friend, James Frodsham, who had charge of the colony. The settlers gave us supper and breakfast."

Parry's company consisted of George W. Hill and seven others. Parry had charge of the company which traveled with three wagons and six yoke of cattle. When Parry traveled northward the previous

June (1855), there were no improvements of any kind in Malad Valley save a shanty or two which had been erected for the accommodation of herders.

After the Fort Limhi exiles had passed through Malad Valley on their return to Utah, the Malad settlers followed them, though it seems that there were only three or four families left in the settlement, including the Barnard family, the Frodsham family and Mrs. Waldron. The rest had become discouraged before and had already left. Now, in the spring of 1858, the last three families left the valley and located temporarily at Call's Ford, immediately north of Brigham City, and afterwards participated in the general move south.

Ezra Barnard returned to Malad Valley in the fall of 1858, after peace had been declared between the inhabitants of Utah and the Johnston Army, and harvested the grain which had matured during the time the valley had been vacated. Besides Barnard, others went up and assisted in harvesting grain and cutting hay for the army. Some of the friendly Indians assisted the men in harvesting their grain and doing other work.

Although the first years were extremely difficult because of the grasshoppers, wolves, snakes, army threats, and some hostile Indian threats, these first settlers showed the courage and determination to persevere in spite of the hardships and loneliness they faced.

Thomas John, a shoemaker by trade, came from Wales to the United States in 1848. He later returned to South Wales, where he was baptized into the Church of Jesus Christ of Latter-day Saints in 1851. He came to Utah in 1861 and was part of a company of pioneers who arrived in Cache Valley on 22 October 1861. The John family moved from Wellsville to the Malad Valley in 1867, and homesteaded one hundred sixty acres of land on the north edge of what is called Portage today.

According to Thelma Gibbs:

> In the early 1900s, railroad tracks were laid through the center of the valley as far north as Malad. On January 1, 1906, the first train rolled through the valley up to Malad, which was the end of the track. A large train depot was built along the tracks at Portage which serviced the area until the late 1940s when the depot was

> discontinued. The building was sold to Harold E. Hall and moved to his property in town.
>
> Until the time of the depression, most of the families in Portage made their living by farming, gardening and raising livestock. Many of the farmers supplemented their income by working at the Utah Idaho Sugar Plant in Garland, Utah during the fall processing the sugar beets into sugar.
>
> As financial conditions worsened and World War II began, many of the small land owners sold their farms to other local farmers and moved to the larger centers, such as Ogden, Utah, where they could find jobs at the military installations such as, Hill Field and the Ogden Defence Depot. People were encouraged to support the war effort and this was a good way to do it.
>
> During this period, the population of Portage decreased from about 450 citizens to around 200 people and it remained at about that level until the late 1970s when new industry such as, the Thiokol Company and the Nucor Company moved in. People could live in Portage and commute to these companies by car. Many new homes were constructed and the population increased.[95]

Portage has, from the beginning, been an LDS community. According to LaVerd and Flora John, "The first Branch of the Church was organized in November of 1867 with Thomas Green as the President. This Branch of the Church was located on the east side of the Malad River opposite the present site of Washakie. In 1872 and 1873, most of the settlers moved to the west side of the Malad River and located at the present site of Portage. The Box Elder Stake of Zion was organized on August 19, 1877. The Portage Ward was organized and became a part of the Box Elder Stake."[96]

Mr. and Mrs. John note that "The first Portage Branch Meeting House was a log structure forty feet long, twenty two feet wide with a nine foot ceiling. The wall logs were hewn on the inside and the roof was lumber slabs. . . . In 1872, this building was moved across the Malad River to the west settlement and was located on the Church Lot where it served as a church meeting house and a school building for 14 years."[97]

The second Portage ward chapel

started as a brick structure in 1882, but due to drought and poor crops little work was accomplished. The construction began again in 1883 and the walls were completed when a wind storm blew the walls down on December 25, 1883. The people were unable to rebuild again until 1885. At that time, a new frame structure was erected on the same foundation. This building was thirty two feet wide, sixty feet long with a twenty foot ceiling. It was located on the Church Lot directly west of the present chapel. The front entrance was on the east end of the building and inside there was a stage on the west end. This building served as the Portage Ward Chapel and as the Malad Stake Center from 1888 to 1911.

In 1936, a contract to construct a brick ward chapel with a cultural hall, a relief society room, six class rooms, a kitchen and a boy scout room was approved at a cost of $24,000.00. The old structure was torn down and all usable lumber and other materials were sold. Church meetings were held in the school house, located on the west end of the Church Lot, while the new building was under construction. The building was dedicated Sunday May 28, 1939 by President Heber J. Grant. An overflow crowd was in attendance.

In March 1987, reconstruction began on the 1939 building under the direction of architect, Wallace N. Cooper and contractor, Jon Z. Thompson. The interior of the chapel, cultural hall, foyer and bishop's office on the main floor were renovated. the cultural hall was converted into a beautiful chapel. The foyer and entrance were enlarged. The old chapel was divided into new offices for bishops and clerks, a mother's lounge, a kitchen and other facilities. A new cultural hall was constructed on the west side of the original building. This building was rededicated on Sunday, April 17, 1988 by Elder Devere Harris of the First Quorum of Seventy, a former bishop of the Portage Ward and a former president of the Malad Stake.[98]

Promontory

Geographically, the Promontory is a mountain range, the southern extension of the North Promontory Mountains. The Promontory, as the name implies, juts out into the Great Salt Lake, dividing its northern half (separated from the southern half by the Southern Pacific causeway) into an eastern and a western arm. Surrounded by three sides by the waters of greater Willard Bay (not the impounded Willard Bay), the Promontory is largely isolated from the rest of Box Elder County.

When speaking of human habitation on the Promontory, we must speak of a number of places. First are the locally well-known Indian Caves on the western side of the Promontory, inhabited in prehistoric times.

There are other caves on Promontory which show signs of ancient habitation, and pictographs which give further evidence.

In historic times there have been several designations for the string of farms and homesteads which dot the east side of Promontory. Most famous, perhaps, is the high valley which divides the Promontory Range from the North Promontory Range. In that valley lies Promontory Summit, the site of the driving of the precious metal spikes marking completion of the nation's first transcontinental railroad on 10 May 1869. The railroad town of Promontory Station is now the site of Golden Spike National Historic Site. Promontory Station lies seven miles west of the Thiokol plant, on the route of the Central Pacific Promontory Branch, running from Corinne around the northern end of Great Salt Lake, passing Monument Point and Kelton, then striking a southwesterly course toward Lucin, just short of the Nevada border.

Thirty miles to the south of Promontory Summit, at the very southern tip of the Promontory Range, is Promontory Point. The Golden Spike was not driven at Promontory Point, nor did rails reach that place until the building of the Lucin Cutoff just after the turn of the twentieth century, more than thirty years after the Union Pacific and Central Pacific's tracks met at Promontory Summit.

At Promontory Point are several places with specific name designations. There is the geographic feature, Promontory Point, a knob of rock at the very tip of the peninsula. That landmark was largely blasted to rubble in the mad rush to keep the Southern Pacific causeway and the Great Salt Lake Minerals' dikes above water during the wet cycle of the mid-1980s.

Where the Southern Pacific causeway meets land on the Promontory is the Southern Pacific "Promontory Point," a siding and trailer camp for railroad maintenance workers. West of Promontory Point and the old FAA landing strip is the site of the old Lake Crystal

Salt Plant at Saline. Saline also had a siding for loading salt onto the railroad. The salt plant closed with the high water cycle of the 1980s, and the plant buildings were demolished and buried in the mid-1990s. Now the site of Saline is marked only by rubble.

Around the tip of the Promontory, west from Saline, is the site of Little Valley Town and the boat docks of Morrison-Knudson's mammoth earth-moving efforts of the 1950s, when the old trestle was replaced by an earth-fill causeway. On the mountain, just southeast of the site of Little Valley Town, is the spot where the world's largest non-nuclear explosion to that time was detonated during the causeway project. North and east of the site of Little Valley Town is Little Valley proper, where thousands of tons of rock and gravel were loaded onto the great conveyor belt for loading onto barges at Little Valley harbor. West of Saline, along the causeway, at the point where the trestle route and the "new" causeway split, is the point known on maps as Bridge. Directly north from Saline is Lead Mountain, site of Lakeview town and the lead-silver mines of the early twentieth century.

Between Promontory Point and Promontory Summit are areas known as East Promontory, North Promontory, and Boothe Valley. At one time there were schools at Boothe Valley and Promontory Station, as well as the one at Little Valley Town in the 1950s.

Riverside

Riverside is a small rural community in northern Box Elder County, located in the southeast quarter of section eleven in Township Twelve North, Range Three West of the Salt Lake Meridian.[99] It is about twenty miles north of Brigham City, the county seat.

Riverside lies on the west side of the Malad River. Along the hills to the west runs a trail which was followed by many early travelers. Early Indians camped nearby, and used a prominent rock outcrop to survey the valley. In 1841 the Bartelson-Bidwell party followed the trail at the base of the hills. Interstate 15 closely follows the old trail.

Riverside is bounded on the south by U.S. Highway 30 leading to the city of Logan, and on the west by I-15 along the foothills. Old Highway 191 cut through Riverside but is now known as State

Highway 13. The Union Pacific Railroad runs along the west side of Riverside by the back or top county road. This was the original road to Garland.

Tom D. Pitt of the Corinne Mill & Livestock Company and William H. Rowe—who represented the Bear River Canal Company—were owners of the land and water in Section 11. They wanted to sell large tracts of land in the area and desired to establish a community. Under Howe's direction, the townsite was surveyed, and 160 acres were laid out in eight-acre blocks. The plan was to have four homesteads on each block. A lane was to run through the middle of each block, with a ten-acre square in the center. The square was to be used for recreation. Around the square would be built a church and a school. The Kennard and Gleason families came to settle Section 14 as early as 1888–89. The townsite was surveyed and laid out in 1894, before any homes were built. That summer John Bowcutt built the first home in the new community, and baby Zina Bowcutt was the first child blessed in Riverside in LDS church services.

As new families came to Riverside, their one- and two-room homes were moved from Plymouth and Fielding. It was customary for the men and boys to help their neighbors in house moving, home building and farm work. Neighbor helped neighbor.

Riverside's existence dates back to 14 October 1894, when LDS apostles Heber J. Grant and Francis M. Lyman came to reorganize the Fielding and South Plymouth wards and form a new ward. Because of the community's location close to the river, the two apostles named the new ward "Riverside." Myron J. Richards—former bishop of Fielding—was named bishop of the new Riverside Ward. By 9 January 1895, seven families were living in Riverside. Richards, Porter, Capener, Bowcutt, Hadfield, Welling, Bourne, Ward, Udy, Tingey, Macfarlane, Kennard, Hess, Miller, Broomhead, Smith, Orwin, Hales, Lillywhite, Cockayne, Nye, Adams, Anderson, Colton, Van Fleet, Hancock, Parke, Jardine, Limb, Monson, Silvester, Doman, and Albert were family names of early settlers. Many of these families came from the Farmington and Centerville areas to the south, a two-day journey by wagon. They were farmers coming to make a living as agriculturists. The Forsberg family came from Sweden. By 1905 the Nishiguchi and Yagi families, both from Japan, settled in Riverside. They found a livelihood in the sugar industry which was established in the area at the turn of the century, with the surrounding farms furnishing sugar beets to the factory in Garland. Descendants of these early families still reside in Riverside, which boasted a population of 450 in 1992, consisting of 123 families.

The farms of the Riverside area were located on the outskirts of town. Each home had a place for animals, chickens, and a garden which helped make the families self-sufficient. When the Depression of 1929 came, the land provided the necessities for these families. Their animals provided milk, butter, and meat. Chickens provided eggs. Fruit trees and gardens filled the root cellars with apples, potatoes, carrots, squash, and cabbage made into sauerkraut. In addition to their vegetables, hundreds of quarts of fruits, pickles, and jams were stored. Wheat from the farm land was taken to the mills in Garland and Honeyville to be ground into flour to make delicious homemade bread.[100] Ruth Forsberg remembers "most homes had a pork barrel where hams and bacon were cured with Morton salt. Our forefathers were able to weather the deep, snowed-in winter and economic depression with a sense of security. Russell Capener remembers early peddlers who would come around to sell their wares. They would come with wagons full of fruit. The Wyatt Brothers of Garland would bring up a one-horse van full of meat, and ring a bell to let people know they were delivering. Also, an Italian peddler would come to sell Kingham (gingham). Now, in the 1990s, we all have automobiles and access to many local grocery stores."

Early landmarks of Riverside included the large barns at the Capener, Richards, Hadfield, and Welling homesteads. The Joseph Hadfield log home was a landmark in Riverside for over 90 years. Another landmark to the north is Plymouth Peak—a beautiful view shared by Riverside and the Bear River Valley.

In 1906, while teaching school in Washakie, Jim Kennard was told the Indian name of Plymouth Peak by Yeager Timbimboo who was Bishop Moroni Ward's first counselor. This is the legend told to Yeager by his father:

> Before the white man came, even before the days of good Chief Washakie who was the white man's friend, there came a famine in the land. No rain, crops burned up, game all died, no deer, no rabbits, people hungry. Indians climbed big mountain; found a herd of mountain sheep, Big Horn. Killed many with bow and arrow. All full of sheep meat. Took plenty down to valley home for hungry women, old men and children. Plenty hungry; plenty eat. Made all people sick—what you call diarrhea. We call it Quoip, plenty bowel run-off. Sheep we call Toqua wee which means sick. Sheep made Indians sick with diarrhea, so Toqua-wee-Quoip. Mountain name in Indian.[101]

Myron J. Richards's journal of 6 September 1900 reads: "Worked on the Canal."[102] The highlight of the valley was the building of the canal which came out of the Bear River Canyon. The ditch was divided into two branches and continued south between the Bear River and Malad River to water that part of the valley. The other branch crossed the Malad River bottoms high up on the hill rim in a huge, trestle flume and watered the west valley. This meant irrigated farms for Riverside. The irrigation system was being developed to enable farmers to plant sugar beets. Richards' entry for 7 May 1901, notes: "I planted sugar beets for a test.[103] The sugar industry also meant work in the winter for the men and some women at the new sugar factory in Garland. During World War II, while our men and boys were serving and fighting in the armed forces, the sugar industry received help from an unexpected source—German prisoners of the war. They were interned at the old C.C.C. Camp in Tremonton which was located where the Bear River Valley Hospital now stands. These prisoners went into the beet fields and topped and harvested the beet crop. The sugar factory also brought a new highway in 1903. The new road soon became the main road south of Riverside. The sugar factory provided livelihood for many until it closed after the last sugar beet "campaign" of 1978–79.[104]

Machines to harvest beets replaced manual labor. Tractors replaced work horses. Combines replaced thrashing machines. Men and women of Riverside were always innovative when it came to working and making a living. Alfred Capener planted a grove of locust trees. They were to be used as wagon tongues. During World

War II, when gasoline was rationed and travel limited, LDS church meetings were held in various homes. Instructions came by mail or telephone from the church headquarters. As the women were at home, they were able to do a lot of welfare sewing for the LDS church. This sewing was sent to Germany and other war-torn countries in 1943–46.[105] Women were always busy making quilts, afghans, dresses, and other hand-sewn items to sell. Cottage industries of the early days would supplement a family income. Now in the 1990s, most women work outside the home to help the family income.

Myron J. Richards recorded in his journal on 20 February 1895: "First well dug water found at 15'7."[106] Each family had its own well for culinary use. Under the direction of Jay U. Macfarlane, the Riverside-North Garland Water Company was formed. On 22 May 1973, a loan was closed to provide a culinary water system for the town.[107] Fresh, clean water was brought down from a deep well on the hill which was purchased from Wendel Welling at Plymouth, Utah. Seventeen miles of pipe were laid to supply 115 families.

Early memories of church house activities include: square dances, basket lunches, ward reunions, or as it was also called, the Budget Dinner, which was held in February. Relief Society bazaars were held in the fall, and then there was always the traditional Christmas party which consisted of a wonderful program with costumes. Each child had a part on the stage. Following the program, Santa came with a present for all. Gold & Green balls were held with a queen and her court.

The first meeting house was built by members of the Church of Jesus Christ of Latter-day Saints and the first meeting was held on 22 December 1895.[108] Red drapes hung on wires formed spaces for classes.[109] A large pot-bellied stove was placed in the middle of the floor. Three-act plays were put on and taken to other wards. Basket dances were held once a year. The women and girls would fill beautifully decorated boxes with good things to eat. The baskets would be auctioned to the highest bidder. Fred and Vera Colton and Fred Nye furnished the music, and Moroni Ward was the caller for the square dances.

On 24 January 1902: "Charley Tingey came for the meeting house benches, and I came home with him, leaving Logan at 2:30 and arriving home at 7:45. Snowed and blew all the way; cold."[110] The building was also used as school, and religion classes were taught once a week by the school teacher.

The Relief Society lot was north of the church house. This Relief Society property was sold to John and Grace Allen in 1941. A picket fence was around the lot with outhouses behind the church.

A tithing lot was in Plat No. 1 in the northwest quarter of town. The lot was 200 feet by 200 feet. The tithing wheat was stored on the lot before being taken to Collinston for shipment to Salt Lake City. It was also used for the needy of the ward. The tithing lot had a board fence around it. There was a granary and hay piled up in the lot for those in need.

A new church building was dedicated by LDS apostle Rudger Clawson on 11 February 1917. "The new building is a frame structure on a solid cement foundation with classrooms and assembly hall in the basement. There is a gallery over the front entrance with a hallway underneath the stairway. A large well-equipped stage with good scenery completes the amusement facilities." The building was heated with an always-smoking furnace. It was completed at a cost of $5,516.97."[111] The majority of the money—over $3,000—was donated by the 250 ward members.

After 1934 some women of the ward (Ellen and Helen Capener, Effie Welling, Grace Hales, and Mina Ward) took on the project of sewing a curtain for the stage. Ward families each donated a dollar toward the project. Forty-four yards of red velour were purchased from Z.C.M.I., and the women sewed the curtains in Effie's living room. Curtain, valance, hooks, and metal track came to $83.52. Effie Welling said, "It fit perfectly and looks so beautiful and worked like a charm." By making the curtain, hundreds of dollars were saved by ward members who didn't have the money.

The community tried to use the old Riverside church as a town center for activities, but after a number of years, they found it too hard to maintain. This meeting house was demolished after the Riverside Ward joined the West Fielding and Plymouth wards to form the Belmont ward on 28 June 1959. The name Belmont was taken from Riverside Railroad siding which had been called Belmont because there was also a Riverside in Idaho. A new church building north of Riverside was dedicated 24 October 1965 by Gordon B. Hinkley, then an LDS apostle. Total cost of the building was $283,706.78. Of this amount, $141, 853.39, or half, was paid by ward members who raised money through building fund projects. The Belmont Building Fund Committee members were: Olene Garn, Gordon Bronson, Douglas Roche, C. M. "Red" Cornwall, Merrill Petty, and Norma Forsberg as secretary. Children brought dimes to Primary. Edna Steed's Primary class made cakes to sell. Gene Cornwall made eleven cakes himself and sold them for $11.00. Chinese dinners filled the cultural hall every year. Maxine Garn put on a "Gay Nineties review" and made $2,900 in ticket sales. There were bake sales and bazaars. Men took calves and pigs to feed and gave the profit to the building fund. Beets were raised behind the building. Members hoed, thinned, and harvested them. Nearly every member who was able worked on the building. They sanded, painted, laid tile, cleaned, worked in the yard and helped in many other ways. The Red Cornwall family painted the power poles. Red set the poles in the ground and hung the lights for the ball park. Darwin Burnett and the Elders Quorum built bleachers for the ball park. Many good ball games were played by children and adults. These projects brought three communities together as never before by the efforts of raising money for their ward meeting house.

The Riverside Ward was part of the Malad Stake. On 11 October 1908 the Malad Stake was divided, and the Bear River Stake was organized. Riverside now belonged to the Bear River Stake which consisted Fielding, Plymouth, Riverside, Beaver, Bothwell, Deweyville, East Garland, Elwood, Garland, and Thatcher wards. The Bear River Stake was divided on 12 May 1985. Riverside then became part of the Fielding Utah Stake which consisted Portage, Belmont I (Plymouth), Belmont II (Riverside), Fielding, Beaver and East Garland wards. The Fielding Ward has since been divided, creating the Hampton Ford Ward.

A two-room brick schoolhouse was begun on 1 September 1901 and completed with the hanging of the bell on 30 November 1903. The cost was $1,850. In 1909 two more rooms and a bell tower were added at a cost of $4,333.[112]

The two rooms were added to the east side—thus changing the

entrance to the north. The bell tower was constructed over the cement entrance. A rope hung down from the bell, and students took advantage of this as the bell was rung many times. The bell is now on a stand of iron in Riverside Park. There was a picket fence around the school yard. Many happy times were had in this yard—trees to climb and yellow johnny jump-up to pick. Games played were red rover, anti-i-over, fox and geese, dare base, and roller skating in one of the unused rooms. On 8 September 1930, grades five through eight were taken to Garland School. One teacher was left in Riverside School to teach grades one through four. About 1946 all students began to travel by bus to the Garland School, and the old school house was torn down. The grounds became a park, with development funded by local women's clubs.

The park, known as "The Square," has always been the center of Riverside recreation. Baseball games with other towns were played on Saturday. Bob Macfarlane had a cooler with cold pop for sale. Fourth of July parades and patriotic programs, which particularly interested the children, were held every year with hamburgers, hotdogs, freezers of homemade ice cream, and plenty of homemade pie to look forward to. The Fourth of July celebrations entailed building a bowery which Jim Kennard said was " . . . a real community project. Posts and logs from farms and ranches. Poles to support the green bough roof, the foliage cut fresh from maple groves in the west hills; plank & log seats and a lumber stand or stage for a program."[113]

On 21 June 1981 the Riverside Community Special Service District was formed. It was funded by tax monies. A bowery and rest rooms have been built, and a beautiful park now graces Riverside.

Myron J. Richards, the first postmaster, recorded that on 18 January 1896 " . . . Mail went from our new Post Office to Collinston for the first time."[114] The post office was located in the L. H. Kennard Store east of the church. Mr. Kennard served as the next postmaster. His daughter, Mary Tingey, succeeded him, followed by John Adams. Robert Macfarlane purchased the Adams home and store, and his wife, Rowane, became the postmistress. The store, now called "Jay's," and the operation of the post office are still in the Macfarlane family.

On 23 August 1905, a business meeting was held at the home of John Bowcutt. The subject of the meeting was to secure land for a cemetery. It was learned that two acres of ground could be purchased from E. T. Capener at a cost of $75.[115] Until this time, children who died were buried on the property owned by their families. In the spring of 1955, Bishop Leland Capener called for a cemetery beautification program. Ralph C. Richards, Russell Capener, and Edmund Udy formed a committee with Clarence E. Smith serving as secretary.[116] Pine trees were planted for a boundary, a well was dug and a pump system installed for watering, grass was planted and a new west side was added. The original price for a grave was $5.00. Lots of twelve graves went from $150 in 1968, to $240 in 1977.

Myron J. Richards chronicled the political beginnings of Riverside. "16 February 1903—Asked for a voting district. Joseph A. Capener appointed Justice of the Peace. Lewis Lillywhite, constable."[117] Riverside is unincorporated and is a predominantly Mormon community. Thus the bishop of the ward is looked upon to lead the community.

In 1905 wires were strung on electric light poles through Riverside.[118] They were put in the middle of the roads which were muddy in wet weather. Later the poles were moved to the sides of the roads which were graveled every spring by the men of the town. In 1960–61 the streets were hard-surfaced. Telephone service came to Riverside in 1906: "The Bear River Valley Phone Company set poles and strung wires in our town."[119]

Every street was lined with gravel sidewalks and poplar trees. After each snow storm, Ward would take his horse which he hooked to a V-shaped plow and cleaned the town's sidewalks. Disease and sickness brought difficulties and concern to Riverside settlers. Sickness in early days brought much misery. Myron J. Richards recorded that on 1 December 1907 no Sunday School on account of scarlet fever." Two weeks later there were thirteen families in quarantine with the measles.[120]

Quarantine meant that a yellow flag would be placed on your home. No one was to enter, and the children were not to leave for two weeks. Joseph Hadfield was the quarantine officer.

Diphtheria was a scourge. An illness that can be treated now brought death to many small children in the early days. When an antitoxin was found, a doctor came from Salt Lake City to administer it. John Ward recalls the time in 1920 when Mina Ward's one-year-old daughter Mary had diphtheria. His wife, Edna, would bake a potato in her stove each day, and John would wrap it up and take it down the street to Mina's and put it on the step. They could not go into the house. Little Mary liked baked potatoes, and a neighbor did all she could do to help, but Mary died on 22 September 1920.[121]

Storms and fires also visited Riverside. A hail storm ruined crops on 13 July 1932. Russell Capener says of the storm: "Windows were broken, chickens killed. Also, seagulls and doves were killed by the hundreds. The town looked like a barren waste. This caused much suffering and loss to land and homes."

In August 1968 Russell and Howard Capener's big barn burned down. The whole town turned out to help fight the fire and save what animals they could. The barn had been a landmark. Its fences on the north and west sides were used each year by Barnum & Bailey Circus to advertise the circus was coming to town. Colored circus pictures were pasted on the board fences. They brought anticipation to the children. Many children slid down the hay and straw and played hide & seek in the old barn. It was a loss to the whole town.

There were also house fires that burned down the homes of Harry Welling, Tracy Welling, Alfred Capener, Marvin Burnett, and Nina Dustin, which burned on 31 October 1975.

Over the years the population of Riverside has increased and the source of income has shifted from agriculture to employment at Thiokol Corporation which manufactures missiles and also boosters for the space shuttle, La-Z-Boy furniture factory in Tremonton, and the Nucor and Vulcraft steel plants.

Russian Settlement

One of the saddest sagas in the history of Box Elder County is the story of the Russian Settlement. It is a story of religious persecution, courage, hard work, death, and eventual defeat. It began in czarist Russia. A movement arose during the seventeenth century, among the peasantry, in reaction to the Orthodox religion. The dissidents held to a "charismatic" theology of Spiritual Christianity, in contrast to the czar-controlled Russian Orthodox church. According to a history of Park Valley, they were led by a Tambose peasant named

Semyon Uklein, who was disaffected by the posh rituals and excessive involvement with the state bureaucracy.[122]

The dissidents believed in personal religion, and felt led by the Holy Spirit to a simpler form of worship, more in line with the Bible than with the rituals, rules, and fast days which had developed in the Orthodox church. They prided themselves on being Bible-centered.

Because they declined to observe the two hundred fast days per year prescribed by the Orthodox calender, and ignored proscriptions against milk, they were given, in derision, the label "Molokani" or milk-drinkers. They were considered a sect, and were branded "sectarian." Instead of shunning the tag, they embraced it, proudly proclaiming that they were drinkers of the spiritual milk of God. The name "Molokani" was first used to describe a group in the Tambov province of Guberniia about 1765.

From their origin in the Caucasus, they were relocated to the undeveloped country of Trancaucasia in the early 1800s. Being "sectarian," they were outside the pale of orthodoxy. Laws in czarist Russia outlawed all but the state church, and the Mokoloni were subjected to persecution for their beliefs. They did not believe in military service. Even so, by the late nineteenth century, the Molokani had grown to between 100,000 and 500,000.

In the years 1905 to 1912, just before the Russian revolution, a number of Molokani migrated to America. It is estimated that perhaps 2,500, or less than three percent of the total Molokani population, joined the migration to the United States.

In Russia the Molokani were all but stamped out under Communism, and especially the Stalinist purges. Their story over the seventy years of Communist rule is the story of many Christians. After the lifting of the Iron Curtain, there were mainly only elderly women (babushki) left to revive the Molokani.

In America most of the Molokani settled on the Pacific Coast, chiefly in eastern Los Angeles and San Francisco, though some later migrated to Mexico and Australia.One small group found that Los Angeles was not all they had wanted to find in America. It was a place where they were constantly at odds with city life, civil law, and modern ways.

It was the civil law which brought things to a head. "Among the persecutions they had to endure was a recent court decision rendered in Los Angeles by a Judge Monroe, who held that a young woman named Sarah Katoff was not legally married to Jacob Ural, who claimed her as his wife, and that the marriage which had been entered into under the Russian colony's customs, was annulled. This action greatly incensed the older Russians, and they at once began their preparations for fleeing from what they termed the 'persecution.'"[123]

They searched for a place where they could begin as a community of believers in the desert, as it were. Unfortunately, it became too much of a reality. They heard the grand advertising of the Pacific Land and Water Company. The company was made up of investors who had purchased 136,949 acres of railroad land in Park Valley. Its principals were James H. Patterson, C. N. Strevell, F. A. Druehl, Harold A. LaFaunt, W. Mont Ferry, Dr. E. D. Woodruff, and Robert LaFaunt.[124] The Pacific Land and Water Company brochure advertised "hundreds of acres of land lying ready to respond most generously to the touch of the husbandman."[125]

The Molokani sent a delegation to Box Elder County to see the land. For some reason, they believed the extravagant claims of the Pacific Land and Water Company, and made a deal. Sarah Yates, who spent eight years researching the history of the Russian colony, writes,

> Need and opportunity meshed. Another migration began.
>
> According to Elizabeth Goodliffe Hirschi and her sister Dorothy Goodliffe Pugsley, whose father Charles Goodliffe ran the Park Valley store, an advance party came to Park Valley to see the property.
>
> "My father's store had the amusement hall upstairs, and it had beds all along the stage. The Russians stayed there when they came the first time to see the land, said Mrs. Hirschi."
>
> "Their leader seemed to have had the money, but I don't know whether it was his or the colony's. Kalpakoff liked my mother and trusted her. He came first and gave her $500 in cash to keep until he came back for it. She locked it in a trunk in the closet and would cheek on it," she added. "She was touched he would trust her so much. If they liked you they trusted you. They were very honest."
>
> The group's arrival was announced in the *Salt Lake Tribune,*

> reprinted in the 9 April 1914, *Box Elder News:* "More than 100 Russians, who for some time past have been members of the Russian colony near Los Angeles, Calif., left the southern California metropolis yesterday for Box Elder county, Utah. Another large contingent, it is said, will follow in a few weeks.
>
> "They are traveling on a special train of four cars—two baggage ears and two passenger coaches. The coaches are fitted up for comfort, and in addition to other conveniences they are supplied with stoves, in order that the Russian women may cook their own meals on the way and not come in contact with Americans," the article continued.[126]

The comfort of their specially-fitted railroad cars may have been the last comfort they experienced for several years. "Upon arrival on the dry sagebrush flats along the lower part of Dove Creek, they set about building wooden plank houses, digging wells and root cellars, and clearing the land for planting. Photographs show board houses, some with porches, plus some outbuildings."[127] It was a bare bones colony of Russian peasants, building simple buildings in a harsh desert. Nor was it a large community.

The Russian colonists bore names unfamiliar in Box Elder County: Kalpakoff, Kobseff, Potapoff, Kobzeff, Shegloff, Chernabeaff, Voldaareff, Danetrieff, Karyakin, Kunakoff, Volkoff, Shubin, Eleen, Rudometkin, Melnikoff, Coepoff, Homenoff, Dofapoff, Slevin.

Within a month of their arrival, tragedy struck the home of Andrew Kalpakoff: "Kalpakoff had just emptied the magazine of his .22 rifle ready to clean it; his wife, who sat at his side, was frightened of the weapon. Mr. Kalpakoff raised the gun to show her it was empty, and with it pointed towards her pulled the trigger, only to find that there remained a cartridge in the barrel, which was discharged. The bullet entered his wife's heart. She fell to the floor and in ten minutes was dead."[128]

According to the Morris history of Park Valley, "The grief stricken husband lost his mind and it was with considerable difficulty that three men who witnessed the accident prevented him from terminating his own life. When he regained self-control, his grief was almost more than he could endure."[129] At the time of her obsequies, it was said of Anna Kalpakoff that she was "an extremely good woman, loved dearly by all who knew her. She was generous and always willing to assist those in need. She could be found with the poor and at the bedside of the sick—a true, devoted wife and loving mother, in the prime of life, being but 36 years of age, and in perfect health and spirits."[130]

Mrs. Kalpakoff was buried in the Park Valley cemetery. According to Mrs. Hirschi, when the Russians came by her father's home, "All the children were watching. They came from burying her and were chanting and crying and huddled in the wagon."[131] In 1915, when Mary Matthew Kalpakoff died in childbirth, the colonists established their own cemetery, and Anna Kalpakoff's grave was removed from the Mormon cemetery to a Russian graveyard, on land owned by Andrew Kalpakoff's father.

The Russian colony struggled in a hostile desert, held there by their faith and their desire to build a utopian community. According to an article in the *Box Elder News,* shortly after their arrival, "the colony of Russians who recently located out there are building up a commonwealth after the pattern of the United Order that was established in this city in the early years. They work together and have everything in common."[132] It is difficult to determine if "the colony's finances were communal, or the people were just cooperative in their farming efforts . . . "[133] One of the problems is that apparently the Pacific Land and Water Company did not record the deed of sale.

Nevertheless, the Russian settlers remained on the land plowing the soil and planting crops on the arid land south of Park Valley. According to Lawrence Carter, "My father had Percheron horses. They came to buy them and took out a wad of bills that would choke a cow. They paid cash for all their purchases. The Russian men pulled peg-tooth harrows and were very hard workers . . . The women wore long black dresses, and veils or scarves over their heads. I don't remember there were many children. They mostly stayed out at that place. The men usually came into town to shop. It was a shame to see all their beautiful belongings from LA out there in the worst dry place in all of Utah."[134]

Elizabeth Goodliffe Hirschi recalled that "They used to come to buy goods at my father's store, everything from groceries to wagon wheels to clothes. I would like to listen to them. It sounded like jibber-jabber to me, and I liked to see their mode of dress, all in black."[135]

The Pacific Land and Water Company allotted two acres for a school in April 1915, and by the start of the school year, the county school board projected a school population of forty, evenly divided among boys and girls. But in November "the superintendent reported the Russian school had hardly enough students to justify its continuence."[136]

According to minutes of the Box Elder County School Board, by 19 October 1915 "member Seely reported that he thought the Russian School would soon have to close because they were all moving away."[137] On 12 November "Supt. Jensen reported that the Russian School would not have enough students to justify keeping it open any longer."[138] Not a year later, on 15 September 1916, the school board discussed building a school on North Promontory. The minutes recount that "After careful consideration it was decided to take the Russian School House apart and have it shipped to North Promontory."[139] According to Pauline Dobrenen, a daughter of one of the Box Elder Molokani, "It did not work out for them, so they came back to L.A. more poor than before they left."[140]

After the settlement was abandoned, many of the houses and other buildings were hauled away to nearby farms or dismantled for their lumber leaving only the schoolhouse foundation, pits with decaying timbers, some rusty farm machinery, tin cans and broken china, and a cemetery with two wooden grave markers bearing inscriptions in Russian honoring the lives of Anna and Mary Kalpakoff. Paul Kalpakoff came from Los Angeles and placed new, granite headstones in 1966, preserving the memory of his mother and aunt.

Ironically, no one from Park Valley who knew the Russians, and no one who has researched the colony has ever discovered its name or can say if it ever had one. It is Box Elder County's ghost town with no name.

Snowville

Snowville is located in the Curlew Valley in far northern Box Elder County, only three miles from the Idaho border, where Utah

Highway 30 splits off from Interstate 15. Before Interstate 15, Highway 30 was the main route to Boise, and went through downtown Snowville.

According to the 1937 *History of Box Elder County:*

> Though some distance from populous centers, the Curlew Valley, even at that time, was a beautiful landscape—a veritable field of waving green grass, dotted here and there with clumps of sagebrush. The grass, however, was so high that the sagebrush was scarcely visible. Then as now Deep Creek ran through almost the center of the valley. President Lorenzo Snow predicted that this stream was one of the everlasting streams whose waters should never diminish, and one from which many should come to drink. Esther Arbon Goodliffe, an old time resident of Snowville, informs us that this prediction has been literally fulfilled, that in very dry seasons its water never decreases.[141]

Settlers came to the site of Snowville shortly after the coming of the railroad. Among the first settlers were George Arbon, his brother, Charles Arbon, Joseph Robbins, and Richard Potter who came from Malad in 1871. "John Houtz came from Salt Lake City to build up a cattle ranch, which project was very successful. William Robbins was a Civil War Veteran who came from New York to Ogden and later moved to Snowville to build a home. William M. Howell came to Snowville at a very early date. In 1877, William Cottam came from Potterville. These men and their families have been prominent factors in the development of this section."[142] Ellen Cottam served for many years as a midwife and delivered three hundred fifty babies without a single loss of life.

Five years after the first settlers arrived, a townsite was laid out on 14 August 1876 and the town named in honor of Lorenzo Snow. Settlers were members of the Mormon faith. An important development occured in 1882 with the organization of the Curlew Irrigation and Reservoir Company. The company directed the construction of two canals, one twelve miles long and the other fifteen miles long, and two reservoirs in Curlew Valley which provided water to thousands of acres of land. The irrigated lands produced fine crops of grain and alfalfa.

In 1937 "Snowville, being centrally located, was headquarters for the Curlew Stake [of the LDS church]; and because of its location on the main auto route to California and western Idaho, it is a popular camping place for tourists. The town has a telephone system, a water system, a post office, three stores, a Union Pacific Stage Line Station, and three garages; also a commodious [LDS]church building and a modern school building."[143]

Snowville is an agricultural town. The coming of the freeway took traffic away from the downtown, but Snowville is not dependant upon tourist traffic. It remains rural and agricultural. Though the old route from Strevell is much less-traveled, Snowville still serves as the northwestern gateway to Box Elder County from Boise.

Standrod

Standrod was originally known as Onemile Valley. It was located at the most southern tip of the Raft River Valley and is tucked back into a large canyon on the north slope of the east-west Raft River Mountains. Sometime in the late nineteenth century the name was changed to Standrod in honor of Judge Stanrod of Malta, Idaho.

When cattlemen entered the valley in the late 1860s, they found that the north side of the Raft River Mountains offered an abundance of grass, several natural springs, and several steams of water flowing down almost every canyon. In the late 1870s the valley became pasture land for the EY Ranch horses and cattle.

Among the first men to settle in the area in the 1870s were John Naf, Calvin Christopher, Richard Barnes, Lorenzo Barnes, William Barners, Alfred Lee, and George McIntire. The latter operated a store and post office in the valley. Other settlers arrived, including Orson Platt and his brother-in-law William Holt in 1882, William and Eliza Freestone about 1883, Thomas Bruckhaw Jones, George Jones, Hovey and Losrenzo and Alazanna Barnes about 1885.

The settlers constructed a good-sized brick school house in 1903 located in the middle of the community and on the state line; part in Utah and part in Idaho. George Jones taught the first school class held in Standrod which was in a log cabin with a dirt roof. In 1920 there were thirty-six people living in the settlement of Standrod, and in 1968 there were seven families. Residents attended Mormon church services in Yost until that church closed in 1977 after which they attended services in Almo, Idaho, twenty-five miles away.

Terrace

Terrace, like Kelton, is located along the route of the old transcontinental railroad grade. It lies twenty-eight miles south and west of Park Valley. It is named for the nearby terraces of ancient Lake Bonneville.[144] Terrace was located on Muddy Creek southwest of Park Valley and southeast of the Grouse Creek Valley about thirty-two miles east of the Nevada border in Box Elder County.

According to a recent historical and archaeological study, "Terrace served the Central Pacific as the maintenance and repair headquarters for the Salt Lake Division (Wells, Nevada to Ogden, Utah). Facilities included a 16-stall roundhouse, machine shop, coal sheds, water tanks, and an eight-track switchyard. Terrace, sustained by the railroad shops, prospered and became a population center in northwestern Utah."[145] Located within Terrace were stores, the Wells Fargo and Company Express, a telegraph, railroad agent, and a school. It was a major supply point for freighters to many western and northern settlements such as Park Valley and Golden. As a stage station into the Boise Basin and Snake River Valley, mail was carried by stage from the post office at Terrace northward. It was said to be, at its zenith, the largest town between Ogden and Elko, Nevada.[146]

Historians Anan Raymond and Richard Fike note that "Business buildings lined a wide avenue north of the tracks. Residential structures, scattered and illogically placed in the earliest years, were normally located south of the tracks. A communal center and structure known as the Athenium contained bath houses and a reading room or library."[147] Residents were asked to pay a tax to support the facility. A large red brick building housed railroad offices and shops.[148]

Other facilities included thirteen saloons, a dance hall, soda fountain, and a Chinatown located in the east end of Terrace that boasted a Buddhist church.[149]

Terrace was waterless as well drilling proved fruitless.[150] Water was obtained from springs that were located in the Grouse Creek Mountains and carried to Terrace along a twelve-mile wooden aque-

Terrace Railroad Station in 1889. (Box Elder County)

duct and stored in three tanks.[151] In October 1887 the wooden aqueduct was "replaced by a 3.5-inch metal pipe."[152]

The Terrace Post Office operated from 28 February 1872 until 15 June 1904 when the Lucin Cutoff across the Great Salt Lake caused most rail traffic to bypass Terrace.

The demise of Terrace came in stages. The railroad shops were moved to Carlin, Nevada, in 1900, perhaps in anticipation of construction of the Lucin Cutoff. After completion of the Cutoff, the decline of Terrace accelerated. Where the trains had passed through Terrace each day before the cutoff was opened, only three trains a week came through afterward. By World War II when the railroad tracks were torn up, Terrace was completely abandoned and today there is little evidence of the once thriving community.

Thatcher

Thatcher is located four miles northeast of Penrose, about six miles southwest of Tremonton, and about nineteen miles from the Box Elder County courthouse in Brigham City. An agricultural community, Thatcher was first settled in the early 1890s and was named for Moses Thatcher (1842–1909), Logan banker and businessman, and an LDS apostle from 1879 to 1896.

An LDS branch was organized in Thatcher on 15 February 1902, upgraded to a ward on 28 September of the same year, reflecting the growth in the valley from the coming of the canals, the sugar industry, and the Malad Valley branch of the OSL. The Penrose and Promontory branches of the LDS Church began as dependencies of the Thatcher Ward.

Tremonton

Tremonton is located roughly in the middle of the Bear River Valley, about fifteen miles north of the Box Elder County courthouse in Brigham City, about twenty miles south of the Idaho border, and just west of the Malad River.[153]

John Petty, at age twenty-eight, took up a homestead of 160 acres here in the year 1888. His farm covered the present south half of town, all south of Main Street, now within the city limits. In 1892 possibilities for Bear River Valley began to look promising for many new settlers.

Toward the beginning of the new century, land agents, including V.S. Peet, went east to induce more people to settle in the Bear River Valley. As a result, a number of families from Nebraska came and bought farms during the years following 1898 and 1899. Fred Nihart came from Cairo, Nebraska, to where Tremonton is now located in the spring of 1899, settling on the northeast quarter of our present townsite. He came because of a desire to farm irrigated land. After tapping the Bear River and building the great canal system, water began to flow over the sterile, thirsty soil. V.S. Peet, the immigration agent for the Union Pacific Railroad Company, was responsible for the arrival of many settlers to this part of the country. Fred Nihart reports that others came from Nebraska and also from Tremont, Illinois, in 1899, including a number of Wyatts and Halls and Ed Porter, who settled near Tremonton. John Summers came to the valley for the first time in 1898, and was so favorably impressed that in 1901 he brought his family here.

As a result of the efforts of V. S. Peet, a German colony came from Tremont, Illinois, in the spring of 1900, and settled on or near the Salt Creek. Among them were Matthew Baer, Henry Baer, Phillip

Getz, Paul Heitz, Lawrence Trukenbrod, Sam, John and Josh Schenk, Jacob Hoerr, Jacob Meister, E.E. Brenkman, and others.

The townsite of Tremonton was laid out early in the spring of 1903 by John Shuman, Fred Nihart, and John Petty on part of their farms. They chose this site because of its location on the Malad branch of the Oregon Short Line Railroad and its being so centrally located on the crossroads in the Bear River Valley.

C.C. Wilson of Bear River City purchased the first lot and built a small room which he used as office and sales room for his hardware business. His lumber was piled at the side of the office in the sagebrush. He opened his doors for business on 14 April 1903.

John Petty of Farmington, Davis County, with John Shuman and Fred Nihart of Nebraska, had been farming there for a number of years. Now they began erecting buildings to attract business to the new townsite. Shuman opened a meat market with George Shuman in charge. He distributed mail from the market. Felix Zesigar opened a barber shop, and Mr. Stohl moved his saloon from Corinne. Mr. Nihart opened an office and started a weekly newspaper, *The Tremont Times,* which he had printed in Logan but distributed from the new townsite which, at the request of the German colony, had been named "Tremont."

Following the first general business boom, and for a year thereafter, businessmen were attracted from all parts of the county. In order of their arrival, they established businesses as follows: Frank Meldrum's blacksmith shop and Sherman's general merchandise store, moved there from North Garland; Cook's Drug Store; Mrs. Cook's Millinery store; Mrs. John Shuman's Boarding House; Proctor Hotel; the Goss Livery Stable; Stohl Furniture Store; Thomas Waldron's general merchandise store; Fishburn & Son's general merchandise store; Consolidated Wagon & Machine Company; Mr. Zimmermans saloon; Wyatt Brothers' Meat Market; and Kent Hotel. Very few homes were built during the first year as most of the families lived in the rear rooms of their places of business.

During the first weeks of its existence, the new town was without a name. Then Fred Nihart, who had sort of fallen into the role of town manager, named it Tremont. This was at the request of Mr. Jacob Hoerr, one of the German colony, who wished to plant in the west the name of his hometown in Illinois. That title was of short duration. Within three or four years, the name of Tremont, Utah, was so frequently confused with Fremont, Utah, that postal authorities requested a name change for the newer town. By simply adding "on" to Tremont, the town became Tremonton and the identity problem was solved.

A town organization was effected 6 January 1906, with J. A. Fishburn, president, and J. C. Gates, D. C. Roush, S. B. Watland, E. M. Wyatt, members of the board, and George Shuman, clerk. They at once began to make improvements. The city park was purchased from John Shuman for $50. In 1909 the old board sidewalks were replaced by cement walks; in 1910 a $6,000 bond was issued and a water system installed using water from the canals; in 1911 the Utah Power and Light Company installed the electric light system.

On 29 March 1912 the Tremonton Commercial Club was organized with Aquilla N. Fishburn, president, Charles McClure, vice-president, Harry L. Gephart, secretary, S. N. Cole, treasurer.

The club voted to organize a hotel commission. David Holmgren was elected chair of the commission, which at once began the erection of the Midland Hotel, and with it began the permanent growth of the town. The contractors soon learned that the underground water was too near the surface to excavate adequate foundations and basements. In response Matthew Baer organized a drainage company in July 1913, and within four months a sewer and drainage system was extended to the greater portion of the town.

From the summer of 1912 to the close of 1914, Tremonton experienced a building boom. Coles Bank, the Shield Hotel Block, Waldron and Harris Mercantile Building, and the Midland Hotel were built at a total cost of $175,000.

On 6 May 1918 Tremonton was incorporated as a city of the third class with Charles McClure as mayor; J. A. King, David Holmgren, W. H. Stone, and H. T. Woodward, city councilmen; Louis Brenkman, clerk; W.E. Getz, treasurer. This same year the city voted a $50,000 bond and installed a new water system using water from the Johnson Spring located just east of Point Lookout. By 1925 the population of Tremonton numbered one thousand people.

The founding of Tremonton differed in many respects from the

Tremonton in the early 1920s. (Utah State Historical Society)

settlement of a vast majority of sister communities in the valley. Most of the families pushing north and west to establish homes were Mormon. The first people of Tremonton and vicinity were non-Mormon. They were people who brought with them a variety of religious beliefs from their former homes. They were an industrious, progressive, and sincere people who, regardless of difference in belief, were willing to cooperate with their neighbors. These qualities were evident when they constructed the first Union schoolhouse to educate *all* their children. They further united (that is what gave Union its name) by sharing that building on Sunday, where several denominations used it for their services on an alternating basis.

Tremonton grew as a twentieth century city. From 1906, when first incorporated as a town, to 1918, when designated a third class city, to 1999, growth has been steady and firm. Educational, recreational, civic, health, medical, and religious services and facilities are updated and have expanded with the steady growth of the city. Economically, the city is a central shopping place for the Bear River Valley. In 1992, 267 businesses were operating with official city licenses.

Employment opportunities have expanded with the Thiokol Plant, twenty-six miles to the west. Nucor Steel is located fourteen miles to the north. La-Z-Boy Chair Co. operates within the city limits. The population in 1992 was 4264 and 4680 in 1996.

Vipont

Vipont was a gold and silver mining settlement established in 1899 in the extreme western part of Box Elder County—five miles east of Goose Creek and one mile north of Birch Creek and only a few miles south of the Idaho border.[154] The area is only two miles south of Granite Pass on the old California Emigrant Trail. It is thirty-five miles north of the railway station at Lucin and twenty-six miles south of the Oregon Short Line railroad as it passes near Oakley, Idaho. From 1899 through the 1920s, the town was a prosperous silver mining camp with as many as three hundred workers at one time.

Vipont began when John Angove found ore in the hills of the area in 1899. In 1900 there were thirty-eight people in the community. A post office was established in 1900, discontinued in 1905, and reestablished on 24 June 1920. It remained in operation until it closed permanently on 22 October 1923.

Willard

Willard, the southern most community in Box Elder County along U.S. 89, is nestled beneath the majestic peaks of the Willard Mountains on the east. Seven miles north is Brigham City with Ogden thirteen miles to the south.[155] To the west are salt flats and the fresh water Willard Bay, created in 1964. The most beautiful sunsets occur here.

Willard had its beginning in 1851 when several companies went out from Salt Lake City for the purpose of founding new settlements. Nineteen souls located on North Willow Creek, seven miles south of where Brigham would soon be. Two years later the settlement was moved to a more eligible site, two miles farther south and named North Willow Creek. A fort wall was built to protect the settlers from the threat of Indian attacks.

In the fall of 1851, North Willow Creek was surveyed by Henry G. Sherwood assisted by Cyril Call. In 1859 it was renamed Willard in honor of Willard Richards, an Apostle of the Mormon church.

Willard received its charter as a city in 1870. The township encompasses seven square miles, being three and a half miles long and two miles wide.

Willard's first settlers were mostly of Welsh, English, Scottish, and Dutch descent. Most were farmers but many were merchants, carpenters, blacksmiths, and school teachers, with an abundance of musicians. Willard has always been noted for its music, claiming Evan Stephens, Mormon Tabernacle Choir director, and Robert B. Baird, hymn writer, as her sons.

Shadrack Jones was a gifted rock mason, and Willard's rock homes reflect his handiwork. Over thirty of these homes are still standing, many of which are on the National Register of Historic Places. A brickyard and the first grist mill in Box Elder County, along with many molasses mills, provided the first citizens with their basic needs.

Electric power came to Willard in the early 1900s with completion of Willard's own power house. A water system was completed in 1912, utilizing water from Willard Canyon. In 1918 Willard was a station on the main line of the Oregon Short Line Railroad. It had a canning factory, a money order post office, general stores, and an estimated population of 800—200 more than Tremonton at that time. It was a city of the third class. Its population in the 1990 census was 1,298, and 1,437 in 1996.

Historically, the economy of Willard centered around agriculture, with fruit crops being the major product. Colorful roadside fruit stands grace Highway 89 as it winds through the area. Buyers travel far to purchase the best fruit in the west.

The construction of Interstate 15 west of Willard eliminated many negative aspects of the "through" traffic on Highway 89 by reducing the noise level and minimizing the hazards of crossing the busy highway. It impacted the local economy by reducing sales at the fruit stands for a time. Patrons have since returned and sales are strong.

Agriculture is now a secondary source of income. Some businesses are located in Willard, but most people seek employment nearby. Hill Air Force Base, the Internal Revenue Service, Utah General Depot, and Thiokol Corp. are within easy commuting distance and employ many citizens. The rural atmosphere and proximity to these facilities make Willard an ideal place to live and raise a family.

Willard is located on an alluvial fan exposed as Lake Bonneville receded and, as such, is an ideal spot for gravel pits which is a constant concern to the town.

Predominately LDS, the three Willard wards are housed in a meetinghouse built in 1973. Willard, along with Perry, now comprise a stake of their own; the Willard Stake being created on 25 November 1984.

The new Willard Elementary School, built in 1986, is of modern energy-efficient design, and is on one level, better serving the needs of the children and faculty. At that time the old school was demolished with its west wing, built in 1964, left intact to serve as Willard's City Hall. It houses the police, courts, and offices. A modern post office was built in 1990.A large fire station was built in 1992 to house the volunteer fire department.

The sheer rock cliffs that rise so majestically east of Willard have, on occasion, contributed to a sudden, swift, and high runoff into the valleys. This situation has been addressed by the Willard City/Box Elder County Drainage and Flood Control District, which has installed reservoirs and pipe lines, helping greatly to reduce the flood problem. Young men in the Civilian Conservation Corps built the dike and spillway in the 1930s to alleviate other problems. They also terraced Willard basin in the upper canyon.

A trip to Willard Peak rewards the visitor with a breathtaking view of the valley below. During the early summer months, over twenty-eight varieties of colorful wild flowers may be seen blooming in profusion along the way.

Willard claims the oldest continuous 4th of July celebration in Utah, beginning with a firemen's ball the night before, races and booths that day, and ending with fireworks in the Willow Creek Park east of town.

Willard Bay State Park, located west of I-80, is a major recreational area for boating and camping. Year-round fishing and its close proximity to the population of the Wasatch Front makes it one of the most popular state parks. Some 269,232 people used its facilities from January-October 1992.

Yost

Yost is one of the most remote of Box Elder County towns, being some eighty-five miles from the courthouse, as the crow flies, and over a hundred and ten miles by road—and that over a gravel road through southern Idaho, via Snowville, Strevell, Naf, and Standrod. The only other road of any note from the south is by way of Lynn and over the pass through Junction Valley. It is commonly said that the town of Yost is so remote that one has to go through Idaho to get there. There are no paved roads into Yost.

According to Merlin Tracy,

> The Yost Valley is located at the extreme southern end of Upper Raft River Valley and is surrounded on three sides by mountains. Today it is mainly accessible by a single dirt/gravel road that enters Utah from the southern edge of Idaho state line. By turning west off oil-paved Idaho State road 42 at the old settlement of Strevell, Idaho (there are no signs), you can travel 22 miles west on the same gravel road that was built in 1939. Segments of that road were once part of the Original Great Salt Lake Cutoff to California as far back as 1848. Traveling from Brigham City, Box Elder's county seat to Strevell, Idaho, via Snowville, Utah, the highway hasn't changed much in its location.
>
> Before the 1900, the road basically followed the Old Salt Lake to California Emigrant Trail into Idaho; after 1900, the Federal Highway 30 (Idaho road 42) crossed over Kelton Pass to the proposed railway settlement of Strevell located just one mile inside Idaho from Utah. Running westward and parallel with the Utah/ldaho state line, the original road passed thru the settlements of Nat and Standrod before reaching the northeast side of Yost Valley via Bally Mountain. After 1939, the road continued west to Almo-Yost-Lynn junction. The road turns south (left) back into Utah and Yost valley; to turn right (north) towards Almo-Malta junction located south-west of the "Lower Narrows" on Raft River; or you can continue westerly towards the settlement of Lynn. At the Almo-Malta junction near the lower Raft River, a left-turn

(west) will head you towards the City of Rocks and settlement of Almo.[156]

It is often forgotten that the town of Yost lies only five miles across the valley, and within sight of Almo, Idaho, and but another mile or so from the City of Rocks, which was the main junction of the main northern branch of the California Trail and the Salt Lake Cutoff.

The famous landmark, the Twin Sisters, or "Steeple Rocks," at the southern edge of the City of Rocks, was the junction of the two main trails, the Salt Lake Cutoff being discovered in 1847 by James Cazier, and pioneered by Captain Samuel J. Hensley and returning members of the Mormon Battalion in the late summer of 1848.

> From 1857 through 1859 the Federal Government had established a free access corridor along the Pacific Wagon Road from the eastern states to California or Oregon via the City of Rocks, which was before the completion of the transcontinental railroad. The purpose of the corridor was to retain grass and good water for the thousands of animals and fire wood for the camp fires. By 1872, the railroad terminus at Kelton and Terrace in Box Elder county were in full operation. Thus greatly reducing the people and wagon traffic, but not the freight wagons that continued to utilize the roads through Yost Valley. By 1878, the Federal Government had released the land within the corridor for homesteaders to set claim on their favorite section of land. Once the news of free land was spread, hundreds of prospective farmers and miners traveled westerly over the Great Salt Lake Cut-off to become "nesters" within the City-of-Rocks region. On the Utah side of the border, the nesters could not set claim as a homesteader until the land had been surveyed. This didn't happen until after 1892.[157]

It is said that one of the earliest white settlers was Charles Yost, who, according to tradition, came to the valley in 1873, along with a man named George. The settlement which grew up with the coming of others in the early 1880s was called George Creek, and then, when Charles Yost obtained a post office for the settlement, it was given his name. According to John Van Cott,

> The first name was George Creek for George, an early range rider

who came into this area with Charles Yost. Yost remained in the area, built the first cabin on George Creek, then became the first postmaster in 1887. Yost and George arrived as cowboys from the Nevada Territory and worked for William Emery. After Yost built his cabin, he lived in it alone for six years until he married Maria Larsen from Terrace, on the south side of the mountains. For four years she was the only woman living in Yost.[158]

Knowing that land in Box Elder County in Utah and Cassia County in Idaho was still available for home-steading, men and women—mostly from the Great Salt Lake Valley, such as North Ogden, Weber County, and Tooele County—pioneered the development of several small settlements in the City-of-Rocks region, i.e., Almo, Malta (Cassia Creek), Albion, Oakley, Rock Creek, George Creek, Clear Creek, Junction, Naf, and Stanrod. Although the settlements were widely scattered within about fifty miles, they enjoyed the free-hearted friendship of their neighbors, who might be as far as ten miles away. The dauntless men and women exercised their talents, foresight, wisdom, and with hard work added luster, brilliance and wealth to their homes. Within a few years, they changed their living conditions from rude comfort of a log cabin to the luxury of a frame house equipped with some modern furnishings.[159]

The first U.S. Post Office came to the area on 2 March 1887 and was given the name "Yost Valley." Merlin Tracy's history notes that

> By 1882, at least six families had built log-cabins, dug ditches, and established wagon-roads that connected several nearby settlements. A community in Yost Valley would be called George-Town. Outsiders would call it George Creek or Junction until about 1900, because a name was never recorded at the county seat in Brigham City. After George had removed from the valley, the settlement received a new name of Yost. But once again, the people didn't record the name, so any State or County business before 1896 was officially recognized and conducted as "Junction" settlement in the County of Box Elder in the Territory of Utah. . . .
>
> Over the years, the valley has been known by four different names, i.e. George Town, George Creek, Junction and "Town of Yost." George Creek so named after early squatter George Davis; Junction, because it was a major emigrant and freighters wagon

> road junction; and Yost, because the first United States Post Office was named after Charles Yost the first postmaster. Then in 1934, the settlers partitioned for a town, and the valley was incorporated as "Town of Yost" in 1935.[160]

The settlement continued to grow in population, and the settlers were chiefly members of the Church of Jesus Christ of Latter-day Saints. "By 1882, there were 15 LDS families living in the Upper Raft River valley. Then one year later Henry R. Cahoon reported that there were between 30 to 35 families in the valley, which included both Yost Valley and Almo areas."[161]

It was not an easy life in the Raft River Valley during the 1880s. Merlin Tracy writes:

> It was the real dry summer of 1886, that left the animals in very poor condition as winter approached. Early snow blizzards raged and temperatures plummeted below zero. This caused the cattle to take shelter in areas, only to find themselves buried in snowdrifts. . . . Theodore Roosevelt wrote in April 1887, "We have had a perfect smashup all through the cattle country." It was after the 1886/1887 cruel winter that large open-range cattle herds quickly disappeared, the larger ranchers were bankrupted.
>
> After the disastrous three winters between 1886–87 thru 1889–90, over 60% of the cattle and 40% of the sheep had died. The method of farming and ranching changed. Each rancher realized that wild meadow grasses, alfalfa hay and grain had to be grown, cut-stacked and grain thrashed to provide winter feed. Winter pastures were fenced to confine the animals; and windmills installed to provided water for the animals. Cattle-raising became an art. It was no longer a time for reckless individual cowboys to work for a big-time rancher.[162]

One of the large ranches in the area has a history which involves Brigham Young himself, the Great Colonizer. According to Russell R. Rich, "Because the mails were so irregular, the situation eventually brought about the organization of the Brigham Young Express and Carrying Company, which began to formulate in Fillmore during the winter of 1855–56 when the legislature and supreme court were in session there. This meeting adjourned to Salt Lake City, where they met on January 26, 1856."[163] Young was chosen president of what became known as the BYX Company, sometimes called the YX Company.[164] The company obtained contracts to carry mail between Independence, Missouri, and Salt Lake City, Utah. The contracts were canceled incident to the troubles which resulted during the Utah War, or "Buchanan's Blunder," of 1857–58, resulting in the "Move South" or the "Abandonment" which affected Brigham City and other Box Elder County communities.

Apparently, the BYX Company had aspirations to establish a route to the west, and to carry the mails toward California.[165]

> The BY Express and Carrying Company was out of business several years before 1878, so Utah Territorial Governor George William Emery had purchased the land and buildings at Clear Creek Stage Station and the stage station at the "Lower Narrows on Raft River" from the stock holders of BY Express. The land on both sides of the river at the Narrows was renamed the EY [Emery and Young] Cattle Ranch. The land at Clear Creek located on both sides of Onemile Creek and adjacent to the Utah/Idaho border, became the EY farm and fenced pastures lands. During the years of operation in the late 1860s and early 1870s, there were several EY Ranch locations in Cassia County that employed several cowboys to ride herd on the thousands of horses and cattle, and Charles Yost was one of those men.[166]

After 1866 the Well's Fargo Stage carried mail from Brigham City to Boise, Idaho via the Lower Narrows Station, Emigrant Canyon/City-of-Rocks, and Oakley stations. Within western territories, a stage station and trading post served as an unofficial United States Post Office. Mail addressed to people in Yost Valley and nearby settlements was via the Twin Sister City-of-Rocks Pony Express and Stage Station or Lower Narrows on Raft River Station.

After the railroad was completed in 1869, the mail was carried via stagecoach from Kelton Terminus and Post Office to Boise via Clear Creek, Lower Narrows, City-of-Rocks and Oakley stations. Mail and express items were dropped off and held at each station for the local settlers to pick up; there were no post offices in the City of Rocks region until 1878. Segments of the old emigrant road were utilized as the stage route. Families took turns going by saddle horse or carriage to the nearest station for their mail.

A change was made in the stage route and stage and old Pony Express station operation in 1878 to better serve the City-of-Rocks region. The population had greatly increased in Marsh Valley; thus new Bridge Post Office was established on 17 December 1878 about ten miles from Sweetzer's Ranch on Raft River in Raft River Valley. Lee Kirk was postmaster for Bridge Post Office. The City-of-Rocks (Twin Sisters) Station and Lower Narrow Station were not used anymore.

The Bridge Post Office served all the people living in Upper Raft River Valley. Before spring 1887, Charles Yost traveled to Bridge Post Office or Almo to collect his mail and that of his neighbors.

The first post office on a scheduled mail route to Almo was established at the Myron B. Durfee place in February 1882. The mail carrier was Robert McCormick.

Many of the settlers who came to Yost Valley took up land in accordance with the Timber and Stone Act of 1878.

One of the early pioneers who visited Yost Valley and made it more accessible was Chester Loveland, the first mayor of Brigham City. Tracy says that

> At 49 years of age, Chester Loveland moved his family to Brigham City in 1865. Over the next few years Colonel Chester Loveland traveled west into Upper Raft River Valley to recover or bury bodies of emigrants, who lost their lives in attacks by the Indians. He would rescue those still alive and dig large trenches to hide personal property of those that lost their life. Chester displayed much skill, energy, sound judgment and friendship in dealing with the issues. His influence with the Indians and leaders allowed him to recover much of the lost property and to gain peace in western Box Elder county. It was his influence that caused the development of several wagon roads in the next few years to be located and improved as we know them today. One of those roads is the County Road through the southern tip of Raft River and Upper Raft River Valleys that included segments of the Old Salt Lake Cut Off wagon road. The western segment of the high road crossed the northern part of Yost Valley.[167]

Among the early pioneer families who came to Yost Valley before 1896 and established homes were the following families: Tracy,

Richardson, Yost, Campbell, Yates, Taylor, Blythe, Blackburn, Montgomery, Randell, Wolter, and Wand.

Across the Upper Raft River Valley at the settlement of Almo in Cassia County, Idaho, the early families included Durfee, King, Eames, Edwards, Jones, Jensen, Brunson, Lowes, Ward, Rice, Spencer, Hubbard, Wakes, and Whittaker. These two neighboring towns became part of one large united community of activity.

One of the reasons for the settling of Yost Valley by Mormons was encouragement from church leaders. "A letter from President John Taylor encouraged the saints to remove into the 'north country' (Snake River Valley) in the winter of 1882, which also included settlements north of Pocatello, Idaho, such as Blackfoot and Eagle Rock (Idaho Falls). The settlements of the Minidoka Region included Albion, Almo, Beecherville (Elba), and Goose Creek (Oakley). The message was to go into the Snake River Valley, found settlements, care for the indians, stand upon an equal footing and make improvements to strengthen the cords of the Stakes of Zion."[168]

The settlers of Yost Valley made their living primarily with cattle, sheep, and milk-cows. Though large in geographic size, the Town of Yost remained small in population and remote in location. There were problems with grazing cattle in the dry valley of the Raft River.

> By the 1930s, too many cattle and sheep feeding on open range in the area during times of dry growth conditions had caused the grass to disappear. This excessive grazing caused poor seed development, hence was no new germination of young grass seedlings. This allowed sagebrush seeds to be scattered and to establishes roots over the vast area, where there was once waving grass.
>
> In 1935, the Town of Yost consisted of about 54 square miles of farm land, mountains and rolling hills with an alkaline desert on the north end adjacent to the Utah/Idaho line. This makes it Utah's largest town geographically. Today, the town's only landmark is the Old Yost Rock Church at the center of town, which is about four miles south of the Utah-Idaho line and located east about twenty-five miles from the Nevada-Utah border.[169]

The full cycle of Yost Valley as a community is complete. After 100 years, the valley has become a large cattle ranch. Under the leadership of the Spencer families, the landscape has been cleared of many houses, barns, and barbed wire fences.

To meet challenges of growth, the cattle operators of the 1870s gave way to sheepmen in the 1900s. The Great Depression of the 1930s allowed the incorporation of the town of Yost on 19 August 1935 as small family-farm community. Poor income conditions forced many young adults to move from the valley. World War II caused many younger generations and several families to move to urban areas for jobs that paid higher wages. By 1968 some ten families remained in a town without a store, post office, or school. Finally, Yost Township was dissolved and disincorporated on 6 January 1984.

ENDNOTES

1. At the inception of this Box Elder County History project, county commissioner Frank Nishiguchi formed a committee to compile histories of the individual communities in the county. He solicited participation from each of the communities, and requested representation from each so that the history of each town in the county would be written by people from that community. Some communities chose to participate, others did not. Support has been exceptional from such places as Rosette, Collinston, Yost, Bothwell, Corinne, and Fielding. Some communities have well-thought-out, well organized, and well-written histories in this section. Some, such as Yost and Park Valley-Rosette, furnished far more information than can be included in this section. For others, information is sparse.

2. See LaRene J. Braegger. *History of Bear River City;* Wallace N. Jibson, *History of Bear River Compact,* November 1991; Lucinda Jensen, *History of Bear River City;* Bear River Town Corporation minutes; Lydia Walker Forsgren, ed., *History of Box Elder County* (Brigham City: Daughters of Utah Pioneers, 1937); John W. Van Cott, *Utah Place Names* (Salt Lake City: University of Utah Press, 1990); Sarah Yates, "Saying goodbye to ward is like losing an old friend," *Box Elder News Journal,* 1 May 1996; and Stacey Kratz, "Church members eulogize meeting hall," Ogden *Standard Examiner,* 19 January 1996.

3. See George Russell Johnson, "Beaver Dam History, 1864–1993" typescript; Forsgren, *History of Box Elder County;* Van Cott, Utah Place Names ; Sarah Yates, "Tractor Patch is a crazy quilt of mechanized iron 'critters'" *Box Elder News Journal,* 28 February 1996; and Jerry Johnston, "A Tractor Menagerie" *Deseret News,* 24 March 1996.

4. This history of Bothwell was prepared by Keith Anderson, with research on Bothwell veterans by Keith Burnhope.

5. Forsgren, *History of Box Elder County*, 265.

6. Stephen L. Carr, *The Historical Guide to Utah Ghost Towns* (Salt Lake City: Western Epics, 1972), 14.

7. This history of Collinston was compiled by Thaine and Gertrude Secrist and their daughter Sonja Secrist Shelton. The Secrists have been among the staunchest supporters of this project. Sadly, Thaine Secrist passed away before the book was published. The Secrists used records from the Box Elder County Courthouse, the Postal Service, the Box Elder County School Board, Utah State University archives, the LDS church archives, and the Utah State Historical Society along with written histories by Gale Welling, Olive White Durfey, Lucille Johnson Roundy, Laurel B. Parkinson and Leonard Hawkes, Stacey Fuhriman, Shirlene Saunders Jones, Arnold R. Standing, and Eugene Bigler.

8. In 1996 a monument was erected near the highway connecting Collinston and Deweyville commemorating a ferry crossing and spring on the Bear River approximately three miles south of the crossing mentioned above. This site was located by the Northern Utah Soil Conservation District supervisors from a map and exploring account made by Captain Howard Stansbury in 1849. The crossing was verified with the help of survey maps in the possession of the Oregon California Trails Association. This crossing is believed by some to be the one used by Samuel J. Hensley in 1848 and later by those pioneers using the Salt Lake Cutoff. William Empey and Abraham Hunsaker ran a ferry at this site in the early 1850s. Possibly this site was used by those traveling east and west, while the northern crossing mentioned above was used by travelers to the north and south.

9. The histories of Collinston and Beaver Dam are intermingled, because of the proximity of the communities and because residents of both communities who attend the LDS church are also members of the same congregation, the Beaver Ward located in Beaver Dam. (See the history of Beaver Dam in this section for related information.)

10. Though the hotel had eighteen rooms, some of the rooms were only accessible by walking through other rooms. Hotel accommodations were different in those days than they are today.

11. Postal Records show that the Collinston Post Office was established on 28 February 1881, indicating that the name of the town had been changed by that time.

12. This history of Corinne is based on the extensive research submitted by Marjorie Mills. See also Brigham D. Madsen, *Corinne: The Gentile Capital of Utah* (Salt Lake City: Utah State Historical Society, 1980).

13. Marjorie Mills, "Corinne History," typescript, 1993, 30.

14. It is erroneously stated that the early name of the settlement was

"Manila Ward in honor of Commodore George Dewey's victory in the Spanish American War." The battle of Manila, in the Philippines, was fought 1 May 1898. Van Cott, *Utah Place Names,* 127.

15. Ibid., 131.

16. Forsgren, *History of Box Elder County,* 297.

17. Van Cott, *Utah Place Names,* 131.

18. This history of Fielding was written by Gale and Rhoda Welling. For a more detailed and in-depth history of Fielding, see Gale Welling's book, *Fielding: The People and the Events that Affected Their Lives* (privately published, 1986).

19. This history of Garland was written by Duane Archibald especially for this project.

20. The information on Golden was provided by Merlin Tracy.

21. This history of Grouse Creek was written by Merlin and Kenna Tanner in 1992.

22. Van Cott, *Utah Place Names,* 169.

23. This history of Harper (known locally as Harper Ward) was written by Arlene Munns for this project.

24. Donna Vest, Kimball Taylor Harper, and Richard Golden Harper Jr., editors "The Thomas Harper Family," 26 April 1982.

25. Wayne 'B' May, "Providing for Education in Harper, Utah—An Historical Study."

26. "The Thomas Harper Family."

27. Wayne B. May, "Providing for Education in Harper." op. cit.

28. Joseph L. Yates, "School Bussing in Harper Ward."

29. Andrew Jenson, "Quarterly Historical Record,." notes in the LDS Church Historian's Office, Salt Lake City, Utah.

30. May, "Providing for Education in Harper."

31. Ibid.

32. Earl H. Peirce, "Assorted Records and Recollections of Harper Ward, Box Elder County, Utah."

33. "The Thomas Harper Family."

34. The compiler is indebted to Eva Bingham for providing a copy of the reminiscences of Norma Grant Gilmore and Ray Boothe: "Memories of our town Honeyville." See also Forsgren, *History of Box Elder County;* and Van Cott, *Utah Place Names.*

35. Gilmore and Boothe, "Memories of our town Honeyville.,"

36. Ibid.

37. Ibid.

38. Ibid.

39. Ibid.

40. Forsgren, *History of Box Elder County,* 321.

41. Ibid.

42. Ibid., 320.

43. Ibid., 321.

44. Rodney A. Morris, Dorothy K. Morris, and LeGrand Morris, "Park Valley History," typescript, 1996, 7.

45. Ibid.

46. Anan S. Raymond and Richard E. Fike, *Rails East to Promontory: The Utah Stations* Cultural Resource Series, No. 8 (Salt Lake City: Bureau of Land Management, 1981), 32.

47. Ibid., 34.

48. Ibid.

49. Ibid.

50. Forsgren, *History of Box Elder County,* 286.

51. This historical sketch of Park Valley and Rosette is excerpted from a seventy-seven page history compiled by LeGrand and Dorothy Morris, and their son Rod. The Morrises went far beyond the call of duty in compiling the history of Park Valley and its communities.

52. Adolf Reeder, ed., *Box Elder Lore of the Nineteenth Century* (Brigham City: Box Elder Chapter, Sons of Utah Pioneers, 1951), 95.

53. Rodney A. Morris, "A Brief History of the Park Valley Livestock Industry," typescript, 1974.

54. Rex R. Pugsley, "An Early History of Park Valley," unpublished manuscript; Tammy Anderson, "Settling of Park Valley, Utah," research paper for an English class at Dixie College, 1985.

55. Personal correspondence from Philbert C. Lind, to the author, 12 September 1975.

56. Norine K. Carter, Letitia W. Palmer, and Dorothy K. Morris, *Our One Hundred Years,1870–1970* (privately published, 1970).

57. *The Salt Flat News,* Wendover, Utah, August 1970.

58. George A. Thompson, *Some Dreams Die: Utah's Ghost Towns and Lost Treasures* (Salt Lake City: Dream Garden Press, 1982), 159.

59. Carter, Palmer, and Morris, *Our One Hundred Years.*

60. Will Higgins, "The Century and the Susannah Mines, Golden, Utah," *The Salt Lake Mining Review* 11 30 November 1909, 16.

61. Carter, Palmer, and Morris, *Our One Hundred Years,* 1870–1970.

62. Ibid.

63. Thompson, *Some Dreams Die,* 159.

64. Degar B. Heylmun, , "Gold in the Raft River Mountains, Utah," *International California Mining Journal,* March 1995.

65. Ibid.

66. Thompson, *Some Dreams Die,* 159.

67. Carter, Palmer, and Morris, *Our One Hundred Years.*

68. Ibid.

69. *The Salt Flat News,* Wendover, Utah (August, 1970).

70. Carter, Palmer, and Morris, *Our One Hundred Years.*

71. Lillian Barrus Nelson, *Juniper and Black Pine: A History of Two Southern Idaho Communities, 1870s to 1995* (Salt Lake City: Publishers Press, 1996).

72. Carter, Palmer, and Morris, *Our One Hundred Years.*

73. This history of Perry depends heavily upon Lois J. Nelson, *History of Three Mile Creek, 1853–1898—Perry, 1898–1993* (Privately published, 1993).

74. Ibid., 1.

75. Ibid., 11.

76. Ibid., 12.

77. Ibid., 13.

78. Ibid., 53.

79. Ibid., 53.

80. Ibid., 78.

81. Ibid., 95.

82. Ibid., 97.

83. Ibid., 105. Legend has it that so many people told Irv Maddox he would never make a go of a restaurant in Perry that he built his place on skids so that it could be hauled away if the business failed.

84. Forsgren, *History of Box Elder County,* 274.

85. *Brigham City Bugler,* 21 May 1898.

86. Forsgren, *History of Box Elder County,* 276. According to Lois J. Nelson, the name was changed in 1898. See Lois J. Nelson, "Perry" in Allan Kent Powell, ed., *Utah History Encyclopedia* (Salt Lake City: University of Utah Press, 1994), 421.

87. Forsgren, *History of Box Elder County,* 308

88. Ibid., 308

89. Ibid., 309. James Cole served as a private in Company D of the Mormon Battalion. He died in 1876, as the result of an accident on his farm

in Plymouth, and is buried on his farm, east of Plymouth town. His grave is marked, though the small marker noting his service in the Mormon Battalion has been stolen.

90. Ibid.

91. Ibid.

92. Ibid.

93. Ibid.

94. This history of Portage is largely excerpted from LaVerd and Flora Hall John, *The Community of Portage, Then and Now: 1855–1995* (Bountiful, UT: Family History Publishers, 1995). Unless otherwise noted, the material herein comes from that book.

95. Thelma Gibbs, "Portage Community Organizations and Businesses" copy in compiler's possession.

96. LaVerd and Flora Hall John, "History of the Portage LDS Ward," copy in compiler's possession. This information also appears in LaVerd and Flora Hall John, *The Community of Portage, Then and Now,* 159–60.

97. Ibid.

98. Ibid.

99. Riverside Township Map, 15 November 1894. This history of Riverside was written by Joyce Cornwall specifically for this history of Box Elder County.

100. Myron J. Richards, Personal Journal.

101. History of James Kennard.

102. Richards, Journal, 6 September 1900.

103. Ibid, 7 May 1901.

104. Norma Forsberg, interview by author.

105. Effie Welling History.

106. Richards, Journal, 20 February 1895

107. Minutes of Riverside-North Garland Water Committee.

108. Richards, Journal, 22 December 1895.

109. Russell Capener, Interview by the author.

110. Richards, Journal, 24 January 1902.

111. *The Garland City Globe,* 15 February 1917.

112. Richards, Journal, 29 May 1901, 2 December 1901, and 8 July 1909.

113. Kennard.

114. Richards, Journal, 8 January 1896.

115. Ibid., 23 August 1905.

116. Minutes of the Riverside Cemetery Committee

117. Richards, Journal, 16 February 1903

118. Ibid., 19 August 1905

119. Ibid., 9 March 1906

120. Ibid., 1 December 1907 and 15 December 1907

121. Interview with John Ward, and Richards, 22 September 1920.

122. Rodney A. Morris, Dorothy K. Morris, and LeGrand Morris, "Park Valley History," typescript, 1996, 55.

123. Ibid., 56.

124. Sarah Yates, "Two graves mark Russian colony site," *Box Elder News Journal,* 29 May 1991, 13.

125. Ibid.

126. Ibid.

127. *Box Elder News,* 9 April 1914.

128. Yates, "Two graves mark Russian colony site." The original article appeared in the *Strevell Times* and was reprinted in the *Box Elder News* 7 May 1914.

129. Rodney A. Morris, Dorothy K. Morris, and LeGrand Morris, "Park Valley History," typescript, 1996, 59.

130. "President of Russian Colony Accidentally Kills His Wife," *Box Elder News,* 7 May 1914, cited in Rodney A. Morris, Dorothy K. Morris, and LeGrand Morris, "Park Valley History," typescript, 1996, 59.

131. Yates, "Two graves mark Russian colony site."

132. Sarah Yates, "Russian colony life went on despite deaths," *Box Elder News Journal,* 5 June 1991, 13.

133. Ibid.

134. Ibid.

135. Ibid.

136. Ibid.

137. Cited in Morris, "Park Valley History," 58.

138. Ibid.

139. Ibid.

140. Sarah Yates, "Russian colony life went on despite deaths," *Box Elder News Journal,* 5 June 1991.

141. Forsgren, *History of Box Elder County,* 292.

142. Ibid.

143. Ibid., 293.

144. Van Cott, *Utah Place Names,* 367.

145. Raymond and Fike, *Rails East to Promontory,* 42.

146. Morris, "Park Valley History," 5.

147. Raymond and Fike, *Rails East to Promontory,* 42.

148. Ibid. See also Frank Tinker, "Utah Chinatown in the Desert," *Salt Lake Tribune* Home Magazine, 26 January 1964, 20–21.

149. Morris, "Park Valley History," 5; Raymond and Fike, *Rails East to Promontory,* 48.

150. Raymond and Fike, *Rails East to Promontory,* 50.

151. Ibid.

152. Ibid.

153. This history of Tremonton was prepared for the present work by LuAnn Adams and is based on the following sources: Reuben D. Law, *History of Tremonton,* 1928; Forsgren, ed., *History of Box Elder County;* Phyllis Christensen *A Glorious Fifty Years, 1928–1978,* 1978 (A brief history of Tremonton, Bear River Valley, and Box Elder County); and Kleon Kerr, *Those Who Have Served, Town of Tremonton, 1906–1917, City of Tremonton, 1918–1992,* 1992.

154. Information on Vipont was provided by Merlin Tracy.

155. This history of Willard was written by Merlene T. Braegger for this volume. See also, Willard Genealogical Committee (David Kunzler et al.) *Willard Centennial: A Brief History of the Past One Hundred Years* (Booklet pub. 1951)

156. Merlin A. Tracy, "Yost Valley History, Land of Our Root Beginning (1841 thru 1945)," typescript, 8–9.

157. Ibid., 9.

158. Van Cott, *Utah Place Names,* 408.

159. Tracy, "Yost Valley History," 29.

160. Ibid., 11.

161. Ibid., 27.

162. Ibid., 27.

163. Russell R. Rich, *Ensign to the Nations: A History of the Church from 1846 to the Present* (Provo: Brigham Young University Publications, 1972), 213.

164. Ibid.

165. Tracy, "Yost Valley History," 30.

166. Ibid.

167. Ibid., 36.

168. Ibid., 5.

169. Ibid., 11.

Selected Bibliography

Aikens, C. Melvin, *Fremont-Promontory-Plains Relationships,* University of Utah Department of Anthropology, Anthropological Paper No. 82 [September 1966].

Alexander, Thomas G., *Utah: The Right Place* (Salt Lake City: Gibbs M. Smith, 1995).

Alexander, Thomas G., *Mormonism in Transition* (Urbana: University of Illinois Press, 1986).

Alexander, Thomas G., *Things in Heaven and Earth: The Life and Times of Wilford Woodruff, a Mormon Prophet* (Salt Lake City: Signature Books, 1991).

Alter, J. Cecil, *Utah: The Storied Domain* (Chicago: The American Historical Society, Inc., 1932).

Anderson, Bernice Gibbs, "The Gentile City of Corinne," *Utah Historical Quarterly* 9 (1941), nos. 3–4.

Arrington, Leonard J., *Beet Sugar in the West* (Seattle: University of Washington Press, 1966).

Arrington, Leonard J., *Brigham Young: American Moses* (New York: Alfred A. Knopf, 1985).

Arrington, Leonard J., "Cooperative Community in the North: Brigham City, Utah," *Utah Historical Quarterly* 33 (Summer 1965).

Arrington, Leonard J., *Great Basin Kingdom* (Lincoln: University of Nebraska Press, 1968).

Arrington, Leonard J, Feramorz Y. Fox, and Dean L. May, *Building the City of God* (Salt Lake City: Deseret Book Co., 1976).

Athearn, Robert G., "Contracting the Union Pacific," *Utah Historical Quarterly* 37 (Winter 1969).

Bancroft, Hubert Howe, *History of Utah* (Salt Lake City: Bookcraft, Inc., 1964) [originally published in 1889 in San Francisco].

Barrett, Ivan J., *Joseph Smith and the Restoration* (Provo: Brigham Young University Press, 1973).

Beadle, John Hanson, *Life in Utah, or The Mysteries and Crimes of Mormonism* (Philadelphia: National Publishing Company, 1870).

Berry, Michael S. "Fremont Origins: A Critique," in David B. Madsen, ed., *Fremont Perspectives,* Utah State Historical Society Antiquities Section Selected Paper (Salt Lake City: Utah State Historical Society, 1980).

Best, Gerald M, *Iron Horses to Promontory* (San Marino, Calif.: Golden West Books, 1969).

Brooks, George R., ed., *The Southwest Expedition of Jedediah S. Smith* (Lincoln: University of Nebraska Press, 1977).

Carlisle, Howard M., *Colonist Fathers, Corporate Sons: A Selective History of the Call Family* (Calls Trust, 1996).

Chronic, Halka, *Roadside Geology of Utah* (Missoula, Mont.: Mountain Press Publishing Co., 1990).

Clark, James R., ed., *Messages of the First Presidency* (Salt Lake City: Bookcraft, 1970).

Conley, Cort, *Idaho for the Curious: A Guide* (Cambridge, Idaho: Backeddy Books, 1982).

Davies, J. Kenneth, *Mormon Gold: The Story of California's Mormon Argonauts* (Salt Lake City: Olympus Publishing Company, 1984).

Davis, Oscar King, "The Lucin Cut-Off: A Remarkable Feat of Engineering across the Great Salt Lake On Embankment and Trestle," *Century* Magazine, January 1906.

Derig, Betty, *Roadside History of Idaho* (Missoula, Montana: Mountain Press Publishing Co., 1996).

Despain, Matthew and Fred R. Gowans, "James Bridger," in Allan Kent Powell, ed., *Utah History Encyclopedia* (Salt Lake City: University of Utah Press, 1994).

Doelling, Helmut H., with Jock A. Campbell, J. Wallace Gwynn, Lee I. Perry, "Geology and Mineral Resources of Box Elder County, Utah," *Utah Utah Geological and Mineral Survey Bulletin* 115 (Salt Lake City: Utah Geological and Mineral Survey, 1980).

Ehat, Andrew F. and Lyndon W. Cook, *The Words of Joseph Smith* (Provo: Brigham Young University Religious Studies Center, 1980).

Eubank, Mark, *Utah Weather* (Bountiful: Horizon, 1979).

Fawcett, Bill and Steve Simms, *Archeological Test Excavations in the Great Salt Lake Wetlands,* Utah State University, no. 14 (1993).

Fiero, Bill, *Geology of the Great Basin* (Reno: University of Nevada Press, 1986).

Fife, Veara S. and Chloe N. Petersen, *Brigham City, Utah Residents, 1850–1877* (Brigham City: Golden Spike Chapter, Utah Genealogical Association, 1976).

Fleming, L. A. and A. R. Standing, "The Road to 'Fortune': The Salt Lake Cutoff," *Utah Historical Quarterly* 33 (Summer 1965).

Forsgren, Lydia Walker, ed., *History of Box Elder County* (Brigham City: Daughters of Utah Pioneers, 1937).

Fowler, Don D., "Introduction," in Howard Stansbury, *Exploration of the Valley of the Great Salt Lake* (Washington, D.C.: Smithsonian Institution Press, 1988).

Frémont, John C., *The Exploring Expedition to the Rocky Mountains* (Washington, D.C.: Smithsonian Institution Press, 1988).

Glines, Carroll V., *Four Came Home* (Princeton, N.J.: D. Van Nostrand Company, Inc., 1966).

Goodwin, S. H. and Committee, *Freemasonry in Utah* (Salt Lake City: Corinne and Corinne Lodge No. 5, F. & A. M., 1926).

Gowans, Fred R., *Rocky Mountain Rendezvous* (Layton, Utah: Gibbs M. Smith, Inc., 1985).

Hardy, B. Carmon, *Solemn Covenant* (Urbana: University of Illinois Press, 1992).

Harrington, Joseph D., *Yankee Samurai: The Secret Role of Nisei in America's Pacific Victory* (Detroit, Mich.: Pettigrew Enterprises, Inc., 1979).

Hartley, William G., "The Priesthood Reorganization of 1877: Brigham Young's Last Achievement," *BYU Studies* 20 (Fall 1979).

Heath, Harvard S., ed., *In the World: The Diaries of Reed Smoot* (Salt Lake City: Signature Books in association with Smith Research Associates, 1997).

Hofsommer, Don L., *The Southern Pacific,* 1901–1985 (College Station: Texas A&M University Press, 1986).

Hoopes, David S. and Roy Hoopes, *The Making of a Mormon Apostle: The Story of Rudger Clawson* (Lanham, N.Y.: Madison Books, 1990).

Huchel, Frederick M., "The Box Elder Flouring Mill," *Utah Historical Quarterly* 56 (Winter 1988).

Hunt, Charles B., ed., "Pleistocene Lake Bonneville, Ancestral Great Salt Lake, as Described in the Notebooks of G. K. Gilbert, 1875–1880," *Brigham Young University Geology Studies* 29 (Provo: Brigham Young University Department of Geology, 1982).

Hunter, Milton R., *Brigham Young the Colonizer* (Salt Lake City: The Deseret News Press, 1940).

Jennings, Jesse D., *Prehistory of Utah and the Eastern Great Basin* [University of Utah Anthropological Papers, Number 98] (Salt Lake City: University of Utah Press, 1973).

Jessee, Dean C., *The Papers of Joseph Smith* (Salt Lake City: Deseret Book Co., 1989).

Journal History of the Church of Jesus Christ of Latter-day Saints, LDS church archives.

Kenney, Scott G., ed., *Wilford Woodruff's Journal* (Salt Lake City: Signature Books, 1983).

Kimball, Stanley B., *Heber C. Kimball: Mormon Patriarch and Pioneer* (Urbana: University of Illinois Press, 1981).

Kirk, Ruth, *Desert: The American Southwest* (Boston: Houghton Mifflin Company, 1973).

Knowlton, Ezra C., *History of Highway Development in Utah* (Salt Lake City: Utah State Department of Highways, 1967).

Kotter, Olive H., "Brigham City to 1900," in *Through the Years* (Brigham City: Brigham City Eighth Ward, 1953).

Kowallis, Bart J., ed., Lehi F. Hintze,"Geologic History of Utah," *Brigham Young University Geology Studies,* Special Publication 7 (Provo: Brigham Young University Department of Geology, 1982).

Kraus, *High Road to Promontory* (Palo Alto, Calif.: American West Publishing Co., 1969).

Larsen, Gustive O., *The "Americanization" of Utah for Statehood* (San Marino, California: Henry E. Huntington Library and Art Gallery, 1971).

Larson, Andrew Karl, *The Red Hills of November* (Salt Lake City: Deseret News Press, 1957).

Larson, Andrew Karl and Katharine Miles Larson, *Diary of Charles L. Walker* (Logan: Utah State University Press, 1980).

Leigh, Rufus Wood, *Five Hundred Utah Place Names* (Salt Lake City: Rufus Wood Leigh, 1961).

Lyman, Edward Leo, *Political Deliverance: The Mormon Quest for Utah Statehood* (Urbana: University of Illinois Press, 1986).

Madsen, Brigham D., *Chief Pocatello: The "White Plume,"* (Salt Lake City: University of Utah Press, 1986).

Madsen, Brigham D., *Corinne: The Gentile Capital of Utah* (Salt Lake City: Utah State Historical Society, 1980).

Madsen, Brigham D., ed., *Exploring the Great Salt Lake: The Stansbury Expedition of 1849–50* (Salt Lake City: University of Utah Press, 1989).

Madsen, Brigham D., *Gold Rush Sojourners in Great Salt Lake City, 1849 and 1850* (Salt Lake City: University of Utah Press, 1982).

Madsen, Brigham D., *The Northern Shoshoni* (Caldwell, Idaho: Caxton Printers, Ltd., 1980).

Madsen, Brigham D. and Betty M., "Corinne, the Fair: Gateway to Montana Mines," *Utah Historical Quarterly* 37 (1969).

Madsen, David B., *Exploring the Fremont* (Salt Lake City: Utah Museum of Natural History, 1989).

Madsen, David B., "Fremont/Sevier Subsistence," in David B. Madsen, ed., *Fremont Perspectives,* Utah State Historical Society Antiquities Section Selected Papers, No. 16 (Salt Lake City: Utah State Historical Society, 1980).

Madsen, David B., "The Human Prehistory of the Great Salt Lake Region," in J. Wallace Gwynn, ed., *Great Salt Lake: A Scientific, Historical and Economic Overview, Utah Department of Natural Resources Bulletin* 116 [June 1980] (Salt Lake City: Utah Geological and Mineral Survey, 1980).

Madsen, Truman G., *Defender of the Faith: The B. H. Roberts Story* (Salt Lake City: Bookcraft, 1980).

Mails, Thomas E., *Hotevilla: Hopi Shrine of the Covenant, Microcosm of the World* (New York: Marlowe & Company, 1995).

Mann, David H., "Tremblors Caused Great Fright in Nineties, Files of 'Brigham Bugler' Show," *Ogden Standard-Examiner,* 25 March 1934.

Mann, David H., "The Undriving of the Golden Spike," *Utah Historical Quarterly* 37 (Winter 1969).

Manuscript History of Box Elder Stake, LDS church archives.

McCarthy, Max R., *The Last Chance Canal Company,* Charles Redd

Monographs in Western History No. 16 (Provo: Charles Redd Center For Western Studies, Brigham Young University, 1987).

McCague, *Moguls and Iron Men* (New York: Harper & Row, 1964).

McKenzie, George, "Cause and Origin of the Walker War," in Peter Gottfredson, *Indian Depredations in Utah* (Salt Lake City: Merlin G. Christensen, 1969).

Merrill, Milton R., *Reed Smoot: Apostle in Politics* (Logan: Utah State University Press, 1990).

Miller, David E. and Della S. Miller, *Nauvoo: The City of Joseph* (Santa Barbara, Calif.: Peregrine Smith, Inc., 1974).

Moody, Raymond A., M.D., Ph.D., *Life After Life* (New York: Bantam, 1975).

Morgan, Dale L., *Jedediah Smith and the Opening of the West* (Lincoln: University of Nebraska Press, 1964).

Morgan, Dale L., supervisor, *Utah: A Guide to the State* (Salt Lake City: Utah Institute of Fine Arts, 1941).

Murphy, Don R., "Drainage," in Wayne L. Wahlquist, ed., *Atlas of Utah* (Ogden and Provo: Weber State College and Brigham Young University Press, 1981).

Murphy, Don R., "Physiographic Provinces," in Wayne L. Wahlquist, ed., *Atlas of Utah* (Ogden: Weber State College, 1981).

Palmer, William R., "Indian names in Utah Geography," *Utah Historical Quarterly* 1.

Pendelton, Mark A., "The Orderville United Order of Zion," *Utah Historical Quarterly 7.*

Porter, Larry C., "Reverend George Lane—Good 'Gifts,' Much 'Grace,' and Marked 'Usefulness'," *BYU Studies* 9 (Spring 1969).

Porter, Larry C., "A Study of the Origins of the Church of Jesus Christ of Latter-day Saints in the States of New York and Pennsylvania, 1816–1831," Ph.D. diss., Brigham Young University, 1971.

Powell, Allan Kent, *Splinters of a Nation: German Prisoners of War in Utah* (Salt Lake City: University of Utah Press, 1989).

Powell, Allan Kent, ed., *Utah History Encyclopedia* (Salt Lake City: University of Utah Press, 1994).

Powell, Allan Kent, *Utah Remembers World War II* (Logan: Utah State University Press, 1991).

Quinn, D. Michael, *The Mormon Hierarchy: Extensions of Power* (Salt Lake City: Signature Books, 1997).

Reeder, Adolph M., ed., Box *Elder Lore of the Nineteenth Century* (Brigham City: Sons of Utah Pioneers, 1951).

Rich, Russell R., *Ensign to the Nations* (Provo: Brigham Young University Publications, 1972).

Richardson, E. Arlo, Gaylen L. Ashcroft, and John K. Westbrook, "Freeze-Free Season," in Wayne L. Wahlquist, ed., *Atlas of Utah* (Ogden and Provo: Weber State College and Brigham Young University, 1981).

Richardson, E. Arlo, Gaylen L. Ashcroft, and John K. Westbrook, "Hours of Sunshine," in Wayne L. Wahlquist, ed., *Atlas of Utah* (Ogden and Provo: Weber State College and Brigham Young University, 1981).

Richardson, E. Arlo, Gaylen L. Ashcroft, and John K. Westbrook, "Precipitation," in Wayne L. Wahlquist, ed., *Atlas of Utah* (Ogden and Provo: Weber State College and Brigham Young University, 1981).

Roberts, B. H., *A Comprehensive History of the Church of Jesus Christ of Latter-day Saints, Century One* (Provo: Brigham Young University Press, 1965).

Roberts, B. H., ed., *History of the Church of Jesus Christ of Latter-Day Saints* (Salt Lake City: Deseret Book Co., 1978)

Roberts, Richard C. and Richard W. Sadler, *A History of Weber County* (Salt Lake City: Utah State Historical Society, 1997).

Robinson, William F., *Abandoned New England* (Boston: New York Graphic Society, 1987).

Romney, Thomas C., *The Life of Lorenzo Snow* (Salt Lake City: S. U. P. Memorial Foundation, 1955).

Roylance, Ward J., *Utah: A Guide to the State* (Salt Lake City: Utah Arts Council, 1982).

Skidmore, Charles H., B. L. M. A., Superintendent of Schools, Administration and *Supervision in the Box Elder School District* (Brigham City: Board of Education, 1921).

Smart, William B., *Old Utah Trails* (Salt Lake City: Utah Geographic Series, Inc., 1988).

Smith, Eliza R. Snow, *Biography and Family Record of Lorenzo Snow, One of the Twelve Apostles of the Church of Jesus Christ of Latter-day Saints* (Salt Lake City: Deseret News Co., 1884).

Stewart, George R., *The California* Trail (Lincoln: University of Nebraska Press, 1962).

Stewart, John J., *The Iron Trail to the Golden Spike* (Salt Lake City: Deseret Book Co., 1969).

Stokes, William Lee, *Geology of Utah* (Salt Lake City: Utah Museum of Natural History and Utah Geological and Mineral Survey, 1986).

Talmage, James E., *The House of the Lord* (Salt Lake City: Bookcraft, 1962).

Tanaka, Chester, *Go For Broke: A Pictorial History of the Japanese American 100th Infantry Battalion and the 442nd Regimental Combat Team* (Richmond, Calif.: Gor For Broke, Inc., 1982).

Toponce, Alexander, *Reminiscences of Alexander Toponce, Pioneer* (Norman: University of Oklahoma Press, 1971) [Originally published in 1923, in Ogden, Utah.]

Towle, Margaret A., "Use of Plant Materials Other Than Maize," in James H. Gunnerson, *The Fremont Culture,* Papers of the Peabody Museum of Archaeology and Ethnology, Harvard University, vol. 59, no. 2 (Cambridge, Mass.: The Peabody Museum, 1969).

Trimble, Stephen, *The Sagebrush Ocean: A Natural History of the Great Basin* (Reno: University of Nevada Press, 1989).

Tykal, Jack B., "Etienne Provost," in Allan Kent Powell, ed., *Utah History Encyclopedia* (Salt Lake City: University of Utah Press, 1994).

Van Cott, John W., *Utah Place Names* (Salt Lake City: University of Utah Press, 1990).

Van Orden, Bruce A., *Prisoner for Conscience' Sake: The Life of George Reynolds* (Salt Lake City: Deseret Book Co., 1992).

Viola, Herman J. and Ralph E. Ehrenberg, "Introduction," to John C. Frémont, *The Exploring Expedition to the Rocky Mountains* (Washington, D.C.: Smithsonian Institution Press, 1988).

Wagoner, Richard S. Van, *Mormon Polygamy: A History* (Salt Lake City: Signature Books, 1986).

Walgamott, Charles S., *Six Decades Back: A Series of Historical Sketches of Early Days in Idaho* (Caxton Printers, 1936).

Walker, Ronald W., "The Panic of 1893," in Allan Kent Powell, ed., *Utah History Encyclopedia* (Salt Lake City: University of Utah Press, 1994).

Walker, Ronald W., "Seeking the 'Remnant': The Native American During the Joseph Smith Period," *Journal of Mormon History* 19 (Spring 1993).

Warrum, Noble, *Utah in the World War* (Salt Lake City: Utah State Council of Defense, 1924).

Webb, Henry J., "The Last Trek Across the Great Salt Desert," *Utah Historical Quarterly* 31 (Winter 1963).

Welling, Gale, *Fielding: The People and the Events that Affected Their Lives* (Fielding: Gale Welling, n.d.).

Index

Abbott, Emily Farley, 379
Abbott, Myron, 379
Adams, D.H., 213
Adams, John, 395
Adams, LuAnn, x, 298
Adams, Maude, 143
Adams-Onis Treaty, 44
Adney, Clarence G., 222, 330
African-Americans, 270
Aldersgate United Methodist Church, 172–73
Allen, Ferrin, ix
Allen, Girard B., 136
Allen, Grace, 393
Allen, John, 393
Alter, J. Cecil, 233
Amalgamated Sugar Company, 228
American Greetings Plant, 297
Amity Lodge 23, 169
Andersen, Keith, 300
Andersen, William, 356
Anderson, Alexander, 359–60
Anderson, Andrew, 311
Anderson, Bernice Gibbs, xi
Anderson, Christian O., 209–11
Anderson, Garren, 326
Anderson, Keith, x
Anderson, Rasmus, 313
Ango, Johnny, 343
Angrove, John, 411
Anthony, Susan B., 302
Apostolic Christian Church, 178–80
Appledale, 23–24, 222
Arbon, Charles, 403
Arbon, George, 403
Armstrong, W.W., 235–36
Arrington, Leonard, 88, 226, 227–28
Ashbrook Mining District, 8
Assembly of God, 185
Atkinson, Ida May Venable, 247
Atkinson, Thomas, 345
Austin, George, 340

Baer, Henry, 179, 407
Baer, Matthew, 407
Bailey, Cyrus W., 356

Bailey, Reed, 245
Baird, John, 154
Baird, Robert B., 412
Baker, Henry C., 350
Bamberger, Simon, 233
Bank of Corinne, 130
Baptist Church 183–84
Barnard, Ezra, 381, 384
Barnard, John, 320
Barnes, Alazanna, 404
Barnes, Hovey, 404
Barnes, Losrenzo, 404
Barnes, William, 404
Baron, James, 98
Bass, James R. "Sam," xi
Bayliss, Edward E., 167
Beadle, John Hanson, 124–25, 126, 127, 128–29, 130, 142
Bear Hunter, 80
Bear Lake and River Water Works and Irrigation Company, 218
Bear River, 4, 14, 22, 44, 51, 123, 126, 130–31, 134, 135, 138, 223, 226, 248, 307, 335
Bear River City, 128, 243, 307–8
Bear River High School, 206, 252, 276, 325
Bear River Irrigation and Ogden Water Work Co., 218, 220
Bear River Land, Orchard and Beet Sugar Company, 221–22, 225
Bear River Massacre, 79–80
Bear River Migratory Bird Reserve, 248
Bear River Water Company, 218
Bear River Water Users Association, 228
Beaver Dam, 308–10
Beecher, Denton, x
Beecher, Elbert, 350
Beet Days, 293–94
Beetal, Levi, 345
Bennett, C. W., 219
Benson, Ezra T., 106, 110
Bentley, J.K., 185
Berlin Candy Bomber, 279–80
Betterridge, James W., 345
Betterridge, William C., 345
Bible Church, 184
Bidwell, John, 47–50
Bidwell-Bartleson Party, 46–50
Bigler, Agnes Standing, 321
Bigler, David, 46
Bigler, Jacob A., 321, 324
Bigler, Mark, 320, 321, 326
Bingham, B. Albert, 355
Bingham, Eva, xi
Bingham, J.S., 206
Bitthell, Charles, 247
Black, Jennie, 137
Blanthorn, Ellen, 346
Blanthorn, George A., 346
Bonneville, B.L.E., 12
Boothe, Emily Orme, 351
Boothe, John M., 355
Boothe, Lewis N., 351, 352
Boothe, Ray, 352–53, 354, 355
Borgstrom, Alben, 272–73
Borgstrom, Boyd, 272–73
Borgstrom, Clyde, 272–73
Borgstrom, Le Roy, 272–73
Borgstrom, Rolon, 272–73
Borgstrom, Rulon, 272–73
Bothwell, 19, 310–14
Bothwell, John R., 217, 222, 297, 311, 338
Bott, John H., 99–100, 302, 309
Boukofsky, N., 125
Bourion, Honore, 180
Bowcutt, John, 389, 395
Bowcutt, Zina, 389
Bowen, Earl, 237
Bowen, Jonathan, 309
Bowen, Louis, 237
Bowers, Ed, 326
Bowers, Orphra, 326
Bowsher, Amos L., 111
Box, E.A., 205
Box Elder Academy of Music and Dancing, 211
Box Elder Canyon, 54
Box Elder Commercial Club, 212
Box Elder County, name, 1; area, 1; boundaries, 2–3; elevation, 3; geology and topography, 4–11; water resources, 14–17; climate, 17–19;

flora and fauna, 19–21; geographic place names, 21–24; courthouse, 73–75, 189, 298–99; united order, 89–100; and gold rush, 197; fair, 293–94
Box Elder County Historical Photo Tour, 299
Box Elder Creek, 15, 66, 90
Box Elder Flouring Mill, 73, 77–78, 99–100
Box Elder Fort, 67–68
Box Elder High School, 206, 209, 325
Box Elder Peak, 3
Box Elder Stake Academy, 206
Box Elder Stake Tabernacle, 19, 120, 146–62, 236, 281
Box Elder Water Conservancy District, 297
Bradford, Kathleen, 270
Bramwell, George, 203
Brelsford, Don, 184
Brenkman, E.E., 408
Brewer, Alexander, 376
Bridger, James, 44, 335
Bridges, 200
Brigham City, 315–17; settled, 65–67, 306; named, 71; during Utah War, 77–78; ground breaking for Utah Northern Railroad, 120
Brigham City LDS Tabernacle, see Box Elder Stake Tabernacle
Brigham City Mercantile and Manufacturing Association, 90–100, 149, 150, 188, 235
Brigham City Opera House, 209–11
Brigham City Sugar Factory, 227, 228
Brigham City Tannery, 90
Brigham City Woolen Mills, 91–92, 93–94
Brizzee, Charles, 345
Broman, Gary, 184
Bronson, Gordon, 394
Brooks, George, 45
Brooks, James, 65, 146, 300, 315
Brown, James, 64
Bryan, William Jennings, 143, 190
Bryant, Edwin, 10
Buckley, James, 92
Buddhist Churches, 175–76
Buel City, 11
Bureau of Land Management, 1
Burgess, M.T., 125
Burke, A.R., 355
Burnett, Darwin, 394
Burnett, Marvin, 397
Busenbark, Alonzo, 319–20
Busenbark, Henry, 319–20
Busenbark, Monroe, 319–20, 322
Bushnell Hospital, 266–72, 281
Bushnell Motel, 268
Bushnell, George E., 267
Buttars, Ann, xi
Butterball, George, 215

Cahoon, Henry R., 417
Calgary, Oliver, 344
Call, Anson, 348
Call, Cyril, 411
Call, Jay, 299
Callahan, Andrew, 364
Callahan, William, 364
Camp Lorenzo, 92–93
Campbell, Lucinda Shipman, 364
Canfield, Chubb, 343
Cannon Structures, 286
Cannon, A. H., 153
Cannon, Fred, x
Cannon, George Q., 157, 159, 191
Capener, A.R., 336, 337, 339
Capener, Alfred, 391, 387
Capener, E.T., 396
Capener, Ellen, 393
Capener, Helen, 393
Capener, Howard, 397
Capener, Joseph A., 396
Capener, Leland, 396
Capener, Russell, 390, 397
Cardon, Alfred, 199
Carr, Stephen, 318
Carroll, Dan, 184
Carson, Kit, 52, 248, 335
Carter, Floyd, 370
Carter, Gordon, 370
Carter, Lawrence, 401

Carter, Simeon, 67, 203
Carter, Will, 369
Casement, Dan, 110
Casement, Jack, 110, 112
Catell, Harvey, 356
Catholic Church, 180–82
Causeway, 282–86
Cazier, James, 415
Cedar Creek, 317–19
Cement Plant, 295
Centennial History Project, xiii
Central Hotel, 142–43
Central Pacific Railroad, 106–20, 140, 192, 229
Century Consolidated Mining and Milling Company, 344
Century Mine, 343, 365
Chadwick, Abraham, 364
Challenger, 289–90
Cheese-making, 96
Chief Pocatello, 79, 81
Chief Sagwitch, 82–83
Chiles, J.B., 57–58
Chinese, 229
Chournos, Nick, 213
Christensen, Tony, 341–42
Christian Reformed Church, 182
Christiansen, Chris, 209–11
Christopher, Calvin, 404
Church of Christ, 185
City of Corinne, 135–39
City of Rocks, 58
Civilian Conservation Corps, 240, 251–52
Clarksston Mountains, 4
Clawson, Hiram B., 160
Clawson, Rudger, 151, 154, 156–57, 151, 161, 191, 300, 309, 356, 393
Climate, 17–19
Clyman, James, 10, 45
Coe, L. W., 117
Cogswell, Milton, 111
Cole, James, 380
Cole, S. N., 409
Coleman, Moroni, 364
Collinston, 319–26
Colton, Fred, 392
Colton, Vera, 392
Compton, Alma, 375
Compton, Matthew, 375
Connor, Patrick Edward, 79–80, 133, 135, 180, 328
Cook, James F., 184
Cooke, Benjamin, 344, 345, 346
Cooksville, 344
Coombs, H. Ross, 355
Cooper, Wallace N., 161, 386
Cooperative Ministry Council, 185
Coprolites, 33–34
Cordon, John, 368
Corey, Amos, 341
Corinne, 23, 123–43, 166, 306, 327–31
Corinne Farm Bureau, 277
Corinne Historical Society, 166, 171
Corinne Methodist Church, 170
Corinne Mill, Canal and Stock Company, 215–16, 218–19, 336, 338
Corinne Opera House, 143
Cornwall, C. M. "Red,," 394
Cornwall, Gene, 394
Cottam, Ellen, 403
Cottam, William, 403
Covert, Julia Bigler, 323
Covert, Timothy, 323
Cragun, Earl, 377
Cragun, Weldon, 377
Craner, John, 330
Crater Island District, 9
Crocker, Charles, 106, 115, 213, 355
Crocker, E.B., 115
Croft, Earl, 245
Crosby, Joseph W., 287–88
Crystal Springs, 16, 53, 354
Curlew Irrigation and Reservoir Company, 403
Curlew Valley, 6, 8
Cutler Dam, 14
Cutler Power Plant, 224
Cutler, John C., 225
Cutler, Thomas R., 224, 225, 226

Dahl, C.A., 135
Dairy, 95–96
Dalton, Mathew W., 199

Danger Cave, 32–33, 34
Dart, Al, 368
Davies, Le Grande, ix
Davis Fort, 67
Davis, Barbara, 182
Davis, Ralph, 182
Davis, Thomas L., 356
Davis, Vinson F., 376
Davis, William, 65, 68, 71, 85, 146, 300, 315
Deep Creek, 15
DeMille, Alan C., xi
Desert Archaic peoples, 31
Dewey, John C., 22
Deweyville, 22
Diefendorf, Fox, 136, 138
Dienger, Fred, 313
Dieter, Jack, 184
Digger Indians, 51
Dillon, Sidney, 110, 119, 141
Division of State History, xiii
Dix, John, 106
Dobrenen, Pauline, 402
Dodge, Grenville M., 106, 108, 110, 113, 117
Doman, Tommy, 337
Dominguez, 44
Dooley, John E., 218
Doty, James Duane, 80–81
Dove Creek, 15
Dowling, Patrick, 180
Dowty, Bob, xi, 121
Dream Mines, 190, 296
Drew, Harry, 314
Druehl, F.A., 176, 399
Dry Farming, 213–14
Dry Lake, 5
Duff, John, 119
Dunn Peak, 3
Dunn, Thomas, 364
Durant, Thomas Clark, 106, 110, 116, 117, 118, 119, 120
Durfey, Francello, 325
Dustin, Nina, 397
Dyer, E.H., 225

E. H. Dywer Company, 228
Earl, Jed, 323, 333
Earl, John, 333
Earl, Milton, 334
Earthquakes, 240–48
East Side Canal, 222
Edwards, Frank, 182
Edwards, Roberta, 182
Electric Power Development, 222–25, 296, 313, 317, 376
Eldridge, H.S., 216–17
Ellis, F. Willis, 323
Ellis, William S., 355
Elwood, 331–32
Emery, George William, 416, 418
Empey Springs, 22
Empey, William, 22, 422
Episcopal Churches, 173–74
Escalante, 43
Eskelsen, Ruel, 361
Etna, 332
Etna Hot Springs, 17
Evans, David, 218, 340
Evans, Henry, 68, 203

Fann, Delbert, 183
Farr, Lorin, 71, 85, 106
Fehlman, Alma, 372
Fennesbeck, Christian, 356
Ferry, W. Mont, 176, 399
Fielding, 19, 23, 332–35
Fike, Richard, 359, 405
First World War, 233–38
Fishburn, Aquilla N., 409
Fishburn, J.A., 409
Fisher, Joseph, 364
Fletcher, Seth, 345
Flint, John K., 352–53
Floods, 238–40
Flora and Fauna, 19–21
Foley, John, 180
Foote, George, 166, 173
Forsberg, Norma, 394
Forsberg, Ruth, 390
Forsgren, David L., 355
Forsgren, Lydia Walker, 68, 197–98, 199, 203, 204
Forsgren, Peter Adolph, 302, 307

Foster, George, 348
Fowler, J.K., 219
Fox, Jesse W., 69
Fraeb, Henry G., 45
Francis, Joseph, xiv
Frank, A.G., 236
Fredricks, W.R., 111
Freestone, Eliza, 404
Freestone, William, 404
Freiday, William G., 323
Freighting, 131–32
Fremont Culture, 30–31, 36–38
Fremont, John C., 14, 50–53, 135, 248, 319, 335
Fridal, K. H., 272
Frodsham, Amelia, 382
Frodsham, James, 383
Fryer, Robert A., 324
Fujinkai, 175, 176
Fuller, Craig, x, xiv
Fulmer, Collins, 322
Fundamentalists, 190

Gallagher, William, 345
Gamble, James, 112
Gambling, 232
Garcia, Abran R., 355
Gardner, Boyd K., 356
Gardner, D. Leon, 355
Garfield, 139
Garfield, James Abram, 139
Garland, 227–28, 335–42
Garland Sugar Factory, 226, 250
Garland, William, 339, 341
Garn, Mary Larelda, 337
Garn, Maxine, 394
Garn, Olene, 394
Gates, J.C., 409
Geographic Place Names, 21–24
Gephart, Harry L., 409
German prisoners of war, 271, 391
German settlers, 178–80
Getz, Bertha, 179
Getz, Philip, 179, 407–8
Getz, Ruth, 179
Getz, W.E., 409
Gibbs, John D., 240, 348, 350
Gibbs, Thelma, 384–85
Gilbert, Grove K., 5, 12
Gillespie, Mattie, 169
Gillespie, Samuel L., 167–69
Gilmore, Norma Grant, 352–53
Gleason, A.H., 337
Godbe, William S., 319, 320, 329
Godfrey, Joseph, 364
Gold Rush, 191
Golden, 343–44
Golden Spike, 106–20
Golden Spike Monument, 201
Gonder, Kathleen, xi
Goodliffe, Charles, 399
Goodliffe, Esther Arbon, 403
Goodwin, S. H., 140
Goose Creek Mountains, 7, 15
Goring, Junior, 326
Goring, Sherrie, 326
Gould, Jay, 141
Graham, J.W., 215
Grant, Heber J., 190, 191, 251, 386, 389
Grant, Jedediah M., 352, 353
Graser, V.M., 239–40
Grasshoppers, 35
Great Basin, 2–3
Great Depression, 249–53
Great Salt Lake, 2, 12–13, 17, 45, 52, 53–56, 124, 192–97, 243–44
Green, Thomas, 385
Grouse Creek, 344–47
Grouse Creek Mountains, 6–7, 8
Grover, Walter, 337, 340
Gunnell, Charles E., 356
Gunnerson, James H., 30, 38
Gunnison, John W., 53
Guthrie, John W., 131–32, 143

H. S. Jacobs and Company, 138
Hadfield, Joseph, 390, 396
Hadfield, Mary, 346
Haight, Hector C., 64
Haines, James W., 108, 114
Hales, Grace, 383
Hall, Harold E., 385
Halling, Lars, 361
Halversen, Gail, 279–80

Hammond Brothers Construction Company, 226, 340
Hammond Canal, 222
Hammond, Datus R., 222
Hammond, James T., 222, 226, 340
Hammond, Lionel, 222
Hampton Stage Stop, 81, 321
Hampton, Benjamin, 200, 319, 320
Hamson, George, 67, 68
Hamson, George Jr., 67
Hamson, Jessie, 377
Hannifin, William J., 174
Hansel Mountains, 8
Hansel Valley, 22–23, 245–46
Hansen, Christian, 70, 95, 102, 307
Hansen, Elizabeth Ericksen, 95, 102
Hansen, H.I., 171
Hansen, Peter Olsen, 361
Hansen, William S., 322
Hanson, Arthur, 240
Hardaway, Robert M., 267
Hardy, Jay, 299
Harkness, Harvey W., 108–9, 114, 116–17
Harper, 347–51
Harper, Thomas, 348, 350
Harris, Devere, 386
Harris, Moses (Black), 45
Harris, Oscar, 337
Harris, William, 183
Harrison, Elias L.T., 329
Hartshorn, A.W., 172
Hawkins, Eli, 313
Haymond, F.O., 272
Haywood, R.F., 223
Henningway, Walter, 345
Heitz, Paul, 408
Hensley, Samuel J., 22–23, 57, 197, 319, 415, 422
Herbert, Margaret Atwood, 270–71
Hernandez, Henry, 185
Hernandez, Maria, 185
Herriman, Edward Henry, 192
Hess, James H., 334
Hess, Jed M., 334
Hess, John W., 333
Hibbard, W.B., 110
Higginson, John, 174
Hill, A.B., 381
Hill, George W., 383
Hill, James J., 80
Hillam, Abraham, 90
Hinckley, Gordon B., 393–94
Hirschi, Christian, 364
Hirschi, Elizabeth Goodliffe, 399, 401–2
Hirschi, Ferd, 369
Hirschi, Fred, 372
Hoerr, Jacob, 408
Hofsommer, Don L., 283
Hogup Cave, 32–33, 34
Hogup Mountains, 7, 8
Holmgren, Albert E., 251
Holmgren, David, 409
Holmgren, Paul, 228
Holt, Nancy, 298
Holton, Fred, 296
Holy Cross Lutheran Church, 184
Honeyville Buddhist Church, 175, 232, 275
Hoover, Herbert, 249, 251
Hopkins, Mark, 108, 115
Hotel Boothe, 236
House, Henry, 132
House, Hiram, 16, 130, 131, 132, 200
House, J.E., 126
House William F., 131
Houtz, John, 403
Howe, Sam, 215
Howell, 23, 355–56
Howell, Joseph, 23, 355
Howell, William M. 403
Hubbard, Elisha, 345
Huchel, Cherie, xi
Huchel, J.L., 377
Hughes, Malanchton, 167
Hunsaker, Abraham, 22, 214, 331, 351, 352, 422
Hunsaker, Allen, 331, 351
Hunsaker, Bryon E., 355
Hunsaker, D.W., 353
Hunsaker, Elazrus, 354
Hunsaker, Eliza Collins, 351
Hunsaker, Enoch, 353
Hunsaker, Horace N., 355

Hunsaker, Isaac, 351
Hunsaker, Israel, 354, 355
Hunsaker, Leo, 355
Hunsaker, Parley, 355
Hunsaker, Paul, 350
Hunt, Duane G., 181
Hunting, 296
Huntington, Collis Potter, 106, 115
Hupfner, Paul, 271
Hussey, Dahler & Co., 130
Hyde, Warren, 294

Idle Isle Restaurant, 268
Imthurn, Samuel, 179
Indian Farm, 96
Indian Hindus, 230
Intermountain Indian School, 181–83, 280–82
Interstate 15 and 84, 201, 294
Iowa String, 356–57
Ipsom, James, 312
Ireland, T.W., 367
Irish, 229–30
Ishidia, Tsunekichi, 175
Italian prisoners of war, 271

J. W. Guthrie and Company, 130
Jackley, August, 182
Jackson, Sheldon, 167
Jackson, W.H., 81
Jacobs, Louis, 111
James, Charles 161
James, David, 368
James, Orson, 364
James, Sam, 364
James, William, 368
Japanese, 175–76, 230–32, 273–79
Jarvis and Conklin Mortgage Trust Company, 217–18, 338
Jarvis, Samuel, 220
Jemmett, Eliza, 322, 323
Jemmett, Henry, 320, 323
Jennings, Jesse D., 29–30, 31, 32–35
Jensen, Carl, 308, 341
Jensen, Hans P., 361
Jensen, Hyrum, 324
Jensen, Lorenzo, 200
Jensen, Mads Christian, 100
Jensen, Wynn K., 275
Jenson, A.J., 324
Jenson, Andrew, 153
John Baxter and Sons, 323
John, Flora, 385
John, LaVerd, 385
John, Thomas, 384
Johnson, Conrad, 310
Johnson, Jarvis, 310
Johnson, Joseph S., 310
Johnson, L. P., 204
Johnson, Rue Corbett, 127
Johnson, Russell, 310
Johnson, William, 337
Johnston, Albert Sidney, 77
Jones, George, 404
Jones, Lewis Howell, Jr., x
Jones, Owen, 68
Jones, Robert Allen, 345
Jones, Shadrack, 302, 412
Jones, Thomas Bruckhaw, 404
Jones, William G. "Bill," xi
Judah, Theodore, 106

Kalpakoff, Andrew, 177–78, 400
Kalpakoff, Anna M., 177–78, 400–1, 402
Kalpkakoff, Mary M., 178, 401, 402
Kalpakoff, Paul, 178, 402
Kate Connor, 135, 136–37, 139
Katoff, Sarah, 399
Kelly, Charles, 98, 157, 211
Kelsey, Benjamin, 47
Kelsey, Eli B., 329
Kelton, 240–41, 357–58
Kennard, Jim, 390, 395
Kennard, L.H., 395
Kennedy, Patrick, 181
Kerr, Clifton, 276
Kerr, John, 213, 215, 217, 338
Kerr, Kleon, 276
Kesler, Frederick, 73, 77
Kidman, Garth, 310
Kidman, Veda, 310
Kiesel, Fred J., 133
Kimball, Hazen, 57–58
Kimball, Heber C., 345

Kimball, Isaac, 345
Kimball, Isadore H., 345
Kimball, Samuel H., 345, 346
Kimber, Charles, 345
Kimber, Charles Jr., 345
Kimber, William, 345
King, Lorus, 340
King, Thomas E., 336–37, 339, 340
Kirk, Lee, 419
Knowlton, Ezra C., 198–99, 200
Knudson, Verabell Call, 268–69
Kondo, Yuki, 175
Kosmo, 247
Koyle, John, 190
Kuipers, Cornelius, 183
Kunzler, Charles, 372
Kunzler, Chester, 370, 373
Kunzler, Harold, 372
Kunzler, Henry, 372
Kunzler, Jacob, 364
Kunzler, Max, 373
Kunzler, Roy, 373

La Plata, 24
LaFaunt, Harold A., 399
LaFaunt, Robert, 176, 399
Laird, John, 97
Lajeunesse, Basil, 51, 248
Lake Bonneville, 3, 12–13, 29
Lakeside Cave, 35
Lakeview Mining Company, 8, 24
Larsen, Adam, 364
Larsen, Doris, 300
Larsen, Howard, 370
Larsen, Jordan, ix
Larsen, Maria, 416
Larsen, Merlin, x, 300
Laurel Cafe, 236
LaVaunt, Corinne, 23, 127, 328
Layton, Christopher, 139
Lazy Boy furniture, 297
Leavitt, Ella Abbot, 379
Leavitt, John Q., 339
Lee, Alfred, 404
Lee, Isaac, 345
Lee, S. N., 157
Legon, Dan, 185
Leonard, Zenas, 9
Lillywhite, Lewis, 396
Lincoln School, 207
Lind, John, 359–60
Lindsay, David Moore, 249
Little Valley shipyard, 284
Little, Jesse C., 63–64, 197, 315
Living Hope Christian Reformed Church, 183
Long, Ella Angebauer, ix
Love, Jonathan, 364
Loveland, C.C., 97
Loveland, Chester, 350, 419
Loveland, Orson, 354
Lowe, George A., 216
Lucin, 358–59
Lucin Cut-Off, 192–97, 282–83
Lutheran Church, 184
Lyman, Amasa, 329
Lyman, Francis M., 389
Lynn, 359–60

M'Master, John B., 157
MacKenzie, Donald, 14, 44
McCabe, C.C., 170
McClure, Charles, 409
McCormick, Robert, 419
McGonagle, G.F., 223
McIntire, George, 404
McKay, David O., 232
McKinley, William
McLaws, Danial, 345
Mabey, Charles, 240
Machebeuf, Joseph Projectus, 180
Macfarlane, Bob, 395
Macfarlane, Jay U., 392
Macfarlane, Rowane, 395
Maddox Ranch House, 377–78
Maddox, Irvin B., 377–78
Maddox, Steven K., 378
Maddox, Wilma K., 378
Madsen Hot Springs, 16, 53, 354
Madsen, Adolphus, 157
Madsen, Brigham D., 59, 78–80, 81, 126
Madsen, David, 28, 35, 36
Madsen, P.W., 367
Madsen, Patty, 82–83

Madsen, Truman, 234
Makepeace, Gerald F., 172–73
Malad River, 14
Malsh, J., 130
Mangelson, Charles, 381
Manila Ward, 332
Mann, Walter G., 288
Manning, David E., 336, 340
Manning, E.E., 337
Manning, Glenn, 340
Mansfield, Jarvis, 381
Mantua, 5, 22, 360–062
Marriot, Frank, 114
Marshall, John, 344, 368
Marwitt, John, 37
Mason, George, 380, 381
Masons, 169–70
Matheson, Scott M., 355
Mathias, Thomas, 70, 375
May, James, 92–93, 350
Mecham, Erastus Darwin, 364
Meacham, F., 125
Meacham, William, 364
Meister, Jacob, 408
Mekkelsen, C.J., 171
Meldrum, Frank, 408
Merrell, Orville, 236
Merrill, Henry, 345
Merrill, Joseph, 379
Merrill, William, 379
Methodist Churches, 170–73
Mexicans, 230
Middleton, C.F., 160
Midland Trail, 200–1
Miller, E.H., 115
Miller, John, 367
Miller, S.L., 341
Miller, Wilford, 367
Miller, William, 341
Mills, Darius Ogden, 108
Mills, Edgar, 108, 110, 113, 117
Minkler, H.H., 112
Minuteman missile, 288
Misaka, Wat, 278
Moench, Louis Frederick, 205
Moeykens, John, xi
Molgard, Lawrence, 377
Molokani, 398–402
Montague, S.S., 115
Morgan, Cecil, 183
Morgan, Willis, 236
Morley, Isaac, 65
Mormon Battalion members, 57, 197
Morris, Charlie, 332
Morris, Dorothy, 300
Morris, James Newberry, 364
Morris, LeGrand, 300, 370
Morris, Royal, 370
Morrison-Knudsen Company, 283
Mortensen, Lars, 154
Morton Airbag Factory, 297
Morton Thiokol, 289–90
Mountain Fuel Supply Company, 296
Moyle, Henry D., 208
Mulder, Al, 183
Munro, W.H., 130

Naf, John, 404
National Guard Armory, 235
Neeley, William, 380
Nelson, Lois, 374, 375
Nelson, Paul, 377
Nelson, Roger, 377
Nessen, Nephi, 356
New Deal, 249–253
Newfoundland Mining District, 9
Newfoundland Mountains, 7, 8–9
Nibley, Hugh, ix-x
Nichols, Alvin, 160, 320
Nielsen, George A., 377, 378
Nielsen, Lola, 378–79
Nihart, Fred, 407, 408
Nishiguchi, Frank, x, 297, 300, 421
North Promontory Mountains, 7
Norton, Alanson, 91, 92
Nottingham, Henry, 114
Nuttall, Keith, 299
Nye, Fred, 392

O'Neil, John, 125, 126
Ogden, Peter Skene, 35, 44
Olague, Antone, 364
Olsen, Adolph, 302–3
Olsen, D.A., ix

Orbit Inn site, 36
Orme, Emily Green, 351
Orme, H. Paul, 355
Orme, Joseph, 351
Ormsby, Oliver, C., 76–77
Osmond, Wes, 377

Pacific Land and Water Company, 177
Pacific Union Express Company, 117
Pack, Frederick J., 244
Paker, Boyd K., 160–61
Palmer, James, 368
Palmer, James W., 368
Palmer, Joseph, 368
Panic of 1873, 94–95
Panic of 1893, 188
Park Valley, 363–73
Parry, Joseph, 383–84
Parsons, George, 363
Paskett, Phillip A., 345, 346
Paskett, William P., 345
Patrick, Joseph C., 287
Patterson, James H., 176, 399
Payne, Thomas, 313
Peace City Apartments, 268
Peacekeeper missile, 289
Peach Days, 211–13, 293–94
Peet, V.S., 356, 407
Penrose, 23, 373
Penrose, Charles W., 23, 373
Pera, Tom, 185
Perry, 373–79
Perry, Gustavus A., 374, 375
Perry, Henry, 374
Perry, Lorenzo, 374, 376
Perry, May W., 376
Perry, Orrin, 374, 379
Person, Harman D., 379
Peters, David Hughes, 375
Peters, John David, 375
Peters, Laura, 375
Peters, Pearl, 375
Petersen, Chase, 334
Peterson, Elmer G., 246
Peterson, James A., 324–25
Peterson, Orlando, 236
Pett, James, 92
Pettingill, Gay, 377
Petty, John, 407
Petty, Merrill, 394
Pierce, Eli Harvey, 71, 85, 349
Pierce, G.M., 170
Pierce, Peter N., 373
Pierce, Thomas, 65, 146, 300, 315
Pilot Peak Mountains, 9–10
Pilot Range, 7
Pioneer, 135
Pitt, Tom D., 389
Pluribathah, 135–36, 139
Plymouth, 379–81
Pocatello (Chief), 79, 81
Polygamy, 189–90
Portage, 381–86
Porter Spring, 22
Porter, Ed, 407
Porter, Larry C., ix
Porter, Richard, 403
Potter, T.W., 324, 326
Potts, Thomas, 320
Powell, Allan Kent, x, xiv
Powell, Bruce, xi
Pratt, Addison, 58
Pratt, Parley P., 65
Prehistory, 28–39
Presbyterian Churches, 167–70
Preston, William B., 159
Preuss, Charles, 53
Priest, Margaret, 312
Prohibition, 232
The Promontory, 194
Promontory, 386–88
Promontory Mountains, 6
Promontory Summit, 107, 192–93
Protestant Student Center, 182
Provost, Etienne, 44, 335
Pugsley, Dorothy Goodliffe, 399
Pugsley, Roy, 372

R. D. Pringle Plant, 377
Raft River Mountains, 6–7, 15
Randstrom, Donald, 184
Rankin, Arthur, 169
Ranshoff, N.S., 125
Ransom, Ira T., 184

Ravenburg, Lorna, x, 300
Raymond, Anan, 359, 405
Reaction Motors, Inc., 288–89
Reed, Samuel B., 106, 112, 119
Reeder, Adolf, 142
Rees, John D., 70
Reynolds, C.A., 125
Rice, Hyrum, 337
Rice, M.Q., 278
Rich, Russell R., 417
Richards, Calvin, 333
Richards, Ezra T., 333
Richards, Franklin D., 98, 153, 159
Richards, Le Grande, 309
Richards, Mary T., 333
Richards, Myron, 340, 389, 391, 392, 395, 396
Richards, Ralph C., 396
Richards, Willard, 22, 411
Richins, Albert F., 345
Richins, Jane, 345
Riverside, 388–97
Riverside-North Garland Water Company, 392
Roads and Highways, 197–202, 294
Robbins, Joseph, 403
Robbins, William, 403
Roberts, Allen, 161
Roberts, Brigham Henry, 233–34
Roberts, Muir, 377
Roche, Douglas, 394
Rock art, 38–39
Rockwell, Merritt, 374
Rockwell, Orrin Porter, 22, 65, 215, 373
Rodeos, 294
Rodgers, Lemuel, 334
Rohwer, Charles J., 364
Roman Catholic Church, 180–82
Romero, Thomas, 185
Roosevelt, Franklin D., 250–51, 268, 273, 294
Rose, Andrew, 364
Rosebud Mining District, 8
Rosenbaum, Morris, 301
Roush, D.C., 409
Rowberry, Ezra, 345
Rowe, William H., 218, 220–21, 389
Rowher, Martin, 242–43
Rucker, William, 324
Russell, William H., 10
Russian Settlement, 397–402

Saal, Mark, 297–98
Sacred Heart Center, 182
Sagwitch, 82–83
Saint Henry's Catholic Church, 181–82
Saint Michael's Episcopal Church, 174
Salt Lake Cutoff, 56–59
Salt Mining, 11
Sanderson, S. William, 108
Sanford, Anson P.K., 108
Saunders, John M., 324, 326
Scandinavian Methodist Church, 171–72
Scandinavians, 69, 171–72
Schenk, John, 408
Schenk, Josh, 48
Schenk, Sam, 408
Schools, 203–9
Secrist, Gertrude, 422
Secrist, Sterling W., 324
Secrist, Thaine, 422
Sessions, Peregrine, 64
Seymour, Silas, 110
Sharp, John, 106, 110
Shearman, William H., 329
Shelton, Sonja Secrist, 422
Sheridan, Philip, 82
Sherman, William G., 108, 114
Sherwood, Henry G., 69, 411
Shesta, John, 289
Shibata, George, 278–79
Shilling, W.N., 111
Shiotani, Sataro, 175
Shore, M.T., 247
Shoshoni Indians, 55–56, 70–71, 78–83, 96, 248
Shoun, Charles, 184
Shoun, Martha, 184
Shuman, George, 408, 409
Shuman, John, 408, 409
Sierra Madre Mining District, 11
Sigler, Howard, 111
Simmonds, Jeff, xi

Simpson, Ellen, 345
Simpson, James R., 345
Silver Island Mining District, 9
Silver Island Mountains, 9
Slatter, Tommy, 297
Sloan, Francis J., 181
Smith, Alice Ann, 334
Smith, Carrie, 77
Smith, Charles Sr., 345
Smith, Charles Jr., 345
Smith, Clarence E., 396
Smith, David A., 246
Smith, Dee Glen, 299
Smith, Eliza R. Snow, 75, 97
Smith, George Albert, 281–82
Smith, Jedediah, 45–46, 335
Smith, Joseph, 63, 88, 97
Smith, Joseph F., 157, 189, 191
Smith, Joseph Fielding, 23, 333
Smith, Robert D., 271–72
Smith, Samuel, 76–77, 99, 307
Smithson, James, 297
Smoot, A.V., 330
Smoot, Reed, 190, 234, 251
Snow, Eugene H., 172
Snow, Lorenzo, 22, 68–69, 71–73, 74–76, 88–89, 90, 92, 93, 97–98, 99–100, 148, 149–51, 153, 159, 161, 189, 191, 204, 215, 300, 301, 308, 315–16, 352, 361, 362
Snow, Oliver G., 149, 352
Snowville, 241, 243, 402–4
Sohn, Heinrich, 238
Sommers, John, 312, 357
Southern Pacific, 192, 283
Spanish American War, 191–92
Spencer, James, 381
Spicer, Wells, 136
Spiral Jetty, 297–98
Springs, 15–16, 52–53
Stage Coach Hotel, 321
Standing, Hyrum, 321
Standing, Jack, 324
Standing, James, 321
Standing, Leonard W., 321
Standing, Mary, 321
Standrod, 404–5
Stanford, A.P., 115
Stanford, Leland, 106, 108, 115, 116–17, 118, 119, 230
Stansbury, Howard, 53–55, 248, 319
Statehood, 189–90
Stayner, Arthur, 225, 333
Steamboats, 135–39
Steed, Edna, 394
Stephens, Evan, 412
Stewart, Daniel, 381
Stewart, James, 381
Stillman, J.D.B., 108
Stimson, Henry, 272
Stinking Hot Springs, 16–17
Stohl, Ola N., 91
Stokes, Joseph M., 311
Stone, W.H., 409
Streets, G.O., 170
Strevell, C.N., 176, 399
Strobridge, J.H., 109, 112, 120
Sugar Beets, 225–29, 235–36, 250
Sugar Factory Hotel, 230
Summer Ranch Mountains, 7
Summers, John, 407
Sun Tunnels, 298
Sunada, Susan, 291
Sweeton, G.G., 323
Swendsen, Warren, 223
Sylvester, L. Jay, 299

Talmage, James E., 244
Tanner, Alma C., 332, 344
Tanner, Valison, 332, 344
Taura, Jutaro, 175
Tawatari, Takematsue, 175
Taylor, John, 225, 379, 420
Taylor, Matt, 141
Tazoi, Jim, 274, 275
Teasdale, Samuel, 217
Telephone, 312
Tenmile Creek, 15
Terrace, 405–6
Terrace Mountains, 8
Thatcher, 23, 406–7
Thatcher, Henry M., 203
Thatcher, Moses, 23, 406
Theater, 72–73, 75

Thiokol, 172, 174, 183–84, 201, 209, 287–90
Thomas, Elbert, 251
Thomas, William (Cotton), 344, 363–64
Thompson, Jon Z., 386
Thumb, Tom, 143
Timbimboo, Moroni, 82
Timbimboo, Yeager, 390
Tiner, Rufus, 244
Tingey, Charley, 392
Tingey, Mary, 395
Tippetts, William Plummer, 374
Todd, John, 110, 113
Tolman, Abinadi, 355
Tolman, Benjamin, 67, 352, 353
Tompkins, Julia Ann, 240
Toohy, Dennis, 136
Toponce, Alexander, 129, 132, 141, 142, 213, 214–17, 219, 230, 338
Tracy, Abraham, 237
Tracy, James Alonzo, 318
Tracy, Margret Melinda Whitaker, 318
Tracy, Merlin, 300, 414–15, 416, 417, 419
Transcontinental Railroad, 105–21
Tremonton, 23, 271, 407–11
Tremonton Methodist Church, 172
Trident missile, 289
Tritle, Fred A., 108, 114
True, A.C., 219
Trukenbrod, Lawrence, 408
Truman, Harry, 268
Tullidge, Edward W., 329
Tuttle, Daniel S., 173

Udy, Edmund, 396
Uklein, Semyon, 398
Union Pacific Railroad, 106–120, 126, 140, 192
United Order Movement, 88
Ural, Jacob, 399
Utah Centennial County History Council, xiii-xiv
Utah Central Railroad, 120
Utah Hot Springs, 16
Utah Idaho Sugar Company, 222, 224, 228
Utah Light and Railway Company, 217
Utah Northern Railroad, 98, 120–21, 140–41, 149, 321–22, 352
Utah Pie Cherry Co-op, 377
Utah Power and Light Company, 223, 224
Utah State Legislature, xiii-xiv
Utah Statehood, 189–90
Utah Sugar Company, 222, 223, 225–26, 340–41

Van Cott, John, 415
Van Denburgh, F. L. 108, 110
Vanfleet, W.R., 337, 340
Vasquez, Louis, 45
Victory Assembly of God Church, 185
Vipont, 411

Wach, Frederick, 324
Wakley, John, 374
Waldon, Benjamin, 382
Waldon, Emmeline, 382
Walker War, 67
Walker, Frank, 334
Walker, Joseph Redford, 335–36
Walker, M. H., 125
Walker, S.S., 125
Walker, William, 374, 376
Walsh, Patrick, 180
Walton, James, 276
Warburton, Richard E., 345
Ward, Agnes M., 239
Ward, Alfred, 239
Ward, Edna, 397
Ward, Ellen, 239
Ward, Elmer "Bear," 299
Ward, John, 396–97
Ward, Mary, 397
Ward, Mina, 393, 397–98
Ward, Moroni, 392
Ward, Sylvia, 239
Warren, Hussey & Co., 130
Wasatch Mountains, 11
Washakie, 80–81, 82
Watanabe, Shoji, 275
Water Resources, 17
Watkins, Susan, 204

Watland, S.B., 409
Watson, Richard S., 174
Weber, John, 44–45
Webster, Jack, 350
Welling, Effie, 393
Welling, Gale, x, 218, 220, 228, 300
Welling, Harry, 397
Welling, Milton H., 232
Welling, Tracy R., 250, 251, 397
Welling, Wendel, 392
Welling, Willard K., 333, 334
Wells, Daniel H., 22
Wells, Lyman, 65
Wellsville Mountains, 4–5, 17, 22
West, Chauncey W., 106, 110
Western Union Telegraph Company, 110–11, 138
Wetmore, Alexander, 249
Wheat Days, 293–94
Wheat, Ron, 161
Wheatley, Abraham, 354
Wheatley, E.C., 352, 353
Wheatley, John G., 355
Wheatley, Thomas, 355
Wheelon collapsible dam, 219–20
Wheelon, J.C., 220, 223
White, Bernard, 376
Wilcox, Ebenezer, 334
Wildcat Hills, 7
Willard, 22, 203, 411–14; flood of 1923, 238–40
Willard Bay, 16, 413–14
Willard Mining District, 11
Willard Peak, 3
Williams, Ben, 18, 323
Williamson, Corinne, 23, 127, 328
Williamson, J. A., 23, 125, 127, 129–30, 328
Wilson, Alice, 376
Wilson, James, 376
Wilson, Rick, xi
Wilson, Woodrow, 207–8
Winzeler, Gideon, 179
Wixom, J.A., 342
Wood, George J., 356
Wood, Oliver, 333, 334
Woodland, John T., 237–38
Woodland, Welton, 237–38
Woodruff, E.D., 399
Woodruff, Ed D., 176
Woodruff, Wilford, 69, 152, 157, 160, 191
Woods, Frank, 271
Woodson, A.E., 125
Woodward, H.T., 409
World War I, 207–8, 233–38
World War II, 266–79
Worley, J. M. 125
Wright, Jefferson, 67
Wright, Jonathan Calkins, 204
Wrighton, William, 302
Wyatt, E.M., 409

Yates, Hyrum, 364
Yates, Sarah, xi, 37, 399
Yates, Thomas, 350
Yeager, Chuck, 289
Yost, 414–21
Yost Valley, 7
Yost, Charles, 415–16, 419
Young, Brigham, 64, 67, 72, 73, 77, 88–89, 92, 97, 105, 110, 120, 129, 134, 140, 142, 146, 148, 149, 191, 215, 233, 238, 306, 307, 315, 327, 330, 347, 374, 379, 417
Young, Brigham, Jr., 110
Young, John W., 110
Young, Joseph A., 110
Young, Malcolm, 213
Young, Richard W., 233
Young, Seymour B., 159–60
Youngville, 71
Yurth, Cindy, 81

Zabriskie, E.B., 125
Zaugg, Fred, 372
Zesigar, Felix, 408
Zion's Cooperative Mercantile Institution, 129
Zollinger, Jacob, 124
Zundel, Elizabeth H., 380
Zundel, Isaac, 333, 379, 380
Zundel, Solomon, 380